T5-BPY-506

The Real in the Ideal

BERKELEY'S RELATION TO KANT

Edited by
R.C.S. Walker

GARLAND PUBLISHING, INC.
NEW YORK & LONDON 1989

For a complete list of the titles in this series,
see the final pages of this volume.

These facsimiles were made from copies in
Yale University Library, with the exceptions of the following:
"Berkeley's Immaterialism and Kant's Trancendental Idealism," by M. R.
Ayers, from a copy in the San Francisco Public Library; "Kant's Trancen-
dental Idealism," by Wilfrid Sellars, from a copy in the University of
Massachusetts Library; and excerpts from *A Commentary to Kant's
Critique of Pure Reason,* by Norman Kemp Smith, from a copy in the New
York Public Library.

Library of Congress Cataloging-in-Publication Data

The Real in the ideal.
        (The Philosophy of George Berkeley ; 4)
        1. Berkeley, George, 1685-1753. 2. Kant, Immanuel,
1724-1804. 3. Idealism—History. I. Walker, Ralph
Charles Sutherland. II. Series.
B1348.R4   1988   192   88-11305
ISBN 0-8240-2447-8

Printed on acid-free, 250-year-life paper.
Printed in the United States of America.

The Philosophy of George Berkeley

A FIFTEEN-VOLUME
FACSIMILE SERIES REPRODUCING
CLASSIC STUDIES AND INCLUDING
FOUR NEVER-BEFORE-PUBLISHED TITLES

EDITED BY
George Pitcher
Princeton University

A GARLAND SERIES

ACKNOWLEDGMENTS

The publisher and editor gratefully acknowledge the permission of the authors and the following journals and organizations to reprint the copyright material in this volume; any further reproduction is prohibited without permission:

The University of California for material from *George Berkeley*; *Journal of the History of Philosophy*; *Idealistic Studies*; the Royal Institute of Philosophy for material from *Idealism Past and Present*; the British Academy for material from *Proceedings of the British Academy*; Walter de Gruyter and Co. for material from *Kant-Studien*; University of Ottawa Press for material from *Proceedings of the Ottawa Congress on Kant*; Macmillan Publishers, Ltd., for material from *A Commentary to Kant's Critique of Pure Reason*; Basil Blackwell for material from *Philosophical Quarterly*; "Idealism: Kant and Berkeley," by R.C.S. Walker, copyright © John Foster and Howard Robinson 1985, reprinted from *Essays on Berkeley*, edited by John Foster and Howard Robinson (1985) by permission of Oxford University Press; Reprinted from Margaret D. Wilson, "The 'Phenomenalisms' of Berkeley and Kant," pp. 157-173, in *Self and Nature in Kant's Philosophy*, edited by Allen W. Wood, copyright © 1984 by Cornell University. Used by permission of the publisher, Cornell University Press.

INTRODUCTION

Berkeley and Kant were both idealists. They both regarded the physical world as being in some way a product of perceptions and thought. At the same time they both held it to be no mere illusion, but real and objective: it was in a sense ideal, but in a different sense also real. This has led some writers, both in Kant's lifetime and since, to conclude that his position and Berkeley's are ultimately much the same. The first review of the *Critique of Pure Reason*, which appeared seven months or so after it was published, took this line; but it was repudiated with great vehemence by Kant himself. He dealt with the review explicitly in an appendix to the *Prolegomena,* and implicitly by designing both the *Prolegomena* itself, and the partially rewritten second edition of the *Critique*, to emphasize his differences from Berkeley: differences both of conclusion and of approach. But despite this the relationship between his idealism and Berkeley's remains unclear. This is largely because it is by no means easy, at least at first sight, to recognize the Berkeley we are familiar with in the Berkeley whom Kant attacks. As a result it often seems that Kant's attempts to clarify the relationship have only made it more obscure.

It was the view of C.M. Turbayne that this was just what Kant was aiming at. Conscious of the similarity between his views and Berkeley's, conscious also that Berkeley's position was widely misunderstood and rejected as absurd, Kant deliberately sought to distance himself from Berkeley. Instead of trying to rehabilitate him and to demand for him the hearing he deserved, Kant—who in Turbayne's view understood Berkeley well, and borrowed his arguments where it suited him—preferred, in bad faith, to condemn him, to bolster his own claim to originality, and to secure a hearing for himself. Turbayne's article sparked off a considerable debate, which has helped towards a better understanding both of Kant and of Berkeley by its exploration of their similarities and difference. It is fair to say that most participants in the discussion have been fairly unsympathetic to Turbayne's conclusion, an exception being Myron Gochnauer, who agrees that Kant's arguments do not tell against Berkeley. He suggests that the Refutation of Idealism might be effective against him, but concludes that it is far from evident that it is, since Berkeley might, as Turbayne claimed, have been willing to accept the existence of things in space in the same sense as Kant does. This volume contains Turbayne's paper and Gochnauer's, and those other articles that have contributed most significantly to the debate, which is still continuing.

It includes also two older contributions. One of these is an extract from N. Kemp Smith's distinguished *Commentary to Kant's Critique of Pure Reason*. Turbayne was in part replying to Kemp Smith, who held that Kant misunderstood Berkeley so badly that he could never have read him. The other older paper is by H.W.B. Joseph, who develops an interesting comparison between Kant and Berkeley without going into the question of how much Kant may have known about his predecessor. Joseph considers that the similarities between them are substantial, but that the role Berkeley assigned to God is divided by Kant between the mind, or consciousness in general, and things as they are in themselves. He also argues that Berkeley cannot explain how we discover the principles of orderliness that govern the world and our inferences about it: these cannot be discovered empirically, but must be known a priori. Kant, on the other hand, cannot account for the way that the *matter* of experience—derived, for Kant, from the world as it is in itself—"is, as it were, sympathetic to mind," and so readily obeys the principles of orderliness that we prescribe to it.

A different suggestion comes from G.P. Adams. Adams sees Berkeley as repudiating the representative theory of perception in favour of the view that we perceive objects directly, but without abandoning the premise—characteristic of the representative theory—that the only things we can perceive directly are our "ideas," the contents of our own experience. Hence Berkeley equates objects with these. Kant also rejects the representative theory, but he rejects this premise too, and can thus hold that we perceive objects directly "not *through* experience but *in* experience." Adams may very well be right, but to leave matters here is to leave a number of crucial questions unanswered, particularly over the status of Kant's *idealism*.

Considerable light is thrown on the problem by Margaret Wilson in two different articles. In opposition to Turbayne—who argued that Kant's conception of space as an a priori form of intuition is strictly irrelevant to his arguments against the idealism he ascribed to Berkeley—she considers that Kant was right to regard his doctrine of space as the key, or at any rate one of the keys, to his difference from Berkeley. He took Berkeley to hold that if real things existed outside the mind they would have to exist in Newtonian absolute space; agreed with him in viewing Newton's conception of space as incoherent; but thought his own account of space provided a viable alternative which would still allow bodies to be real and objective. Space for Kant is ideal in that it is a form of our intuition, but he nevertheless accepts the scientific picture of bodies in space as causing our perceptions of them, perceptions which in the case of secondary qualities by no means resemble properties of the physical objects themselves. Here he contrasts sharply with Berkeley, one of the aims of whose phenomenalism was to reject that scientific picture of things in favour of a more commonsense view which assigned to secondary qualities the same status as to primary.

George Miller agrees with Wilson over the importance of Kant's account of space, and over the inadequacy of Turbayne's dismissal of it. He examines in some depth both Turbayne's theory that Kant deliberately presented a distorted picture of Berkeley, and what he calls the traditional theory, the view of Kemp Smith that Kant misunderstood Berkeley because he knew him only at second hand. He finds severe difficulties in both of these theories, and two that they have in common. In the first place neither can properly explain why Kant should say, as he does in the second edition of the *Critique* (B 274),[1] that Berkeley's idealism is undermined in the Transcendental Aesthetic. The traditional theory ignores it, and Turbayne fails to understand that without space as an a priori form of intuition Kant thinks Berkeley incapable of giving an account of objectivity. In the second place neither theory can explain why Kant should apparently promise a refutation of Berkeley in the first edition of the *Critique* (A 377) and then fail to supply one. Miller has his own answer to this, though it is one he develops only in an article that is not included in this collection because its relevance to the Berkeley-Kant problem is more indirect:[2] what Kant promises to do is to refute the "dogmatic idealist," and Miller suggests that although the dogmatic idealist of the second edition and the *Prolegomena* is explicitly identified as Berkeley, the dogmatic idealist of the first edition is not Berkeley but Leibniz.

Henry Allison and Gale Justin both emphasize the importance for Kant of the a priori character of space. Allison points out that he requires a priori forms of sensibility as a condition of the possibility of a mathematical science of nature, and that it is of central importance to Kant's conception of a physical reality—in contrast to Berkeley's—that such a science should be possible. He also argues that even in the first edition, when at first sight he seems to be at his most Berkeleian, Kant's appearances are not "in us" in anything like the sense in which Berkeley's ideas are; indeed, from his point of view Berkeley is a transcendental realist. A Kantian appearance requires a real correlate that a Berkeleian idea could never have. The real correlate is the thing in itself, with which—on Allison's reading of Kant, and indeed Justin's also—the appearance is strictly identical: appearance and thing in itself are one and the same thing regarded in two different ways.

Two articles by Justin are included in the collection. In the first of them he distinguishes Kant's reply to Berkeley in the *Prolegomena* from his reply in the second edition of the *Critique*. In the latter Kant focusses on Berkeley's rejection of the reality of space, in contrast to his own account, which allows it to be empirically real while also transcendentally ideal. It is in the *Prolegomena* that he makes the related point—picked up, as we have seen, by Miller—that by failing to recognize any a priori elements in experience Berkeley prevents himself from giving any adequate account of the distinction between reality and illusion. Justin goes rather further than Miller did into exploring why Kant should have thought this. In his second paper he argues vigorously against construing Kant as a phenomenalist in the sense in which Berkeley is. Kant is not offering any reduction of objects to sensory states: when he says appearances are "in us" his purpose is to distinguish sharply between things as they appear and things as they are in themselves.

According to Wilfrid Sellars, Kant regards Berkeley as holding that not only colours but also shapes and all the other properties we ascribe to physical things are to be construed like pains, in the sense that they are nothing more than modifications of the mind—just as there is nothing more to the existence of a pain than its being felt, there is nothing more to the existence of a shape than its being perceived. That is why he thinks Berkeley cannot distinguish between what is real and what is imaginary. Sellars argues that Kant has some justification for claiming that Berkeley is committed to this, though Berkeley's own statements on the subject are not consistent. His reply to Berkeley consists in distinguishing between an act of representation and its content: if what is represented is a house, the house may or may not be actual. Its actuality does not follow from the fact of its being represented, but that does not mean it must consist in a reality independent of us and of our representations. What makes it actual, rather, is that the representations of it exhibit a certain kind of rule-governed connectedness. No empiricist account of this connectedness, which sought to generate the relevant rules from experience, could be adequate; the rules Kant regards as indispensable are provided by the Analytic of Principles, and they are essentially rules governing the relations of object and perceiver in a spatio-temporal system.

Richard Aquila's view has something in common with Sellars's, and he starts, as Sellars also does, from an examination of Kant's conception of intuition. He is prepared to call Kant a phenomenalist, but distinguishes his position from reductive phenomenalism: he does hold that all statements about objects can in principle be translated into statements about actual and possible intuitions, but denies that the translation can be reductive, because each intuition is identifiable only as the intuition of such and such an object. Sellars would, I take it, agree with the latter point, but might be less ready to accept the possibility of a translation.

Michael Ayers similarly points out that Kant's appearances are "necessarily appearances *of* something, whereas Berkeley's ideas have no such intrinsic intentionality." For Kant it is through space as a form of sensibility that things in themselves impinge on us, and space is indispensable, because only space allows us to identify and individuate particular objects. Berkeley's dissatisfaction with any objective conception of space Ayers relates to the thought that it would involve an incoherent notion of infinite divisibility; and he similarly rejects an objective conception of time, which as Ayers observes would, if consistently carried through, clearly render it impossible for him to give any account of the reality of bodies and justify Kant's accusation that he "degrades bodies to mere illusion." Throughout this wide-ranging article Ayers casts considerable light on the details of Kant's and Berkeley's arguments by relating them to the arguments and the conclusions—often ill understood nowadays—of such predecessors as Descartes, Hobbes, Malebranche, Bayle, Leibniz, and Locke.

Many of the contributors discuss the likely state of Kant's actual knowledge of Berkeley. The fullest examination of this is provided by G.J. Mattey. He establishes that Kant's lectures of 1762–64 show a knowledge of Berkeley's *Dialogues*, but through a German translation which presents him as explicitly denying the reality of bodies. In lectures of the late 1770s he does not mention Berkeley, and the "dogmatic idealist" he is concerned with there is Leibniz, which supports Miller's suggestion that Leibniz was the dogmatic idealist of the first edition of the *Critique*. Mattey thinks his attention returned to Berkeley only after the review which so irritated him and provoked the reply in the *Prolegomena*; difficulties in understanding why he characterizes Berkeley as he does in that work are overcome if we suppose that the Berkeley he has in mind there is the more mystical and visionary Berkeley of *Siris*, rather than the younger, and in Kant's view perhaps less mature and interesting, Berkeley of the *Three Dialogues*. The greater emphasis on the account of space in the second edition of the *Critique* is based on a reading of the *De Motu*.

My own article, which concludes the collection, arose from the feeling that it was still not really clear why Kant should have thought that Berkeley's type of idealism was incapable of providing a criterion for distinguishing reality from illusion, despite some useful work on this by several writers and by Justin in particular. Berkeley's rejection of objective time does, indeed, lead him into incoherence, but as Ayers agrees there is no particular reason to think Kant was aware of it or would have regarded it as more than an inessential feature of his system. Berkeley does, of course, offer several criteria of reality; Kant's objection to them, I suggest, is that they either take us beyond the limits of possible experience (by referring to God) or else inevitably rest upon principles of inference that Kant regards, quite rightly, as synthetic a priori and as therefore unavailable to an empiricist. What I have to say on this score may perhaps be seen as complementing Joseph. We have the right to use such principles if, and only if, they can be justified transcendentally. Berkeley, like other phenomenalists, relies on induction without seeing the need for any such defence; once the need for it is recognized, Kant thinks it clear that a similar defence can equally be provided for other a priori principles, which are constitutive of experience and of the distinction between illusion and reality within it. They yield an account of the physical world sharply different from any phenomenalist's. I end, however, by suggesting a possible line of reply for a Berkeleian to make against Kant.

What I have said above amounts only to a brief and sketchy introduction of the contributions to the debate that make up this volume. It may be felt that an editor should address himself more directly to the issues themselves. But since the collection ends with a paper of my own, and since I have not (yet) changed my mind about what I say there, to say more in my own voice at this stage would be redundant. It does, however, seem to me that a fitting introduction to a collection on Berkeley and Kant might be the review that, in a sense, started the whole issue off, long before Turbayne's time: the review that so irritated Kant.

It was published in the *Zugabe zu den Göttingischen Anzeigen von gelehrten Sachen* for 19 January 1782, and appears as pp. 40–48 of the first volume for that year. Although it mentions Berkeley only once, and although (as Kant points out in the Appendix to the *Prolegomena*) its overall philosophical drift is somewhat confused, it clearly does treat Kant as an idealist of a Berkeleian kind. The confusion may be partly due to the fact that the review is not the product of a single hand. The editor of the *Anzeigen*, J.G. Feder, gave the book to Christian Garve to review, and Garve's review was too long for the journal. It was therefore very substantially reduced in length by Feder, who also added passages of his own, despite the fact that he had apparently only leafed rather briefly through the *Critique*.[3] It was Feder who called the *Critique* a system of *higher* idealism, something to which Kant took particular exception, and it was Feder who added another passage that much annoyed him, to the effect that the categories and principles of pure understanding are nothing but "the widely recognized principles of logic and ontology, set out in accordance with the author's idealistic restrictions." It was Feder also who added the reference to Berkeley. All the same, and despite the fact that

xiv

in correspondence with Kant Garve disowned the Göttingen review and blamed Feder for its overall tone,[4] Garve's own version, published a year later in the *Allgemeine deutsche Bibliothek*, makes much the same criticisms and shares the same fundamental misunderstanding of what Kant was seeking to do. Although he does not mention Berkeley by name, Garve constantly treats Kant as a textbook idealist who tries to build a world out of ideas. He reduces to nothing the role of the thing in itself, and he completely fails to understand Kant's problem as to how synthetic a priori knowledge, or indeed knowledge of any kind, is possible. The idea of a transcendental argument or a transcendental deduction passes him by entirely. As in the Göttingen review, therefore, he provides a very external account of the *Critique* through an examination of what he took to be its salient conclusions, construing these in a roughly Berkeleian fashion; he shows no grasp of the arguments that drove Kant to them.

The review, which follows, is headed "Riga" because that is where the *Critique* was published. All of the footnotes are mine; words in bold type are in bold type in the original, and words in italics are in Roman type (the rest being in Gothic). I have taken the liberty of dividing up some of the longer sentences, and I am very grateful to my colleague, Mr. P.L. Gardiner, for help with the translation. I have used the sign I [page-number] I to mark the start of each new page.

R.C.S. Walker

I 40 I
Riga.
Critique of Pure Reason. By Imman. Kant. 1781. 856
pp. octav. This work, which always exercises, even if it does not always instruct, its reader's understanding, often strains his attention to the point of weariness, but sometimes comes to its aid with the help of felicitous images, or rewards it with unexpected conclusions which are of general utility. It is a system of higher, or as the author calls it, of transcendental [transcendentellen] idealism; an idealism which embraces spirit and

xv

matter in the same fashion, changes the world and ourselves into representations, and makes all objects arise out of appearances through the understanding's connecting them together in a single experiential series, and through reason' attempting necessarily, though vainly, to extend and unite them into a single full and complete system of the world. The author's system depends on roughly the following main principles. All our knowledge has its source in certain modifications of ourselves, which we call sensations. What these modifications belong to, what they depend on—those are matters that are fundamentally quite unknown to us. If there exists a real thing in which the representations inhere; or real things independent of us, which produce them; in neither case do we know the slightest predicate of the things in question. Nevertheless we assume there are objects; we speak of ourselves, we speak of bodies, as real things; we believe we know them, we make judgements about them. The cause of this is merely that many appearances have something in common with one another. Through this they unite themselves one with another, and differentiate themselves from what we call **ourselves.** Thus we regard the intuitions of the outer senses | 41 | as things and events outside us; because they all take place side by side in a determinate space and one after another in a determinate time. That is real for us, which we represent to ourselves as at some place and at some time. Space and time themselves are nothing real outside us, nor are they relations, nor concepts acquire by abstraction, but rather subjective laws of our capacity of representation, forms of sensations, subjective conditions of sensible intuition. On these concepts, of sensations as mere modifications of ourselves (on which also **Berkeley** principally constructed his idealism), and of space and of time, rests the one foundation pillar of the Kantian system.

Out of **sensible appearances**, which are distinguished from other representations only through the subjective condition that space and time are bound up with them, the **understanding** makes objects. It **makes** them. For it is the understanding that first unites several successive little alterations of

xvi

the soul into whole complete sensations. It is again the understanding which so combines these wholes with one another in time that they succeed one another as cause and effect, so that each of them acquires its determinate place in infinite time, and all of them together acquire the character and fixity of real things. It is the understanding, finally, that through an additional exercise of connecting differentiates objects that exist simultaneously, as reciprocally acting on one another, from those that are successive, as depending on one another in one direction only. In this way, by bringing to the intuitions of the senses order, regularity of succession, and reciprocal influence, the understanding literally creates nature and determines its laws in accordance with its own. These laws of the understanding are prior to the appearances in which they are applied | 42 | thus there exist *a priori* concepts of the understanding. We pass over the author's attempt to illuminate the whole business of the understanding yet further, by a reduction of it to four key functions, and four key concepts depending on them, namely quality, quantity, relation, and modality; those again are supposed to include simpler concepts under them, and in combination with the representations of time and space to yield the principles of empirical knowledge. These are the widely recognized principles of logic and ontology, set out in accordance with the author's idealistic restrictions. It is incidentally shown how Leibniz arrived at his Monadology, and remarks are made against it which for the most part can be sustained independently of the author's transcendental idealism. The main result of all the author's observations about the business of the understanding is therefore supposed to be this: that the right use of the pure understanding consists in applying its concepts to sensible appearances, and to forming **experiences** by combining the appearances and concepts together; and that it is a misuse of it, which can never be successful, to draw conclusions from concepts about the existence and properties of objects that we can never experience. (Experiences, in contrast with mere imaginings and dreamings, are for the author sensible intuitions, combined with concepts of the understanding. But we confess that we do not see how the distinction of what is real from what is imagined and merely possible, a distinction which is in general so easy for the human understanding, can be adequately based **just** in the application of the concepts of the understanding, without supposing that a single mark of reality is to be found in sensation itself. For even visions and fantasies, whether sleeping or waking, | 43 | can present themselves as outer appearances in space and in time, and as altogether combined with one another in the most orderly fashion; sometimes in a more orderly fashion, on the face of it, than real events.)

Besides the understanding, however, there now enters a new force that operates on representations, **reason**. Reason relates to the concepts of the understanding, collected together, in the same way as the understanding relates to the appearances. Just as the understanding contains the rules by which individual phenomena are marshalled into the ordered series of a coherent experience, reason seeks the highest principles through which these ordered series can be united into a complete world whole. Just as the understanding makes out of sensations a chain of objects attached to one another, as the parts of time and space are, where the last member always points back to earlier or more distant members, reason wants to extend this chain to its first or outermost member—it seeks the beginning and the limit of things. The first law of reason is that where there is something conditioned, the series of its conditions must be completely given or must ascend to something unconditioned. In consequence of this reason goes out beyond experience in a twofold manner. For one thing it wants to extend the series of things that we experience much further than experience itself reaches, because it wants to have the series complete. On the other hand it also wants to lead us to things the like of which we have never experienced, to the unconditioned, the absolutely necessary, the unlimited. But all principles of reason lead to illusion, or to contradictions, when they are stretched into exhibiting real things and their natures; for they ought merely | 44 | to serve the understanding as a rule requiring it **to advance without end** in the exploration of nature. This universal judgement the author brings to bear on all the main investigations of speculative psychology, cosmology, and theology. How he employs it throughout, and seeks to justify it, will be made in some measure comprehensible, though not completely, by the following observations. In the theory of the soul fallacious inferences arise when determinations that apply to thoughts merely as thoughts are taken as properties of the thinking being. The proposition **I think**, the one source of the whole of rational [räsonnirenden] psychology, contains no predicate of the **I**, of the being itself. It expresses merely a certain determination of the thoughts, namely their interconnection through consciousness. Thus nothing can be inferred from it about the real properties of the being which is represented by "I." From the fact that the concept of **myself** is the subject of many propositions, and can never be the predicate of any, it is inferred that **I**, the thinking being, am a substance; though this word "substance" is properly used only for the permanent in outer intuition. From the fact that within my thoughts there are no parts outside one another, the simplicity of the soul is inferred. But there can be no simplicity in what should properly be regarded as real, i.e., as an object of outer intuition, because the condition of it is that it be in space, that it fill a space. From the identity of consciousness the personality of the soul is inferred. But could not a series of substances transfer their consciousness and their thoughts one to another, as they communicate their movements one to another? (An | 45 | objection that was already used by Hume and long before him.) Finally from the difference between the consciousness of ourselves and the intuition of outer things a fallacious inference is made to the ideality of the latter; though inner sensations do not give us absolute predicates of ourselves any more than outer sensations give us absolute predicates of bodies. Thus ordinary, or as the author calls it empirical, idealism is meant to be refuted, not through the proven existence of bodies, but through the disappearance of the advantage that the conviction of our own existence is supposed to have over the belief in bodies.

The contradictions in cosmology are held to be unavoidable, as long as we treat the world as an objective reality and seek to grasp it as a complete whole. The infinity of its past duration, of its extension, and of its divisibility are held to be incomprehensible to the understanding and to be an offence against it, because it fails to find the resting-place it seeks. And reason finds no adequate ground for stopping at any point. The solution that the author discovers, the true law of reason, is supposed, if we understand him rightly, to consist in this, that reason should direct the understanding to seek causes of causes and parts of parts endlessly, with the aim of achieving completeness in the system of things; but that the understanding should at the same time warn reason never to take as final and ultimate any cause or any part which it arrives at through experience. It is the law of approximation, which includes both unattainability and continual drawing nearer.

The result of the critique of natural theology is very similar to the previous cases. Propositions that appear to express reality are turned into rules that only prescribe a certain procedure to the understanding. | 46 | The one new thing the author adds here is, that he calls on the assistance of practical interest, and allows moral ideas to turn the scale where speculation has left both pans of the balance equally weighted, or rather equally empty. What this amounts to is as follows. All thought about a limited reality is similar to thought about a limited space. Just as a limited space would not be possible unless there were an infinite universal space, so no determinate finite reality would be possible unless there were a universal infinite reality, which provided a basis for the determinations, i.e., the limitations, of individual things. But neither of these considerations is true except of our concepts, as a law of our understanding, in so far as a representation presupposes others. All other proofs that purport to show more the author finds by examination to be mistaken or inadequate. We prefer entirely to pass over the way in which the author ultimately tries to use moral concepts to provide grounds for the ordinary way of thinking, after he has removed the speculative grounds for it, for we do not know what to make of it in the least. There is indeed a way to connect the conceptions of the true and the most general laws of thought with the most general concepts and principles of right conduct; this has its foundation in our nature, and it can guard us against the extravagances of speculation or bring us back from them. But we do not recognize it in the author's phraseology and mode of expression

           *   *   *

The last part of the work, which contains the Doctrine of Method, shows first what pure reason must guard itself against—that is the **Discipline**; | 47 | secondly it gives the rules by which it must govern itself, and that is the **Canon** of pure reason. We cannot analyse its content more exactly; to a large extent it can be derived from what has already been said. The whole book can indeed serve to make the reader familiar with the considerable difficulties of speculative philosophy, and to hold up much material for salutary reflection to those builders and defenders of metaphysical systems who trust themselves all too proudly and boldly to the conceits of pure reason. But the middle way between the extravagances of scepticism and dogmatism, the proper way to get back—with reassurance even if not with complete satisfaction—to the most natural way of thinking: this middle way, it seems to us, the author has not chosen. In our view, though, both scepticism and dogmatism are marked by reliable criteria. First the right use of the understanding must correspond to the most general concept of right conduct, to the fundamental law of our moral nature, and thus to the promotion of happiness. From this it soon becomes clear that the understanding must be applied in accordance with its own fundamental laws, which make contradiction intolerable and which require us to have grounds for what we assent to —grounds which must be preponderant and lasting when there are also considerations pointing the other way. It follows from this, then, that we must attach ourselves to the strongest and most lasting **sensation**, or the strongest and most lasting appearance [Schein],[5] as to our most external reality. This is what the ordinary human understanding does. And how can the sophistic reasoner do otherwise? By bringing together the **two kinds of sensation**, inner and outer, | 48 | and by fusing them together or changing one into the other. Hence materialism, anthropomorphism, etc., if one changes the knowledge of inner sensation into the form of outer sensation or muddles the two together. Hence also idealism, if one impugns the validity or the distinctiveness of outer sensation in contrast to inner. Scepticism sometimes does one of these things and sometimes the other, so as to confuse everything together and to make it totter. To some extent our author does this too; he fails to recognize the rights of inner sensation by seeking to regard the concepts of substance and reality[6] as belonging to outer sensation alone. But his idealism conflicts still more with the laws of outer sensation, and with the ways of representing and talking that arise out of them and that are in accordance with our nature. If, as the author himself asserts, the understanding only operates on sensations and does not yield us new knowledge, it acts in accordance with its basic laws if in everything that concerns reality it allows itself more to be guided by the sensations than to guide them. And if we suppose the idealist is right in his most extreme claims, and that everything about which we can know or say anything is only representation and law of thought; if what we call objects and world are nothing more nor less than representations in us, modified and ordered following certain laws; what then is the point of objecting to our commonly assumed way of talking? What is the **point** and what is the **source** of the idealist's distinction?[7]

[End of the Göttingen review.]

NOTES

1. I follow the common convention of referring to the first edition of the *Critique* as A and to the second as B.

2. G. Miller, "Kant's First Edition Refutation of Dogmatic

xxii

Idealism." *Kant-Studien* 62 (1971).

3. For details see B. Erdmann, *Kant's Prolegomena* (Voss, Leipzig, 1878), introduction; and the introduction to K. Vorländer's edition of the *Prolegomena*, which appears in vol. 3 of the edition of Kant's works edited by O. Buek, K. Vorländer et al. (Felix Meiner, Leipzig, 2nd ed. 1905). Vorländer reprints the Göttingen review in full as an appendix.

4. Though he did not mention Feder by name. See Garve's letter to Kant of 13 July 1783, and Kant's reply, in vol. X of the Academy edition of Kant's works; also reprinted in Vorländer's edition of the *Prolegomena*. Garve's own version appeared in the *Anhang zu dem 37sten bis 52sten Bande der allgemeinen deutschen Bibliothek*, IIte Abtheilung, 1783, pp. 838–62.

5. This word is generally used by Kant to mean *illusion*, and that is how Lucas translates it in his own reference to this passage in the Appendix to the *Prolegomena* (p. 147 in Lucas's translation). In Kant's time, however, the word did not necessarily carry the implication of falsity, and could more neutrally mean "appearance": cf. Kemp Smith's *Commentary*, p. 153.

6. *Wirklichkeit*. I have translated this word throughout as "reality," as the context demands. In his translation of the *Critique* Kemp Smith sometimes translates it in this way too, but the category of *Wirklichkeit*—which is being referred to here—he renders as the category of *actuality*, to distinguish it from the category of *Realität*.

7. The text does not make it fully clear what "the idealist's distinction" is; this is one of the consequences of Feder's abridgement. From Garve's version in the *Allgemeine deutsche Bibliothek* it is clear that it is the distinction between representations and objects. Garve's point is not itself a very clear one, but it seems to be that although the idealist, like anyone else, must obviously make some distinction between the two, he deprives

himself of the means to do so. He equates objects with representations (of a certain kind); but "in that case it is equivalent whether we reduce things to ideas, or change ideas into things. The latter is more in accordance with the laws of nature—and it is also so woven into our language, that we do not know how to express ourselves otherwise." (p. 861.)

BIBLIOGRAPHY

The standard edition of Berkeley's works is *The Works of George Berkeley, Bishop of Cloyne*, ed. by A.A. Luce and T.E. Jessop (Nelson: London and Edinburgh, 1948–57). The standard edition of Kant's is the one by the Königlich Preussische Akademie der Wissenschaften and its successors, *Kant's gesammelte Schriften* (Berlin, 1902–); it is often referred to by the abbreviation "Ak." The best translation of the *Critique of Pure Reason* is the one by N. Kemp Smith (Macmillan, London, 1929); there are good translations of the *Prolegomena* by P.G. Lucas (Manchester University Press, 1953) and L.W. Beck (Library of Liberal Arts, Indianapolis, 1950).

What follows is not a general bibliography on Berkeley and on Kant, but a list of references of particular relevance to the relationship between them.

Adams, R.M., "Berkeley and Epistemology." In E. Sosa, ed., *Essays on the Philosophy of George Berkeley*. Reidel, Dordrecht etc., 1987.

Adickes, E., *Kant und das Ding an Sich*. Pan, Berlin, 1924.

Adickes, E., *Kants Lehre von der doppelten Affektion unseres Ich als Schlüssel zu seiner Erkenntnistheorie*. Mohr, Tübingen, 1929.

Allison, H.E., "Transcendental Idealism and Descriptive Metaphysics." *Kant-Studien* 60 (1969).

Allison, H.E., "Kant's Refutation of Realism." *Dialectica* 30 (1976).

Allison, H.E., *Kant's Transcendental Idealism.* Yale University Press, 1983. Esp. parts I and IV.

Ameriks, K., *Kant's Theory of Mind.* Oxford University Press, 1982. Esp. chs. 3 and 7.

Aquila, R.E., *Representational Mind.* Indiana University Press, 1983. Esp. chs. 1 and 4.

Armstrong, D.M., *Berkeley's Theory of Vision.* Melbourne University Press, 1960.

Ayers, M.R., "Berkeley and the Meaning of Existence." *History of European Ideas* 7 (1986).

Ayers, M.R., "Divine Ideas and Berkeley's Proofs of God's Existence." In E. Sosa, ed., *Essays on the Philosophy of George Berkeley.* Reidel, Dordrecht etc., 1987.

Barker, S.F., "Appearing and Appearances in Kant." *Monist* 51 (1967). Reprinted in L.W. Beck, ed., *Kant Studies Today.* Open Court, La Salle, 1969.

Beck, L.W., *Early German Philosophy.* Belknap Press, Cambridge, Mass., 1969. P.476 n.

Bennett, J.F. *Kant's Analytic.* Cambridge University Press, 1966. Esp. sections 7–8, 18, 32, 52.

Bennett, J.F. *Kant's Dialectic.* Cambridge University Press, 1974. Esp. sections 16–17.

Bird, G., *Kant's Theory of Knowledge*. Routledge & Kegan Paul, London, 1962. Esp. chs. 1–5.

Bracken, H.M., *The Early Reception of Berkeley's Immaterialism: 1710--1733*. Nijhoff, The Hague, 1959.

Buchdahl, G., *Metaphysics and the Philosophy of Science*. Blackwell, Oxford, 1969. Esp. pp. 532–52.

Buchdahl, G., "Transcendental Reduction." In G. Funke, ed., *Akten des 4. Internationalen Kant-Kongresses*. De Gruyter, Berlin and New York, 1974–75.

Cassirer, E., *Das Erkenntnisproblem in der Philosophie und Wissenschaft in der neueren Zeit*. Bruno Cassirer, Berlin, 2nd ed. 1911. Vol. II, pp. 325 ff.

Erdmann, B., *Immanuel Kant's Prolegomena*. Voss, Leipzig, 1878. Einleitung.

Fernandes, S.L. de C., *Foundations of Objective Knowledge*. Reidel, Dordrecht etc., 1985. Esp. ch. 6.

Foster, J., "Berkeley on the Physical World." In J. Foster and H. Robinson, eds., *Essays on Berkeley*. Oxford University Press, 1985.

Furlong, E.J., "Berkeley and the Tree in the Quad." In C.B. Martin and D. Armstrong, eds., *Locke and Berkeley*. Doubleday, New York, 1968.

Glouberman, M., "The Dawn of Conceptuality." *Idealistic Studies* 9 (1979).

Harper, W., "Kant on Space, Empirical Realism, and the Foundations of Geometry." *Topoi* 3 (1984).

Herring, H., *Das Problem der Affektion bei Kant. Kant-Studien* Ergänzungsheft 67 (1953).

Jammer, M., *Concepts of Space.* Harper, New York, 1960. Pp.133–34.

Janitsch, J., *Kants Urteile über Berkeley.* Diss. Strassburg, 1879.

Lambert, R.T., "Berkeley's Commitment to Relativism." In C.M. Turbayne, ed., *Berkeley: Critical and Interpretive Essays.* Manchester University Press, 1982.

Lascola, R.A., "Ideas and Archetypes: Appearances and Reality in Berkeley's Philosophy." *The Personalist* 54 (1973).

Luce, A.A., *Berkeley's Immaterialism.* Nelson, London etc., 1945.

Mattey, G.J., *The Idealism of Kant and Berkeley.* Diss. Pittsburgh, 1979.

Matthews, H.E., "Strawson on Transcendental Idealism." *Philosophical Quarterly* 19 (1969). Reprinted in R.C.S. Walker, ed., *Kant on Pure Reason.* Oxford University Press, 1982.

Melnick, A., *Kant's Analogies of Experience.* University of Chicago Press, 1973. Esp. ch. 4.

Miller, G., "Kant's First Edition Refutation of Dogmatic Idealism." *Kant-Studien* 62 (1971).

Pappas, G., "Berkeley, Perception, and Common Sense." In C.M. Turbayne, ed., *Berkeley: Critical and Interpretive Essays.* Manchester University Press, 1982.

Park, D., "Kant and Berkeley's 'Idealism'." *Studi Internazionali di Filosofia* 2 (1970).

Paton, H.J., *Kant's Metaphysic of Experience*. Allen & Unwin, London, 2 vols, 1936. Esp. chs. 22 and 51.

Pippin, R.B., *Kant's Theory of Form*. Yale University Press, 1982. Esp. ch. 7.

Pitcher, G., *Berkeley*. Routledge & Kegan Paul, London etc., 1977. Esp. chs. 8–10.

Popkin, R.H., "Berkeley and Pyrrhonism." *Review of Metaphysics* 5 (1951–52).

Posy, C., "Dancing to the Antinomy: a Proposal for Transcendental Idealism." *American Philosophical Quarterly* 20 (1983).

Prauss, G., *Erscheinung bei Kant*. De Gruyter, Berlin, 1971.

Robinson, H., "The General Form of the Argument for Berkeleian Idealism." In J. Foster and H. Robinson, eds., *Essays on Berkeley*. Oxford University Press, 1985.

Robinson, L., "Contributions à l'histoire de l'évolution philosophique de Kant." *Revue de Métaphysique et de Morale* 31 (1924).

Sellars, W., *Science and Metaphysics*. Routledge & Kegan Paul, London, 1968. Esp. chs. 1 and 2.

Skorpen, E., "Kant's Refutation of Idealism." *Journal of the History of Philosophy* 6 (1968).

Smith, A.D., "Berkeley's Central Argument Against Material Substance." In J. Foster and H. Robinson, eds., *Essays on Berkeley*. Oxford University Press, 1985.

Smith, N. Kemp, *A Commentary to Kant's Critique of Pure Reason*.

Macmillan, London, 2nd ed. 1923. Esp. pp. 270–84, 298–321.

Sosa, E., "Berkeley's Master Stroke." In J. Foster and H. Robinson, eds., *Essays on Berkeley*. Oxford University Press, 1985.

Stäbler, E., *George Berkeley's Auffassung und Wirkung in der deutschen Philosophie bis Hegel*. Diss. Tübingen, 1935.

Strawson, P.F., *The Bounds of Sense*. Methuen, London, 1968. Esp. parts J and IV.

Stroud, B., *The Significance of Philosophical Scepticism*. Oxford University Press, 1984. Esp. ch. 4.

Taylor, C.C.W., "Berkeley on Archetypes." *Archiv für Geschichte der Philosophie* 67 (1985).

Thomas, G.H., "Berkeley's God Does Not Perceive." *Journal of the History of Philosophy* 14 (1976).

Tipton, I.C., *Berkeley: The Philosophy of Immaterialism*. Methuen, London, 1974.

Topitsch, E., "Transzendentaler und Empirischer Idealismus bei Kant." *Grazer Philosophische Studien* 4 (1977).

Turbayne, C.M., editor's introduction to Berkeley's *Treatise Concerning the Principles of Human Knowledge*. Library of Liberal Arts, New York, 1957.

de Vleeschauwer, H.J., "Les Antinomies kantiennes et la *Clavis Universalis* d'Arthur Collier." *Mind* N.S. 47 (1938).

Vorländer, K., introduction to the *Prolegomena*, in the edition of Kant's *Werke* edited by O. Buek, Vorländer et al., Felix Meiner, Leipzig, new ed. 1905. Vol. III.

Walker, R.C.S., *Kant*. Routledge & Kegan Paul, London, 1978.

Esp. chs. 8 and 9.

Walsh, W.H., *Kant's Criticism of Metaphysics*. Edinburgh University Press, 1975. Esp. sects. 6, 17, 29.

Werkmeister, W.H., "Notes to an Interpretation of Berkeley." In W. Steinkraus, ed., *New Studies in Berkeley's Philosophy*. Holt Rinehart & Winston, New York etc., 1966.

Wilkerson, T., *Kant's Critique of Pure Reason*. Oxford University Press, 1976. Esp. ch. 9.

Wilson, M., "The Phenomenalisms of Leibniz and Berkeley." In E. Sosa, ed., *Essays on the Philosophy of George Berkeley*. Reidel, Dordrecht etc., 1987.

Wolff, R.P., "Kant's Debt to Hume via Beattie." *Journal of the History of Ideas* 21 (1960).

Wolff, R.P., *Kant's Theory of Mental Activity*. Harvard University Press, 1963.

CONTENTS

III. (Second Part) B 70.—Kant urges that his doctrine of the ideality of space and time, so far from reducing objects to mere illusion, is the sole means of defending their genuine reality. If space and time had an independent existence, they would have to be regarded as more real than the bodies which occupy them. For on this view space and time would continue to exist even if all their contents were removed ; they would be antecedent necessary conditions of all other existences. But space and time thus interpreted are impossible conceptions.[1] The reality of bodies is thereby made to depend upon *Undinge*. If this were the sole alternative, "the good Bishop Berkeley [could] not be blamed for degrading bodies to mere illusion." We should, Kant maintains, have to proceed still further, denying even our own existence. For had Berkeley taken account of time as well as of space, a similar argument, consistently developed in regard to time, would have constrained him to reduce the self to the level of mere illusion. Belief in the reality of things in themselves, whether spiritual or material, is defensible only if space and time be viewed as subjective. In other words, Berkeley's idealism is an inevitable consequence of a realist view of space. But it is also its *reductio ad absurdum*.

["Berkeley in his dogmatic idealism] maintains that space, with all the things of which it is the inseparable condition, is something impossible in itself, and he therefore regards the things in space as merely imaginary entities (*Einbildungen*). Dogmatic idealism is inevitable if space be interpreted as a property which belongs to things in themselves. For, when so regarded, space, and everything to which it serves as condition, is a non-entity (*Unding*). The ground upon which this idealism rests we have removed in the *Transcendental Aesthetic*."[2]

The term *Schein* is not employed throughout this passage in either of the two meanings of the appended note, but in that of the main text. It signifies a representation, to which no existence corresponds.

---

[1] Cf. above, A 39 = B 57. This is, however, merely asserted by implication ; it is not proved. As already noted, Kant does not really show that space and time, viewed as absolute realities, are " inconsistent with the principles of experience." Nor does Kant here supply sufficient grounds for his description of space and time as *Undinge*. Kant, it must be observed, does not regard the conception of the actual infinite as in itself self-contradictory. Cf. below, p. 486.
[2] B 275.

KANT'S RELATION TO BERKELEY

By idealism [1] Kant means any and every system which maintains that the sensible world does not exist in the form in which it presents itself to us. The position is typified in Kant's mind by the Eleatics, by Plato, and by Descartes, all of whom are rationalists. With the denial of reality to sense-appearances they combine a belief in the possibility of rationally comprehending its supersensible basis. Failing to appreciate the true nature of the sensible, they misunderstand the character of geometrical science, and falsely ascribe to pure understanding a power of intellectual intuition. Kant's criticisms of Berkeley show very clearly that it is this more general position which he has chiefly in view. To Berkeley Kant objects that only in sense-experience is there truth, that it is sensibility, not understanding, which possesses the power of *a priori* intuition, and that through pure understanding, acting .in independence of sensibility, no knowledge of any kind can be acquired. In other words, Kant classes Berkeley with the rationalists. And, as we have already seen, he even goes the length of regarding Berkeley's position as the *reductio ad absurdum* of the realist view of space. Kant does, indeed, recognise [2] that Berkeley differs from the other idealists, in holding an empirical view of space, and consequently of geometry, but this does not prevent Kant from maintaining that Berkeley's thinking is influenced by certain fundamental implications of the realist position. Berkeley's insight—such would seem to be Kant's line of argument—is perverted by the very view which he is attacking. Berkeley appreciates only what is false in the Cartesian view of space ; he is blind to the important element of truth which it contains. Empiricist though he be, he has no wider conception of the function and powers of sensibility than have the realists from whom he separates himself off ; and in order to comprehend those existences to which alone he is willing to allow true reality, he has therefore, like the rationalists, to fall back upon pure reason. [3]

---

[1] Cf. below. p. 298 ff., on Kant's *Refutations of Idealism*. This is also the meaning in which Kant employs the term in his pre‐Critical writings. Cf. *Dilucidatio* (1755), prop. xii. *usus* ; *Träume eines Geistersehers* (1766), ii. 2, *W.* ii. p. 364. These citations are given by J '~ch (*Kant's Urtheile uber Berkeley*, 1879. p. 20), who also points out that the '-eady used in this sense by Bülffinger as early as 1725, *Dilucidationes* 'his is also the meaning in which the term is employed in B xxxiv. Cf. ∧ _ 3 44.

[2] *Prolegomena* ; *Anhang. W.* iv. pp. 374·5.

[3] In his *Kleine Aufsätze* (3. *Refutation of Problematic Idealism*, Hartenstein, v. p. 502) Kant would seem very inconsistently to accuse Berkeley of maintaining

■2■

That Kant's criticism of Berkeley should be extremely external is not, therefore, surprising. He is interested in Berkeley's positive teaching only in so far as it enables him to illustrate the evil tendencies of a mistaken idealism, which starts from a false view of the functions of sensibility and of understanding, and of the nature of space and time. The key to the true idealism lies, he claims, in the Critical problem, how *a priori* synthetic judgments can be possible. This is the fundamental problem of metaphysics, and until it has been formulated and answered no advance can be made.

" My so-called (Critical) idealism is thus quite peculiar in that it overthrows ordinary idealism, and that through it alone *a priori* cognition, even that of geometry, attains objective reality, a thing which even the keenest realist could not assert till I had proved the ideality of space and time." [1]

In order to make Kant's account of Berkeley's teaching really comprehensible, we seem compelled to assume that he had never himself actually read any of Berkeley's own writings. Kant's acquaintance with the English language was most imperfect, and we have no evidence that he had ever read a single English book.[2] When he quotes Pope and Addison, he does so from German translations.[3] Subsequent to 1781 he could, indeed, have had access to Berkeley's *Dialogues between Hylas and Philonous* [4] in a German translation; but in view of the account which he continues to give of Berkeley's teaching, it does not seem likely [5] that he had availed himself of this opportunity. As to what the indirect sources of Kant's knowledge of Berkeley may have been, we cannot decide with any certainty, but amongst them must undoubtedly be reckoned Hume's statements in regard to Berkeley in the *Enquiry,*[6] and very probably also the references to Berkeley in Beattie's *Nature of Truth.*[7]   From

---

a solipsistic position. " Berkeley denies the existence of all things save that of the being who asserts them." This is probably, however, merely a careless formulation of the statement that thinking beings alone exist. Cf. *Prolegomena,* § 13, Anm. ii.

[1] *Prolegomena,* W. iv. p. 375 ; Eng. trans. p. 148.

[2] Borowski (*Darstellung des Lebens und Charakters Immanuel Kant*, in Hoffman's ed. 1902, p. 248 ff.) gives a list of English writers with whom Kant was acquainted. They were, according to Janitsch (*loc. cit.* p. 35), accessible in translation. Cf. above, pp. xxviii *n.* 3, 63 *n.* 1.

[3] Cf. *W.* i. pp. 318, 322. When Kant cites Hume in the *Prolegomena* (Introduction), the reference is to the German translation.

[4] This was the first of Berkeley's writings to appear in German. The translation was published in Leipzig in 1781.

[5] Cf. below, pp. 307-8. The opposite view has, however, been defended by Vaihinger : *Philos. Monatshefte,* 1883, p. 501 ff.

[6] *Enquiry Concerning the Human Understanding* (sec. xii. at the end of pt. i. and of pt. ii.).   [7] Sixth edition, pp. 132, 214, 243 ff.

the former Kant would learn of Berkeley's empirical view of space and also of the sceptical tendencies of his idealist teaching.   From it he might also very naturally infer that Berkeley denies all reality to objects.   By Beattie Kant would be confirmed in this latter view, and also in his contention that Berkeley is unable to supply a criterion for distinguishing between reality and dreams.   Kant may also have received some impressions regarding Berkeley from Hamann.

To take Kant's criticisms of Berkeley more in detail.   In the first edition of the *Critique*[1] Kant passes two criticisms, without, however, mentioning Berkeley by name: first, that he overlooks the problem of time, and, like Descartes, ascribes complete reality to the objects of inner sense.   This is the cause of a second error, namely, that he views the objects of outer sense as mere illusion (*blosser Schein*).   Proceeding, Kant argues that inner and outer sense are really in the same position.   Though they yield only appearances, these appearances are conditioned by things in themselves.   Through this relation to things in themselves they are distinguished from all merely subjective images.   Berkeley is again referred to in the fourth *Paralogism*.[2]   His idealism is distinguished from that of Descartes.   The one is dogmatic; the other is sceptical.   The one denies the existence of matter; the other only doubts whether it is possible to prove it.   Berkeley claims, indeed, that there are contradictions in the very conception of matter; and Kant remarks that this is an objection which he will have to deal with in the section on the *Antinomies*.   But this promise Kant does not fulfil; and doubtless for the reason that, however unwilling he may be to make the admission, on this point his own teaching, especially in the *Dialectic*, frequently coincides with that of Berkeley.   So little, indeed, is Kant concerned in the first edition to defend his position against the accusation of subjectivism, that in this same section he praises the sceptical idealist as a "benefactor of human reason."

"He compels us, even in the smallest advances of ordinary experience, to keep on the watch, lest we consider as a well-earned possession what we perhaps obtain only in an illegitimate manner. We are now in a position to appreciate the value of the objections of the idealist.   They drive us by main force, unless we mean to contradict ourselves in our commonest assertions, to view all our perceptions, whether we call them inner or outer, as a consciousness only of what is dependent on our sensibility.   They also compel us to regard the outer objects of these perceptions not as things in

---

[1] A 38.   [2] A 377.

themselves, but only as representations, of which, as of every other representation, we can become immediately conscious, and which are entitled outer because they depend on what we call 'outer sense' whose intuition is space. Space itself, however, is nothing but an inner mode of representation in which certain perceptions are connected with one another."[1]

These criticisms are restated in A 491-2 = B 519-20, with the further addition that in denying the existence of extended beings "the empirical idealist" removes the possibility of distinguishing between reality and dreams. This is a new criticism. Kant is no longer referring to the denial of unknowable things in themselves. He is now maintaining that only the Critical standpoint can supply an immanent criterion whereby real experiences may be distinguished from merely subjective happenings. This point is further insisted upon in the *Prolegomena*,[2] but is nowhere developed with any direct reference to Berkeley's own personal teaching. Kant assumes as established that any such criterion must rest upon the *a priori*; and in this connection Berkeley is conveniently made to figure as a thoroughgoing empiricist.

The *Critique*, on its publication, was at once attacked, especially in the Garve-Feder review, as presenting an idealism similar to that of Berkeley. As Erdmann has shown, the original plan of the *Prolegomena* was largely modified in order to afford opportunity for reply to this "unpardonable and almost intentional misconception."[3] Kant's references to Berkeley, direct and indirect, now for the first time manifest a polemical tone, exaggerating in every possible way the difference between their points of view. Only the transcendental philosophy can establish the possibility of *a priori* knowledge, and so it alone can afford a criterion for distinguishing between realities and dreams. It alone will account for the possibility of geometrical science; Berkeley's idealism would render the claims of that science wholly illusory. The Critical idealism transcends experience only so far as is required to discover the conditions which make empirical cognition possible; Berkeley's idealism is 'visionary' and 'mystical.'[4] Even sceptical idealism now comes in for severe handling. It may be called "dreaming idealism"; it makes things out of

---

[1] A 377-8. Though Kant here distinguishes between perceptions and their "outer objects," the latter are none the less identified with mental representations.
[2] Cf. below, p. 305 ff.
[3] *Prolegomena*, § 13, *Remark* III.; and *Anhang* (*W.* iv. p. 374).
[4] Kant's description of Berkeley's idealism as visionary and mystical is doubtless partly due to the old-time association of idealism in Kant's mind with the spiritualistic teaching of Swedenborg (*W.* ii. p. 372). This association of ideas was further reinforced owing to his having classed Berkeley along with Plato.

mere representations, and like idealism in its dogmatic form it virtually denies the existence of the only true reality, that of things in themselves. Sceptical idealism misinterprets space by making it empirical, dogmatic idealism by regarding it as an attribute of the real. Both entirely ignore the problem of time. For these reasons they underestimate the powers of sensibility (to which space and time belong as *a priori* forms), and exaggerate those of pure understanding.

"The position of all genuine idealists from the Eleatics to Berkeley is contained in this formula : 'All cognition through the senses and experience is nothing but mere illusion, and only in the ideas of pure understanding and Reason is there truth.' The fundamental principle ruling all my idealism, on the contrary, is this : 'All cognition of things solely from pure understanding or pure Reason is nothing but mere illusion and only in experience is there truth.'"[1]

This is an extremely inadequate statement of the Critical standpoint, but it excellently illustrates Kant's perverse interpretation of Berkeley's teaching.

To these criticisms Kant gives less heated but none the less explicit expression in the second edition of the *Critique*. He is now much more careful to avoid subjectivist modes of statement. His phenomenalist tendencies are reinforced, and come to clearer expression of all that they involve. The fourth *Paralogism* with its sympathetic treatment of empirical idealism is omitted, and in addition to the above passage Kant inserts a new section, entitled *Refutation of Idealism*, in which he states his position in a much more adequate manner.

---

[1] *Prolegomena, Anhang, W.* iv. p. 374 ; Eng. trans. p. 147.

THE DISTINCTION BETWEEN PHENOMENALISM AND SUBJECTIVISM

A wider set of considerations than we have yet taken into account must be borne in mind if certain broader and really vital implications of Kant's enquiry are to be properly viewed. The self has a twofold aspect. It is at once animal in its conditions and potentially universal in its powers of apprehension. Though man's natural existence is that of an animal organism, he can have consciousness of the spatial world out of which his organism has arisen, and of the wider periods within which his transitory existence falls.   Ultimately such consciousness would seem to connect man cognitively with reality as a whole. Now it is to this universal or absolutist aspect of our consciousness, to its transcendence of the embodied and separate self, that Kant is seeking to do justice in his transcendental deductions, especially in his doctrine of the transcendental unity of apperception.   For he views that apperception as conditioned by, and the correlate of, the consciousness of objectivity.   It involves the consciousness of a single cosmical time and of a single cosmical space within which all events fall and within which they form a whole of causally interdependent existences.   That is why he names it the *objective* unity of apperception.   It is that aspect in which the self correlates with a wider reality, and through which it stands in fundamental contrast to the subjective states and to the conditions of its individual, animal existence.   The transcendental self, so far from being identical with the empirical self, would seem to be of directly opposite nature.   The one would seem to point beyond the realm of appearance, the other to be in its existence strictly natural. The fact that they are inextricably bound up with one another, and co-operate in rendering experience possible, only makes the more indispensable the duty of recognising their differing characters. Even should they prove to be inseparable aspects of sense-experience, without metaphysical implications, that would not obviate the necessity of clearly distinguishing them. The distinction remains, whatever explanation may be adopted of its speculative or other significance.

Now obviously in so fundamental an enquiry, dealing as it does with the most complicated and difficult problem in the entire field of metaphysics, no brief and compendious answer can cover all the various considerations which are relevant and determining. The problem of the deduction being what it is, the section dealing with it can hardly fail to be the most difficult portion of the whole *Critique*. The conclusions at which it arrives rest not merely upon the argument which it contains but also upon the results more or less independently reached in the other sections. The doctrine of the empirical object as appearance requires for its development the various discussions contained in the *Aesthetic*, in the sections on *Inner Sense* and on the *Refutation of Idealism*, in the chapters on *Phenomena and Noumena* and on the *Antinomies*. The metaphysical consequences and implications of Kant's teaching in regard to the transcendental unity of apperception are first revealed in the chapter on the *Paralogisms*. The view taken of productive imagination is expanded in the section on *Schematism*. In a word, the whole antecedent teaching of the *Critique* is focussed, and the entire subsequent development of the Critical doctrine is anticipated, in this brief chapter.

But there are, of course, additional causes of the difficulty and obscurity of the argument. One such cause has already been noted, namely, that the *Critique* is not a unitary work, developed from a previously thought-out standpoint, but in large part consists of manuscripts of very various dates, artificially pieced together by the addition of connecting links. In no part of the *Critique* is this so obvious as in the *Analytic of Concepts*. Until this is recognised all attempts to interpret the text in any impersonal fashion are doomed to failure. For this reason I have prefaced our discussion by a statement of Vaihinger's analysis. No one who can accept it is any longer in danger of underestimating this particular cause of the obscurity of Kant's deduction.

But the chief reason is one to which I have thus far made

only passing reference, and to which we may now give the attention which its importance demands, namely, the tentative and experimental character of Kant's own final solutions. The arguments of the deduction are only intelligible if viewed as an expression of the conflicting tendencies to which Kant's thought remained subject. He sought to allow due weight to each of the divergent aspects of the experience which he was analysing, and in so doing proceeded, as it would seem, simultaneously along the parallel lines of what appeared to be the possible, alternative methods of explanation. And to the end these opposing tendencies continued side by side, to the confusion of those readers who seek for a single unified teaching, but to the great illumination of those who are looking to Kant, not for clear-cut or final solutions, but for helpful analysis and for partial disentanglement of the complicated issues which go to constitute these baffling problems.

The two chief tendencies which thus conflicted in Kant's mind may be named the subjectivist and the phenomenalist respectively. This conflict remained, so to speak, underground, influencing the argument at every point, but seldom itself becoming the subject of direct discussion. As we shall find, it caused Kant to develop a twofold view of inner sense, of causality, of the object of knowledge, and of the unity of apperception. One of the few sections in the *Critique* where it seems on the point of emerging into clear consciousness is the section, added in the second edition, on the *Refutation of Idealism*. But this section owes its origin to polemical causes. It represents a position peculiar to the maturer portions of the *Analytic* ; the rest of the *Critique* is not rewritten so as to harmonise with it, or to develop the consequences which consistent holding to it must involve.[1]

I shall use the term *subjectivism* (and its equivalent *subjective idealism*) in the wide sense [2] which makes it applicable to the teaching of Descartes and Locke, of Leibniz and Wolff, no less than to that of Berkeley and Hume. A common element in all these philosophies is the belief that subjective or mental states, "ideas" in the Lockean sense, are the objects of consciousness, and further are the sole possible objects of which it can have any direct or immediate awareness. Knowledge is viewed as a process entirely internal to the individual mind, and as carrying us further only in virtue of some additional supervening process, inferential, conjectural, or instinctive. This subjectivism also tends to combine with a view of consciousness as an ultimate self-revealing property

[1] Cf. below, Appendix C.
[2] The same wide sense in which Kant employs "empirical idealism."

of a purely individual existence.[1] For Descartes consciousness is the very essence, both of the mind and of the self. It is indeed asserted to be exhaustive of the nature of both. Though the self is described as possessing a faculty of will as well as a power of thinking, all its activities are taken as being disclosed to the mind through the revealing power of its fundamental attribute. The individual mind is thus viewed as an existence in which everything takes place in the open light of an all-pervasive consciousness. Leibniz, it is true, taught the existence of subconscious perceptions, and so far may seem to have anticipated Kant's recognition of non-conscious processes ; but as formulated by Leibniz that doctrine has the defect which frequently vitiates its modern counterpart, namely that it represents the subconscious as analogous in nature to the conscious, and as differing from it only in the accidental features of intensity and clearness, or through temporary lack of control over the machinery of reproductive association. The subconscious, as thus represented, merely enlarges the private content of the individual mind ; it in no respect transcends it.

The genuinely Critical view of the generative conditions of experience is radically different from this Leibnizian doctrine of *petites perceptions*. It connects rather with Leibniz's mode of conceiving the origin of *a priori* concepts. But even that teaching it restates in such fashion as to free it from subjectivist implications. Leibniz's contention that the mind is conscious of its fundamental activities, and that it is by reflection upon them that it gains all ultimate *a priori* concepts, is no longer tenable in view of the conclusions established in the objective deduction. Mental processes, in so far as they are generative of experience, must fall outside the field of consciousness, and as activities dynamically creative cannot be of the nature of ideas or contents. They are not subconscious ideas but non-conscious processes. They are not the submerged content of experience, but its conditioning grounds. Their most significant characteristic has still, however, to be mentioned. They must no longer be interpreted in subjectivist terms, as originating in the separate existence of an individual self. In conditioning experience they generate the only self for which experience can vouch, and consequently, in the absence of full and independent proof, must not be conceived as individually circum-

---

[1] Cf. above, pp. xliii-v, 208 ; below, pp. 295-6, 298 ff. Malebranche, Hume, and Spinoza are the only pre-Kantian thinkers of whose position the last statement is not strictly descriptive, but even they failed to escape its entangling influence.

scribed. The problem of knowledge, properly conceived, is no longer how consciousness, individually conditioned, can lead us beyond its own bounds, but what a consciousness, which is at once consciousness of objects and also consciousness of a self, must imply for its possibility. Kant thus obtains what is an almost invariable concomitant of scientific and philosophical advance, namely a more correct and scientific formulation of the problem to be solved. The older formulation assumes the truth of the subjectivist standpoint; the Critical problem, when thus stated, is at least free from preconceptions of that particular brand. Assumptions which hitherto had been quite unconsciously held, or else, if reflected upon, had been regarded as axiomatic and self-evident, are now brought within the field of investigation. Kant thereby achieves a veritable revolution; and with it many of the most far-reaching consequences of the Critical teaching are closely bound up.

This new standpoint, in contrast to *subjective* idealism, may be named *Critical*, or to employ the term which Kant himself applies both to his transcendental deduction and to the unity of apperception, *objective* idealism. But as the distinction between appearance and reality is no less fundamental to the Critical attitude, we shall perhaps be less likely to be misunderstood, or to seem to be identifying Kant's standpoint with the very different teaching of Hegel, if by preference we employ the title *phenomenalism*.

In the transcendental deduction Kant, as above noted, is seeking to do justice to the universal or absolutist aspect of our consciousness, to its transcendence of the embodied and separate self. The unity of apperception is entitled *objective*, because it is regarded as the counterpart of a single cosmical time and of a single cosmical space within which all events fall. Its objects are not mental states peculiar to itself, nor even ideal contents numerically distinct from those in other minds. It looks out upon a common world of genuinely independent existence. In developing this position Kant is constrained to revise and indeed completely to recast his previous views both as to the nature of the synthetic processes, through which experience is constructed, and of the given manifold, upon which they are supposed to act. From the subjectivist point of view the synthetic activities consist of the various cognitive processes of the individual mind, and the given manifold consists of the sensations aroused by material bodies acting upon the special senses. From the objective or phenomenalist standpoint the synthetic processes are of a noumenal character, and the given manifold is similarly viewed as being due to noumenal agencies acting, not upon the sense-organs, which as appearances are themselves noumenally conditioned, but upon what may be called "outer sense." These distinctions may first be made clear.

Sensations, Kant holds, have a twofold origin, noumenal and mechanical. They are due in the first place to the action of things in themselves upon the noumenal conditions of the self, and also in the second place to the action of material bodies upon the sense-organs and brain. To take the latter first. Light reflected from objects, and acting on the retina, gives rise to sensations of colour. For such causal interrelations there exists, Kant teaches, the same kind of empirical evidence as for the causal interaction of material bodies.[1] Our sensational experiences are as truly events in time as are mechanical happenings in space. In this way, however, we can account only for the existence of our sensations and for the order in which they make their appearance in or to consciousness, not for our awareness of them. To state the point by means of an illustration. The impinging of one billiard ball upon another accounts causally for the motion which then appears in the second ball. But no one would dream of asserting that by itself it accounts for our consciousness of that second motion. We may contend that in an exactly similar manner, to the same extent, no more and no less, the action of an object upon the brain accounts only for the occurrence of a visual sensation as an event in the empirical time sequence. A sensation just as little as a motion can carry its own consciousness with it. To regard that as ever possible is ultimately to endow events in time with the capacity of apprehending objects in space. In dealing with causal connections in space and time we do not require to discuss the problem of knowledge proper, namely, how it is possible to have or acquire knowledge, whether of a motion in space or of a sensation in time. When we raise that further question we have to adopt a very different standpoint, and to take into account a much greater complexity of conditions.

[1] Cf. A 28-9 ; also *Lectures on Metaphysics* (Pölitz's edition, 1821), p. 188 ff. In Kant's *Opus Postumum*, his *Transition from the Metaphysical First Principles of Natural Science to Physics*, it is asserted in at least twenty-six distinct passages that sensations are due to the action of "the moving forces of matter" upon the sense-organs. Cf. below, p. 283 n. 2. In his *Ueber das Organ der Seele* (1796) (Hartenstein, vi. p. 457 ff.), Kant agrees with Sömmerring in holding that the soul has virtual, *i.e.* dynamical, though not local, presence in the fluid contained in the cavities of the brain. Cf. below, Appendix C.

Kant applies this point of view no less rigorously to feelings, emotions, and desires than to the sensations of the special senses. All of them, he teaches, are 'animal'[1] in character. They are one and all conditioned by, and explicable only in terms of, the particular constitution of the animal organism. They one and all belong to the realm of appearance.[2]

The term 'sensation' may also, however, be applied in a wider sense to signify the material of knowledge in so far as it is noumenally conditioned. Thus viewed, sensations are due, not to the action of physical stimuli upon the bodily organs, but to the affection by things in themselves of those factors in the noumenal conditions of the self which correspond to "sensibility." Kant is culpably careless in failing to distinguish those two very different meanings of the phrase 'given manifold.' The language which he employs is thoroughly ambiguous. Just as he frequently speaks as if the synthetic processes were conscious activities exerted by the self, so also he frequently uses language which implies that the manifold upon which these processes act is identical with the sensations of the special senses. But the sensations of the bodily senses, even if reducible to it, can at most form only part of it. The synthetic processes, interpreting the manifold in accordance with the fixed forms, space, time, and the categories, generate the spatial world within which objects are apprehended as causally interacting and as giving rise through their action upon the sense-organs to the various special sensations as events in time. Sensations, as mechanically caused, are thus on the same plane as other appearances. They depend upon the same generating conditions as the motions which produce them. As minor incidents within a more comprehensive totality they cannot possibly represent the material out of which the whole has been constructed. To explain the phenomenal world as constructed out of the sensations of the special senses is virtually to equate it with a small selection of its constituent parts. Such professed explanation also commits the further absurdity of attempting to account for the origin of the phenomenal world by means of events which can exist only under the conditions which it itself supplies. The manifold of the special senses and the primary manifold are radically distinct. The former is due to material bodies acting upon the material sense-organs. The latter is the product of noumenal agencies acting upon "outer sense," *i.e.* upon those noumenal conditions of the self

---

[1] Cf. *Critique of Practical Reason*, Bk. i. ch. i. § iii.
[2] Cf. below, pp. 279 ff., 293-6, 312 ff., 321, 361 n. 3, 384-5, 464-5, 476.

which constitute our "sensibility"; it is much more comprehensive than the former; it must contain the material for all modes of objective existence, including many that are usually regarded as purely mental.[1]

To turn, now, to the other aspect of experience. What are the factors which condition its form? What must we postulate in order to account for the existence of consciousness and for the unitary form in which alone it can appear? Kant's answer is again ambiguous. He fails sufficiently to insist upon distinctions which yet are absolutely vital to any genuine understanding of the new and revolutionary positions towards which he is feeling his way. The synthetic processes which in the subjective and objective deductions are proved to condition all experience may be interpreted either as conscious or as non-conscious activities, and may be ascribed either to the agency of the individual self or to noumenal conditions which fall outside the realm of possible definition. Now, though Kant's own expositions remain thoroughly ambiguous, the results of the Critical enquiry would seem— at least so long as the fundamental distinction between matter and form is held to and the temporally sequent aspect of experience is kept in view—to be decisive in favour of the latter alternative in each case. The synthetic processes must take place and complete themselves before any consciousness can exist at all. And as they thus precondition consciousness, they cannot themselves be known to be conscious; and not being known to be conscious, it is not even certain that they may legitimately be described as mental. We have, indeed, to conceive them on the analogy of our mental processes, but that may only be because of the limitation of our knowledge to the data of experience. Further, we have no right to conceive them as the activities of a noumenal self. We know the self only as conscious, and the synthetic processes, being the generating conditions of consciousness, are also the generating conditions of the only self for which our experience can vouch. Kant, viewing as he does the temporal aspect of human experience as fundamental, would seem to be justified in naming these processes "synthetic." For consciousness in its very nature would seem to involve the carrying over of content from one time to other times, and the construction of a more comprehensive total consciousness from the elements thus combined. Kant is here analysing in its simplest and most fundamental form that aspect of consciousness which William James has

---

[1] Cf. below, pp. 279-80, and pp. 293-4, on inner sense.

described in the *Principles of Psychology*,[1] and which we may entitle the telescoping of earlier mental states into the successive experiences that include them. They telescope in a manner which can never befall the successive events in a causal series, and which is not explicable by any scheme of relations derivable from the physical sphere.

Obviously, what Kant does is to apply to the interpretation of the noumenal conditions of our conscious experience a distinction derived by analogy from conscious experience itself—the distinction, namely, between our mental processes and the sensuous material with which they deal. The application of such a distinction may be inevitable in any attempt to explain human experience; but it can very easily, unless carefully guarded, prove a source of serious misunderstanding. Just as the synthetic processes which generate consciousness are not known to be themselves conscious, so also the manifold cannot be identified with the sensations of the bodily senses. These last are events in time, and are effects not of noumenal but of mechanical causes.

Kant's conclusion when developed on consistent Critical lines, and therefore in phenomenalist terms, is twofold: positive, to the effect that consciousness, for all that our analysis.can prove to the contrary, may be merely a resultant, derivative from and dependent upon a complexity of conditions; and negative, to the effect that though these conditions may by analogy be described as consisting of synthetic processes acting upon a given material, they are in their real nature unknowable by us. Even their bare possibility we cannot profess to comprehend. We postulate them only because given experience is demonstrably not self-explanatory and would seem to refer us for explanation to some such antecedent generative grounds.

Kant, as we have already emphasised, obscures his position by the way in which he frequently speaks of the transcendental unity of apperception as the supreme condition of our experience. At times he even speaks as if it were the source of the synthetic processes. That cannot, however, be

[1] i. p. 339: "Each pulse of cognitive consciousness, each Thought, dies away and is replaced by another. . . . Each later Thought, knowing and including thus the Thoughts which went before, is the final receptacle—and appropriating them is the final owner—of all that they contain and own. Each Thought is thus born an owner, and dies owned, transmitting whatever it realized as its Self to its own later proprietor. As Kant says [cf. below, pp. 461-2], it is as if elastic balls were to have not only motion but knowledge of it, and a first ball were to transmit both its motion and its consciousness to a second, which took both up into *its* consciousness and passed them to a third, until the last ball held all that the other balls had held, and realized it as its own."

regarded as his real teaching. Self-consciousness (and the unity of apperception, in so far as it finds expression through self-consciousness) rests upon the same complexity of conditions as does outer experience, and therefore may be merely a product or resultant. It is, as he insists in the *Paralogisms*, the emptiest of all our concepts, and can afford no sufficient ground for asserting the self to be an abiding personality. We cannot by theoretical analysis of the facts of experience or of the nature of self-consciousness prove anything whatsoever in regard to the ultimate nature of the self.

Now Kant is here giving a new, and quite revolutionary, interpretation of the distinction between the subjective and the objective. The objective is for the Cartesians the independently real; [1] the subjective is that which has an altogether different kind of existence in what is entitled the field of consciousness. Kant, on the other hand, from his phenomenalist standpoint, views existences as objective when they are determined by purely physical causes, and as subjective when they also depend upon physiological and psychological conditions. On this latter view the difference between the two is no longer a difference of kind; it becomes a difference merely of degree. Objective existences, owing to the simplicity and recurrent character of their conditions, are uniform. Subjective existences, resting upon conditions which are too complex to be frequently recurrent, are by contrast extremely variable. But both types of existence are objective in the sense that they are objects, and immediate objects, for consciousness. Subjective states do not run parallel with the objective system of natural existences, nor are they additional to it. For they do not constitute our consciousness of nature; they are themselves part of the natural order which consciousness reveals. That they contrast with physical existences in being unextended and incapable of location in space is what Kant would seem by implication to assert, but he challenges Descartes' right to infer from this particular difference a complete diversity in their whole nature. Sensations, feelings, emotions, and desires, so far as they are experienced by us, constitute the empirical self which is an objective existence, integrally connected with the material environment, in terms of which alone it can be understood. In other words, the distinction between the subjective and the objective is now made to fall within the system of natural

---

[1] I here use "objective" in its modern meaning: I am not concerned with the special meaning which Descartes himself attached to the terms *objective* and *formaliter*.

law. The subjective is not opposite in nature to the objective, but is a subspecies within it.

The revolutionary character of this reformulation of Cartesian distinctions may perhaps be expressed by saying that what Kant is really doing is to substitute the distinction between appearance and reality for the Cartesian dualism of the mental and the material. The psychical is a title for a certain class of known existences, *i.e.* of appearances ; and they form together with the physical a single system. But underlying this entire system, conditioning both physical and psychical phenomena, is the realm of noumenal existence ; and when the question of the possibility of knowledge, that is, of the experiencing of such a comprehensive natural system, is raised, it is to this noumenal sphere that we are referred. Everything experienced, even a sensation or desire, is an event ; but the experiencing of it is an act of awareness, and calls for an explanation of an altogether different kind.

Thus Kant completely restates the problem of knowledge. The problem is not how, starting from the subjective, the individual can come to knowledge of the independently real ; but how, if a common world is alone immediately apprehended, the inner private life of the self-conscious being can be possible, and how such inner experience is to be interpreted. How does it come about that though sensations, feelings, etc., are events no less mechanically conditioned than motions in space, and constitute with the latter a single system conformed to natural law, they yet differ from all other classes of natural events in that they can be experienced only by a single consciousness. To this question Kant replies in terms of his fundamental distinction between appearance and reality. Though everything of which we are conscious may legitimately be studied in terms of the natural system to which it belongs, consciousness itself cannot be so regarded. In attempting to define it we are carried beyond the phenomenal to its noumenal conditions. In other words, it constitutes a problem, the complete data of which are not at our disposal. This is by itself a sufficient reason for our incapacity to explain why the states of each empirical self can never be apprehended save by a single consciousness, or otherwise stated, why each consciousness is limited, as regards sensations and feelings, exclusively to those which arise in connection with some one animal organism. It at least precludes us from dogmatically asserting that this is due to their being subjective in the dualistic and Cartesian sense of that term—namely, as constituting, or being states of, the knowing self.

A diagram may serve, though very crudely, to illustrate Kant's phenomenalist interpretation of the cognitive situation.

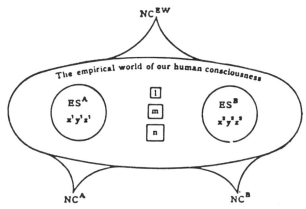

ES^A = Empirical self of the conscious Being A.
ES^B = Empirical self of the conscious Being B.
NC^A = Noumenal conditions of the conscious Being A.
NC^B = Noumenal conditions of the conscious Being B.
l, m, n = Objects in space.
x^1, y^1, z^1 = Sensations caused by objects l, m, n acting on the sense-organs of the empirical self A.
x^2, y^2, z^2 = Sensations caused by l, m, n acting on the sense-organs of the empirical self B.
NC^{EW} = Noumenal conditions of the empirical world.

Everything in this empirical world is equally open to the consciousness of both A and B, save only certain psychical events which are conditioned by physiological and psychological factors. x^1, y^1, z^1 can be apprehended only by A ; x^2, y^2, z^2 can be apprehended only by B. Otherwise A and B experience one and the same world ; the body of B is perceived by A in the same manner in which he perceives his own body. This is true *a fortiori* of all other material existences. Further, these material existences are known with the same immediacy as the subjective states. As regards the relation in which NC^A, NC^B, and NC^{EW} stand to one another, no assertions can be made, save, as above indicated,[1] such conjectural statements as may precariously be derived through argument by analogy from distinctions that fall within our human experience.[2]

Kant's phenomenalism thus involves an objectivist view of

---

[1] Pp. 277-8.
[2] On this whole matter cf. above, p. xlv ; below, pp. 312-21 on Kant's *Refutation of Idealism* ; pp. 373-4 on the *Second Analogy*; pp. 407 ff., 414 ff. on *Phenomena and Noumena* ; p. 461 ff. on the *Paralogisms* ; p. 546 ; and below, Appendix C. Cf. also A 277-8 = B 334.

individual selves and of their interrelations. They fall within the single common world of space. Within this phenomenal world they stand in external, mechanical relations to one another. They are apprehended as embodied, with known contents, sensations, feelings, and desires, composing their inner experience. There is, from this point of view, no problem of knowledge. On this plane we have to deal only with events known, not with any process of apprehension. Even the components of the empirical self, the subject-matter of empirical psychology, are not processes of apprehension, but apprehended existences. It is only when we make a regress beyond the phenomenal as such to the conditions which render it possible, that the problem of knowledge arises at all. And with this regress we are brought to the real crux of the whole question — the reconciliation of this phenomenalism with the conditions of our self-consciousness. For we have then to take into account the fundamental fact that each self is not only an animal existence within the phenomenal world, but also in its powers of apprehension coequal with it. The self known is external to the objects known; the self that knows is conscious of itself as comprehending within the field of its consciousness the wider universe in infinite space.

Such. considerations would, at first sight, seem to force us to modify our phenomenalist standpoint in the direction of subjectivism. For in what other manner can we hope to unite the two aspects of the self, the known conditions of its finite existence and the consciousness through which it correlates with the universe as a whole? In the one aspect it is a part of appearance; in the other it connects with that which makes appearance possible at all.

Quite frequently it is the subjectivist solution which Kant seems to adopt. Objects known are " mere representations," "states of the identical self." Everything outside the individual mind is real; appearances are purely individual in origin. But such a position is inconsistent with the deeper implications of Kant's Critical teaching, and would involve the entire ignoring of the many suggestions which point to a fundamentally different and much more adequate standpoint. The individual is himself known only as appearance, and cannot, therefore, be the medium in and through which appearances exist. Though appearances exist only in and through consciousness, they are not due to any causes which can legitimately be described as individual. From this standpoint Kant would seem to distinguish between the grounds and conditions of phenomenal existence and the special

determining causes of individual consciousness. Transcendental conditions generate consciousness of the relatively
permanent and objective world in space and time ; empirical
conditions within this space and time world determine the
sensuous modes through which special portions of this infinite
and uniform world appear diversely to different minds.

This, however, is a point of view which is only suggested,
and, as we have already observed,[1] the form in which
it is outlined suggests many objections and difficulties.
Consciousness of the objective world in space and time does
not exist complete with one portion of it more specifically
determined in terms of actual sense-perceptions. Rather the
consciousness of the single world in space and time is gradu-
ally developed through and out of sense experience of limited
portions of it. We have still to consider the various sections
in the *Analytic of Principles* (especially the section added in
the second edition on the *Refutation of Idealism*) and in the
Dialectic, in which Kant further develops this standpoint.
But even after doing so, we shall be forced to recognise
that Kant leaves undiscussed many of the most obvious
objections to which his phenomenalism lies open. To the
very last he fails to state in any really adequate manner how
from the phenomenalist standpoint he would regard the
world described in mechanical terms by science as being
related to the world of ordinary sense-experience,[2] or
how different individual consciousnesses are related to one
another. The new form, however, in which these old-time
problems here emerge is the best possible proof of the
revolutionary character of Kant's Critical enquiries. For

[1] P. 267 ff.

[2] Though Kant's *Opus Postumum*, parts of which have been published by
R. Reicke in the *Altpreussische Monatsschrift* (1882-4), under the title *Transition
from the Metaphysical First Principles of Natural Science to Physics*, exists only
in the form of preliminary studies and detached notes, and though in its later
sections it bears in some degree the marks of weakening powers, it enables us to
appreciate the extent to which Kant had come to be preoccupied with the problem
as to how the world of physical science stands related, on the one hand to the
sensible world of ordinary consciousness, and on the other to the world of things
in themselves. As above noted (p. 275 *n.*), Kant asserts in at least twenty-six
distinct passages that sensations are due to the action of "the moving forces of
matter" upon the sense-organs. What is especially significant is the adoption
and frequent occurrence (*op. cit.* (1882), pp. 236, 287, 289, 290, 292, 294, 295-6,
300, 308, 429, 436, 439) of the phrase "*Erscheinung von der Erscheinung.*"
Kant attaches to this phrase very varying meanings, according as he has metaphysical or physical existence in view, and according as he is considering the
material or the formal aspect of experience. In a few passages the phrase
"*Erscheinung vom ersten Range*" (*op. cit.* p. 436) (*i.e.* appearance as such) quite
definitely denotes the objective world as determined by physical science.
"*Erscheinung vom zweiten Range*" (*i.e.* appearance of the appearance) is then
taken as meaning the sensations, the secondary sense-qualities, generated in the
empirical self through the action of physical bodies on the sense-organs. Cf.
below, Appendix C.

these problems are no longer formulated in terms of the individualistic presuppositions which govern the thinking of all Kant's predecessors, even that of Hume. The concealed presuppositions are now called in question, and are made the subject of explicit discussion. But further comment must meantime be deferred.[1]

---

[1] Cf. below, pp. 312-21, 373-4, 414 ff., 425 ff., 558 ff., and Appendix C.

KANT'S REFUTATIONS OF IDEALISM

Kant has in a number of different passages attempted to define his Critical standpoint in its distinction from the positions of Descartes and Berkeley. Consideration of these will enable us to follow Kant in his gradual recognition of the manifold consequences to which he is committed by his substitution of inner sense for direct self-conscious intuition or reflection, or rather of the various congenial tenets which it gives him the right consistently to defend and maintain. In Kant's Critical writings we find no less than seven different statements of his refutation of idealism : (I.) in the fourth *Paralogism* of the first edition of the *Critique* ; (II.) in section 13 (*Anm.* ii. and iii.) of the *Prolegomena* ; (III.) in section 49 of the *Prolegomena* ; (IV.) in the second appendix to the *Prolegomena* ; (V.) in sections added in the second edition at the conclusion of the *Aesthetic* (B 69 ff.) ; (VI.) in the "refutation of idealism" (B 274-8), in the supplementary section at the end of the section on the *Postulates* (B 291-4), and in the note to the new preface (B xxxix-xl) ; (VII.) in the "refutation of problematic idealism" given in the *Seven Small Papers* which originated in Kant's conversations with Kiesewetter. Consideration of these in the above order will reveal Kant's gradual and somewhat vacillating recognition of the new and revolutionary position which alone genuinely harmonises with Critical principles. But first we must briefly consider the various meanings which Kant at different periods assigned to the term idealism. Even in the *Critique* itself it is employed in a great variety of diverse connotations.

In the pre-Critical writings[1] the term idealism is usually employed in what was its currently accepted meaning, namely, as signifying any philosophy which denied the existence of an independent world corresponding to our subjective representations. But even as thus used the term is ambiguous.[2] It may signify either denial of a *corporeal* world independent of our representations or denial of an immaterial world "corresponding to" the represented material world, *i.e.* the denial of *Dinge an sich.* For there are traceable in Leibniz's writings two very different views as to the reality of the material world. Sometimes the monads are viewed as purely intelligible substances without materiality of any kind. The

[1] Cf. above, p. 155.
[2] Cf. Vaihinger in *Strassburger Abhandlungen zur Philosophie* (1884), p. 106 ff.

kingdom of the extended is set into the representing subjects; only the immaterial world of unextended purely spiritual monads remains as independently real. At other times the monads, though in themselves immaterial, are viewed as constituting through their coexistence an independent material world and a materially occupied space. Every monad has a spatial sphere of activity. The material world is an objective existence due to external relations between the monads, not a merely subjective existence internal to each of them. This alternation of standpoints enabled Leibniz's successors to deny that they were idealists; and as the more daring and speculative aspects of Leibniz's teaching were slurred over in the process of its popularisation, it was the second, less consistent view, which gained the upper hand. Wolff, especially in his later writings, denounces idealism; and in the current manuals, sections in refutation of idealism became part of the recognised philosophical teaching. Idealism still, however, continued to be used ambiguously, as signifying indifferently either denial of material bodies or denial of things in themselves. This is the dual meaning which the term presents in Kant's pre-Critical writings. In his *Dilucidatio* (1755)[1] he refutes idealism by means of the principle that a substance cannot undergo changes unless it is a substance independent of other substances. Obviously this argument can at most prove the existence of an independent world, not that it is spatial or material. And as Vaihinger adds, it does not even rule out the possibility that changes find their source in a Divine Being. In the *Dreams of a Visionseer* (1766)[2] Swedenborg is described as an idealist, but without further specification of the exact sense in which the term is employed. In the inaugural *Dissertation* (1770)[3] idealism is again rejected, on the ground that sense-affection points to the presence of an intelligible object or *noumenon*.

In Kant's class lectures on metaphysics,[4] which fall, in part at least, between 1770 and 1781, the term idealism is employed in a very different sense, which anticipates its use in the *Appendix* to the *Prolegomena*.[5] The teaching of the *Dissertation*, that things in themselves are knowable, is now described as dogmatic, Platonic, mystical (*schwärmerischer*) idealism. He still rejects the idealism of Berkeley, and still entitles it simply idealism, without limiting or descriptive predicates. But now also he employs the phrase "problematic

---

[1] Section III., Prop. *XII Usus.*
[2] Theil II. Hauptstück II. *W.* ii. p. 364.
[3] § 11.
[4] Pölitz's edition (1821), pp. 100-2.
[5] *W.* iv. p. 373 ff.

idealism" as descriptive of his own new position.   This is, of course, contrary to his invariable usage elsewhere, but is interesting as showing that about this time his repugnance to the term idealism begins to give way, and that he is willing to recognise that the relation of the Critical teaching to idealism is not one of simple opposition.   He now begins to regard idealism as a factor, though a radically transformed factor, in his own philosophy.

Study of the *Critique* reinforces this conclusion.   In the *Aesthetic* Kant teaches the " transcendental ideality " of space and time ; and in the *Dialectic* (in the fourth *Paralogism*) describes his position as idealism, though with the qualifying predicate transcendental.[1]   But though this involves an extension of the previous connotation of the term idealism, and might therefore have been expected to increase the existing confusion, it has the fortunate effect of constraining Kant to recognise and discriminate the various meanings in which it may be employed.   This is done somewhat clumsily, as if it were a kind of afterthought.   In the introductory syllogism of the fourth *Paralogism* Descartes' position and his own are referred to simply as idealism and dualism respectively.   The various possible sub-species of idealism as presented in the two editions of the *Critique* and in the *Prolegomena* may be tabulated as follows :

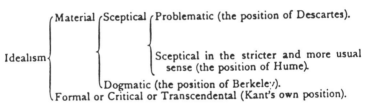

Idealism
- Material
  - Sceptical
    - Problematic (the position of Descartes).
    - Sceptical in the stricter and more usual sense (the position of Hume).
  - Dogmatic (the position of Berkeley).
- Formal or Critical or Transcendental (Kant's own position).

The distinction between problematic idealism and idealism of the more strictly sceptical type is not clearly drawn by Kant.[2]   Very strangely Kant in this connection never mentions Hume : the reference in B xxxix *n.* is probably not to Hume but to Jacobi.   Transcendental idealism is taken as involving an empirical realism and dualism, and is set in opposition to transcendental realism which is represented as involving empirical idealism.   In B xxxix *n.* Kant speaks of " psychological idealism," meaning, as it would seem, material or non-Critical idealism.

[1] It may be noted that in the *Aesthetic* (A 38 = B 55) Kant employs the term idealism, without descriptive epithet, in the same manner as in his pre-Critical writings, as signifying a position that must be rejected.
[2] Cf. below, p. 301 ff.

In the second appendix to the *Prolegomena* Kant draws a further distinction, in line with that already noted in his lectures on metaphysics. Tabulated it is as follows:

Idealism
- Mystical, in the sense of belief in and reliance on a supposed human power of intellectual intuition. It is described as idealism in the strict (*eigentlich*) sense—the position of the Eleatics, of Plato and Berkeley.
- Formal or Critical—Kant's own position.

This latter classification can cause nothing but confusion. The objections that have to be made against it from Kant's own critical standpoint are stated below.[1]

Let us now consider, in the order of their presentation, the various refutations of idealism which Kant has given in his Critical writings.

I. Refutation of Idealism as given in First Edition of " Critique " (A 366-80). — This refutation is mainly directed against Descartes, who is mentioned by name in A 367. Kant, as Vaihinger suggests, was very probably led to recognise Descartes' position as a species of idealism in the course of a re-study of Descartes before writing the section on the *Paralogisms*. As already pointed out, this involves the use of the term idealism in a much wider sense than that whioh was usually given to it in Kant's own day. In the development of his argument Kant also wavers between two very different definitions of this idealism, as being denial of *immediate* certainty and as denial of all certainty of the existence of material bodies.[2] The second interpretation, which would make it apply to Hume rather than to Descartes, is strengthened in the minds of his readers by his further distinction[3] between dogmatic and sceptical idealism, and the identification of the idealism under consideration with the latter. The title problematic which Kant in the second edition[4] applies to Descartes' position suffers from this same ambiguity. As a matter of fact, Kant's refutation applies equally well to either position. The teaching of Berkeley, which coincides with dogmatic idealism as here defined by Kant, namely, as consisting in the contention that the conception of matter is inherently contradictory, is not dwelt upon, and the appended promise of refutation is not fulfilled.

Descartes' position is stated as follows: only our own existence and inner states are immediately apprehended by us; all perceptions are modifications of inner sense; and

[1] Pp. 307-8.   [2] Cf. A 368-9 and 372.
[3] A 377 : a passage which bears signs of being a later interpolation.
[4] B 274.

the existence of external objects can therefore be asserted only by an inference from the inner perceptions viewed as effects.   In criticism, Kant points out that since an effect may result from more than one cause, this inference to a quite determinate cause, viz. objects as bodies in space, is doubtfully legitimate.   The cause of our inner states may lie within and not without us, and even if external, need not consist in spatial objects.   Further, leaving aside the question of a possible alternative to the assumption of independent material bodies, the assertion of the existence of such objects would, on Descartes' view, be merely conjectural.   It could never have certainty in any degree equivalent to that possessed by the experiences of inner sense.

"By an idealist, therefore, we must not understand one who denies the existence of outer objects of the senses, but only one who does not admit that their existence is known through immediate perception, and who therefore concludes that we can never, by way of any possible experience, be completely certain of their reality."[1]

No sooner is the term idealist thus clearly defined than Kant, in keeping with the confused character of the entire section, proceeds to the assertion (*a*) that there are idealists of another type, namely, transcendental idealists,[2] and (*b*) that the non-transcendental idealists sometimes also adopt a dogmatic position, not merely questioning the immediacy of our knowledge of matter, but asserting it to be inherently contradictory.   All this points to the composite origin of the contents of this section.

Transcendental idealism is opposed to empirical idealism. It maintains that phenomena are representations merely, not things in themselves.   Space and time are the sensuous forms of our intuitions.   Empirical idealism, on the other hand, goes together with transcendental realism.   It maintains that space and time are given as real in themselves, in independence of our sensibility.   (Transcendental here, as in the phrase "transcendental ideality,"[3] is exactly equivalent to transcendent.)   But such a contention is inconsistent with the other main tenet of empirical idealism.   For if our inner representations have to be taken as entirely distinct from their objects, they cannot yield assurance *even of the existence* of these objects.   To the transcendental idealist no such difficulty is presented.   His position naturally combines with empirical realism, or, as it may also be entitled, empirical

---

[1] A 368-9.   [2] A 369.
    [3] A 28 = B 44.   Cf. above, pp. 76, 116-17.

dualism. Material bodies in space, being merely subjective representations, are immediately apprehended. The existence of matter can be established "without our requiring to issue out beyond our bare self-consciousness or to assume anything more than the certainty of the representations in us, *i.e.* of the *cogito ergo sum*." [1] Though the objects thus apprehended are outside one another in space, space itself exists only in us.

"Outer objects (bodies) are mere appearances, and are therefore nothing but a species of my representations, the objects of which are something only through these representations. Apart from them they are nothing. Thus outer things exist as well as I myself, and both, indeed, upon the immediate witness of my self-consciousness. . . ." [2]

The only difference is that the representation of the self belongs only to inner, while extended bodies also belong to outer sense. There is thus a dualism, but one which falls entirely within the field of consciousness, and which is therefore empirical, not transcendental. There is indeed a transcendental object which "in the transcendental sense may be outside us," [3] but it is unknown and is not in question. It ought not to be confused with our representations of matter and corporeal things.

From this point [4] the argument becomes disjointed and repeats itself, and there is much to be said in support of the contention of Adickes that the remainder of the section is made up of a number of separate interpolations. [5] First, Kant applies the conclusion established in the *Postulates of Empirical Thought*, viz. that reality is revealed only in sensation. As sensation is an element in all outer perception, perception affords immediate certainty of real existence, Kant next enters [6] upon a eulogy of sceptical idealism as "a benefactor of human reason." It brings home to us the utter impossibility of proving the existence of matter on the assumption that spatial objects are things in themselves, and so constrains us to justify the assertions which we are at every moment making. And such justification is, Kant here claims, only possible if we recognise that outer objects as mere representations are immediately known. In the next paragraph we find a sentence which, together with the above eulogistic estimate of the merits of idealism, shows how very

---

[1] A 370.   [2] *Loc. cit.*   [3] A 372.
[4] A 373 : *Weil indessen*, etc.
[5] Adickes regards them as *later* additions. To judge by their content (cf. above, pp. 204 ff., 215-16, on Kant's doctrine of the transcendental object), they are more probably of quite early origin.
[6] A 377-8.

far Kant, at the time of writing, was from feeling the need of differentiating his position from that of subjectivism. The sentence is this :

"We cannot be sentient of what is outside ourselves, but only of what is in ourselves, and the whole of our self-consciousness therefore yields nothing save merely our own determinations."

It is probable, indeed, that the paragraph in which this occurs is of very early origin, prior to the development of the main body of the *Analytic* ; for in the same paragraph we also find the assertion, utterly at variance with the teaching of the *Analytic* and with that of the first and third *Paralogisms*, that " the thinking ego " is known phenomenally as *substance*.[1] We seem justified in concluding that the various manuscripts which have gone to form this section on the fourth *Paralogism* were written at an early date within the Critical period. We may note, in passing, two sentences in which, as in that quoted above, a distinction between representations and their objects is recognised in wording if not in fact.

"All outer perception furnishes immediate proof of something actual in space, or rather is the actual itself. To this extent empirical realism is beyond question, *i.e.* there corresponds to our outer perceptions something actual in space."[2]

Again in A 377 the assertion occurs that "our outer senses, as regards the data from which experience can arise, have their actual corresponding objects in space." Certainly these statements, when taken together with the other passages in this section, form a sufficiently strange combination of assertion and denial. Either there is a distinction between representation and its object or there is not ; if the former, then objects in space are not merely representations ; if the latter, then the "correspondence" is merely that of a thing with itself.[3]

This refutation of idealism will not itself stand criticism. For two separate reasons it entirely fails to attain its professed end. In the first place, it refutes the position of Descartes only by virtually accepting the still more extreme

[1] Adickes argues that this paragraph is subsequent to the main body of the *Analytic*, but that is in keeping with the tendency which he seems to show of dating passages, which cannot belong to the " Brief Outline," later rather than earlier.

[2] A 375.

[3] The remaining passages in the fourth *Paralogism*, together with the corresponding passages in B 274 ff., in Kant's note to B xxxix, and in B 291-3, are separately dealt with below, pp. 308 ff., 322 ff., 462-3.

position of Berkeley. Outer objects, Kant argues, are immediately known because they are ideas merely. There is no need for inference, because there is no transcendence of the domain of our inner consciousness. In other words, Kant refutes the problematic idealism of Descartes by means of the more subjective idealism of Berkeley. The "dogmatic" idealism of Berkeley in the form in which Kant here defines it,[1] namely, as consisting in the assertion that the notion of an independent spatial object involves inherent contradictions, is part of his own position. For this reason he was bound to fail in his promise[2] to refute such dogmatic idealism. Fortunately he never even attempts to do so. In the second place, Kant ignores the fact that he has himself adopted an "idealist" view of inner experience. Inner experience is not for him, as it was for Descartes, the immediate apprehension of genuine reality. As it is only appearance, the incorporation of outer experience within it, so far from establishing the reality of the objects of outer sense, must rather prove the direct contrary. No more is really established than Descartes himself invariably assumes, namely, the actual existence of mental representations of a corporeal world in space. Descartes' further assertion that the world of things in themselves can be inferred to be material and spatial, Kant, of course, refuses to accept. On this latter point Kant is in essential agreement with Berkeley.

It is by no means surprising that Kant's first critics,[3] puzzled and bewildered by the obscurer and more difficult portions of the *Critique*, should have based their interpretation of Kant's general position largely upon the above passages; and that in combining the extreme subjective idealism which Kant there advocates with his doctrine that the inner life of ever-changing experiences is itself merely ideal, should have come to the conclusion that Kant's position is an extension of that of Berkeley. Pistorius objected that in making outer appearances relative to an inner consciousness which is itself appearance, Kant is reducing everything to mere illusion. Hamann came to the somewhat similar conclusion, that Kant, notwithstanding his very different methods of argument, is "a Prussian Hume," in substantial agreement with his Scotch predecessor.

II. "Prolegomena," Section 13, Notes II. and III.—In the *Prolegomena* Kant replies to the criticism which the first edition of the *Critique* had called forth, that his position is an

---

[1] A 377.   [2] *Loc. cit.*   [3] *E.g.* Garve.

extension of the idealism of Descartes, and even more
thoroughgoing than that of Berkeley. Idealism he redefines
in a much narrower sense, which makes it applicable only to
Berkeley

". . . as consisting in the assertion that there are none but thinking
beings, and that all other things which we suppose ourselves to
perceive in intuition are nothing but representations in the thinking
beings, to which no object external to them corresponds in fact."[1]

In reply Kant affirms his unwavering belief in the reality
of *Dinge an sich*

". . . which though quite unknown to us as to what they are in
themselves, we yet know by the representations which their influence
on our sensibility procures us. . . . Can this be termed idealism?
It is the very contrary."[2]

Kant adds that his position is akin to that of Locke, differing
only in his assertion of the subjectivity of the primary as
well as of the secondary qualities.

"I should be glad to know what my assertions ought to have
been in order to avoid all idealism. I suppose I ought to have said,
not only that the representation of space is perfectly conformable to
the relation which our sensibility has to objects (for that I have said),
but also that it is completely similar to them—an assertion in which
I can find as little meaning as if I said that the sensation of red has
a similarity to the property of cinnabar which excites this sensation
in me."[3]

Kant is here very evidently using the term idealism in the
narrowest possible meaning, as representing only the position
of Berkeley, and as excluding that of Descartes and Leibniz.
Such employment of the term is at variance with his own
previous usage. Though idealism here corresponds to the
" dogmatic idealism " of A 377, it is now made to concern the
assertion or denial of things in themselves, not as previously
the problem of the reality of material objects and of space.
Kant is also ignoring the fact, which he more than once points
out in the *Critique*, that his philosophy cannot prove that the
cause of our sensations is without and not within us.   His
use of " body "[4] as a name for the thing in itself is likewise
without justification.   This passage is mainly polemical ; it is
hardly more helpful than the criticism to which it was designed
to reply.

In Section 13, Note iii., Kant meets the still more

[1] § 13, *W.* iv. pp. 288-9 : Eng. trans. p. 42.   [2] *Loc. cit.*
[3] *Op. cit.* pp. 289-90 : Eng. trans. pp. 43-4.   [4] In Note II.

extreme criticism (made by Pistorius), that his system turns
all the things of the world into mere illusion (*Schein*). He
distinguishes transcendental idealism from "the mystical and
visionary idealism of Berkeley" on the one hand, and on the
other from the Cartesian idealism which would convert mere
representations into things in themselves. To obviate the
ambiguities of the term transcendental, he declares that his
own idealism may perhaps more fitly be entitled Critical. This
distinction between mystical and Critical idealism connects
with the contents of the second part of the Appendix, treated
below.

III. "**Prolegomena**," **Section 49.**—This is simply a repetition
of the argument of the fourth *Paralogism*. The Cartesian
idealism, now (as in B 274) named material idealism, is alone
referred to. The Cartesian idealism does nothing, Kant says,
but distinguish external experience from dreaming. There is
here again the same confusing use of the term "corresponds."

"That something actual without us not only corresponds but
must correspond to our external perceptions can likewise be
proved. . . ."[1]

IV. "**Prolegomena**," **Second Part of the Appendix.**—Kant here
returns to the distinction, drawn in Section 13, Note iii.,
between what he now calls "idealism proper (*eigentlicher*),"[2]
i.e. visionary or mystical idealism, and his own.

"The position of all genuine idealists from the Eleatics to Bishop
Berkeley is contained in this formula: 'All cognition through the
senses and experience is nothing but mere illusion, and only in the
ideas of pure understanding and Reason is there truth. The
fundamental principle ruling all my idealism, on the contrary, is
this: 'All cognition of things solely from pure understanding or
pure Reason is nothing but mere illusion and only in experience is
there truth.'"[3]

This mode of defining idealism can, in this connection,
cause nothing but confusion. Its inapplicability to Berkeley
would seem to prove that Kant had no first-hand knowledge
of Berkeley's writings.[4] As Kant's Note to the Appendix to
the *Prolegomena*[5] shows, he also had Plato in mind. But the
definition given of "the fundamental principle" of his own
idealism is almost equally misleading. It omits the all-
essential point, that for Kant experience itself yields truth
only by conforming to *a priori* concepts. As it is, he proceeds

---

[1] § 49, *W.* iv. 336: Eng. trans. p. 99.   [3] *Anhang*, *W.* iv. p. 375 *n.*
[2] *W.* iv. p. 374: Eng. trans. p. 147.   [4] Cf. above, p. 155 ff.
[5] *W.* iv. p. 375.

to criticise Berkeley for failure to supply a sufficient criterion of distinction between truth and illusion. Such criterion, he insists, is necessarily *a priori*. The Critical idealism differs from that of Berkeley in maintaining that space and time, though sensuous, are *a priori*, and that in combination with the pure concepts of understanding they

". . . prescribe *a priori* its law to all possible experience : the law which at the same time yields the sure criterion for distinguishing within experience truth from illusion. My so-called idealism—which properly speaking is Critical idealism—is thus quite peculiar in that it overthrows ordinary idealism, and that through it all *a priori* cognition, even that of geometry, now attains objective reality, a thing which even the keenest realist could not assert till I had proved the ideality of space and time."[1]

V. **Sections added in Second Edition at the Conclusion of the Aesthetic.** (B 69 ff.)—Kant here again replies to the criticism of Pistorius that all existence has been reduced to the level of illusion (*Schein*). His defence is twofold : first, that in naming objects appearances he means to indicate that they are independently grounded, or, as he states it, are "something actually given." If we *mis*interpret them, the result is indeed illusion, but the fault then lies with ourselves and not with the appearances as presented. Secondly, he argues that the doctrine of the ideality of space and time is the only secure safeguard against scepticism. For otherwise the contradictions which result from regarding space and time as independently real will likewise hold of their contents, and everything, including even our own existence, will be rendered illusory. "The good Berkeley [observing these contradictions] cannot, indeed, be blamed for reducing bodies to mere illusion." This last sentence may perhaps be taken as supporting the view that notwithstanding the increased popularity of Berkeley in Germany and the appearance of new translations in these very years, Kant has not been sufficiently interested to acquire first-hand knowledge of Berkeley's writings.[2] The epithet employed, if meant to be depreciatory, is characteristic of the attitude which Kant invariably adopts in speaking of Berkeley.

VI. **"Refutation of Idealism" in Second Edition of the "Critique."** (B 274-9, supplemented by note to B xxxix.).— The refutation opens by equating idealism with material idealism (so named in contradistinction to his own "formal or rather Critical" teaching). Within material idealism Kant

---

[1] *W.* iv. p. 375 : Eng. trans. p. 147-8.   [2] Cf. above, p. 156.

distinguishes between the problematic idealism of Descartes, and the dogmatic idealism of Berkeley. The latter has, he says, been overthrown in the *Aesthetic.* The former alone is dealt with in this refutation. This is the first occurrence in the *Critique* of the expression " problematic idealism ": it is nowhere employed in the first edition.[1] Problematic idealism consists in the assertion that we are incapable of having experience of any existence save our own ; only our inner states are immediately apprehended ; all other existences are determined by inference from them. The refutation consists in the proof that we have experience, and not mere imagination of outer objects. This is proved by showing that inner experience, unquestioned by Descartes, is possible only on the assumption of outer experience, and that this latter is as immediate and direct as is the former.

Thesis.—The empirically determined consciousness of my own existence proves the existence of objects in space outside me.[2]

Proof.—I am conscious of my own existence as determined in time. Time determination presupposes the perception of something permanent. But nothing permanent is intuitable in the empirical self. On the cognitive side (*i.e.* omitting feelings, etc., which in this connection are irrelevant), it consists solely of representations ; and these demand a permanent, distinct from ourselves, in relation to which their changes, and so my own existence in the time wherein they change, may be determined.[3] Thus perception of this permanent is only possible through a thing outside, and not through the mere representation of a thing outside. And the same must hold true of the determination of my existence in time, since this also depends upon the apprehension of the permanent. That is to say, the consciousness of my existence is at the same time an immediate awareness of the existence of other things outside me.

In the note to the *Preface* to the second edition [4] occurs the following emphatic statement.

" Representation of something permanent in existence is not the same as permanent representation. For though the representation [of the permanent] may be very changing and variable like all our other representations, not excepting those of matter, it yet refers to

---

[1] As already noted above, p. 299, it is employed by Kant in his lectures on Metaphysics.

[2] Kant's phrase "in space outside me" is on Kant's principles really pleonastic. Cf. *Prolegomena*, § 49 ; Eng. trans. p. 101 : "the notion 'outside me' only signifies existence in space." Cf. A 373.

[3] Cf. text as altered by note to B xxxix. [4] B xxxix.

something permanent. This latter must therefore be an external thing distinct from all my representations, and its existence must be included in the determination of my own existence, constituting with it but a single experience such as would not take place even internally if it were not also at the same time, in part, external. How this should be possible we are as little capable of explaining further as we are of accounting for our being able to think the abiding in time, the coexistence of which with the variable generates the conception of change."

The argument of this note varies from that of B 274 ff. only in its use of an ambiguous expression which is perhaps capable of being taken as referring to things in themselves, but which does not seem to have that meaning. "I am just as certainly conscious that there are things outside me which relate to my sense. . . ."

In B 277-8 Kant refers to the empirical fact that determination of time can be made only by relation to outer happenings in space, such as the motion of the sun. This is a point which is further developed in another passage which Kant added in the second edition.

". . . in order to understand the possibility of things in conformity with the categories, and so to demonstrate the objective reality of the latter, we need not merely intuitions, but intuitions that are in all cases outer intuitions. When, for instance, we take the pure concepts of *relation*, we find firstly that in order to obtain something *permanent* in intuition corresponding to the concept of substance, and so to demonstrate the objective reality of this concept, we require an intuition in space (of matter). For space alone is determined as permanent, while time, and therefore everything that is in inner sense, is in constant flux. Secondly, in order to exhibit *change* as the intuition corresponding to the concept of *causality*, we must take as our example motion, *i.e.* change in space. Only in this way can we obtain the intuition of changes, the possibility of which can never be comprehended through any pure understanding. For change is combination of contradictorily opposed determinations in the existence of one and the same thing. Now how it is possible that from a given state of a thing an opposite state should follow, not only cannot be conceived by any reason without an example, but is actually incomprehensible to reason without intuition. The intuition required is the intuition of the movement of a point in space. The presence of the point in different spaces (as a sequence of opposite determinations) is what first yields to us an intuition of change. For in order that we may afterwards make inner changes likewise thinkable, we must represent time (the form of inner sense) figuratively as a line, and the inner change through the drawing of this line (motion), and so in this manner by means of outer intuition make comprehensible the successive existence of ourselves in different states. The reason of this is that all change, if it is indeed to be perceived as change, presupposes something permanent in intuition, and that in inner sense no permanent intuition is to be met with. Lastly, the possibility of the category of *community* cannot be comprehended through mere reason alone. Its objective reality is not to be understood without intuition and indeed outer intuition in space."[1]

In this passage Kant is modifying the teaching of the first edition in two very essential respects. In the first place, he is now asserting that consciousness of both space and motion is necessary to consciousness of time;[2] and in the second place, he is maintaining that the *categories* can acquire meaning only by reference to outer appearances. Had Kant made all the necessary alterations which these new positions involve, he would, as we shall find,[3] have had entirely to recast the chapters on *Schematism* and on the *Principles of Understanding*. Kant was not, however, prepared to make such extensive alterations, and these chapters are therefore left practically unmodified. This is one of the many important points in which the reader is compelled to reinterpret passages of earlier date in the light of Kant's later utterances. There is also a further difficulty. Does Kant, in maintaining that the categories can *acquire* significance only in reference to outer perception, also mean to assert that their subsequent employment is limited to the mechanical world of the material sciences? This is a point in regard to which Kant makes no quite direct statement; but indirectly he would seem to indicate that that was not his intention.[4] He frequently speaks of the states of inner sense as mechanically conditioned. Sensations,[5] feelings, and desires,[6] are, he would seem to

---

[1] B 291-2. The remaining points in B 274 ff. as well as in B xxxix *n.* are separately dealt with below, p. 322 ff.

[2] The nearest approach to such teaching in the first edition is in A 33 = B 50. Cf. above, pp. 135-8.

[3] Cf. below, pp. 333, 341, 360, 384-5.

[4] Adamson (*Development of Modern Philosophy*, i. pp. 241 ff.) takes the opposite view as to what is Kant's intended teaching, but remarks upon its inconsistency with Kant's own fundamental principles. "Now, in truth, Kant grievously endangers his own doctrine by insisting on the absence of *a priori* elements from our apprehension of the mental life; for it follows from that, if taken rigorously, that according to Kant sense and understanding are not so much sources which unite in producing knowledge, as, severally, sources of distinct kinds of apprehension. If we admit at all, in respect to inner sense, that there is some kind of apprehension without the work of understanding, then it has been acknowledged that sense is *per se* adequate to furnish a kind of apprehension." As pointed out above (p. 296), by the same line of reasoning Kant is disabled from viewing inner consciousness as merely reflective. In other words it can neither be more immediate nor less sensuous than outer perception. Cf. below, pp. 361, *n.* 3, 384-5.

[5] Above, pp. xlvi, 275-82; below, pp. 313-14, 384-5.

[6] Above, pp. 276, 279-80; below, pp. 312, 384-5.

assert, integral parts of the unitary system of phenomenal existence. Such a view is not, indeed, easily reconcilable with his equating of the principle of substance with the principle of the conservation of matter.[1]   There are here two conflicting positions which Kant has failed to reconcile: the traditional dualistic attitude of Cartesian physics and the quite opposite implications of his Critical phenomenalism. When the former is being held to, Kant has to maintain that psychology can never become a science;[2] but his Critical teaching consistently developed seems rather to support the view that psychology, despite special difficulties peculiar to its subject matter, can be developed on lines strictly analogous to those of the material sciences.

We may now return to Kant's main argument.   This new refutation of idealism in the second edition differs from that given in the fourth *Paralogism* of the first edition, not only in method of argument but also in the nature of the conclusion which it seeks to establish.   Indeed it proves the *direct opposite* of what is asserted in the first edition.   The earlier proof sought to show that, as regards immediacy of apprehension and subjectivity of existence, outer appearances stand on the same level as do our inner experiences.   The proof of the second edition, on the other hand, argues that though outer appearances are immediately apprehended they must be existences distinct from the subjective states through which the mind represents them.   The two arguments agree, indeed, in establishing immediacy, but as that which is taken as immediately known is in the one case a subjective state and in the other an independent existence, the immediacy calls in the two cases for entirely different methods of proof. The first method consisted in viewing outer experiences as a subdivision within our inner experiences.   The new method views their relation as not that of including and included,

---

[1] Cf. below, p. 361.
[2] Cf. *Metaphysical First Principles of Natural Science* (1786), *W.* iv. pp. 470-1. It should be observed, however, that the reasons which Kant gives in this treatise for denying that psychology can ever become more than a merely historical or descriptive discipline are not that the objects of inner sense fall outside the realm of mechanically determined existence.   Kant makes no assertion that even distantly implies any such view.   His reasons are—(1) that, as time has only one dimension, the main body of mathematical science is not applicable to the phenomena of inner sense and their laws; (2) that such phenomena are capable only of a merely ideal, not of an experimental, analysis; (3) that, as the objects of inner sense do not consist of parts outside each other, their parts are not substances, and may therefore be conceived as diminishing in intensity or passing out of existence without prejudice to the principle of the permanence of substance (*op. cit.* p. 542, quoted below, p. 361, *n.* 2); (4) that inner observation is limited to the individual's own existence; (5) that the very act of introspection alters the state of the object observed.

but of conditioning and conditioned ; and it is now to outer experience that the primary position is assigned. So far is outer experience from being possible only as part of inner experience, that on the contrary inner experience, consciousness of the flux of inner states, is only possible in and through experience of independent material bodies in space. A sentence from each proof will show how completely their conclusions are opposed.

"Outer objects (bodies) are mere appearances, and are therefore nothing but a species of my representations, the objects of which are something only through these representations. Apart from them they are nothing."[1] "Perception of this permanent is possible only through a *thing* outside me, and not through the mere *representation* of a thing outside me."[2]

The one sentence asserts that outer objects are representations ; the other argues that they must be existences distinct from their representations. The one inculcates a subjectivism of a very extreme type ; the other results in a realism, which though ultimately phenomenalist, is none the less genuinely objective in character. This difference is paralleled by the nature of the idealisms to which the two proofs are opposed and which they profess to refute. The argument of the *Paralogism* of the first edition is itself Berkeleian, and refutes only the problematic idealism of Descartes. The argument of the second edition, though formally directed only against Descartes, constitutes a no less complete refutation of the position of Berkeley. In its realism it has kinship with the positions of Arnauld and of Reid; while, in attempting to combine this realism with due recognition of the force and validity of Hume's sceptical philosophy, it breaks through all previous classifications, formulates a profoundly original substitute for the previously existing theories, and inaugurates a new era in the theory of knowledge.

As already pointed out,[3] Kant restates the distinction between the subjective and the objective in a manner which places the problem of knowledge in an entirely new light. The subjective is not to be regarded as opposite in nature to the objective, but as a subspecies within it. It does not proceed parallel with the sequence of natural existences, but is itself part of the natural system which consciousness reveals. Sensations, in the form in which they are consciously apprehended by us, do not constitute our consciousness of nature,

[1] A 370.
[2] B 275. These two sentences are cited in this connection by Vaihinger · *Strassburger Abhandlungen sur Philosophie* (1884), p. 131.
[3] Above, pp. xlv-vii, 279 ff.

but are themselves events which are possible only under the conditions which the natural world itself supplies.[1] The Cartesian dualism of the subjective and the objective is thus subordinated to the Critical distinction between appearance and reality. Kant's phenomenalism is a genuine alternative to the Berkeleian teaching, and not, as Schopenhauer and so many others have sought to maintain, merely a variant upon it.

The striking contradiction between Kant's various refutations of idealism has led some of Kant's most competent critics to give a different interpretation of the argument of the second edition from that given above. These critics take the independent and permanent objects which are distinguished from our subjective representations to be things in themselves. That is to say, they interpret this refutation as based upon Kant's semi-Critical doctrine of the transcendental object (in the form in which it is employed for the solution of the *Antinomies*), and so as agreeing with the refutation given in the *Prolegomena*.[2] Kant is taken as rejecting idealism because of his belief in things in themselves. This is the view adopted by Benno Erdmann,[3] Sidgwick,[4] A. J. Balfour.[5]

As Vaihinger,[6] Caird,[7] and Adamson [8] have shown, such an interpretation is at complete variance with the actual text. This is, indeed, so obvious upon unbiassed examination that the only point which repays discussion is the question, why Benno Erdmann and those who follow him should have felt constrained to place so unnatural an interpretation upon Kant's words. The explanation seems to lie in Erdmann's convinced belief, plainly shown in all his writings upon Kant, that the *Critique* expounds a single consistent and uniform standpoint.[9] If such belief be justified, there is no alternative save to interpret Kant's refutation of idealism in the manner which Erdmann adopts. For as the subjectivism of much of Kant's teaching is beyond question, consistency can be obtained only by sacrifice of all that conflicts with it. Thus, and thus alone, can Erdmann's rendering of the refutation of the second edition be sustained; the actual wording,

<hr>

[1] Cf. also above, pp. 275-7, and below, Appendix C.
[2] § 13, *Anmerkung II.*   [3] *Kriticismus*, p. 197 ff.   Cf. below, Appendix C.
[4] *Mind* (1879),iv. p. 408 ff. ; (1880), v. p. 111.
[5] *A Defence of Philosophic Doubt* (1879), p. 107 ff. ; *Mind* (1878), iii. p. 481 ; v. p. 115; vi. p. 260.   [6] *Op. cit.* p. 128 ff.
[7] *Critical Philosophy*, i. 632 ff. ; *Mind* (1879), iv. pp. 112, 560-1 ; v. p. 115.
[8] *The Philosophy of Kant*, p. 249 ff.
[9] The one fundamental question to which Erdmann would seem to allow that Kant gives conflicting answers is as to whether or not categories can be transcendently employed.   The assumption of a uniform teaching is especially obvious in Sidgwick's comments ; cf. *Mind* (1880), v. p. 113 ; *Lectures on the Philosophy of Kant* (1905), p. 28.

taken in and by itself, does not support it. Kant here departs from his own repeated assertion, in the second hardly less than in the first edition of the *Critique*, of the subjectivity of outer appearances. But, as Vaihinger justly contends, Kant was never greater than in this violation of self-consistency, "never more consistent than in this inconsistency." Tendencies, previously active but hitherto inarticulate, are at last liberated. If the chrysalis stage of the intense brooding of the twelve years of Critical thinking was completed in the writing of the first edition of the *Critique*, the philosophy which then emerged only attains to mature stature in those extensions of the *Critique*, scattered through it from *Preface* to *Paralogisms*, which embody this realistic theory of the independent existence of material nature. For this theory is no mere external accretion, and no mere reversal of subordinate tenets, but a ripening of germinal ideas to which, even in their more embryonic form, the earlier Critical teaching owed much of its inspiration, and which, when consciously adopted and maturely formulated, constitute such a deepening of its teaching as almost amounts to transformation. The individual self is no longer viewed as being the bearer of nature, but as its offspring and expression, and as being, like nature, interpretable in its twofold aspect, as appearance and as noumenally grounded. The bearer of appearance is not the individual subject, but those transcendental creative agencies upon which man and nature alike depend. Both man and nature transcend the forms in which they are apprehended ; and nothing in experience justifies the giving of such priority to the individual mind as must be involved in any acceptance of subjectivist theory. Though man is cognisant of space and time, comprehending them within the limits of his consciousness, and though in all experience unities are involved which cannot originate within or be explained by experience, it is no less true that man is himself subject to the conditions of space and time, and that the synthetic unities which point beyond experience do not carry us to a purely individual subject. If man is not a part or product of nature, neither is nature the product of man. Kant's transcendentalism, in its maturest form, is genuinely phenomenalist in character. That is the view which has already been developed above, in the discussion of Kant's transcendental deduction. I shall strive to confirm it by comparison of the teaching of the two editions of the *Critique* in regard to the reality of outer appearances.

Schopenhauer, to whom this new development of the Critical teaching was altogether anathema, the cloven hoof of the Hegelian heresies, denounced it as a temporary and ill-judged distortion of the true Critical position, maintaining that it is incapable of combination with Kant's central teaching, and that it finds no support in the tenets, pure and unperverted, of the first edition. Kant, he holds, is here untrue to himself, and temporarily, under the stress of polemical discussion, lapses from the heights to which he had successfully made his way, and upon which he had securely established, in agreement with Plato and in extension of Berkeley, the doctrine of all genuine philosophical thinking, the doctrine of the *Welt als Vorstellung*.

We may agree with Schopenhauer in regarding those sections of the first edition of the *Critique* which were omitted in the second edition as being a permanently valuable expression of Kantian thought, and as containing much that finds no equally adequate expression in the passages which were substituted for them ; and yet may challenge his interpretation of both editions alike. If, as we have already been arguing, we must regard Kant's thinking as in large degree tentative, that is, as progressing by the experimental following out of divergent tendencies, we may justly maintain that among the most characteristic features of his teaching are the readiness with which he makes changes to meet deeper insight, and the persistency with which he strives to attain a position in which there will be least sacrifice or blurring of any helpful distinction, and fullest acknowledgment of the manifold and diverse considerations that are really essential. Recognising these features, we shall be prepared to question the legitimacy of Schopenhauer's opposition between the teaching of the two editions. We shall rather expect to find that the two editions agree in the alternating statement and retraction of conflicting positions, and that the later edition, however defective in this or that aspect as compared with the first edition, none the less expresses the maturer insight, and represents a further stage in the development of ideas that have been present from the start. It may perhaps for this very reason be more contradictory in its teaching ; it will at least yield clearer and more adequate formulation of the diverse consequences and conflicting implications of the earlier tenets. It will be richer in content, more open-eyed in its adoption of mutually contradictory positions, freer therefore from unconscious assumptions, and better fitted to supply the data necessary for judgment upon its own defects. Only those critics who are blind to the stupendous difficulties of the tasks which Kant here sets himself, and credulous of their speedy and final completion, can complain of the result.

Philosophical thinkers of the most diverse schools in Germany, France, and England, have throughout the nineteenth century received from the *Critique* much of their inspiration.   The profound influence which Kant has thus exercised upon succeeding thought must surely be reckoned a greater achievement than any that could have resulted from the constructing of a system so consistent and unified, that the alternative would lie only between its acceptance and its rejection.   Ultimately the value of a philosophy consists more in the richness of its content and the comprehensiveness of its dialectic, than in the logical perfection of its formal structure.   The latter quality is especially unfitted to a philosophy which inaugurated a new era, and formulated the older problems in an altogether novel manner.   Under such conditions fertility of suggestion and readiness to modify or even recast adopted positions, openness to fuller insight acquired through the very solutions that may at first have seemed to satisfy and close the issues, are more to be valued than the power to remove contradictions and attain consistency.   This is the point of view which I shall endeavour to justify in reference to the matters now before us.   In particular there are two points to be settled : first, whether and how far the argument of the second edition is prefigured in the first edition ; and secondly, whether and to what extent it harmonises with, and gives expression to, all that is most central and genuinely Critical in both editions.

In the first place we must observe that the fourth *Paralogism* occurs in a section which bears all the signs of having been independently written and incorporated later into the main text.   It is certainly of earlier origin than those sections which represent the third and fourth layers of the deduction of the first edition, and very possibly was composed in the middle 'seventies.   Indeed, apart from single paragraphs which may have been added in the process of adapting it to the main text, it could quite well, so far as its refutation of idealism is concerned, be of even earlier date.   The question as to the consistency of the refutation of the second edition with the teaching of the first edition must therefore chiefly concern those parts of the *Analytic* which connect with the later forms of the transcendental deduction, that is to say, with the transcendental deduction itself, with the *Analogies* and *Postulates*, and with particular paragraphs that have been added in other sections.   We have already noted how Kant from the very first uses terms which involve the drawing of a distinction between representations and their objects.   Passages in which this distinction occurs can be cited from both the *Aesthetic* and the *Analytic*, and two such· occur in the fourth *Paralogism* itself.[1] Objects, he says, "correspond" to their representations. A variation in expression is found in such passages as the following :

". . . the objects of outer perception also actually exist (*auch wirklich sind*) in that very form in which they are intuited in space. . . ."[2]

Such language is meaningless, and could never have been chosen, if Kant had not, even in the earlier stages of his thinking, postulated a difference between the existence of an object and the existence of its representation. He must at least have distinguished between the representations and their content. That, however, he could have done without advancing to the further assertion of their independent existence. Probably he was not at all clear in his own mind, and was too preoccupied with the other complexities of his problem, to have thought out his position to a definite decision. When, however, as in the fourth *Paralogism*, he made any attempt so to do, he would seem to have felt constrained to adopt the extreme subjectivist position. Expressions to that effect are certainly very much more common than those above mentioned. This is what affords Schopenhauer such justification, certainly very strong, as he can cite for regarding subjectivism as the undoubted teaching of the first edition.

When, however, we also take account of the very different teaching which is contained in the important section on the *Postulates of Empirical Thought*, the balance of evidence is decisively altered. The counter-teaching, which is suggested by certain of the conflicting factors of the transcendental deduction and of the *Analogies*, here again receives clear and detailed expression. This is the more significant, as it is in this section that Kant sets himself formally to define what is to be understood by empirical reality. It thus contains his, so to speak, official declaration as to the mode of existence possessed by outer appearances. The passage chiefly relevant is as follows :

"If the existence of the thing is bound up with some perceptions according to the principles of their empirical connection (the Analogies), we can determine its existence antecedently to the perception of it, and consequently, to that extent, in an *a priori* manner. For as the existence of the thing is bound up with our perceptions in a possible experience, we are able in the series of possible perceptions, and under the guidance of the Analogies, to make the transition from our actual perception to the thing in

---

[1] Cf. above, pp. 303·4.   [2] A 491 = B 520.

question. Thus we discover the existence of a magnetic matter pervading all bodies from the perception of the attracted iron filings, although the constitution of our organs cuts us off from all immediate perception of that matter. For in accordance with the laws of sensibility and the connection of our perceptions in a single experience, we should, were our senses more refined, actually experience it in an immediate empirical intuition. The grossness of our senses does not in any way decide the form of possible experience in general." [1]

Now it cannot, of course, be argued that the above passage is altogether unambiguous. We can, if we feel sufficiently constrained thereto, place upon it an interpretation which would harmonise it with Kant's more usual subjectivist teaching, namely as meaning that in the progressive construction of experience, or in the ideal completion which follows upon assumption of more refined sense-organs, possible empirical realities are made to become, or are assumed to become, real, but that until the possible experiences are thus realised in fact or in ideal hypothesis, they exist outwardly only in the form of their noumenal conditions. And as a matter of fact, this is how Kant himself interprets the teaching of this section in the process of applying it in solution of the antinomies.

"Accordingly, if I represent to myself the aggregate of all objects of the senses existing in all time and all places, I do not set them, antecedently to experience, in space and time. The representation is nothing but the thought of a possible experience in its absolute completeness. Since the objects are mere representations, only in such a possible experience are they given. To say that they exist prior to all my experience, can only be taken as meaning that they will be met with, if, starting from actual perception, I advance to that part of experience to which they belong. The cause of the empirical conditions of this advance (that which determines what members I shall meet with, or how far I can meet with any such in my regress) is transcendental, and is therefore necessarily unknown to me. We are not, however, concerned with this transcendental cause, but only with the rule of progression in that experience in which objects, that is to say, appearances, are given. Moreover, in outcome it is a matter of indifference whether I say that in the empirical progress in space I can meet with stars a hundred times farther removed than the outermost now perceptible to me, or whether I say that they are perhaps to be met with in cosmical space even though no human being has ever perceived or ever will perceive them. For though they might be given as things in themselves, without relation to possible experience, they are still nothing to me, and therefore are not objects, save in so far as they are contained in the series of the empirical regress." [2]

---

[1] A 225-6 = B 273.   Cf. below, Appendix C.   [2] A 495-6 = B 523-4.

But though this is a possible interpretation of the teaching of the *Postulates*, and though further it is Kant's own interpretation in another portion of the *Critique*, it is not by any means thereby decided that this is what the section itself actually teaches. Unbiassed study of the section, in independence of the use to which it is elsewhere put, can find within it no such limitation to its assertion of the actual independent existence of non-perceived bodies. We have to remember that the doctrine and solution of the *Antinomies* was completed prior to the writing of the central portions of the *Critique*. The section treating of their *solution* seems, indeed, in certain parts to be later [1] than the other main portions of the chapter on the *Antinomies*, and must have been at least recast after completion of the *Postulates*. But the subjectivist solution is so much simpler in statement, so much more fully worked out, and indeed so much more capable of definite formulation, and also so much more at one with the teaching developed in the preceding chapter on the *Paralogisms*, that even granting the doctrine expounded in the section on the *Postulates* to be genuinely phenomenalist, it is not surprising that Kant should have been unwilling to recast his older and simpler solution of the *Antinomies*. In any case we are not concerned to argue that Kant, even after formulating the phenomenalist view, yields to it an unwavering adherence. As I have already insisted, his attitude continues to the very last to be one of alternation between two opposed standpoints.

But the most significant feature of Kant's treatment of the argument of the *Postulates* still remains for consideration. It was in immediate succession to the paragraph above quoted [2] that Kant, in the second edition, placed his "*Refutation of Idealism*" with the emphatic statement that this (not as in the first edition in connection with the *Paralogisms*) was its "correct location." It is required, he says, as a reply to an objection which the teaching of the *Postulates* must at once suggest. The argument of the second edition in proof of the independent reality of material bodies, and in disproof of subjectivism, is thus given by Kant as a necessary extension and natural supplement of the teaching of the first edition.

There is therefore reason for concluding that the same preconception which has led to such radical misinterpretation of Kant's *Refutation of Idealism* has been at work in inducing a false reading of Kant's argument in the *Postulates*, namely the belief that Kant's teaching proceeds on consistent lines, and that it must at all costs be harmonised with itself.

---

[1] Cf. below, p. 506.   [2] Viz. A 225·6 = B 273.

Finding subjectivism to be emphatically and unambiguously inculcated in all the main sections of the *Critique*, and the phenomenalist views, on the other hand, to be stated in a much less definite and somewhat elusive manner, commentators have impoverished the Critical teaching by suppression of many of its most subtile and progressive doctrines. Kant's experimental, tentative development of divergent tendencies is surely preferable to this artificial product of high-handed and unsympathetic emendation.

A COMPARISON OF KANT'S IDEALISM WITH THAT OF BERKELEY

By H. W. B. JOSEPH

Read July 3, 1929

WHEN I reflect how much is said and written, and how little certainty is reached, on questions of philosophy, I can but doubt the wisdom of the invitation with which I have been honoured, to lecture before you to-day. Great indeed must be the attraction of our problems, and the interest of our pursuit, to support us in the endurance of so many disappointments.

We have seen in recent years an active output of new philosophical theories, and much of it has claimed the name of realism. When I was an undergraduate there were very few teachers in Oxford who did not regard the case for realism as finally disposed of: for realism, I mean, in the sense that the things we perceive, with which science is concerned, are independent of any knowing mind. That things known are independent of mind is asserted on all sides to-day.

Some who assert it are primarily interested in maintaining what is rather different, that the object of any man's knowledge is what it is and what he knows it to be, independently of any knowing of it. To maintain this, if mind is active in some other way than knowing, is not to maintain that the thing known is independent of mind in every way. Others are primarily interested in bringing the mind within the sweep of scientific, and particularly of biological, investigation; but that is an old story. Others, among whom are the so-called New Realists, take a more original position. They assert to be independent of mind the very objects of apprehension which in the idealist tradition were held most obviously dependent: sounds, colours, scents, and what we distinguish, as the shifting appearances of the same thing to different observers, from the supposed identical thing. These sense-data or sensa, they say, are no otherwise mental than a man is a French citizen, by membership of a particular aggregate. He can lose his citizenship but remain the same man; and a sensum can lose the relations to others which make it mental, and still remain the same item. What collects certain of those items into minds, and at other times or even at the same time into bodies, is not clear; and certainly is not made clearer by what we are told about processes of logical construction, since products of construction can hardly do the constructing. *Mutatis mutandis*, Bradley's question is still pertinent: 'Mr. Bain collects that the mind is a collection; has he ever thought who collects Mr. Bain?' [1]

No philosopher has more uncompromisingly rejected realism, in the sense in which I am taking the word, than Berkeley, and none has claimed more confidently to have refuted Berkeley than Kant. Kant's *Refutation of Idealism* in the second edition of the *Critique of Pure Reason* is notoriously at variance with much of his teaching elsewhere; particularly with passages of the first edition which he omitted from the second. Some find in it an abandonment of the fundamental doctrine that our knowledge is only of appearances, not of things by themselves; another sees in its 'realistic theory of the independent existence of material nature' the ripening of the germinal ideas which give to the critical philosophy its real originality and value.[2] To me it seems that the argument of it is singularly weak. But if we reject it, what are we to say of the relation of Berkeley's thought to Kant's? That is the question which I wish to discuss, for it seems to me to have some points of interest which I have not found worked out.

[1] *Ethical Studies*, 2nd ed., p. 39.
[2] N. K. Smith, *A Commentary on Kant's Critique of Pure Reason*, p. 315.

Let us first examine Kant's *Refutation*. It runs as follows: 'The bare, but empirically determined consciousness of my own existence proves the existence of objects in space outside me.' That is his thesis; here is his proof. It is not long. 'I am conscious of my existence as determined in time. All time-determination presupposes something permanent in perception. But this permanent cannot be something in me, just because my existence in time cannot be determined except through it. Therefore the perception of this permanent is possible only through *a thing* without me, not through the bare *presentation* of a thing without me. Consequently the determination of my existence in time is possible only through the existence of real things which I perceive outside myself. Now consciousness in time is necessarily connected with consciousness of the possibility of this time-determination; therefore it is also necessarily connected with the existence of things outside me, as a condition of time-determination, *i.e.* the consciousness of my own existence is at the same time an immediate consciousness of the existence of other things outside me.' [1]

The general character of the argument is this: that consciousness of one thing, A (my existence in time), is impossible without consciousness of another, B (things outside

---

[1] B. 275–6. The *Refutation* professes to be directed against the 'problematic idealism' of which Kant takes Descartes as spokesman, not the 'dogmatic idealism' of Berkeley; that, Kant says, is unavoidable, if space be supposed to be a property of things; but his doctrine, that space is a form of our sensibility, has removed the ground for it. The removal, however, of an assumption whose truth would make idealism necessary still leaves it possible that idealism may be established on other grounds; and the *Refutation* must have rather had in mind Berkeley, who explicitly rejected the reality of material substance, and is elsewhere by Kant taken as an outstanding exponent of idealism, than Descartes, who, though denying that we *immediately* apprehend bodies in space, taught that we had conclusive reasons for asserting their existence. Kant's *Refutation* professes to show that our apprehension of them is immediate; so far, therefore, it contradicts Descartes; but if sound, it would on the main point refute rather Hume and Berkeley, who did deny the reality of material substance, than Descartes who did not.

me); the consciousness of A being admitted, that of B, and
therefore the existence of B, must be admitted also. This
is why Kant concludes a proof of the *existence* of objects in
space outside me with the statement that my consciousness
of my own existence in time is at the same time an *immediate
consciousness* of their existence.[1] His procedure is reflection,
and really dogmatic; but none the worse for that.   But let
us turn to the detail.

The statement that I am conscious of my existence as
determined in time must mean, I think, merely that I am
conscious that my states, or what Kant elsewhere calls the
phenomena of my inner sense, are successive; time relation is a form of relatedness in which they occur.   But the
interpretation of the next sentence, 'All time-determination
presupposes something permanent in perception', is more
difficult.   If, as Kant is trying to prove, there are real things
outside me which may exist and change unperceived, their
existence is also determined in time; but as their existence,
and so the time-relatedness involved in their existence, do
not presuppose perception, they do not presuppose anything
permanent in perception.   Of their relatedness in time, therefore, the sentence would not be true, and Kant must have
meant here by time-determination perception or consciousness of time-determination.   But what did he mean by saying
that it presupposes something permanent in perception:
that it presupposes something permanently perceived, or
perceiving something permanent?   The first alternative may
draw support from empirical psychology.   We are told that
the apprehension of change in our states is possible only
if there is some unchanging state with which their changes
may be noticed to contrast.   The somatic consciousness,
or coenaesthesia, is said to furnish the contrast required;
and when anything occurs to interrupt the continuous
qualitative identity of this state of feeling it is said that pro-

---

[1] It is also why he describes his argument as a refutation of the
problematic idealism of Descartes, which rests on the denial that our
consciousness of their existence is immediate.

found psychical disturbances arise. But whatever be the empirical facts about coenaesthesia, it hardly provides an unchanging state of feeling, nor anything with the permanence that Kant's argument on this interpretation of it would require. Moreover, not only had Kant denied, in the first edition[1], that any empirical state is thus unchanging, but the next sentence seems to exclude such an interpretation, for it says that 'this permanent cannot be something in me'; and 'something in me' should mean some state of myself of which I am conscious, some phenomenon of my inner sense. Kant must therefore be taken to have meant that the consciousness of the time-determination of my states presupposes the perception of something permanent; and this permanent is not in me—that is, it is not one of my states; for if it were, it would be merely one of the items, the consciousness of which presupposes that of something else. But why may not the permanent be the self which is not any of its states? Until this is shown, the argument cannot proceed. It is fair enough to say that the perception of this permanent is not possible through the bare *presentation* of a thing without me. For, the bare presentation, or *Vorstellung*, would be a state in me; and when Kant argues that the consciousness of my successive states is only possible through something permanent in perception, *i.e.* (as we have seen) through perceiving something permanent, he means through being aware of a permanent that is none of my states. But why must it therefore be a *thing without me*? Why may it not be myself? This is the crucial point. The rest of the proof seems only to say that if consciousness of A is not possible without consciousness of B, I am immediately, and not subsequently and inferentially, conscious of B in being conscious of A.

It would seem that Kant was uneasy about assuming *sub silentio* that it is not enough, in order to be conscious of succession in my states, to be aware of the permanence of my actively conscious self. For in the first two *Remarks* that

[1] *Kritik der reinen Vernunft*, A. 107.

follow the *Proof*, he alleges, without establishing, its insufficiency; indeed, in the second *Remark* he states that we can only set before ourselves (or, according to another text, perceive) a time-determination through the movement of something permanent in space. No doubt we measure durations this way; but consciousness of succession is possible without it, as in hearing a tune. The doctrine of the synthetic unity of apperception teaches that I could not be conscious of any relatedness among my presentations—and therefore not of my existence in time—if the 'I think' could not accompany them all: if, that is, I could not be conscious of the one self whose they all are. This permanent is therefore apprehended. Kant indeed warns me against ascribing to it any further permanence than is needed in order that it may be the correlative of my successive states; that would be to make a transcendent use of the conception of the self. But equally the permanence of the permanent in space is only correlative with experience.

Nor is it of any use to point out that the self is not an object of empirical intuition (which was the reason why Hume rejected it); for equally what is permanent in space, as distinguished from its changing qualities, which Kant regards, at least from one point of view, as presentations, or states in me, is not an object of empirical intuition. It is true that he alleges impenetrability to serve thus as the intuitable in our apprehension of matter. But impenetrability is not really sensible. As he points out elsewhere, a body may seem to disappear, *e.g.* when consumed by fire; and not empirical intuition, but only the conviction that there is something permanent which changes, makes us confident that it has not disappeared. True, we go on to say that it has been *dispersed*; *i.e.* we think of its parts, if taken small enough, as unchanged. But this is to make figure, rather than impenetrability, the sensible to be submitted to the conception of permanence; and even figure only serves on the supposition that there are atoms of unchanging shape preserved in all their movements. Some have believed that bodies, however small, may change shape as well as place. If that were so, there would be no sensible correlate for permanence at all; and if it be not so, there is still a great difficulty presented by the question of the atom's real and permanent size. That only the permanent can change, as maintained by Kant elsewhere, is a proposition in metaphysics; it cannot be verified by observation any more of things without me than of myself. There may be reasons, and I believe there are, for assigning to things without me a reality which Berkeley denies them. But they are not produced in the argument before us.

The *Refutation of Idealism* therefore, I think, fails. Kant has not succeeded here in dragging the root of his doctrine to light. Yet I believe we may discover the thought that guided him, and that we may be helped to this discovery by a comparison of his teaching with Berkeley's. I put aside any considerations which rest upon discarded passages of the first edition, as that whereas Kant says, in the *Fourth Paralogism*,[1] that space itself, with all its appearances, as presentations, is only in me, Berkeley in his *Siris*[2] says that 'those who would penetrate into the real and true causes' will 'speak of the world as contained by the soul, and not the soul by the world'. I shall take Kantian doctrine that is unwithdrawn, and (as I think) for Kant fundamental. I wish to call attention to a remarkable agreement between their accounts of what the reality of things consists in, and again of their distinctions between reality and illusion within experience; and at the same time to call attention to certain connected differences in their doctrines.

Berkeley finds the reality of things in the order and connexion of our ideas.[3] 'Mechanical laws of nature or motion direct us how to act, and teach us what to expect.'[4] 'Natural philosophers excel, as they are more or less acquainted with the laws and methods observed by the Author of

[1] A. 375. [2] § 285.
[3] *Principles of Human Knowledge*, §§ 60-6.
[4] *Siris*, § 234.

Nature,'[1] but observed, if we would speak strictly, in causing men's ideas. For a spirit is the only real cause; what we call the relation of cause and effect in nature is properly a relation of sign and thing signified. 'Ideas are not anyhow and at random produced.'[2] But they are not produced by bodies. 'We are chained to a body,' says Philonous; 'that is to say, our perceptions are connected with corporeal motions. By the law of our nature, we are affected upon every alteration in the nervous parts of our sensible body; which sensible body,' he however continues, 'is nothing but a complexion of such qualities or ideas as have no existence distinct from being perceived by a mind; so that this connexion of sensations with corporeal motions means no more than a correspondence in the order of nature between two sets of ideas, or things immediately perceivable.'[3] This system of signs he calls the Language of the Author of Nature. But it should be noted that there is a certain confusion in his use of that metaphor. He first employs it in his *New Theory of Vision*, where he speaks of a visual language.[4] But tangibles are there treated as 'without the mind', and the metaphor, on this basis, is appropriate enough. Afterwards sign and thing signified are equally ideas; but in language words do not stand for one another. Hence he also treats the order of ideas in its entirety as a language in which the Author of Nature declares to us himself; and what they signify is not one another but their Author.[5] The metaphor is now at fault; for it is the words of a language that have meaning, not a language in its entirety. This failure of the metaphor is, as we shall see, important. It betrays a failure to think out the necessities of his doctrine.

Meanwhile it is clear what answer Berkeley held himself entitled to give to any one asking him how he distinguished

---

[1] *Siris*, § 243. [2] *Principles of Human Knowledge*, § 64.
[3] *Works*, vol. i, p. 459, ed. Oxford, 1901. *Dialogues between Hylas and Philonous*, III.
[4] § 147, cf. *Principles of Human Knowledge*, § 44, &c.
[5] *e.g., Siris*, § 254.

between real and illusory perception. If I really see a man before me, the occurrence of my present visual idea is connected with that of other ideas in my own mind, such as I might name by saying that I heard the sound of his approaching footsteps, saw his footmarks, shook him by the hand, and so forth; it is connected again with the occurrence in other finite minds of ideas more or less like mine, and with the possibility of such ideas in other finite minds as might be named by saying that they saw the reflection of his body in the cornea of my eye. But if I merely have the illusion of seeing him, then the occurrence of the same present visual idea is connected with that of none of those others; but only perhaps with that of some past emotional ideas, hopes and fears, of mine, and with future ideas in other minds that might be named by saying that they saw marks of disease in my brain at a *post-mortem*. Now what is Kant's doctrine? 'To know the *reality* of things requires *perception*, and consequently sensation, of which one is conscious: conscious not indeed immediately of the object whose existence is to be known, but yet of its connexion with some real perception according to the analogies of experience; it is these which exhibit to us in general all real connexion in an experience.'[1] The analogies of experience require us to regard our presentations as occurring in connexion with physiological conditions; these are events in nature; and nature we must conceive as a system of bodies in space, determining changes one in another according to laws or rules. To perceive something real therefore is to have a presentation or *Vorstellung* (the word is the equivalent here of Berkeley's 'idea'), whose occurrence is connected according to the order of nature with that of other presentations, our own or other people's. The illusory, as before, would be differently connected. If we ask what difference there is between the two doctrines in their cash value (to use William James's phrase), the answer is—none.

But, it will be said, there is this great difference, that

[1] *Kritik der reinen Vernunft*, B. 272.

Berkeley allows nothing except the cash of ideas and the Author of Nature; Kant distinguishes our perceptions or ideas alike from things by themselves (what he sometimes calls the transcendental object, an unknown x) and from objects of experience—real things in space without me. In his system, the cash of ideas will buy goods that can be delivered.

Doubtless he thought so. But when we consider how Berkeley's account needs supplementing, if it is to be made intelligible, and what Kant tells us of the real nature of the goods, or phenomena, the difference between them will appear less great.

About the nature of phenomena, and their distinction from our presentations on the one hand, and things by themselves on the other, Kant makes so many inconsistent statements that any account of what he really meant is disputable. I will be bold enough to offer an account of what I believe he wanted to say, though he never quite succeeded in saying it. It concerns chiefly his theory of causation.

Time-order in our presentations is, according to Kant, the mind's work, a result of synthesis, and so is the imagination of time-order among them. But that one presentation precedes another in my apprehension is not that I apprehend a cause followed by its effect; nor is a sequence of ideas in imagination the thought of a causal sequence. This is Kant's starting-point, his demonstration of the failure of Hume's derivation of the idea of cause and effect from the principles of association. For if Hume were right, to think that A causes B is merely that the impression or idea A is followed in the imagination by the idea B; but by the principles of association, the impression or idea B is as readily followed by the idea A; and I ought, when that happens, to be thinking that B causes A—when, for example, a sound calls up the idea of a swinging bell I ought to think that the sound rings the bell. Except on the presupposition that in nature all succession is determined in accordance with some rule, I could never come by the thought of an order of events to which more belongs than the series of my own presentations, whether impressions or ideas; whereas I manifestly do. That is the answer to any empiricist theory of causality; to J. S. Mill's, for example, when he alleges that we directly know that there is uniformity of succession among by far the greater number of phenomena.[1] If phenomena be our presentations, the statement is patently false; and in his *Examination of the Philosophy of Sir William Hamilton* he allows that the uniform antecedent of a phenomenon is generally only a possible perception.[2] But possible perceptions are not directly known; we cannot appeal for their occurrence to experience, as Mill understands experience. The belief in rules of causality then is not the result either of custom or induction. That all events in nature conform to some rule is an *a priori* principle.

But it is also synthetic; and therefore cannot, according to Kant, be asserted of a nature independent of mind—of things by themselves. It is true, because nature is conformed to the principles of synthesis demanded by the understanding. How is this conformity possible?

The conformity is possible, because these principles are exhibited in a manifold that is permeated by relations of space and time, and relatedness in space and time is the result of work done, in the synthesis of sense, by the same mind that understands. If the sensible did not exhibit relatedness in space and time, it would not even be sensible. We may say also that what exhibited neither quality nor quantity would not even be sensible; it would be for us nothing. That is why these categories are said to determine

[1] *System of Logic*, III, xxi. 4.

[2] 'As already remarked, the constant antecedent of a sensation is seldom another sensation, or set of sensations, actually felt. It is much oftener the existence of a group of possibilities, not necessarily including any actual sensations, except such as are required to show that the possibilities are really present. Nor are actual sensations indispensable even for this purpose, for the presence of the object (which is nothing more than the immediate presence of the possibilities) may be made known to us by the very sensation which we refer to it as its effect.' Ch. xi, 5th ed., 1878, p. 237.

objects, but those of relation and modality the existence of objects.[1] A presentation is an object of the inner sense; but I do not apprehend anything real, an existing object, or phenomenon, unless it is connected with other such according to the laws of a possible experience. Now, since the mind is to give to the manifold of sense its relatedness in space and time, it may do so under the direction of the understanding, and so as to suit its requirements; and only because the synthesis of understanding works through that of sense can it secure the conformity of nature to its requirements. Any arrangement of the sensible in time and space must consist with the forms of temporal and spatial order. But time and space are not like other forms of order, which are constituted by the natures of the terms ordered in them, so that in them it is absurd to suggest that a given term might be related to others of the order in more than one way; that 7, for example, might not come between 6 and 8, or that the blue of a forget-me-not might be darker than that of a star-gentian, and yet both be the colours they are. Time and space each provide an order of places, but are indifferent to the quality of what shall occupy them. And it is upon the qualities of what is ordered in space and time that the exhibition of regularity in nature depends. Even our modern physicists, who most of all abstract from quality, must admit this. For if there were no more by which to distinguish one body from another than there is by which to distinguish one place from another, they must declare the motion of one body among others a phrase as meaningless as the motion of one body in otherwise empty space.

The mind indeed is not responsible, according to Kant, for quality, nor for differences of quality, in the sensible, beyond the formal condition that all quality must exhibit degree. The rest, what he calls the material character, is given: it depends somehow on the thing by itself, the unknowable x. But given it is. What then is the task of understanding, in directing the synthesis of sense? To fill

[1] B. 110, 199.

the places in the time-scheme of sense with presentations so qualitied that it may be able to regard their occurrence as connected with events in nature whose succession is determined, in this very time, always in accordance with some rule. The order of my presentations will then, and only then, be understandable; and it will be so because we can then regard them as events, connected according to rules with other events, that are not presentations, but phenomena whose occurrence conforms to other rules. Taken apart from their connexion with these phenomena, the order of my presentations would appear to conform to no rules among themselves; there is no empirical regularity in the succession of my ideas. That they have such an order that, when taken in connexion with the phenomena, they are seen to conform in their occurrence to rules, is the work of the understanding, which gave them the order that such connexion would require of them. Whatever may be said about the reality of the phenomena on this view, the thought of them has been real; for it has guided the mind, though blindly and unconsciously, in its synthesis of sense.

Let us now return to Berkeley. The function divided by Kant between mind working in us and the thing by itself is assigned by Berkeley altogether to the Author of Nature. It is a mistake to call God in his system a *deus ex machina*, any more than is *Bewusstsein überhaupt* in Kant's, or Spirit in Hegel's. Also it is true that Berkeley became a Bishop; but when he published his *New Theory of Vision* he had only just become a deacon, and he must have thought out his main position while yet an innocent layman.

There is, according to Berkeley, no cause but a spirit. Finite spirits can produce in themselves imaginations; but ideas or things sensible are produced in them only by God. This however not at random, but in a regular course, arbitrary indeed, yet consistent. Ideas in finite minds must be conceived therefore to occur in connexions which these rules require; and whereas each of us perceives only his own ideas, the complete system with which the several ideas of

xv   G g

all finite conscious beings are connected is eternally known to God. 'All objects are eternally known by God or, which is the same thing, have an eternal existence in His mind: but when things, before imperceptible to creatures, are, by a decree of God, perceptible to them, then are they said to begin a relative existence with respect to created minds.'[1] 'There is an *omnipresent, eternal mind*, which knows and comprehends all things, and exhibits them to our view in such a manner, and according to such rules, as He Himself hath ordained, and are by us termed the *Laws of Nature*.'[2]

But we are not to suppose that world to exist in the eternal mind as if this mind perceived it from all points of view at once. It is not such a 'logical construction' of 'private worlds' as Mr. Russell would have it to be. 'To know everything knowable is certainly a perfection; but to endure, or suffer, or feel anything by sense, is an imperfection. The former, I say, agrees to God, but not the latter. God knows or hath ideas; but His ideas are not conveyed to Him by sense, as ours are'.[3] So in *Siris*: 'God knoweth all things, as pure mind or intellect; but nothing by sense, nor in nor through a sensory.'[4] 'As understanding perceiveth not, . . . so sense knoweth not . . . sense or soul, so far forth as sensitive, knoweth nothing.'[5]

How are we to put this theory to ourselves? that God conceives a system of bodies in space, variously composed and interacting according to laws, with definite time-relations between the events therein; and that at such times at which certain events are conceived to occur therein in a particular sensory, he exhibits some idea to a particular finite mind. It will be noted that time, on this view, must be allowed a singleness and reality which Berkeley denies to it, when he says that it is merely the succession of ideas, so that there is no more a single or common time than there are ideas common to different minds.[6]

---

[1] *Dialogues between Hylas and Philonous*, III: *Works*, i. 472.
[2] *Ib., Works*, i. 447.   [3] *Ib., Works*, i. 459.
[4] § 289.   [5] § 305.   [6] *Principles of Human Knowledge*, §§ 97, 98.

Now Kant would object to such a theory at the outset, that space and time are inconceivable to a being whose ideas are not conveyed to him by sense, and therefore pure intellect could not conceive this scheme. The objection is formidable; yet does it not recoil upon himself? for the understanding that directs the synthesis of sense is equally called upon to conceive such a scheme. It is true that Kant speaks in this connexion of the productive *imagination*, and imagination is sensuous. The mind in its synthetic activities, he may have thought, is one: it is at once sensuous and understands. But a blending of the activity directed with that directing it is not easy to realize; and we have a problem here which neither Berkeley nor Kant has solved, nor perhaps any one else.

In any case they are agreed so far as this, that our several ideas, or presentations, occur in such an order as they would, if their occurrence were connected according to laws with events in sensories which are themselves bodies along with other bodies in space and time, mutually affecting each other according to rules which we call laws of nature. I perceive something real, *i.e.* my idea or presentation is an idea or presentation of an object, not a mere state in me, if its occurrence can be thus interpreted. But if asked whether this object has a reality independent of mind, they both must answer no. Berkeley will reply that it exists in the divine mind; it belongs to a scheme conceived by God to guide him in producing the cash of our ideas. Kant, notwithstanding the *Refutation of Idealism*, will reply that it belongs to a scheme that mind in each one of us is bound to think, in order so to order his presentations that he can say that through them he has experience. To ascribe other reality to it than this would be to make it a thing by itself, no longer transcendentally ideal.

And this is really a remarkable extent of agreement. But when we look for the differences, we find them, I think, to be partly to Berkeley's disadvantage, and partly to Kant's. Berkeley does not see that he has not shown how we should ever discover the plan in accordance with which our several ideas are produced. 'Without a regular course nature could never be understood';[1] but what directs my mind to the discovery of this regular course? It is here that his metaphor of the language of nature betrays him. He calls nature the language, and either God or else nature again what the language tells us of; whereas he unconsciously thinks of nature as telling us of herself in the language of ideas. But mere observation of the order of my ideas, as we have seen, would never discover to me nature and her regular course. Unless it belongs to finite minds to think with the divine mind, so far at least as to conceive the general principles of orderliness in nature which God conceives, they would never find out the detailed rules observed by the Author of Nature. And here Kant has the advantage over Berkeley; for the categories are principles, the conception of which is native to mind, to that *Bewusstsein überhaupt* which is one in us all. The mind works in accordance with them in that blind synthesis, through which it comes about that there is at the outset of consciousness an order of its presentations. Small wonder if in considering these it becomes conscious of the plan on which it has worked unconsciously.

But on another count the advantage seems to rest with Berkeley. Kant claims to have shown that the principle of causality, and other categories, are valid for all possible experience. We may allow this for the mathematical categories, as he calls them, of quality and quantity. Of what has neither quality nor quantity, as we have seen, there can be no perception at all, and we can never be troubled with the intrusion of such nonconforming items into the order of our presentations. But the other categories, the dynamical, require that there be set in relations of time and space sensibles of definite kinds. It is not enough that the sensibles should barely conform to the forms of spatial and temporal order. That they might do, whatever their sensible qualities. If grapes grew on thorns, and figs on thistles,

[1] *Siris*, § 160.

there would be no more breach of the rules of Euclidean geometry than if a wag had hung them there. Our presentations in their order exhibit to us events in nature only if the quality of what is sensible now and here is such as the laws of nature require. Now such sensible quality is given, and is not due to the synthetic activity of mind. If the order of my presentations is to be such that I can suppose them connected in their occurrence with events in nature determined according to rules, I ought after seeing a flash (say) to hear a sound of definite quality. Allow that the mind can give duration and date, and some degree of its quality, whatever that quality be, to material of sense that would not otherwise have them; yet how am I to be sure that the material will be such that what is sensible to me at the date and for the time in question shall be a sound of the sort required? Unless the unknown *x* responsible for this given factor which analysis discovers in the objects of sense is, as it were, sympathetic to mind, this need not be. Kant does indeed suggest that what lies at the base of external phenomena, what ' so affects our sensibility, that it acquires presentations of space, matter, figure, and so forth,' may be also at the same time the subject of our thoughts.[1] In the *Critique of Pure Reason* such remarks occur mainly in the section on the *Paralogisms* discarded from the second edition; but they are frequent again in the *Critique of Judgement*. In the second remark appended there to § 57, for example, it is said that the supersensible which underlies the sensible may be the intelligible substrate of nature both without and within us. But he cannot afford to leave this an open question. If it be not so, the task of the understanding in giving to what would otherwise be mere manifold of sense the form of objects of experience is like that of a man called upon to arrange in sentences that shall express his thought letters which he must take as they are given; the task may be impossible of fulfilment.

Now this particular difficulty does not arise on Berkeley's

[1] A. 358.

theory; for God, to whom the formative function belongs which Kant assigns to mind in us, determines also the sensible characters for which mind in us is not held by Kant to be responsible; as a man who can determine not only the order but the quality of the articulate sounds he utters is free to form the sentences required to express his thought.

We may now summarize the results of our comparison. Both Berkeley and Kant deny that there is a world of bodies in space independent of mind. Both affirm our sensible experience to be such as would arise if there were such a world, and to be only intelligible to us, only not a mere flux of feeling, when we think of it as connected with the events of such a world. Berkeley accounts for this by supposing that God, to whom the thought of such a world is eternally present, excites in finite minds those sensible experiences which a world, the scheme of which God thinks of, would require; but he leaves unexplained how this world becomes the object also of their thought. Kant imputes to the spontaneity of mind in finite beings both the fact that the scheme of such a world is an object of their thought, and an activity in ordering their sensible experiences accordingly; but he fails to explain how the material of these experiences is such as to admit of being so ordered. Kant, it may be said, asks of mind in us more than, on his theory, it could achieve; Berkeley, in a sense, asks too little. Kant should have allowed to the principle which is not in us more kinship with the intelligence which is; Berkeley to us more kinship with the intelligence which is not. But there is not such difference between them as might justify Kant's half-pitying disparagement of the 'man in Ireland'.

What, however, is the importance of showing the extent of their agreement, if it is only agreement in error? Are not both, if what has been said is true, unable to defend the ascription of any reality to nature, even when their doctrines have been developed in the ways suggested? Though the *Refutation of Idealism* may have failed to prove it, is it not a fact that we are as immediately aware of a world of things in space as we are of our own states?

I think we must say that we are immediately aware of a world of things in space. By calling our awareness immediate, I do not mean that it comes at once, or is unconditioned. But the conditions which may be assigned are of two sorts. There are, first, what may be called the empirical conditions: a body, physiological stimuli, intercourse with other persons; all these belong to the world of which we become aware, and our awareness of them must not be held privileged. We cannot take them for granted in attempting to account for our awareness of the rest. But secondly, there are the metaphysical—or what perhaps we may call in Kantian language the transcendental—conditions. To know these would be to know the nature of that reality within which our life and knowledge arise and to which the world in space and its history belong. And if we can discover them, it can only be by reflective thinking, which thinking itself is not the least notable matter with whose possibility our account of this reality must be consistent. It would be foolish therefore to offer an account which would make of this reflective thinking something incapable of discovering it. I suppose that what I am calling reflective thinking is (at least in its employment upon the problem of the conditions of our knowledge of the physical world) what Kant meant by criticism; but he was surely mistaken in the antithesis he drew between criticism and dogmatism. Dogmatism is an ugly word, because it suggests assertion without reflection; but when we reflect, we have no better or worse reason to give for the assertions reached than that we apprehend the truth of them.

Now this activity of reflective thinking seems to me different in nature both from the thinking by which knowledge advances either in the inductive sciences or in mathematics and from what is called logical construction. Logical construction, if I understand rightly, is supposed to bring us to the thought of those objects whose relations are then investigated in inductive or mathematical science; but it brings us to the thought of them by somehow constructing them out of sense-data. I cannot recognize, in such construction, a process of development; and the transition from the sensitiveness of infancy to that awareness of objects without which neither inductive nor mathematical thinking can begin seems to me to be a process of development. Until this has taken place, reflection also cannot begin.

Reflection, as I have said, may be directed to the question what that reality can be, within which our life and knowledge arise, and to which the world in space and its history belong. But it may also be directed to questions short of that. For example, reflection shows (and there too, the activity might be called critical) that my belief in other selves cannot have come about, as Berkeley and others have supposed, by an argument from analogy; and that no complication of psychological association, or of logical construction, nor yet any inference in which we could distinguish premises and conclusion, could suffice to lead us from a knowledge of sense-data and their temporal and qualitative relations to a knowledge, or apprehension, of bodies in space. It is for this reason that I call such knowledge or apprehension immediate.

It would surely be a mere misdescription of the facts to put all so-called sensa on one level, and say that when we feel pain or hear sounds, and when we see or touch, what occurs can equally well be described as apprehending phenomena of the inner sense. The relation of what we feel or hear to the feeling or hearing it is not the same with that of what we see or touch to the seeing or touching it. Where the apprehension of figure and space-relation enters, there enters the thought of a difference between what is, and how it appears to us, which is immediate; this, and not 'the consciousness of my existence as determined in time' (as Kant's *Refutation of Idealism* would have it) is what presupposes the existence of 'things outside me'.

And there one is tempted to leave the matter, and say that these things are real and independent of mind, and that we come along and get to know them. Yet we cannot be so easily quit of the idealist. In the first place there are the difficulties (to be mentioned again) about the infinity and continuity of space, and what distinguishes a body from a geometrical solid; and secondly there is this difficulty. In that immediate apprehension, in which is involved the distinction between what is and how it appears to us, we seem to apprehend bodies of sensible magnitude and continuous surface. The real figure of what looks differently to observers from different angles or at different distances is, we say, a cube when we look at a tea-chest, a disk when we look at a penny. But when we investigate the empirical conditions of our awareness of these real things without us, we are driven to give quite a new account of them. We seemed immediately aware of something continuous and cubic or discoid, appearing diversely from different points of view; and now we are told there is only a collection of separate minute particles, whose shapes are unknown, darting about with unimaginable rapidity at intervals vast in comparison of their diameters, though like these minute in comparison of any length sensible to us. And when the physicists tell us that mass may disappear in radiant energy, material substance is wearing very thin. There is some plausibility in the distinction between space and the impenetrable body that fills a volume of it, so long as we think of mass as quantity of matter or of what fills space; but what is there extensive about energy? Is it not intensive rather?

Our common-sense realism is thus rudely shaken, and we cannot leave the matter where we were tempted to leave it. The bodies in space of which I seemed to be conscious in the same act of seeing or touching which involved the apprehension of something private to myself, some phenomenon of my inner sense, have been dissipated into something extraordinarily unlike them. I am left indeed with space, but with nothing in it that really has the real shapes of which I seemed to be conscious in that perception, wherein was

xv   H h

234 PROCEEDINGS OF THE BRITISH ACADEMY

involved the distinction of the real body and its shape from how they appeared. Even space is being as it were rebuilt by the physicists and mathematicians: with what justification cannot be discussed now. And space is an unsatisfactory thing by itself, and not made satisfactory by having bodies in it. For it is infinite and infinitely divisible, and therefore neither a genuine whole nor with genuine unit-parts. No portion of it therefore, nor body occupying any portion, has a size that can be stated as being any fraction of the spatial whole or multiple of the spatial unit; we can only state its ratio to some other portion; and to such ratio size is indifferent. The intelligible ratio is displayed in something, the apprehension of which is bound up with sense, if not merely sensuous, and whose being, I confess, seems to be inseverable from the being of sensuous or imaginative mind. Certainly the real things without me are not private like the pains I feel or the sounds I hear. But perhaps, as these are bound up with my feeling or hearing them, so are those with the being of knowing and perceiving minds. The empirical conditions of the apprehension of them by finite minds, and the development in finite minds of that apprehension, may depend together upon a reality or intelligence which shows itself in nature to itself in minds. This is of course an old theory or, if you will, romance; for truly it has not been made understandable in detail. And if anything easier can be shown sufficient, well and good. Meanwhile all that I ask you to consider to-day is whether it be not true that something of this sort emerges both from Berkeley's doctrine, and from Kant's who thought himself and Berkeley so opposed, when we supplement them in certain ways which their weaknesses seem to require—from Berkeley's, if it is to be made intelligible that we should divine in common the system of nature to which our several private courses of ideas all point; from Kant's, if it is to be made intelligible that the understanding working in us all alike should not be baffled in its activity by the alien nature of that with which it has to busy itself.

KANT'S REFUTATION OF DOGMATIC IDEALISM

I

It is commonly held that because of his obvious misinterpretations of Berkeley's philosophy, which he called dogmatic or visionary and mystical idealism, Kant thereby betrayed a gross misunderstanding of that philosopher. The theory advanced to explain this is that Kant was not acquainted with any of Berkeley's writings, but obtained his knowledge from inadequate second-hand sources.[1] This theory is supported by the fact that Kant's knowledge of the English language was most imperfect. He never read a single English book. Coupled with this is the apparently acceptable fact that there were no German translations of Berkeley's works in existence before 1781, the year of publication of the first edition of the *Critique of Pure Reason*.[2] In that year, there appeared a German translation of Berkeley's *Three Dialogues between Hylas and Philonous*.[3] This work was therefore available to Kant before he published his *Prolegomena to any Future Metaphysics* (1783)[4] and the second edition of the *Critique* (1787). But such is the nature of Kant's account of Berkeley's doctrine in these works that, on the common view, Kant neglected to avail himself of the opportunity to read it. Thus, previous assessments of the evidence, internal and external, have produced the view that Kant knew nothing of Berkeley's writings at first hand and, accordingly, misunderstood and misinterpreted his teaching. From this, it follows, although the commentators have omitted to stress this conclusion, that Kant's many attempted refutations of dogmatic idealism fail before they begin. The above is not only the accepted view, backed by seemingly strong evidence ; it is the most plausible. Nevertheless, it is almost wholly mistaken, as I shall show.

II

First, let us banish the idea that Kant could not have read any of Berkeley's writings before he published the first edition of the *Critique*. On the contrary, he could have read at least two. These are Berkeley's *Three Dialogues between Hylas and Philonous* and his *De Motu*. Professor Kemp Smith indicates that a German translation of the *Three Dialogues* was published

---

[1] See N. Kemp Smith, *A Commentary on Kant's Critique of Pure Reason*, pp. 156-7. Cf. also A. C. Ewing, *A Short Commentary on Kant's Critique of Pure Reason*, p. 182 ; H. J. Paton, *Kant's Metaphysic of Experience*, II, p. 376 ; T. D. Weldon, *Introduction to Kant's Critique of Pure Reason*, pp. 9-10 ; A. D. Lindsay, *Kant*, p. 15 ; *et. al.*

[2] References to the first and second editions will be by page numbers and the letters A and B respectively.

[3] Hereafter referred to in notes by dialogue number as *Hylas*. Berkeley's *Principles of Human Knowledge* will be referred to in notes by paragraph numbers as *Prin.*

[4] Hereafter referred to in notes by section numbers as *Proleg.*

at Leipzig in 1781, and asserts that this was the first of Berkeley's writings to appear in German.[5] Authorities on Kant have ignored a much earlier translation of the same work which was published at Rostock in 1756. Their oversight is understandable because the translation lies hidden in a larger work entitled *Die Würklichkeit der Körper*[6] which contains also Arthur Collier's *Clavis Universalis*. Hence, the *Three Dialogues*, which contains the whole of Berkeley's main doctrine, was available to Kant long before he began to compose his *Critique*. Moreover, the fact that the editor and translator of the *Dialogues*, Johann Christian Eschenbach I, was also a professor of philosophy at Rostock, who sought to refute Berkeley's doctrine and who subsequently published works of his own on logic and metaphysics,[7] increases the chances that the book attracted Kant's attention. Laying aside, for the time being, all the claims adduced from the internal evidence to the effect that Kant was wholly unacquainted with Berkeley's writings, it seems to me highly unlikely that Kant, who lived with the book-dealer Kanter for a considerable time prior to the eighties,[8] and who was sufficiently curious to buy and study Swedenborg's *Arcana Coelestia*,[9] should not have availed himself of the opportunity to examine a book containing the official doctrines of two other exponents of ' mystical and visionary idealism ',[10] and indeed, as the title indicates, the most eminent repudiaters of the reality of the entire corporeal world.

Another important work of Berkeley's which Kant might also have read, is the former's *De Motu*, published in London in 1721 and again in 1752. This Latin treatise did not have a wide circulation on the continent. However, it opposes the doctrines of Newton and Leibniz on the subject of motion in space, a subject which was Kant's special concern in his pre-

[5]*Op. cit.*, p. 156.

[6]I have examined a copy of this work from the library of the University of Southern California. Its full title is : *Samlung der vornehmsten Schriftsteller die die Würklichkeit ihres eignen Körpers und der ganzen Körperwelt läugnen. Enthaltend des Berkeleys Gespräche zwischen Hylas und Philonous und des Colliers Allgemeinen Schlüssel. Uebersetzt und mit wiederlegenden Anmerkungen versehen nebst einem Anhang worin die Würklichkeit der Körper erwiesen wird von Joh. Christ. Eschenbach, Prof. Philos. zu Rostock*. (Rostock bey Unton Ferdinand Röse. 1756.) Eschenbach states in the Preface that since it was impossible to come upon the English original his translation of the *Dialogues* is based on the French translation of Amsterdam, 1750. T. E. Jessop, *Bibliography of George Berkeley*, no. 73, gives the same title. However, in Kayser, *Bücher-Lexicon* (now Bücherverzeichnis), V (S-T), Leipzig, 1835, pp. 34b-35a, an abbreviated title of undoubtedly the same book is given. It omits reference to Berkeley's and Collier's works, also the phrase *und der ganzen Körperwelt*, and names the publisher as Cnobloch of Leipzig.

[7]*Metaphysik, oder Hauptwissenschaft* (1757) ; *Elementa Logices* (1766) ; both written at Rostock and published at Leipzig by Cnobloch.

[8]See F. Paulsen, *Immanuel Kant*, Scribners (1902), p. 45.

[9]Kant's work on Swedenborg, *The Dreams of a Visionseer*, appeared in 1766. Kant was, of course, extremely sceptical of Swedenborg's theories. However, the Russian philosopher, Vladimir Sergeivitch Soloviev, in his article on Kant (Brockhaus and Ephron's encyclopaedic dictionary) attributes Kant's renunciation of Newton's absolute space and his corresponding adoption of the ideality of space in his *Dissertation* (1770) to the influence of Swedenborg. See A. V. Vasiliev, *Space, Time, Motion* (1924), pp. 74-5.

[10]Kant uses this phrase to describe Berkeley's position in *Proleg.* 13. Kemp Smith notes that such a description is doubtless partly due to the old-time association of idealism in Kant's mind with Swedenborg's teaching. *Op. cit.*, p. 158, note 4.

Critical period. To a diligent enquirer, Berkeley's *De Motu*, which, as far as Kant was concerned, required no translation, would most assuredly have been accessible.

Having removed the supposed impossibility of Kant's direct acquaintance with Berkeley's works prior to the publication of the first edition of the *Critique*, by showing that at least two of them were available to Kant, and one of these readily so, let us now proceed to examine Kant's attempted refutations of idealism.

III

There are eight separate passages in the first and second editions of the *Critique* and in the *Prolegomena* which are specific attempts by Kant to refute idealism. These passages, approximately in the order in which they were written, and accompanied by brief comments upon the kinds of idealism Kant opposes, are as follows :

FIRST EDITION OF *CRITIQUE*

I   *Section 7 of the Transcendental Aesthetic* (A36-41).
     Explicit against ' idealism '.

II   *The Fourth Paralogism : Of Ideality* (A366-80).
     Explicit against all ' empirical ' idealism, and, in particular, against the ' sceptical ' idealism of Descartes. ' Dogmatic ' idealism is merely mentioned.

III   *Section 6 of the Antinomy of Pure Reason* (A491-97).
     Explicit against ' empirical ' idealism.

THE *PROLEGOMENA*

IV   *Section 13, Remarks II and III.*
     Explicit against the ' mystical and visionary ' idealism of Berkeley. The ' empirical ' or ' dreaming ' idealism of Descartes is mentioned.

V   *Section 49.*
     Explicit against ' material, or Cartesian ' idealism.

VI   *Appendix, Second Part.*
     Explicit against all ' genuine ' idealism from the Eleatics, through Plato, to Berkeley, and particularly against the ' dogmatic ' idealism of Berkeley. The ' sceptical ' idealism of Descartes is mentioned.

SECOND EDITION OF *CRITIQUE*

VII   *Section 8, Parts III and IV of the Transcendental Aesthetic* (B69-72).
     Explicit against Berkeley.

VIII   *Refutation of Idealism* (B274-9) supplemented by *note to Preface* (Bxxxix-xli).
     Explicit against the ' problematic ' idealism of Descartes. The ' dogmatic ' idealism of Berkeley is described. Both are called instances of ' material ' idealism.

The idealism which Kant seeks to refute is material or empirical idealism, that is, any doctrine which doubts or denies the existence of objects in space outside us. The former is called 'sceptical' or, though not until the last passage, 'problematic' idealism. Descartes' name is the only one explicitly associated with it. The latter is the dogmatic idealism of Berkeley. It is only once described as 'mystical and visionary'. From the above, Kant distinguishes his own critical or transcendental idealism, a doctrine which denies the *absolute* reality of space and time and the external bodies in them. It involves empirical realism or dualism, according to which, bodies in space outside us, as well as ourselves who perceive them, are considered to be empirically real. In the first edition of the *Critique*, the most important passage is the fourth *Paralogism* which, by adopting a position resembling Berkeley's, tries to refute Descartes. Although Kant promises to deal with dogmatic idealism, Berkeley is neither named nor opposed in this edition. The first edition of the *Critique* appeared in the early summer of 1781. Kant waited many anxious months for the response of the learned world. He was most disappointed by the contents of the first, the Garve-Feder or Göttingen review, which appeared in January, 1782. Garve described the *Critique* as 'a system of higher idealism', and classified Kant with Berkeley. This was anathema to Kant. Accordingly, in the *Prolegomena* (published Easter, 1783), Kant, for the first time, is at pains to show that his position is the 'very contrary' of Berkeley's. Two of the three 'refutations' in the *Prolegomena* are directed against Berkeley. Kant asserts that Berkeley's doctrine is 'an objectionable idealism', against which and other such 'chimeras of the brain', his *Critique* contains the 'proper antidote'. In the second edition of the *Critique* (1787), Kant suppresses what Schopenhauer called 'the principal idealistic passage', i.e., the fourth *Paralogism*, and replaces it by the *Refutation of Idealism* which answers Descartes' view without appearing to fall into subjectivism. The other passage, added to the *Aesthetic*, is, as we have seen, directed against Berkeley. In these passages, occur those well-known obvious misinterpretations of Berkeley. To 'the good Berkeley' is ascribed the view that the things in space are 'merely imaginary entities' or that he degrades bodies in space to 'mere illusion'.

It appears from the above summary that the eight 'refutations' of idealism are directed against either Descartes or Berkeley. This, however, is mere appearance. If one ponders on these passages in the order in which they were written, one may discern an underlying central argument to which the attacks on Descartes and Berkeley are merely incidental. This central argument begins by outlining a position common to most previous metaphysicians and natural philosophers. It is, in fact, the prime feature of the Newtonian World-View. Kant calls it 'transcendental realism'. Omitting details, the argument continues by showing that such a view leads inevitably to idealism, and culminates by turning the argument of idealism against itself to provide a positive proof of the external world. This is the real argument of the ' refutations '. Depending on the point of emphasis, it has been regarded either as a refutation of realism or (as Kant treats it) as a refutation of idealism with its corresponding proof of the external world which exhibits his empirical realism. Although the argument is discernible in all the ' refutations ' except the last, it is most clearly seen in the fourth *Paralogism*. In the last ' refutation ', Kant uses a method of proof of the external world different from that of the preceding seven. Because only one of these passages was subsequently suppressed by Kant, the central argument must be considered official Kantian doctrine. In this paper I shall, accordingly, ignore the *Refutation of Idealism* except in so far as it presents Kant's views on Berkeley.

It is my view that the central argument of the ' refutations ' has a systematic similarity, in its principal features, with the main argument of Berkeley's *Principles* and *Dialogues*. Berkeley is concerned to expose the fallacies inherent in a certain way of thinking to which the metaphysicians and physicists of his age were prone. He calls this doctrine ' materialism ' and those who teach it, ' materialists ', or, more often, ' the philosophers '. He shows that it leads inevitably to scepticism, and, in fact, joins the sceptics for much of the way. Then he turns the argument of scepticism against itself to provide (up to his time) a unique proof of the external world. Since Berkeley's death, commentators have tended to emphasize the first half of his argument, which they have seen as an attempt to refute materialism or realism, and have been notorious in their neglect of the last. Consequently, Berkeley has been presented to the world as an idealist. Few have dwelt upon his refutation of scepticism and his corresponding proof of the external world which exhibits his empirical realism. The whole argument appears most clearly in that paradigm of dramatic unity, the *Three Dialogues*. It is seen, of course, in the *Principles*, but here the dissentient side of immaterialism is so protested at the expense of Berkeley's empirical realism that one can readily understand the mistaken judgement of history.

IV

In order to prove my point, I shall now present, in more detail, the main steps of this argument. I shall juxtapose the key assertions of Kant and Berkeley. For reasons only of conciseness, quotations from the *Principles* will preponderate over those from the *Dialogues* :

First Step

The philosophers assert the absolute reality of space and time, and hold that external objects exist by themselves independently of our senses.

> Kant : [The transcendental realists] . . . maintain the absolute reality of space and time, whether as subsistent or only as inherent (A39) . . . wrongly supposing that objects of the senses, if they are to be external, must have an existence by themselves, and independently of the senses (A369).
> Berkeley : [The philosophers assert] the being of an absolute space, distinct from that which is perceived by sense (*Prin.* 116). (They hold that) there are certain objects really existing without the mind, or having a subsistence distinct from being perceived (*Prin.* 56).

Kant specifically refers to certain 'mathematical' and 'metaphysical' students of nature ; probably Newton and Leibniz. Berkeley elsewhere refers to 'absolute space, that phantom of the mechanic and geometrical philosophers' (Siris 271). However, in the above passages, he has in mind, not only Newton, but Locke, Descartes, Malebranche, More and Raphson. The views of these thinkers and many others (whom I shall continue to refer to as 'the philosophers') make them advocates of the prevailing doctrine, called by Kant, 'realism' and by Berkeley, 'materialism'. Berkeley only barely considers the subject of time, but doubtless intends to ascribe to his opponents the belief in absolute time, which notion he calls 'duration in abstract' (Prin. 97).

Kant and Berkeley observe that the transcendental realist or materialist distinguishes between the primary and the secondary qualities of bodies. The former, such as extension and shape, really inhere in external bodies. The latter, such as heat, colour and taste, belong only to appearances and are held to have no proper existence 'outside us' (in the transcendental sense) but to be entirely relative to our sensibility (Proleg. 13, A373 ; Prin. 9).[11]

Second Step

This doctrine of the philosophers makes them victims of the common delusion that the human mind can venture beyond all possible experience.

> Kant : [Transcendental realism involves] the transcendental illusion, by which metaphysics has hitherto been deceived and led to the childish endeavour of catching at bubbles, because appearances, which are mere ideas,[12] were taken for things in themselves (Proleg. 13. Cf. A369, 491).

> Berkeley : When we do our utmost to conceive the existence of external bodies, we are all the while only contemplating our own ideas. But the mind taking no notice of it self, is deluded to think it can and doth conceive bodies existing unthought of or without the mind ; though at the same time they are apprehended by or exist in it self (Prin. 23).

Kant and Berkeley provide similar analyses of the error committed by the philosophers ; it is manifested in the deluded attempt to venture beyond the limits of possible experience. Dealing directly with this symptom, Kant observes that 'our knowledge of the existence of things reaches only so far as perception' (A226), and that, 'in the absence of perception even imagining and dreaming are not possible' (A377). Berkeley notices the same truth, 'My conceiving or imagining power does not extend beyond the possibility of real existence or perception' (Prin. 5), and again, 'Many things, for aught I know, may exist . . . but then those things must be possible' (Hylas III). Kant names the error, 'the transcendental illusion', here defined as treating ideas as things in themselves. This instance of the illusion he calls, on one occasion, 'dreaming idealism' (Proleg. 13). On

[11]This observation by Kant and Berkeley oversimplifies Locke's official position. For him, the secondary qualities are not in us, but are powers of the primary qualities which produce *ideas of* secondary qualities in our minds.

[12]Throughout this paper, following Caird, *The Critical Philosophy of Kant*, I translate the term *Vorstellung* by 'idea'. This is more appropriate than the 'representation' of most translations because Kant is referring to the same entities as Locke, Berkeley and the Cartesians, who use the term 'idea' or 'idée'.

Berkeley's analysis also, our supposed conception of external bodies (material substance) in absolute space outside us[13] is shown to be nothing but a contemplation of our own ideas. The error of the philosophers is therefore revealed as interpreting these ideas as external bodies. Yet for him, the analysis goes further. In the quoted passage, he describes the source of the error as ' the mind taking no notice of itself '. We forget that we are chained to a human sensibility. We forget ourselves as observers.[14]

Third Step

The philosophers' distinction of things from ideas leads inevitably to scepticism.

> Kant : Transcendental realism inevitably falls into difficulties, and finds itself obliged to give way to empirical idealism, in that it regards the objects of outer sense as something distinct from the senses themselves (A 371). [On this view] it is quite impossible to understand how we could arrive at a knowledge of their reality outside us, since we have to rely merely on the idea which is in us (A378. Cf. *Proleg.* 49).
>
> Berkeley : All this scepticism follows from our supposing a difference between *things* and *ideas.* . . . So long as we attribute a real existence to unthinking things, distinct from their being perceived, it is not only impossible for us to know with evidence the nature of any real unthinking being, but even that it exists. . . . We see only the appearances, and not the real qualities of things (*Prin.* 87-8).

As we have seen, Kant is opposed to empirical or material idealism. Its two sub-divisions are sceptical idealism (that which doubts) and dogmatic idealism (that which denies) the existence of bodies in space outside us The meaning Kant intends to give to ' idealism ' is partially obscured by his various definitions and by the ambiguity of the phrase ' bodies in space outside us '. Is Kant referring to material substance or to sensible things in empirical space ? A careful reading of all the ' refutations ' indicates that Kant intends the latter. We shall see that Kant's own official doctrine, transcendental idealism, denies the absolute reality of bodies in absolute space. Moreover, Kant's use of the title ' empirical ' reveals the nature of the idealism he opposes. Finally, although on one occasion Kant defines ' dogmatic idealist ' as ' one who denies the existence of matter ', and ' sceptical idealist ' as ' one who doubts its existence ' (A377), in the same passage he defines ' matter ' as ' only a species of ideas ' (A370). From all this it is evident that the idealism Kant opposes is the doctrine which doubts or denies the reality of the sensible world. Since once transcendental realism is upheld, sceptical idealism is ' inevitable ' (A371) and dogmatic idealism ' unavoidable ' (B274), it follows that Kant regards these doctrines as two different stages in the logical decline of transcendental realism.

On my view, in spite of a different terminology, the same two stages can be distinguished in Berkeley's analysis of the logical decline of materialism. This is true of the *Dialogues*, not of the *Principles* in which only one stage

[13] ' Your belief in matter ', Philonous remarks to Hylas, ' makes you *dream* of those unknown natures in everything ' (*Hylas* III).

[14] Berkeley discovered this Idol of the Tribe whilst working on a particular problem in the psychology of vision, viz., the problem of the inverted retinal image, in which he exposes the same delusion in the writers of optics, including Newton and Molyneux. (See his *New Theory of Vision*, 116-118.)

is discernible. Hylas vacillates between doubt and denial of the reality of
the external world. The former position, Berkeley calls ' scepticism '.
However, when Hylas is ' plunged yet deeper in uncertainty ' and is forced,
' positively to deny the real existence of any part of the universe ', Berkeley
names this further stage, ' the deepest and most deplorable scepticism '
(*Hylas* III). Thus, that position which Kant calls ' sceptical idealism ',
Berkeley calls ' scepticism ', and what Kant calls ' dogmatic idealism ',
Berkeley calls ' the deepest scepticism '. It is the latter position of extreme
scepticism that both men are most anxious to ridicule and escape from.
The one thinks of it as a chimera of the brain, the other, as an extravagancy.

In similar fashion, Kant and Berkeley expose the consequences of the
philosophers' corresponding distinctions between two spaces and two times
—absolute and relative. Kant observes that absolute space and time, ' two
eternal and infinite self-subsistent non-entities (*Undinge*) . . . must be the
necessary condition of the existence of all things, and moreover must continue to exist, even although all existing things be removed. . . . As conditions of all existence in general, they must also be the conditions of the
existence of God ' (A39, B71). Since the existence of all things thus depends
on nothing, the whole universe is thereby ' transformed into mere *illusion* '
(B70). This consequence would belong to a doctrine lying beyond even
extreme scepticism or dogmatic idealism since our own selves would also
vanish from existence. All such notions, Kant calls ' absurdities ' (B70).
Berkeley's account is similar. As we have seen, he barely considers time.
He ascribes to the philosophers the view that ' absolute space continues
to exist after the annihilation of all bodies '. He remarks that it ' necessarily
exists of its own nature ' (*De Motu* 54), and that we are, accordingly, reduced
to thinking that ' there is something beside God which is eternal, uncreated,
infinite, indivisible, immutable ' (*Prin.* 117). Since all its attributes are
negative, he concludes, ' it seems therefore to be nothing ' (*De Motu* 53).
All such views, Berkeley calls ' absurd notions ' (*Prin.* 117).

We have arrived at that stage of the argument in which the diagnosis
of the malady afflicting modern philosophy is complete. Dogmatic idealism
(extreme scepticism) is seen as the inevitable consequence of a certain way
of thinking (transcendental realism or materialism) which must be deluded
because its consequences are either absurd or impossible. The last half of
the argument contains the remedy. So deceptive in nature are the early
stages of this remedy that it appears as though Kant and Berkeley are
victims of a self-inflicted malady—the very same malady they seek to cure.
The argument proceeds by accepting, what are, in fact, idealist or sceptical
premisses.

Fourth Step

The remedy consists first, in pointing out to the philosophers a truth they
already know, namely that the *esse* of ideas or appearances is *percipi*.

Kant : Sceptical idealism thus constrains us to have recourse to the only refuge
still open, namely, the ideality of all appearances . . . for we cannot be

sentient of what is outside ourselves, but only of what is in us (A378).
All appearances are not in themselves *things* ; they are nothing but ideas,
and cannot exist outside our mind (A492).

Berkeley : The philosophers '. . . being of the opinion that . . . the things
immediately perceived are ideas which exist only in the mind (*Hylas*
III).

The philosophers must admit the truth of this premiss because it is their
own. They had used it whilst correcting the views of the common man, who
holds that the things immediately perceived are external bodies which exist
independently of being perceived. The philosophers corrected this ' mistake
of the vulgar '.[15] In the above passages, Kant and Berkeley use the terms
' *Vorstellung* ' and ' idea ' to refer to the immediate data of sense. Things
immediately perceived, i.e., appearances, are identified with these ideas.
No claim is made at this stage that these ideas are real or permanent. No
criterion is provided to distinguish reality from the idle visions of fancy
or from dreams. As a result of the next step, the denotation of ' idea '
increases enormously.

Fifth Step

The remedy continues by assimilating the so-called external bodies of the
philosophers into the realm of ideas or appearances.

Kant : External bodies are mere appearances, and are therefore nothing but a
species of my ideas, the objects of which are something only through
these ideas. Apart from them they are nothing (A370. Cf. A491, *Proleg.*
13).

Berkeley : As to what is said of the absolute existence of unthinking things
without any relation to their being perceived, that seems perfectly
unintelligible. Their *esse* is *percipi*, nor is it possible they should
have any existence, out of the minds or thinking things which perceive
them (*Prin.* 3).

This is the point of departure from the doctrine of the philosophers, and it
would seem to plunge Kant and Berkeley even deeper into scepticism.
Berkeley may be conscious of this association but does not admit it. Kant,
however, concedes, ' Up to this point I am one in confession with the above
idealists ' (*Proleg.* Appx.). In fact, the above passage is Kant's explicit
formulation of what he calls his ' transcendental idealism ' (A491). In this
step, the realm of ideas has been extended radically to accommodate the
contents of all possible outer experience. Its significance is most clearly
grasped in its application to the distinction of the philosophers between the
primary and secondary qualities. Kant observes that since Locke's time
it has been generally assumed that the secondary qualities of bodies, such
as heat, colour and taste, belong only to their appearances and do not exist
outside our ideas. He adds, ' I go farther and, for weighty reasons, rank as
mere appearances the remaining qualities of bodies also, which are called
primary—such as extension, place, and, in general, space, with all that which
belongs to it ' (*Proleg.* 13). Berkeley has at least three different arguments

[15]E.g., Malebranche, *Recherche* . . ., VIe *Éclaircissement*, ' Les hommes ont toujours
consulté leurs yeux pour s'assurer de l'existence de la matière. . . . Ils pensent qu'il
ne faut qu'ouvrir les yeux pour s'assurer qu'il y a des corps. . . Cependant il est certain
(que toutes les qualités sensibles dans les corps qui semblent les exhaler ou les répandre)
ne sont point hors de l'âme qui les sent '.

against this distinction, but the one which is uniquely his, and on which he rests his whole case, is the argument : ' It is evident . . . that extension, figure and motion are only ideas existing in the mind, and that an idea can be like nothing but another idea, and that consequently neither they nor their archetypes can exist in an unperceiving substance ' (*Prin.* 9). This is an application of Berkeley's main argument against the doctrine of material substance. The latter is used repeatedly in the *Principles* and the *Dialogues*. It is a sceptical or idealist argument, but has more power than any of the relevant arguments of the great sceptical precursors of Berkeley, such as Bayle. Their arguments from relativity cannot affect Locke's official position (see above, note 11), whereas I think Berkeley's argument demolishes it.

From all this, it is readily seen that the fourth and fifth steps of this central argument represent the idealism of Kant and Berkeley. The fourth step showed that the *esse* of ideas or appearances is *percipi*. The fifth shows that the *esse* of the external bodies of the philosophers is also *percipi*. The term ' idea ' or ' *Vorstellung* ' has snowballed in meaning. As before, no claim is yet made that these ideas are real or permanent. They are phantasms, of the same stuff as dreams, having the same ontological status as the ideas of Locke and the Cartesians. All that has occurred is a notable increase in the denotation of the term. The early critics of Kant and Berkeley evidently interpreted this temporary stage as their final position. We have noticed this response in Kant's case (see above p. 228). It was voiced more confidently and widely in the case of Berkeley. James Beattie wrote of ' this absurd doctrine '.[16] David Hume considered Berkeley the best of all teachers of scepticism : ' All his arguments, though otherwise intended, are, in reality, merely sceptical '.[17] Either Hume neglected the important final step in the whole argument, or he thought it failed.

Sixth Step

And all these appearances are real.

> Kant : I leave things as we obtain them by the senses their reality (*Proleg.* 13). In order to arrive at the reality of outer objects, I have just as little need to resort to inference as I have in regard to the reality of the object of my inner sense. . . . For in both cases alike the objects are nothing but ideas, the immediate perception of which is at the same time a sufficient proof of their reality (A371).
> An empirical realist allows to matter, as appearance, a reality which does not permit of being inferred, but is immediately perceived (A371).
> Berkeley : I am of a vulgar cast, simple enough to believe my senses, and leave things as I find them (*Hylas* III).
> I might as well doubt of my own being, as of the being of those things I actually see and feel. . . . Those immediate objects of perception, which, according to you, are only appearances of things, I take to be the real things themselves (*Hylas* III).

[16]In his *Essays* (Edinburgh 1776), p. 183, he continued, ' If all men were in one instant deprived of their understanding by almighty power, and made to believe that matter has no existence but as an idea in the mind, all other earthly things remaining as they are . . . I am certain that, in less than a month after, there could not without another miracle, be one human creature alive on the face of the earth ', and added in a footnote that whilst a blind or deaf man can survive, it would be impossible for all mankind if they lost their percipient faculties.

[17]*Enquiry*, XII, i, note.

> If by *material substance* is meant only sensible body, that which is
> seen and felt . . . then I am more certain of matter's existence than
> you, or any other philosopher, pretend to be (*Hylas* III).

This step concludes the argument. Having consorted with idealism in
order to refute transcendental realism, a procedure which was, for Kant,
the 'only alternative' (B72), a 'recourse to the only refuge' (A378), and
for Berkeley, an appeal to a truth, 'so near and obvious to the mind' (*Prin.*
6); and, on the face of it, having left no avenue of escape from the negative
conclusions of the sceptics, the two men now divorce themselves from it.
Accordingly, this final step in the central argument constitutes Kant's and
Berkeley's refutation of idealism or scepticism and, by the same token,
their proof of the external world. From it, emerges their empirical realism.
The argument achieves this in a most ingenious yet simple way, by accepting
the sceptical conclusion of one such as Hylas, that all we can ever know of
the external world is certain ideas or appearances, and then admitting, as
any consistent empiricist must, that these appearances are real. After all,
it is a jest to hold, as do the philosophers, that the things we see and touch
are mere illusions.[18]

There are, of course, difficulties in such a proof of the external world
as this, the main one being the problem of error or illusion. If external
bodies are reduced to mere ideas, it might seem that the external world is
thereby reduced to the level of dreams. Locke had said, 'To make our
knowledge real, it is requisite that the ideas answer their archetypes'.[19] It
might seem that neither Kant nor Berkeley, in spite of the ingenuity of
their final step, has escaped from that extreme form of scepticism which
each was most anxious to avoid, to wit, dogmatic idealism. Both men posed
and answered this objection (in the first edition of the *Critique* and in the
Principles, respectively) long before it was made in fact by their detractors.
Berkeley had the prescience, remarkable but unavailing, to give it pride of
place as the First Objection in the *Principles* (34-40). The critics, however,
in both cases, proved to be either negligent or unconvinced. As Kant said
about Hume, both men 'suffered the usual misfortune of metaphysicians,
of not being understood'. In answering the critics, Kant asserts that the
above objection rises from an 'almost intentional misconception, as if my
doctrine turned all things of the world of sense into mere illusion' (*Proleg.*
13). The same objection prompts Berkeley's: 'It is a misapprehension
that I deny the reality of sensible things' (*Hylas* III). Both men then proceed to reaffirm their pervious answer.

[18] This final step illuminates the irony inherent in Dr. Johnson's notorious ostensive
refutation of Berkeley's 'ingenious sophistry', by exclaiming, while 'striking his foot
with mighty force against a large stone, till he rebounded from it " I refute it thus " '.
Such an argument, and also G. E. Moore's celebrated proof of an external world, 'By
holding up my two hands, and saying, as I make a certain gesture with the right hand,
" Here is one hand ", and adding, as I make a certain gesture with the left, " and here
is another " ', amount to nothing but vindications of the empirical realism of Kant and
Berkeley. See *Life of Johnson*, Globe Edition, Macmillan, London, 1929, p. 162; and
G. E. Moore, 'Proof of an External World', *Proceedings of the British Academy*, Vol.
25, 1939, p. 295.
[19] *Essay*, IV, iv ,8.

The distinction between reality and illusion retains its full force. Its criterion is not the futile correspondence of our ideas with external archetypes, but merely their coherence within our experience. In effect, there are no illusions of sense, only delusions of the understanding, because the senses tell no lies. Kant declares, ' It is not the senses, however, which must be charged with the illusion, but the understanding ' (*Proleg.* 13). Error occurs on the level of judgment. Thus, when we connect our ideas ' according to the rules of the coherence of all knowledge in experience, illusion or truth will arise according as we are negligent or careful '.[20] He illustrates an ' illusion of sense ' by the apparent progressive and retrogressive motion of the planets (*ibid.*). Berkeley tells us that the objection vanishes once we but place ' the reality of things in ideas, fleeting indeed, and changeable ; however not changed at random, but according to the fixed order of Nature ' (*Hylas* III). Real things are ' more strong, orderly and coherent ' than the irregular visions of fancy (*Prin.* 33). A man's ' mistake lies not in what he perceives immediately ', for error here is impossible, ' but in the wrong judgment he makes '. He illustrates an ' illusion of sense ' by the apparent lack of motion of the earth (*Hylas* III).

V

The central argument, which I have drawn attention to, constitutes the common ground of Kant and Berkeley. They did, of course, proceed to supplement it along different lines peculiar to their separate systems. Before we consider what conclusions may be drawn from the fact that the two men share the central argument, let us notice the important ways in which Kant differs from Berkeley as exhibited in the passages of the ' refutations '. These ways are concerned with Kant's treatment of : the self, the reality of common things and the nature of space.

First, although Kant and Berkeley agree that we know the external world as immediately as we know ourselves, the self which Kant refers to here is merely the empirical self. From it he distinguishes the self proper, the transcendental subject, which is an unthinking, and, to us, an entirely unknown, being (A380, 492). Berkeley makes no such distinction, holding that we know our real selves, not in the same way as we know ideas, but, still immediately, by reflex act and notionally (*Hylas* III). This important difference does not affect the central argument because, in it, the nature of that self which is known immediately is not in question. All that is sought is the equality in immediacy of knowledge of the outside world with it.

Secondly, at the close of the argument, we saw that the reality of common things was secured by appealing to the criteria of their immediate perception and their coherence within experience. The questions of their cause and of the ground of the coherence of our ideas were not treated, because in these matters, Kant and Berkeley differ. In Berkeley's case, the cause of

---

[20]*Cf.* B69, ' It would be my own fault, if out of that which I ought to reckon as appearance, I made mere illusion ', also A376-7, A492, *Proleg.* 49.

the sensible world is God. He is the ground of its 'steadiness, order, and coherence '. Our ideas change, not at random, but according to the fixed order of Nature, the rules or laws of which, open to discovery by us, constitute God's will. For Kant, the non-sensible, but purely intelligible, ' cause of appearances in general ' is the transcendental object. This is not material substance, but is the ' ground (to us unknown) of the appearances '. To it ' we can ascribe the whole extent and connection of our possible perceptions ' (A380, 494). It is, therefore, the cause, not only of real things (those connected in accordance with the laws of empirical advance) but of the fixed order of Nature. The transcendental object, therefore, replaces Berkeley's God.[21]

Kant, however, provides additional criteria of the reality of outer objects. I have so far considered only those which he shares with Berkeley. The first of these was immediate perception. Kant often speaks as if nothing else is needed. He asserts that it is ' a sufficient proof ' of the reality of outer objects. He accepts the existence of matter on the ' unaided testimony of our mere self-consciousness '. The other criterion shared with Berkeley was coherence within experience. This involves, not only actual perception, but judgment by the understanding. Thus, for example, the dagger before Macbeth's eyes is certainly perceived. However, unlike the dagger which he draws, it lacks objective reality, and Macbeth is able to correct his earlier judgment, and to regard the former dagger as a mere ' dagger of the mind '. Whilst this example illustrates the criterion of coherence within experience for both men, the coherence is differently explained. Berkeley rests it upon the comparison of ideas. Kant accepts such comparison, but states that *a priori* concepts of the understanding must be ' superadded ' (*Proleg.* 20). In the passages of the ' refutations ', however, the formal conditions underlying the criterion are implied, rather than stated, giving the impression that they are, indeed, superadded.[22] A typical statement of the criterion is : ' Whatever is connected with a perception according to empirical laws, is actual ' (A376).[23] This accords with the second *Postulate of Empirical*

[21]Whether Kant intends to identify the transcendental object with the thing-in-itself is doubtful. Authorities differ. Kemp Smith, *op. cit.*, p. 204, regards the doctrine of the transcendental object as a pre-Critical, or semi-Critical, survival. Paton, *op. cit.*, p. 423, disagrees, and identifies it with the thing-in-itself. Whether Kant intends to identify it with God is equally doubtful. However, Kant's God, whose existence ' we not only may, but *must*, assume ', has the same role as that of the transcendental object as described in the text to this note. Not in any of the passages of the ' refutations ' but in the appendix to the *Transcendental Dialectic*, Kant argues that ' the world is a sum of appearances ; and there must therefore be some transcendental ground of the appearances ', responsible for ' the order of the world and of its connection in accordance with universal laws '. But, by assuming this ' all-sufficient cause ', Kant asks, ' Do we then extend our knowledge beyond the field of possible experience ? ' and answers, ' *By no means*. All that we have done is merely to presuppose a something, a merely transcendental object, of which, as it is in itself, we have no concept whatsoever ' (A696-8). It is needless to indicate, however, that for Kant, such an object is only an ' object in *idea* and not in reality ', which must be used regulatively and not constitutively.

[22]For example, *Proleg.* 49, ' This doubt (regarding reality) may easily be disposed of, and we always do so in common life by investigating the connection of appearances in both space and time according to universal laws of experience '.

[23]*Cf.* A493 ; *Proleg.* 13, 49.

Thought,[24] in which it is shown that, under the guidance of the *Analogies of Experience*, we can know that an object is real. In the *Analogies*, it is shown that knowledge must conform to *a priori* concepts.[25] According to Kant, we are thus able to make the transition from awareness of our own ideas to cognition of outer objects, or, in other words, from our perceptions to objectively valid judgments. Apart from this condition, there can be no knowledge, but merely ' a rhapsody of perceptions '.[26] The above criterion is stressed in the early ' refutations '.[27] It is used directly against the sceptical idealism of Descartes on three occasions. Since the formal conditions of this criterion are, as Kant states, 'superadded,' the central argument is not affected thereby. They do mark an important divergence from Berkeley's ' pre-Critical ' doctrine, but Kant never directly developed it against Berkeley. An additional criterion is the assumption of the thing-in-itself. In the passages of the ' refutations ' this is stressed on only one occasion (*Proleg.* 13). It is the existence of the things behind the appearances, causing these appearances in us, which makes Kant's doctrine ' the very contrary ' of idealism. Berkeley's idealism fails because it denies, not the existence of bodies in space, but things-in-themselves. This recourse is completely out of line with the other ' refutations ', and indeed, with the Critical philosophy. The illegitimate appeal to this criterion, coming as it does, just after Kant had read the Garve-Feder review, gives the impression of desperation. Kant has not yet found his ' certain criterion ' which distinguishes his doctrine from that of Berkeley.

Thirdly, although in the penultimate step of the central argument we saw that Kant and Berkeley are as one on the question of the *ideality* of space and its appearances (that is, all things perceived or perceivable have no existence outside our minds), Kant proceeds to superimpose his characteristic doctrine that space (but not the things in it) is not only ideal, but inheres in us as a pure form of sensibility prior to all experience. Kant uses the *a priori* character of space as an additional criterion of reality, but not until late in the ' refutations '. It turns out to be the essence of Kant's answer to Berkeley. Unlike the other divergences, which occur after the conclusion of the central argument, this one may affect the final step. It is, therefore, significant to my thesis, and will be considered in the next section.

[24]' That which is bound up with the material conditions of experience, that is, with sensation, is actual ' (A218).
[25]Specifically, to the ' *a priori* transcendental unity of apperception ' (A177).
[26]In spite of such seemingly sure guidance, Kant encounters difficulties in distinguishing, in fact, an objectively valid judgment from a subjective perception. In the *Prolegomena*, he distinguishes between judgments of perception and judgments of experience. The former, e.g., ' Sugar is sweet ', involves merely the comparison of ideas and contains no necessity or universality. The latter, e.g., ' The sun warms the stone ', has undergone the addition of a concept of the understanding, and is inter-subjectively valid (*Proleg.* 19, 20). This tenuous distinction is relinquished in the second edition of the *Critique*, for it is clear that if one kind of judgment must conform to the formal condition, so must the other.
[27]See note 22 and accompanying text.

In spite of these differences, the central argument is unified and complete. Before we proceed to consider Kant's direct treatment of Berkeley's doctrine, let us see what conclusions may be drawn from the fact that the above argument, as it now stands, is shared by both men. In the history of philosophy, this argument is the unique property of Kant and Berkeley. Whilst no other philosopher, to my knowledge, has produced it, many have asserted some of the individual steps, some, like the sceptics or idealists, more than others ; but none has either presented these steps in such a characteristic fashion or conjoined them. First, there is the incisive analysis of the existing situation, which, by its complete antagonism to the tone of the age, separates Kant and Berkeley from the vast majority of other thinkers. Allied to this, is their exclusive disclosure of the source of the delusion inherent in modern philosophy, and their singular deduction of its inevitable consequences, temporarily in sceptical, and ultimately in dogmatic, idealism. Next, there is the deliberate acceptance (one may almost add, exploitation) of sceptical arguments. Kant and Berkeley develop this stage in different directions,[28] but what they share, viz., ' the ideality of all appearances ', and the consequent assimilation of the external bodies of the philosophers into the realm of mere appearance, they share only with the sceptics. Finally, in their refutation of dogmatic idealism (the deepest scepticism) with its attendant proof of an external world, they leave the whole field far behind. Berkeley's refutation of scepticism, with his parallel vindication of common-sense, was one of his main aims. His argument to implement it, developed in the *Dialogues* rather than in the *Principles*, is perhaps the most singular feature in his whole philosophy. This simple, but devastating, turning of the game played by scepticism against itself[29] was original with Berkeley. When this is conjoined with the other steps to make his main argument, Berkeley's contribution must be considered as unique up to his time.

Seventy years later, Kant developed an argument in which the parallel with Berkeley's is exact in some features and close in others. This becomes more evident once we realize the fact (strangely neglected by commentators) that Kant most often uses the term ' idealism ' (a word which Berkeley never used) to mean what Berkeley means by the term ' scepticism '. Kant shares with Berkeley what is perhaps the latter's most singular feature and uses it to turn the tables on idealism. He conjoins with it the other steps of the argument in a fashion characteristic of none of his precursors (including Hume) except Berkeley.

From the considerations summarized above, and, for the time being, from these alone, I may say at once that Berkeley anticipated Kant in the latter's central argument of the ' refutations '. I go further and, for weighty reasons, conclude that it is inherently likely that Kant was thoroughly familiar with Berkeley's doctrine and learned from it.

[28] As we have seen, and as Hume implies, Berkeley provides stronger arguments than any of his sceptical precursors. (See above, p. 234.)

[29] See Richard H. Popkin, ' Berkeley and Pyrrhonism ', *Review of Metaphysics*, V, 2, (Dec., 1951), which brings out this point with great clarity.

VI

There are four difficult sets of facts which my theory must explain. These are : (1) Kant's many obvious misinterpretations of Berkeley's doctrine ; (2) Kant's vehement denial that his own doctrine resembles Berkeley's ; (3) Kant's extreme animus, reserved, amongst philosophers, for Berkeley alone ; (4) Kant's omission of any direct treatment of Berkeley's doctrine in the first edition of the *Critique* ; his promise to deal with it, and his failure to do so ; his belated indication, in the appendix of the *Prolegomena* and in the second edition of the *Critique*, that Berkeley's doctrine had already been undermined in the *Aesthetic*. Of these, the first three are readily accounted for on the accepted theory, according to which, Kant was largely ignorant of Berkeley's philosophy. This theory can, not quite so readily, explain the fourth. On the face of them, none of them supports my theory. The most important is the first, which seems to demolish my theory. Clearly, Berkeley did not deny the reality of the sensible word ; Kant says that he did. Such gross misinterpretation surely indicates profound misunderstanding. However, this first set of facts, when properly assessed and interpreted, yields a contrary view. The remaining facts are so illuminated thereby, that the accepted theory is rendered improbable, whilst my view, that Kant was thoroughly familiar with Berkeley's doctrine and understood it well, becomes the only adequate explanation.

Kant's official view of Berkeley's doctrine is found in five short passages, one in the first edition of the *Critique*, and two each in the *Prolegomena* and the second edition of the *Critique*.[30] The objection to Berkeley's doctrine, common to all the passages, is that it is a philosophy of illusionism : Berkeley denies the reality of bodies. In only one passage (*Proleg.* 13),[31] are these bodies held to be external, in the sense of being transcendentally outside us. Therefore, the burden of Kant's official view is that Berkeley denies the reality of bodies *in space*, or, in Kant's words, he ' regards the things in space as merely imaginary entities (*Einbildungen*) ' (B274). Kant's official view does seem to arise from a misconception of Berkeley's doctrine, and therefore to stem from ignorance. This accords with the accepted theory. However, such a theory loses weight immediately, when it is pointed out that Kant rarely agrees with anyone,[32] and that his customary procedure in discussing the views of other philosophers, is to present, not their real views, but rather the consequences he considers to be entailed by them. These Kantian consequences are then ascribed to the philosophers as their own views. For example, although Kant studied Leibniz's works carefully, he ascribes to him views which Leibniz never held.[33] Therefore, even if

[30] Numbered by me, II, IV, VI, VII, VIII. See above, p. 227.
[31] See above, p. 238.
[32] Hume is about the only philosopher to whom he acknowledges a debt. See *Proleg.*, Introduction.
[33] Cf. A39-40. On this matter, Kemp Smith, *op. cit.*, p. 140, note 6, observes : ' Kant, following his usual method in the discussion of opposing systems, is stating what he regards as being the logical consequences of certain of Leibniz's tenets, rather than his avowed position '. Similar considerations apply to Kant's account of Newton (A39-40).

Kant had studied Berkeley's writings as carefully as he studied those of Leibniz, it is likely that his account of Berkeley's doctrine would be distorted. From this consideration, it may be safely observed that Kant's misinterpretations of Berkeley's doctrine are, at least, compatible with the theory that he was thoroughly familiar with it.

Of the five passages, the last three are most relevant, because, not until he began them, had Kant finally settled on a way to treat Berkeley. Although they seem to indicate misconception, nevertheless they secrete Kant's real view of Berkeley. Kant's final account of Berkeley's doctrine is as follows :

> He maintains that space, with all the things of which it is the inseparable condition, is something which is in itself impossible ; *and he therefore regards the things in space as merely imaginary entities.* Dogmatic idealism is unavoidable, if space be interpreted as a property that must belong to things in themselves. For in that case space, and everything to which it serves as condition, is a nonentity. The ground on which this idealism rests has already been undermined by us in the Transcendental Aesthetic [B274, my italics].

It will be noticed that this passage contains an essential part of Kant's own doctrine. It is, in fact, a summary of the logical decline of transcendental realism, presented in the first three steps of the central argument of the ' refutations ' : doctrine which, as we have seen, is just as much Berkeley's as it is Kant's. The important question is : Does Kant know that Berkeley shares it ? I think he does. It is certain that Kant ascribes to Berkeley his own denial of the absolute reality of space and the external bodies in it, i.e., his denial of transcendental realism. This is evident from the first sentence. But Kant holds also that Berkeley had drawn the ultimate logical consequence from the realist position, viz., dogmatic idealism, with its denial, not only of the reality of absolute space, but of the reality of the whole sensible world. In other words, Kant ascribes to Berkeley his own doctrine, that once transcendental realism is upheld, dogmatic idealism (complete illusion), is unavoidable. The only other passage which treats of Berkeley directly in the second edition of the *Critique* bears this out. The passage was added at the end of the *Aesthetic*. Here, Kant asserts that his principle of the ideality of appearances does not entail illusion. The contrary is the case : ' It is only if we ascribe objective reality ' to space and time, 'that it becomes impossible for us to prevent everything being transformed thereby into mere illusion ' (B70). Then, after indicating the absurdities involved in the notion of such entities, he concludes that, accordingly,

> We cannot blame the good Berkeley for *degrading bodies to mere illusion* [B71, my italics].

Since Kant asserts by implication that dogmatic idealism or illusionism is avoidable if one does not uphold the absolute reality of space, it follows that a way of escape is left open for himself and Berkeley ; not so for the transcendental realists. Kant would have to admit that we must ' blame ' Newton, Leibniz, More, Clarke and Locke for inconsistency, and Descartes and Malebranche for refraining from taking the last logical step ; he would have to admit that we must ' blame ' all transcendental realists for not seeing what he and Berkeley saw. From all this, it is evident that Kant is consciously ascribing to Berkeley his own insights which are presented in the first three steps of the central argument of the ' refutations '.[34]

We have seen that another essential part of Kant's doctrine is his principle, called by him, ' the ideality of all appearances ', a principle also shared with Berkeley. But of even more significance than the fact that they share it, is the additional fact that Kant is aware of it. This is evident from the remaining relevant passage on Berkeley in the appendix to the *Prolegomena*. Here, Kant makes a striking admission—one he makes nowhere else. He attributes to Berkeley the view that space and its contents have no absolute reality, but instead, are nothing but appearances ; then he admits that he is ' one in confession ' with Berkeley on this doctrine. In other words, Kant is here consciously ascribing to Berkeley what amounts to his own insights embodied in the fourth and fifth steps of the central argument.[35] In the same passage Kant reveals additional knowledge :

> Berkeley regarded space as a more empirical idea that, like the appearances it contains, is, together with its determinations, known to us only by means of experience or perception.

A line later, he adds that ' Berkeley did not consider ' the subject of time. Kant's account of Berkeley on space is accurate, and his remark on time would be accurate, had he read only the *Dialogues*[36] and *De Motu*. We now know, therefore, not only that Kant and Berkeley hold in common the central argument, but that Kant is aware he shares almost all of it with Berkeley : and we also know that Kant has reliable additional knowledge. My assessment of the evidence reveals on Kant's part, not ignorance of Berkeley's philosophy, but sure comprehension.

Although Kant must admit that illusionism is avoidable by himself and Berkeley, he means that, while he succeeds, Berkeley fails. The italicized portions of the above passages reveal this. Since Berkeley does not intend to degrade bodies to mere illusion, Kant's assertion that he does is a misinterpretation. Kant, almost throughout, speaks as though he really believes that Berkeley intends to be a whole-hearted dogmatic idealist ; but there is one exception. In the last passage we have been considering, Kant gives more detailed treatment of the difference between him and Berkeley than anywhere else. Here we see that Kant departs from Berkeley's view, not on the question of the ideality of space and its appearances, but on its *a priori* nature. The distinction between *ideality* and the *a priori* (often neglected by authorities) is clarified in this passage. Kant agrees with Berkeley that space is ideal, but whereas the latter holds that it is learned from experience, Kant holds he has proved that ' it inheres in us as a pure form of our sensibility before all perception or experience '. Because of this, it can ' afford the certain criterion for distinguishing truth from illusion therein '. He adds :

[34]See above, pp. 229-32.

[35]See above, pp. 232-4.

[36]In these, however, occurs the one significant observation : ' Do I not acknowledge a two-fold state of things, the one ectypal or natural, the other archetypal and eternal ? The former was created in time ; the latter existed from everlasting in the mind of God ' (*Hylas* III). The subject is accorded only two paragraphs (97-8) in the *Principles*.

It follows from this that . . . experience, according to Berkeley, can have no criteria of truth because its phenomena (according to him) have nothing *a priori* at their foundation, whence *it follows* that experience is nothing but sheer illusion [my italics].

Kant thus holds that illusion is a necessary consequence of Berkeley's view, not that it is Berkeley's view. His highly significant admission makes it more than likely that Kant's repeated assertions elsewhere to the effect that Berkeley actually believes in dogmatic idealism are instances of Kant's habit of ascribing to other philosophers what are, in fact, consequences drawn by Kant himself.[37] It follows that Kant's knowledge of Berkeley's philosophy is still more accurate than was previously thought. Since the misinterpretations stem from accurate knowledge, they are deliberate, and are, therefore, more properly called ' perversions '. The same analysis comprehends Kant's denial that his doctrine at all resembles Berkeley's. For this just is not so. We have Kant's own admission that it is not. One would also expect misinterpretation and denial of resemblance, both of which stem from full knowledge, to be symptoms of animus. This is most likely the case. We have already noticed remarks which indicate that Kant desires his readers to know that he finds Berkeley's teaching abhorrent.[38]

This brings us to the question of Kant's promise, in the first edition of the *Critique*, to deal with Berkeley's doctrine, and his failure to do so. In the fourth *Paralogism*, Kant's position is made to resemble Berkeley's more closely than anywhere else. We now know that there is, not only resemblance, but Kant's awareness of it. If he had sought to refute Berkeley in the next section, he must have ended in hopeless confusion, for he would have been refuting himself. He therefore did not even try. A niggardly description of Berkeley's doctrine was his only recourse. However, the Göttingen review and similar criticisms made it imperative for Kant to define his difference from Berkeley. He appealed first, to his assumption of the thing-in-itself, and then to the *a priori* character of space. Although the latter is a legitimate difference, Kant's appeal to it in this connection (as a guard against illusion, which Berkeley lacked), creates difficulties. We have seen that, throughout the ' refutation ', transcendental realism entails illusion, not because it lacks the assumption of space as a prior condition of all experience (because it already makes this assumption), but because it distinguishes outer appearances from the senses. The Kantian antidote to this is not the *a priori* nature of space, but its ideality or subjectivity, which assimilates space and its contents into the realm of ideas, and thus *prevents* illusion.[39]

[37] See above, note 33 and text. In the case of Newton and Leibniz, however, Kant is usually more careful. For them, he uses phrases such as : ' They have to admit ', and ' They are obliged to deny '. Cf. A39-40.

[38] See above, p. 228. In addition, the epithet, ' the good Berkeley ', should be contrasted with ' the illustrious ' or ' the celebrated ', which are reserved for other philosophers. He calls the sceptical idealist ' a benefactor of human reason '.

[39] This is made clear at A378, *Proleg.* 13, B69-70. It is, moreover, the principle of ideality which saves *all* outer appearances, i.e. all possible experience, for the application of mathematical knowledge. Kant's additional doctrine of the *a priori* character of

Finally, my suggestion that Kant's deliberate misinterpretations of Berkeley's doctrine were prompted by animus calls for further explanation. The vulgar view of Berkeley, then as now, was of a befooled enthusiast who sought notoriety by his paradoxes.[40] Moreover, Kant abhorred all things mystical[41] and visionary, and classified Berkeley's idealism as such. To acknowledge debt to such a man, or even to admit affinity, was quite out of the question for Kant. However, in the history of philosophy, instances of Horace's *odi et amo* are by no means rare ; the prime example being the relation between Aristotle and Plato. As a result of my reassessment of the evidence, I hold that Kant carefully studied and fully comprehended the writings of the eccentric Irishman. I also suggest that, whilst he may very well have deplored some of Berkeley's conclusions, nevertheless he noted those insights which contributed to the solution of the problem of modern philosophy, and made them his own. My thesis is summarized by Ernst Mach : ' Berkeley's point of view (was) secretly preserved by Kant '.[42]

COLIN M. TURBAYNE

University of Washington.

space is designed to give this mathematical knowledge its apodeictic certainty. However, in certain passages of the second edition (particularly B44), Kant seeks to confuse the *a priori* and the *subjective* elements, using the word ' ideality ' to embrace both.

[40]The remark of Leibniz is representative : ' I suspect that he is one of those people who seek to become famous by their paradoxes ' (Letter to des Bosses, 15 Mar. 1715).

[41]Kant's reactions to the impressions of his friend, George Hamann, after reading the first edition of the *Critique*, are recorded : ' Owing to its high ideals, he thought the book might be called " Mysticism " as well as the *Critique of Pure Reason*. He told Kant that he liked his work, " all except the mysticism ". Kant, who had a dread of everything of the kind, was astonished ' (J. H. W. Stückenberg, *Life of Immanuel Kant*, Macmillan, London, 1862, p. 269).

[42]Quoted by A. V. Vasiliev, *op. cit.*, p. 85.

BERKELEY AND KANT

GEORGE P. ADAMS

To say anything in these present circumstances, here and now, about the philosophy of Bishop Berkeley is, of course, but carrying coals to Newcastle. Perhaps it is by way of offering a slight justification for presenting another paper in this series that I have, very timorously, appended to the title of this paper the name of another philosopher. There is another source of discomfort on my part. The problems with which Berkeley dealt appear at best to have worn thin and threadbare. And, at worst, they may appear to concern questions which ought never to have been asked, and which were asked by Berkeley because of ambiguities and confusions in ordinary linguistic usage. Once these confusions are cleared up, the puzzles evaporate. So many of the troublesome ghosts which have haunted the arena of philosophical thought are to be exorcized by verbal incantations fetched from the proper understanding of verbal usage.

I *shall* have something to say about Berkeley and, very brashly, about Kant. But I should like, first of all, to ask why it was that they asked the questions, or certain of them, which stand out so prominently in their thinking. What lies behind the questions which for them were so central and urgent?

Berkeley and Kant belong to the eighteenth century. By the eighteenth century the main outline and contours of the epoch we speak of as "modern" had become fairly clear. The foundations upon which a new kind of life and society, different from both the ancient and medieval worlds, were to be built had been laid down. Fresh energies, both of life and of thought, had been released. It may be that we are witnessing the close of an era, the breakup of that framework of life and of thought, of ideas and of institutions, characteristic of this classical modern period; for the energies which fashion a historic epoch breed conflicts and problems. The great philosophers do not invent their problems, making them up like chess problems for the sheer fun of solving them.

But it will not do to exaggerate the problems uniquely characteristic of any one historic epoch; for there are perennial and ever-recurring features of man's life and experience, of the total situation within which men find themselves. The rhythm of birth, life, and death, the practical need of reckoning with the things in one's environment, the

[189]

■ 89 ■

recognition of selves and interests other than one's own, the weight of custom and tradition, the need of satisfying the basic needs of man's nature, needs and demands recurrent in each generation, such as these and much besides, constitute the constant background of the enterprise of man's living in the ever-changing epochs of his history. I make mention of this because I am going to single out two formative forces strikingly characteristic of our modern age, and I should not wish to overstress their uniqueness and novelty within this one historic epoch. They have always been resident within the human scene. But they happen to have taken on an additional increment of energy and meaning with the breakup of the medieval world, and the problems generated by their encounter acquired a fresh urgency and pathos.

Berkeley and Kant share the preoccupation of all philosophers belonging to the great tradition with the global, perennial problem of the nature of man's life and experience, with the cosmic setting and environment which is his habitat, and with the relation between these two poles of the total situation within which men find themselves. It may be that one of the signs of the end of our era is the fact that we tend no longer to ask of philosophy that it undertake any such task as this, and that many philosophers seem to welcome this release.

There must always have been some sense of the contrast between that which arises and is enacted in man's experience and that which belongs to the nonhuman world of nature. The contrast may have been blurred under the spell of primitive animism, but the radical distinction between persons and things could never have been wholly in abeyance. Theories of hedonism in Ethics, which lie tolerably close to the spontaneous attitudes and persuasions of common sense, in all ages, imply the notion of conscious life, of feelings of pleasure and pain immediately experienced by the individual. And Lucretius' saying that when we are, death is not, and that when death is, we are not, moves within the orbit of the conscious life of the individual self. And so I think it a mistake to ascribe a sense of this momentous contrast between experience consciously lived through by an individual, and surrounding things which have being but no experience, solely to the peculiar vagaries of modern thought. But unquestionably it is within the modern period that this dualism becomes markedly enhanced. The moderns neither discovered nor invented the notion of the inner conscious life of the experiencing individual. But by the eighteenth century it and the problems which it posed had come to play a dominant role. Recall the shift in the titles of philosophical writings when one goes from the ancient to the modern period. The ancients wrote περὶ φύσει and *de rerum natura*. The moderns write essays on The Human Understanding (the eighteenth-century equivalent of the term "experience"). The Greek thinkers from the Ionians to Plato and beyond asked the question, "What makes nature intelligible?" Kant, in this respect a spokesman for modern philosophy, asks, "What makes experience possible?" But over against the experience which the individual lives through, there is nature, material bodies in space, the system of the physical world. So great was the discrepancy between these two domains, these two opposite poles of our total human situation, that the problem of their relation to one another became inevitable and central. Our two eighteenth-century philosophers could well have borrowed the title, if not the contents, of Dewey's best book, *Experience and Nature*. The dualism of conscious life and unthinking, extended things was not foisted upon modern thought by the paternal zeal of Descartes. Descartes was but the spokesman for the energies and moving forces which he sensed as transforming and shaping the world in which he lived. The dualism of *res cogitans* and *res extensa* was already there to be reckoned with.

I should like to carry this one step further before coming to our two philosophers. This accentuation and primacy of the conscious life of the individual and the problems for philosophy to which it gave rise is one of the forms assumed by the massive sweep of the motives and forces commonly comprised within the term "modern individualism." The central problems of modern morals and politics are analogues of the theoretical problems which bothered the philosophers. How discover a common good which will appeal to the individual and also at the same time transcend his individual self-interest? How shall men organize a political order which will elicit the obedience and allegiance of individuals without, at the same time, trespassing upon the individual's own domain, his rights, and his interests? And the theoretical problem which the philosophers set out to answer, what was it but the question whether, and if so, how, the individual can transcend the boundaries set by his own individual experience and acquire authentic knowledge of the independent world out there, lying beyond all the possessions of his individual experience.

The sweep of this mighty current of individualism engulfs all the provinces of man's life and interests. But there is that other force transforming all his ways of thinking and the whole gamut of his beliefs and attitudes, denoted by the term "science," destined in due time completely to transform the scene of our daily lives. Not experience, lived through by the individual, not *res cogitans,* but *res extensa* is now the theme. Yet this outer world which goes its own way independently of anything which transpires in the inner life of conscious selves is nevertheless accessible to our minds. Its components, its structure, and the laws which govern its motions can be discovered. The achievements of Newton stand as proof. We encounter physical objects in our everyday perceptions. We see and touch and manipulate them directly, face to face. The outer world of nature transcends all that belongs to the experience of individual minds. Nevertheless, it is directly accessible to us. How?

When philosophers in the seventeenth and eighteenth centuries ask questions and write about human understanding and experience, about our perception of material things belonging to the world out there, and about our scientific knowledge of the physical universe, their analysis and thinking moves within an orbit whose two poles are individualism and science. All experience is the possession of individual selves. What is owned and enacted in experience belongs not to the world out there, but to some mind, ineluctably individual. But there is the world out there, inescapable, accessible to sensory perception and so successfully explored by the new sciences. These are two tacit premises of seventeenth- and eighteenth-century philosophy. They have no need of being explicitly formulated and defended, because they are taken for granted.

Philosophers are not exempt from the requirement that whenever anyone asks any specific question there is always hovering in the background something unquestioned, in the absence of which just that question could not be asked. If this unquestioned background and premise itself becomes subject to question and doubt, as it always can be, then the horizon of the unquestioned shifts and recedes to some further region which makes possible the new questioning. The tacit assumptions and premises of philosophers lying in this unquestioned background compromise, in a sense, what Cornford has called their "unwritten philosophies." They don't need to write them, because they and their readers take them for granted. They belong to the accepted ways of thinking, to the "common sense" of the age. The two unwritten philosophies of the age which now concerns us are telescoped within the two terms "individualism" and "science." Experience in all its modes, impressions and sensations, feelings, thoughts and ideas, volitions, hopes and fears, are possessions of an individual mind. They all lie within the boundary defined by the circumference of his individual life and experience. Beyond this boundary is the physical world, material bodies which exist and change independently of the fluctuating stream of perceptions and ideas which transpire in the career of individual experience. Although it is so completely other and independent, it is directly accessible to experience, to observation and perception, and to the enormously refined procedures of the astronomer and mathematician. How is all this possible? Here is the problem of perception and of knowledge, on all fours with the problems of morals, politics, and economics, confronting thinkers carried along by the ground swell of these two energies, individualism and science.

And now, after this too long a prologue, to Berkeley and Kant. That there exists an order of nature, independent of the ebb and flow of individual sensations and perceptions, both Berkeley and Kant, in accordance with what Berkeley calls "the plain dictates of nature and common sense," take for granted. That material objects, chairs and tables, exist and continue in existence when we cease to perceive them, is not in doubt. The sole question is, *what* they are. What sort of things are they, must they be, in the light of the unquestioned assumption that they are directly accessible to our experience, that they are immediately knowable? That they are thus knowable is demonstrated by common-sense perception and by science. But what sort of entity is it that is directly knowable? Here the motive of individualism comes into play. Anything immediately knowable must be actually experienced; it must be an ingredient in the felt possessions of an individual mind. What is directly and primarily known exists and can exist only "in the mind," in the phrase repeatedly used by Berkeley. What is directly known, face to face, must be actually experienced. Only that which is actually experienced has presence, immediacy, "warmth and intimacy," in James's phrase. When it ceases to be felt and experienced it ceases to exist. Its *esse* is *percipi*. Berkeley's "subjectivism," rightly so called, is his version of individualism. After all, the two terms, "subject" and "individual," appear interchangeable. Every subject is an individual, and every human individual is a subject. It is important to remember, however, that Berkeley's subjectivism pertains to *what* material objects are and not to the fact *that* they are. Material things, the entire furniture of earth and choir of heaven are experienced and perceived as congeries of particular sensible qualities; and sensible qualities, as we experience them, are sensations and perceptions, on all fours with feelings and emotions. They are "ideas" in the eighteenth-century use of that term. Like feelings, they exist only as they are felt and sensed, only when they are actually being experienced. Their *esse* coincides

with their *percipi*. All of this is, of course, but a small hodful of coal
being brought to Newcastle.

Berkeley constantly falls back upon the belief that this doctrine, and
this alone, is consonant with the beliefs and persuasions of unsophisti-
cated common sense. "I am," says Philonous, "of a vulgar cast, simple
enough to believe my senses, and leave things as I find them. To be
plain, it is my opinion that the real things are those very things I see,
and feel, and perceive by my senses." Berkeley is, I think, quite on the
right track in wanting to formulate a theory which explicates and
justifies so fundamental and pervasive a belief of common sense. If any
philosophical theory purports to show that a belief, woven into the
texture of man's experience throughout, is groundless or illusory, so
much the worse for that philosophical theory. That the plain man also,
at times, entertains beliefs incompatible with the belief "that real things
are the very things I see and feel," I shall want presently to note. If we
dignify this belief, held to both by common sense and by Berkeley, by
speaking of it as a theory, it is, of course, the theory of direct perception. And this theory, viewed in the light of Berkeley's predecessors,
both in philosophy and the new sciences, wears something of a revolutionary aspect. Berkeley breaks with the representative theory of perception, held to, in different ways, by Galileo, Descartes, and Locke.
This theory states that sense data, the contents of immediate sensory
experience, can never be identical with real material things out there
in our world. They are the effects produced in us by a chain of physical,
mechanical happenings which originate in something out there. But
the something out there isn't the thing we perceive. We perceive only
the impressions produced in us, initiated by the external, unperceived
thing and carried along through intervening media until, at the very
end of this causal chain, there is something which reaches us. It alone
is given to us, is our datum. This is all we possess, all that we experience.
Our perceptions are messages. We are aware of the sources of these
messages only indirectly. External things are never encountered
directly, face to face. All that we encounter immediately belongs to us,
and we are cut off from the senders of these messages by a complex
sequence of physical transactions and energy transformations hidden
from us. Berkeley sweeps all of this away. There is nothing in physical
nature which necessarily escapes our direct grasp and awareness. All
of nature is immediately accessible to perceiving minds. If much or

---

¹ *Dialogues between Hylas and Philonous*, Third Dialogue, in Berkeley's *Works*,
ed. A. C. Fraser (Oxford: Clarendon Press, 1901), Vol. I, p. 445.

Berkeley and Kant

most of nature escapes our finite human minds, then surely there are other spirits and, above all, a universal mind to which the whole of nature directly appears and lies wholly open like an open book.

But there seems to be something queer and odd in this procedure. Berkeley throws overboard the whole perspective of representative perception and the causal theory of perception. But isn't the only ground upon which he rejects this theory fetched from the very theory itself? It is only because he first assumes that our perceptions are the causal effects of physical processes outside of us that he is led to say that perceptions belong wholly to the mind that has them, that they are subjective modifications, ideas residing in the mind. These ideas are the only things we experience and know, the only things we need be concerned about. But why locate these things "in the mind"? Why identify them with ideas, save on the single premise that they are effects in us, generated by causes external to us? The apparent perversity of this situation has been often observed, notably by Kemp Smith. He writes: "Subjective idealism has its source, exclusively, in a supposedly necessary deduction from the belief that sensations are mechanically generated through brain-processes.... [The subjectivist] can only prove things perceived to be subjective by proving them to be externally related to objects as their mechanical effects, and yet this can only be done by simultaneously interpreting the things perceived in a manner which the realist standpoint can alone justify."[1] And quite in line with this account of the sources of Berkeley's subjectivism is the statement made by Mr. Pepper, if I remember rightly, that Berkeley's philosophy is an "inverted materialism."

Now, undoubtedly, this mechanical, causal theory of representative perception gave a powerful push to the development of Berkeley's subjectivism. But this is not, I think, quite the whole story. This contradiction between subjectivism and the premises from which it is here said to issue exhibits the discrepancy and tension between the claims of individual experience and the claims arising from the perspective of seventeenth- and eighteenth-century science. Had there been no representative theory of perception, supposedly required by science and taught by Galileo, Descartes, and Locke, Berkeley would still be driven to hold that everything accessible to human experience comes to life, is enacted and possessed by an individual mind. All experience, all its ingredients and phases, are possessions of an individual self or mind.

[1] Smith, *Prolegomena to an Idealist Theory of Knowledge* (London: Macmillan, 1924), p. 52.

They are encompassed and enclosed within the boundaries of his individual life and experience. They are "in the mind." It is this drive of individualism, taken by itself, which pushes Berkeley into his subjectivism. The only world that concerns me immediately, that I can know directly, is *my* world. Any other world, *your* world, *the* world, is at best problematic. It lies across the border of any one individual's experience.

I have mentioned Berkeley's persistent desire to stick as closely as possible to the beliefs and attitudes implicit within common sense, the experience of the plain man. "The wisest way," says Philonous, "[is] to follow nature, trust your senses, and, laying aside all anxious thought about unknown natures or substances, admit with the vulgar those for real things which are perceived by the senses." Yet this complete identification of real things with sensa and ideas as actually experienced is a bit troublesome for Berkeley. In general the plain man does believe that the contents of his own immediate experience are real physical things. But the plain man also recognizes that sometimes what he immediately experiences and real things are quite different. They do not always coincide. At a distance large objects look small. What is then directly present in visual experience is really small. As one approaches the object, the visual presentation becomes larger. But, of course, the real object hasn't increased in size. The ordinary language of common sense takes care of this situation by having two sets of expressions which are interchangeable. One may say either "I see yonder tower" or "I have a perception of yonder tower." The former expression is shorter and more convenient. Implicit in the second form of expression, in the phrase "perception of the tower," is the belief that there are two things, not coincident, the tower out there which I don't have as I possess my perception, and the perception which is my own possession. But Berkeley will have none of any two things. When I have what I call a "perception of the table," Berkeley warns us to stick to what I actually have and not go beyond that. When I see a table, all that I have and experience is a tabular perception.

Berkeley does recognize that the complete identification of material objects with experienced contents does diverge from common sense, at least from its language. The plain man supposes that an object seen under a microscope is the very same object which is seen with the naked eye, with its details seen more clearly. Not so, says Berkeley. "When I look through a microscope," says Philonous again, "it is not that I may perceive more clearly what I perceived already with my bare eyes; the

---

* *Dialogues,* Third Dialogue, Fraser ed., Vol. I, p. 466.

object perceived by the glass being quite different from the former." This vulgar prejudice, that these are two different visions of the same thing, Berkeley ascribes to the confusion which takes its rise "from not rightly understanding the common language of men, speaking of several distinct ideas as united into one thing by the mind." Words, he says, were framed by the vulgar, "merely for conveniency and dispatch in the common actions of life, without any regard to speculation."[4]

There are other discrepancies between the outcome of Berkeley's position and common-sense beliefs, together with the ordinary language in which they get expressed. Thomas Reid pointed out that on Berkeley's principles "the ideas in my mind cannot be the same with the ideas in any other mind; therefore, if the objects I perceive be only ideas, it is impossible that two or more such minds can perceive the same things."[5] This question, how can different minds know the same thing, is the epistemological variant of the central modern problem: how can the experiences and possessions of individual minds be transcended so that many minds may discover a common, sharable world, a common good, and build an enduring community?

Berkeley departs from the teachings of his modern predecessors in rejecting the theory of representative perception. But in another respect Berkeley agrees with his predecessors. He shares their acceptance of another assumption and premise which forms part of their unwritten philosophy. It is with respect to this tacit assumption that we may come in sight of some aspects of the philosophy of Kant, and I turn now to him. I am not unmindful of the pitfalls which here dog my steps. There are different strands and strata displayed in the development of his thought and writings. These lend themselves to various and conflicting interpretations. And I must keep as far as possible from the cumbersome apparatus which Kant employs throughout. But I think it possible to state, in fairly simple language, one of the conclusions at which he arrived and which bears directly upon that tacit assumption of his predecessors, including Berkeley, to which I just now referred. It is the assumption that the only things which one can immediately and directly know and be certain of are the present contents of actual experience. It is the premise that one can be cognizant of these without knowing anything else. Any knowledge of anything other than or beyond what is immediately experienced is problematic and precarious. There can be no immediate knowledge of anything except the contents

---

[4] *Ibid.*, p. 464.
[5] Reid's *Works*, ed. Sir William Hamilton (Edinburgh, 1852), p. 284.

of immediate experience. Descartes supposes that these contents are representative of things other than themselves. Berkeley wonders why anyone should bother about any such unperceived things. This premise—we may call it the premise of "immediacy"—seemed to Kant's predecessors to be self-evident because this was their reading of what was implied by the acceptance of the whole drive of modern individualism. It is just this which Kant comes to question, and if this be individualism, if individualism is wholly synonymous with subjectivism, then Kemp Smith is wholly right in saying that the "revolutionary character of Kant's critical inquiries" is shown by the fact that "these problems [the problems of perception and of knowledge as formulated by Descartes and Berkeley] are no longer formulated in terms of the individualistic presuppositions which govern the thinking of all Kant's predecessors, even that of Hume. The concealed presuppositions are now called in question, and are made the subject of explicit discussion."*

Kant too, like all modern thinkers, is carried along by the forces and implications which I have subsumed under the rubric "individualism." But there is that other perspective and motive, stemming from the promise and achievements of the new sciences of the physical world. Besides all that is to be alloted to the career of individual experience and mind, there is the system of nature, independent of any of the mind's possessions, which had to be reckoned with in any attempt to understand our total human situation. For Berkeley, "all those bodies which comprise the mighty frame of the world" are dissolved into the order of actual and possible sensations. Berkeley here sets the pace for the nineteenth-century positivism of Mill, Mach, and Karl Pearson. With this difference, that, for Berkeley, what for us is a congeries of possible sensations—the other side of the moon and the chair in the next vacant room—is a system of actual sensations in the mind of God. For Mill and the others, possible sensations are left hanging in the air as mere possibilities which need never be actualized.

The theory to which Kant's analysis of experience points is, on the other hand, something like this. He rejects the premise of immediacy, that nothing can be directly known save what is actually experienced. In being conscious of the contents of immediate experience we are at the same time cognitively aware of something other and distinct from that which lives in our immediate enjoyment. Real things, independent of the stream of individual experience, are known directly and not

---

* Smith, *A Commentary to Kant's Critique of Pure Reason* (London: Macmillan, 1923), pp. 283–284.

through inference. They are known *through* experience but not *in* experience.

Kant added to the second edition of his *Critique* "his refutation of Idealism." He did this because his first edition was commonly taken to be a variant of subjectivism, a restatement of Berkeley's position. In this refutation of Idealism, Kant labels the position of Descartes, that we can use the immediate certainty of self-consciousness as a basis from which eventually to infer the existence of bodies in space, "problematic Idealism." Berkeley's doctrine, which locates spatial bodies within the mind, is "dogmatic Idealism." He undertakes to point out the flaw which, he thinks, is common to both of these types of subjectivism. He comes to the conclusion that we cannot be aware of anything in our immediate experience, of anything "in the mind," as Berkeley puts it, unless we are at the same time aware of something which is no item of immediate experience, but has an independent status. In his own words, "the consciousness of my own existence is, at the same time, an immediate consciousness of the existence of other things." What Kant calls "internal experience" covers, for Berkeley, the entire range of all that the individual mind possesses in its actual experience. "When we do our utmost," says Berkeley, "to conceive the existence of external bodies, we are all the while only contemplating our own ideas."* What Kant calls "external experience," the immediate awareness of things other than our own ideas, is, for Berkeley, wholly engulfed within and swallowed by "internal experience." Kant, on the other hand, insists, in his own words, that "internal experience is possible only through external experience." We are conscious of our own being, our own possessions, our own ideas, only so far as we are also aware of bodies in space which are not our own ideas.

I shall not venture here to recount the steps in the analysis and argument which Kant employs in his "refutation of Idealism." I should like instead to set forth, in a very free way, that aspect of the situation in which we find ourselves when we reflect upon this thing called "human experience," an aspect to which Kant seems to be directing attention in his own way. If it is Kant who puts his finger upon this aspect of our experience, and not some of his commentators who have read it into Kant, then Kant did inaugurate something of a revolution. He drew attention to a feature of all experience pretty generally, if not entirely, overlooked by his predecessors.

---

[7] Kant, *Critique of Pure Reason*, trans. Max Müller (New York: Macmillan, 1902), p. 779.
[8] *Principles of Human Knowledge*, Fraser ed., Vol. I, p. 270.

Kant is saying, I think, that the range of what we attend to, are aware of, are cognizant of, is vastly larger than the range of actual experience. Is this a truism, contingent upon an initial and arbitrary definition of the term "experience"? If I become interested in, study, and learn something about the French Revolution, does it make sense to say that I know something which transcends my experience? Isn't it trivial to point out that I wasn't alive then and, of course, could not have experienced the French Revolution as contemporary Frenchmen did?

The range of what we are concerned with, interested in, attentive to, aware and cognizant of, is vastly larger than the range of what we experience. Suppose you object to this statement and prefer to say that anything I attend to thereby comes within the range of experience. Experience is utterly catholic and inclusive. It specifies no one kind of existence contrasted with other kinds. There is more involved here than the definition of a term. To identify experience with anything and everything which confronts and concerns us, with whatever one attends to, is to move entirely away from the perspective of modern individualism. In that perspective, experience is what an individual mind enacts, undergoes, and lives through in the course of the life of that mind. I shall not argue the question of whether this perspective is, historically, an ephemeral episode of a particular epoch, or whether it is a perennial ingredient of our human situation as such, which is what I believe it to be. In any case, the issue as between Berkeley and Kant arises within this perspective.

Experience, like life, is throughout temporal. It is the kind of thing that James discusses in his chapter on "The Stream of Consciousness." The live portion of the stream of individual experience is the present. All actual experience is experience of the present. There is no experience of the past, nor of the future. No experience ever literally comes to life and is relived after it is experienced and fades into the past. Yet we are concerned with the past; we study archeology and history and acquire some knowledge of a real past.

But what is present is not only set over against the past and the future; it is also that which in any way is near at hand, immediate, set over against the distant, the remote, the absent. To be present in both these ways is just what Berkeley meant by something being "in the mind." The contents of immediate experience, sense data, impressions, everything that Ward puts into the class of "presentations" such as these, are present, neither past nor future, neither distant nor absent.

Had the roll been called to ascertain who was present and who was absent, all these would have answered "Present." But how many absences there would be! All my past and future, all the pasts which antedate my past, other minds, material bodies in space, none of these would be there to answer "Present." It seems hardly worth while to spend time in calling the roll when you realize how small is the number of those present, and there are those philosophers who think it just isn't worth bothering about and that we had better skip the roll call and get on to the agenda at hand.

But, in order to be fair to this content of immediate experience which has come into the mind and answers "Present," I think we ought to let it tell its own story and in its own words. Of course, we cannot expect so primitive and elemental a thing to use language at all elevated and refined. It hasn't quite grown up yet. "Yes," it would say when the roll is called, "I answer 'Present.' But, if you don't mind—you see I can use you as a verb and not only as the name of a geographical place,—I think I ought to tell you a little bit more about myself and about some of the adventures I have had when I have found myself inside of one mind or another.

"At one time I was present in the mind of Mr. Berkeley. He called me an 'idea.' I happened then to be the idea of triangularity, not of any particular triangle nor even of any particular kind of triangle, but just the idea of *any* triangle. Now of course, I wanted to bring with me inside his mind that part of me which was the idea of triangle in general. That belonged to me; it was my meaning. But I discovered, on trying, that I couldn't get it through the door. When I told Mr. Berkeley what I had tried to do, he said, 'All I know about you is what you have brought with you. If there is anything else belonging to you which you have left outside, go get it, bring it in and let's look at it. I only know what gets inside.' I told him that I was only an image or picture, perhaps only the sound of a word, but of course I had a meaning and if my meaning was too big for me to bring in, I was sorry. How would you like it if your teacher told you to go to the blackboard and draw just triangle, but no particular triangle? I began to suspect that Mr. Berkeley was asking too much of me. But I was getting lonely without my meaning, and so I left to rejoin it.

"On another occasion I wandered into the mind of Mr. Hume. I had always wanted to get inside of his mind because I had been told that his was the kind of mind that Mr. Berkeley's mind would be when it became fully grown. Mr. Hume called me an 'impression.' That seemed odd to me because I thought an impression required something outside which made an impress upon something else. But Mr. Hume told me that he didn't know about anything outside of me. He knew nothing about my ancestors nor where I came from. He said he had just picked me up on the doorstep like a foundling. And he said that if I didn't like to be called an impression, he would be perfectly willing to call me an object. It wouldn't make any difference.

"He said he liked me and had confidence in me because I had force and vivacity. He told me to stay around a while or go hide somewhere and come back. I would have lost most of my force and vivacity, but that was all right because I would then be an idea and in so far as I resembled what I was in the first blush of youth he would still trust me. And he added that I might come across some freshly arrived impression with all its youthful force and vivacity, get hitched up with this, and become a belief. And beliefs, he said, are pretty useful things. We can't get along without them, especially the belief in causality. 'I use it every time I brew a cup of tea,' he said.

"Then one warm afternoon a lot of us impressions were lying around all over the place, helter-skelter, taking things easy, and we heard his voice. 'Come along now,' he said, 'you've been lying around here long enough. It's time to get going. Stand up, fall in line, and start marching. I want you to follow one another in regular succession. It won't be too easy for you, for you are all loose and separate. There is no necessary connection, no real connection at all, between any two of you, so I can't expect too much of you. But do the best you can. And when you get going, following one another in regular succession, we are going to play a little game of make-believe. I've gotten Custom and Imagination to help out. In fact, they are going to do most of the playing, and with their help we are going to put something over. We are going to make it look as if you weren't the loose and separate impressions which you really are, but were items of some orderly system. After Custom and Imagination have played their part, you can pretend to be something that you really aren't, and that's our game.'

"Then one day he came to me with a troubled look. 'I am bothered,' he said, 'about one thing. There are a lot of ideas hanging around and cluttering up the place which have no right to be here. They haven't proper credentials and visas. They are ideas like the idea of substance, causality, and self. All respectable ideas have impressions to vouch for them, but these haven't. They are security risks. But I'll tell you what I've decided to do. These ideas have been around for a long time. I don't want to deport them. They don't seem to be doing any harm, though I'm not sure that they earn their keep. So what I'm going to do is cook up some artificial visas for them. Custom and Imagination are going to help me—I always call on Custom and Imagination for any odd jobs around the place. I know that this is a fraud, but ideas are apt to be pretty persuasive, and I hope it won't be discovered. But I can't have these ideas around without any credentials at all!

"I had about decided that I had better leave Mr. Hume's mind. He had hinted to me that before long he was going to splinter his self into a heap of loose and separate bits. Now I had become very fond of his self. It was kindly, gentle, and generous, and I didn't want to stay around and see it all shattered to pieces. I was just about to leave when he appeared and said to me, 'Now don't be bothered about anything I've been telling you. Don't worry. I'm going off presently to converse with my friends and play backgammon. I've put a lot of impressions in my pocket for lunch and for playing backgammon. I'll be all right. Don't worry. What I've been telling you is just speculation, speculative philosophy, nothing more. It has nothing to do with conversing with ones friends and playing backgammon. It stands just as loose and separate from them as any one impression is loose and separate from any other impression. So don't worry about how a heap of loose and separate bits can understand the rules of backgammon, to say nothing of winning the game. Philosophy hasn't anything to do with life! Then, as he waved good-bye to me, I could still see the familiar, kindly, and wistful gleam in his eyes.

"But I must tell you about the exciting adventures I had when I was in the mind of Mr. Kant. I had set my watch by seeing him take his daily walk, so I knew I would find his mind at home. He welcomed me warmly, but said that even before I came in he knew a good deal about me. He knew that I had come from a world where there was a whole lot of space and time, a lot more than I had brought with me. He must have had my dossier all the time. Then he said he was very glad I had come; in fact, that I was indispensable. There was a time, he said, when he was caught up in the philosophy of Leibniz, when he thought he could get along without me and rely entirely upon thought and reason. He didn't just stare at me and feel my presence as the other minds had done. He asked me a lot of questions and said that, really to get acquainted with the whole of me and not only with that part of me which I had brought into his mind, he would have to use thought, judgment, and understanding, and even some things which he said he

had stolen from the Logic of Aristotle and which he called 'categories'.
I had never been treated quite in this way before. He said he was
going to use me to discover the kind of world from which I came and
to learn about the relatives I had left behind. My dossier, which he
had all the time, contained some of that information—for instance,
that I came from a world organized in terms of substance, causality,
and reciprocity. But these were formal and relational, and he needed
just me to provide the filling, like sausage meat you put into a casing.
When he said he was going to use me, I don't think he intended to be
cruel and mistreat me, use me just as grist for his mill, grinding me
up and making me into sausage meat in the machinery of his mind.
Sometimes he did seem to say this. He used long words and I was often
confused. But sometimes I thought he was saying that just as that
part of me which was in his mind was incomplete, so the whole world
for which I was a sort of spokesman was itself incomplete and fragmentary. He called that world the world of 'phenomena'. He didn't try
to tell me very much about the kind of world which would round out
and complete the world of phenomena. Perhaps he wanted to leave
that for some other time. He did hint that perhaps we would have to go
elsewhere than to the intellectual pursuit of knowledge, to come in sight
of any such world. It was all very puzzling, and I rather think that he
himself wasn't at all sure of what all this might lead to. But I had heard
enough to keep me out of mischief for a long time and so I left.

"I wish there were time to tell you about my visits elsewhere and my
entrance into other minds, especially about one time when I got into
the mind of Mr. Alexander. He told me right off that he didn't see why
I thought I had to come into his mind, or into any mind; that I could
have just as healthy and normal an existence outside of any mind as
I would inside of some mind. I took this as a broad hint that I wasn't
wanted and so I left.

"Once, I got into what had been advertised as the mind of Mr.
Russell. But you know what advertisements are like. When I got inside
he told me that being a mind wasn't so very different from being a
chunk of matter, and that what had been advertised as his mind, and
matter too, were all made up of what he called 'neutral stuff' because,
I suppose, it always stayed on the fence and never took sides. The only
difference between what was advertised as mind and what was advertised as matter was in the kind of company that neutral stuff kept. I
was a bit puzzled when told that being a mind or being material was,
like guilt, something that could be acquired by mere association. But

I'm getting a little tired and, if you don't mind, I guess that, in spite of what Mr. Alexander told me, I had better find some mind into which I can retire and rest a while."

I should like, in conclusion, to revert to one or two matters. I have said that the premise of eighteenth-century empiricism is the thesis that the basic and original data from which we have to start in any pursuit of knowledge and understanding consists solely in the present contents of immediate experience, and that one is cognizant of these without being aware of anything else. In one important respect, however, as Stout has pointed out, Hume departs from this assumption. He presupposes memory. Now, memory, Stout points out, "provides at least one clear example of immediate knowledge of existence which is not actually experienced at the time and in the process of knowing it.—Suppose a thirsty man who has just quenched his thirst. What he is then immediately cognizant of is the bygone actual experience of being thirsty, not any present simulacrum or image of it with the sting extracted. The object, or part of the object, of his thought and attention in remembering is the actual occurrence of the felt thirst as he lived through it in the past, distinguished from and contrasted with his present situation. He is not living through it while he is remembering it as past. Thirst satisfied and thirst unsatisfied are so far incompatible that they cannot both be actually experienced together." Here is a clear case of immediate, noninferential knowledge of something which, as known, is no content of immediate experience, but lies beyond and outside. Something is here directly known which is not being immediately and actually experienced.

Material objects, belonging to physical nature, have the same status. All that we immediately experience is sense data and the like. But we know physical objects without actually experiencing them. This we do because the immediate felt possession of sensa and presentations is the apprehension of their incomplete and fragmentary nature. It is they which ask that they be rounded out and completed in an objective, physical world.

Kant locates the system of physical nature neither in the mind, as does Berkeley, nor in the transcendent realm of things-in-themselves, as Descartes does. There is a third territory distinct both from the fleeting possessions of individual minds and from the region of things-in-themselves inaccessible to our experience. Kant's phenomenalism is

---

* G. F. Stout, *Mind and Matter* (Cambridge Univ. Press, 1931), pp. 215–216. My indebtedness to the writings of Stout is evident throughout.

neither the subjectivism of Berkeley nor the transcendent realism of Descartes.

Of course, the term "phenomenon" and still more the term "appearance" readily carry the implication that what appears before the mind as a phenomenon is a mere appearance, really different from what it seems to be. Although this sense of phenomenon, this contrast between what things seem to be but are not and what they really are, dogs the thought and language of Kant, it does not express the radical and revolutionary character of Kant's philosophy. He points to the conclusion that the phenomenal order of physical nature is no mere seeming. It is to be taken to be really just what it is perceived and known as being. It is appearance only in the innocent sense that it appears, just as one watching for the sunrise might say, "There it is, it has appeared." The phenomenal order is known *through* experience. Only a tiny fragment is known *in* experience.

For Berkeley, nature is fairly transparent. Nature is composed of sensations and perceptions, and what these are is fully disclosed in the experience of them. Nature harbors little of mystery. It is different with Kant. Nature baffles us, and our human experience to which nature presents itself is likewise disconcerting and baffling. The world of phenomena in space and time holds conflicts and antinomies. Kant points to the conclusion that nature, as known both by perception and the sciences, isn't quite all there is to nature. If man is a child of nature, a part of nature, as we now say, then the nature of which man is a part, from which he derives the ideals in terms of which he seeks to organize his life and his world, *that* nature is more and other than nature as envisaged within the framework of the sciences. Nature isn't quite an open book written in clear-cut visual language, decipherable in principle by anyone who has hands to touch and eyes to see.

Kant and
"The *Dogmatic* Idealism
of Berkeley"

MARGARET D. WILSON

I

I̶N̶ ̶T̶H̶E̶ "CRITIQUE OF PURE REASON" Kant maintains that space and time are
(merely) *a priori* conditions of our perceptual experience—mere "forms" under
which our sensible objects must appear. Thus space and time have no claim to
reality independent of us, of our experience: they are "transcendentally ideal."
Similarly, the objects we perceive *in* space and time are also said to be transcendentally ideal: since their character is determined by the spatial and temporal
conditions of our experience, they have an intrinsic dependence on *us*. Kant
contrasts these mind-dependent or conditional perceptual objects ("appearance")
with the realm of the unconditioned, transcendentally real "thing in itself." Our
knowledge is limited to sensible objects, to appearance.[1]

One of Kant's most insistent claims is that his "transcendental" idealism differs
radically from all previous idealisms, and indeed vindicates "empirical realism"
against them. Whereas earlier idealisms deny or call into question the reality of the
physical world, Kant contends that transcendental idealism provides a uniquely
secure basis for the claim that we do have knowledge of real things in space. He
holds that knowledge of spatial reality is possible if and only if space is regarded
as a condition of our perception, and things in space are distinguished from things
in themselves.

Specifically, Kant represents himself as a defender of realism against *two*
idealist positions. One is "problematic idealism"—defined as the doctrine that we
can have no *immediate knowledge* of objects in space; that such objects can at best
be inferred as *causes* of the immediately perceived ideas in our own mind. Kant
claims that such inference can never lead to certainty; hence on this view the
existence of outer objects would always remain problematic or doubtful. Not
too surprisingly, Kant associates problematic idealism with Descartes and his

---

[1] Kant characterizes his position as "transcendental idealism" at A 369 ff. Cf. A 28=B 44;
A 36=B 52. The quotations in this paper are from Norman Kemp Smith's translation (London: Macmillan, 1958).

followers.[2] He discusses this position in the first edition of the *Critique* ("Paralogisms" section),[3] in the *Prolegomena*,[4] and in a new section inserted in the second edition of the *Critique*, titled "Refutation of Idealism." [5] (As we shall have occasion to note below, there is a clear change in Kant's manner of replying to problematic idealism in the course of these three works.)

The other idealist position to which Kant explicitly contrasts his own is called "dogmatic idealism." The dogmatic idealist is said to hold that there *can be* no real things in space, that space (and everything in it) is "false and impossible," or that spatial appearances are mere "illusion." Dogmatic idealism is mentioned only briefly in the first edition (in the course of the reply to Descartes); [6] it is not attributed to any particular philosopher. In the *Prolegomena* and second edition, however, Kant repeatedly associates this doctrine with the name of Berkeley.[7] And he seeks to emphasize the merits of his own position, and especially his conception of space, as an answer to the "dogmatic idealist." As Kant openly indicates, the new polemical interest in Berkeley resulted from the critical reception of the first edition: more than one reader, to Kant's displeasure, thought there were significant affinities between transcendental idealism and Berkeley's philosophy.[8]

Kant's conception of problematic idealism is quite perspicuous. Further, while there are points of obscurity in all of Kant's anti-Cartesian passages the general line of attack is sufficiently clear in each case. His treatment of dogmatic or

---

[2] The attribution of problematic idealism to Descartes does involve some license, of course, since Descartes himself concluded that the transcendental causal inference can be guaranteed. But Kant, like many post-Cartesian philosophers, evidently felt that the most significant of Descartes' arguments were those developed in the first two *Meditations*.

[3] A 366 ff.

[4] *Prolegomena to Any Future Metaphysics*, § 49. The *Prolegomena* (1783) was published between the first (1781) and second (1787) editions of the *Critique*.

[5] B 274 ff. Cf. Kant's note on this passage in the Preface to the second edition, B xxxix ff. In this note Kant seems to use the expression "psychological idealism" as an alternative to "problematic idealism."

[6] A 377. Kant here says that the dogmatic idealist will be answered in the next section after the "Paralogisms"—i.e., the "Antinomies." He does not mention dogmatic idealism in the latter section.

[7] *Prolegomena*, Appendix: *Critique*, B 274; cf. B 69 ff. In Remark III at the end of § 13 of the *Prolegomena* Kant speaks of the "mystical and visionary" idealism of Berkeley.

[8] Cf. *Prolegomena*, Appendix. As this passage shows, the prime offender was the (now infamous) Garve-Feder review, published in the *Göttinger gelehrten Anzeigen* of January 19, 1782 (Zugabe, Stück III). The passage in this review which contains the comparison with Berkeley reads as follows:

Auf diesen Begriffen, von den Empfindungen als bloßen Modificationen unserer selbst (worauf auch Berkeley seinen Idealismus hauptsächlich baut) vom Raum und von der Zeit berüht der eine Grundpfeiler des Kantschen Systems.

B. Erdmann has written in detail about the impact of this review on Kant, in the introduction to his edition of the *Prolegomena* (Leipzig: Voss, 1878). (But see introduction to Karl Vorländer's edition [Hamburg: F. Meiner, 1957] for evaluation of Erdmann's results.)

It is perhaps worth stressing that this is the *sole* mention of Berkeley in the entire (nine page) review, since one often encounters exaggerations in the Kant literature. A. C. Ewing, for instance, can only have this review in mind when he writes: "Kant was considerably offended by a review of the first edition which accused him of being an idealist and of out-Berkeleying Berkeley. . . ." (*A Short Commentary on Kant's Critique of Pure Reason* [London: Methuen, 1961; first ed. 1938], p. 182.)

"Berkeleyan" idealism, on the other hand, is full of difficulties. The aim of this paper is to present and deal with some of the most serious of these difficulties. (The replies to Descartes will be considered just in so far as they are bound up with questions about Kant's relation to Berkeley.)

There is, first, an obvious historical problem connected with Kant's remarks about dogmatic idealism. For Kant's allegation that "Berkeley degraded bodies to mere illusion" [9] appears to be altogether without foundation in Berkeley's actual position; it is certainly in contradiction to Berkeley's own understanding of his position. Another thesis that Kant attributes to Berkeley is, if anything, even more incongruous: in the *Prolegomena* Kant cites Berkeley as a latter-day Eleatic who believed that "only in the ideas of the pure understanding and of reason is there truth." [10] Such characterizations make it very doubtful whether Kant's repudiations of dogmatic idealism can have any significant relevance to the position of the historical Berkeley.

Apart from the issue of historical relevance, moreover, one is forced to question whether Kant had *any* plausible conception of what he was attacking and repudiating under the rubric "dogmatic idealism." The difficulty here is that Kant's different remarks on dogmatic idealism in general, and Berkeley in particular, do not seem to add up to any coherent position. Thus, in the *Prolegomena* Kant first groups Berkeley with the Eleatic rationalists, placing in contrast his own position that knowledge depends on sensory experience.[11] Immediately afterwards he comments approvingly that Berkeley, like Kant himself, treated space as mere appearance:

Space and time, together with all that they contain, are not things in themselves or their qualities, but belong merely to the appearances of the things in themselves. Up to this point I am one in confession with the above idealists [i.e. "all genuine idealists, from the Eleatic school to Bishop Berkeley," who hold that "only in the ideas of . . . reason is there truth"].[12]

However, Kant goes on to say that Berkeley was unable to avoid illusionism because he regarded space as merely empirical:

But these [idealists], and among them more particularly Berkeley, regarded space as a mere empirical representation that, like the appearances it contains, is, together with its determinations, known to us only by means of experience or perception. . . . It follows from this that, as truth rests on universal and necessary laws as its criteria, experience, according to Berkeley, can have no criteria of truth because its phenomena (according to him) have nothing *a priori* at their foundation, whence it follows that experience is nothing but sheer illusion. . . .[13]

---

[9] *Critique*, B 71.
[10] *Loc. cit.*
[11] *Ibid.*
[12] *Ibid.* Quotations from the *Prolegomena* follow the L. W. Beck translation (Indianapolis: Bobbs-Merrill, 1950 [Library of Liberal Arts]).
[13] *Ibid.*

In this passage Kant claims that the way to avoid Berkeley's "illusionist" conclusions is by accepting the Critical conception of space as an *a priori* form of sensibility.

In the second edition of the *Critique,* on the other hand, Kant twice seems to allege that Berkeley drew illusionist conclusions because he could not free himself from the *transcendental realist* conception of space.[14] That is, he concluded that a real world in space was impossible on the grounds that the very notion of space leads to absurdities, conceiving space as an independently existing entity, or as a property of things in themselves. Here Kant indicates that the remedy to Berkeleyan illusionism or dogmatic idealism lies in the view that space is ideal. The following passage is representative:

[Berkeley, as dogmatic idealist] maintains that space, with all the things of which it is the inseparable condition, is something which is in itself impossible; and he therefore regards the things in space as merely imaginary entities. Dogmatic idealism is unavoidable, if space be interpreted as a property that must belong to things in themselves. For in that case space, and everything to which it serves as condition, is a non-entity.[15]

It seems, then, that taking together the *Prolegomena* and the second edition of the *Critique* Kant attributes to Berkeley (1) mainstream rationalism; (2) some form of empiricism; (3) the view that space is a property of appearances only (or ideal); and (4) the view that space is a property of things in themselves (or transcendentally real). Kant's claims that his own system provides a bulwark *against* dogmatic idealism reflect these varying (and apparently inconsistent) characterizations.

In this paper I will try to show that Kant's various characterizations of Berkeley's "dogmatic idealism" can, despite appearances, be reconciled with each other in a rather interesting way. I will also suggest some ways in which Kant' replies to "dogmatic idealism" do happen to reflect significant differences betwee his conception of the problem of external reality and that of Berkeley—eve though Berkeley's position is hardly what Kant represents it to be.

It is not strictly essential to this part of my thesis that Kant *genuinely believe* Berkeley to have held the views attributed to him in the *Prolegomena* and th *Critique.* Nevertheless, the supposition is both significant and convenient for m purposes, and I will begin my discussion by defending it.

It may at first seem unlikely that this supposition needs much defense. For th

---

14 B 69 ff. and B 274.
15 B 274. The statement relating to Berkeley at B 69 is very similar:

It would be my own fault, if out of that which I ought to reckon as appearance, I ma mere illusion. That does not follow as a consequence of our principle of the ideal of all our sensible intuitions—quite the contrary. It is only if we ascribe *objective real* to these forms of representation [i.e. space and time], that it becomes impossible for to prevent everything being thereby transformed into mere *illusion.* For if we rega space and time as properties which, if they are to be possible at all, must be found things in themselves, and if we reflect on the absurdities in which we are then invol [Kant here itemizes absurdities], . . .—we cannot blame the good Berkeley for degrad bodies to mere illusion.

assumption that Kant's misrepresentations of Berkeley as an illusionist result from ignorance is surely a natural one, and has been made almost automatically by many commentators.[16] However, certain features of Kant's successive treatments of *Cartesian* idealism do seem to suggest a different view of Kant's relation to Berkeley. Thus, the first edition reply to Descartes ("Fourth Paralogism," A 366 ff.) turns on the reduction of objects in space to representations or ideas. It does have, therefore, a distinctly Berkeleyan character. In this passage Kant accepts the Cartesian premiss that we have immediate knowledge only of our own ideas (representations), but argues that this premiss does *not* lead to the conclusion that we have at best inferential knowledge of objects in space. If space is transcendentally ideal, then spatial objects are *nothing but* a "species of representations."[17] Hence the transcendental idealist ". . . may admit the existence of matter without going outside his mere self-consciousness, or assuming anything more than the certainty of his representations, that is, the *cogito ergo sum*."[18] This explicitly reductionist line of reply is not relied on in the *Prolegomena*, however, and in the second edition of the *Critique* the passage in which it had originally occurred is suppressed. (Kant therefore seems to move away from this argument just at the time he becomes interested in repudiating charges of Berkeleyanism.) The new Refutation in the second edition is an argument for the seemingly opposite conclusion that "I have immediate consciousness of a permanent (substance) in space *distinct from* my representations."[19] *This* argument can easily be construed as unBerkeleyan or even as anti-Berkeleyan.

Such considerations have led commentators to some of the following conclusions: (a) Kant did not reply to Berkeley in the first edition because he could not do so without refuting himself; (b) Kant, in developing his first refutation of Descartes, was directly influenced by Berkeley's rejection of causal realism; (c) Kant abandoned the first edition argument for immediate knowledge of material things *because* he recognized the difficulty of distinguishing his original reply from Berkeley's position; (d) the second edition argument, which concludes that I have immediate knowledge of a real thing in space distinct from my ideas, is Kant's actual answer to Berkeley.[20]

Each of these propositions carries the implication that Kant was not as ignorant of Berkeley as his remarks on that philosopher suggest. At least three of them imply that Kant could not seriously have regarded his doctrine of space as itself the basis for an adequate answer to Berkeley.

In the next sections I will briefly consider the views of two scholars, Norman Kemp Smith and Colin Turbayne, who accept some of the four propositions listed

[16] See, for instance, Ewing, *loc. cit.*; H. J. Paton, *Kant's Metaphysics of Experience* (London: George Allen and Unwin, 1936), Vol. II, p. 376; T. D. Weldon, *Kant's Critique of Pure Reason*, second ed. (Oxford: Clarendon Press, 1958), pp. 9 f.
[17] A 370.
[18] *Ibid.*
[19] Cf. B 274 ff. This is a paraphrase of Kant's conclusion, not an exact quotation.
[20] See sections II and III, below, for some references; cp. Robert Paul Wolff, *Kant's Theory of Mental Activity* (Cambridge: Harvard University Press, 1963), pp. 200, 300; also Ewing, *loc. cit.*

above. I will try to show that neither offers compelling reasons to believe that Kant was aware of the "realist" intentions of Berkeley's empiricism. Once this point has been made clear, we can go on to consider what Kant may really have had in mind in his various remarks about Berkeley.

II

In his *Commentary* Kemp Smith concludes from Kant's misrepresentations of Berkeley's philosophy that Kant was essentially ignorant of his predecessor's position.[21] (He suggests that Kant must have relied on inadequate secondary sources, such as Beattie and Hume.) However, Kant's successive arguments against *Cartesian* idealism do lead Kemp Smith to accept (a), (c), and (d) of the above propositions. His account of *these* arguments therefore involves a much more positive view of Kant's understanding of Berkeleyan doctrine. (Kemp Smith himself seems unaware of this apparent inconsistency in his interpretation.) With respect to the first edition reply to Descartes, Kemp Smith writes:

Kant refutes the problematic idealism of Descartes by means of the more subjective idealism of Berkeley. The "dogmatic" idealism of Berkeley in the form in which Kant here defines it, namely, as consisting in the assertion that the notion of an independent spatial object involves inherent contradiction, is part of his own position. For this reason he was bound to fail . . . to refute such dogmatic idealism. Fortunately he never even tries to do so.[22]

According to Kemp Smith, the conclusion of the second edition Refutation is "the direct opposite of what is asserted in the first edition." "This difference," he continues,

is paralleled by the nature of the idealismus to which the two proofs are opposed and which they profess to refute. The argument of the *Paralogisms* of the first edition is itself Berkeleyan, and refutes only the problematic idealism of Descartes. The argument of the second edition, though formally directed only against Descartes, constitutes a no less complete refutation of the position of Berkeley.[23]

In these passages Kant is represented as attributing to Berkeley the denial of bodies in space *conceived as distinct from perceptions*, rather than the denial of physical reality or matter *simpliciter* (illusionism). On this view, the doctrine Kant attributes to the "dogmatic idealist" is very close to, though not quite the same as his own position in the first edition Paralogisms, and also very close to a central

---

[21] *A Commentary to Kant's* Critique of Pure Reason (New York: Humanities Press, 1962; reprint of second ed. [1923]), pp. 156-157.
[22] *Ibid.,* p. 305; cp. p. 157, where Kemp Smith observes that Kant does not keep his promise to answer Berkeley's idealism in the "Antinomies," "doubtless for the reason" that his own teaching "frequently coincides with that of Berkeley."
[23] *Ibid.,* p. 313.

tenet of the historical Berkeley. In the second edition, we are to believe, Kant finds it necessary to "refute Berkeley" by arguing that there is *immediate knowledge* of a distinct spatial entity—thereby negating his own earlier position.

Inspection of Kant's text, however, reveals little or no real basis for such an interpretation. In the first place (and most importantly) Kant does *not* in fact define dogmatic idealism as the doctrine that "the notion of an independent spatial object involves inherent contradiction." If this *were* Kant's definition his own position would indeed satisfy it. But what Kant actually says in the first edition Paralogisms is that the dogmatic idealist regards *matter* as a notion involving contradiction.[24] It is precisely Kant's point in this passage that one can deny the possibility of "independent spatial objects," in the transcendental realist sense, while affirming the existence of matter—*provided* Kant's transcendental idealism is accepted. In other words, Kant is insisting that a distinction must be recognized between independent or non-representational existence, and external (spatial) reality. Without such a distinction, discovery of contradiction in spatial existence as conceived by the transcendental realist might well seem to entail the general denial of physical reality. (As I shall try to make clear below, this is exactly what Kant regards as the dogmatic idealist's error.)

Contrary to Kemp Smith, then, Kant's denial of *independent spatial objects* in the first edition Paralogisms by no means commits him to "dogmatic idealism" (or the outright denial of "matter"). Nor does Kant's first edition definition of dogmatic idealism bring it closer to the position of the historical Berkeley than his characterizations in the later works.

It may further be noted against Kemp Smith's view, that the *second* edition Refutation in no way "professes" to refute any position except Descartes'. (Berkeley, Kant claims, has already been answered in the Transcendental Aesthetic.)[25] Indeed, this Refutation has an *intrinsic* feature that marks it as a specifically anti-Cartesian argument. Having remarked in this passage that Berkeley regards space, "with all the things of which it is the inseparable condition" as "impossible," Kant continues:

Problematic idealism, which makes no such assertion, but merely pleads incapacity to prove, through immediate experience, any existence save our own, is, in so far as it allows of no decisive judgment until sufficient proof has been found, reasonable. . . . The required proof must, therefore show that we have experience, and not merely imagination of outer things; and this, it would seem, cannot be achieved save by proof that even our inner experience, which for Descartes is indubitable is possible only on the assumption of outer experience.[26]

Kant then proceeds to the proof itself, which begins with the premiss, "I am conscious of my own existence as determined in time." He thus rests his proof on a premiss which (he stresses) Descartes himself would accept. At no point, however,

---

[24] A 377.
[25] B 274 f.
[26] B 274-275.

does he attempt to establish a connection between this premiss (or any other part of the argument) and Berkeleyan doctrine.

In general, Cartesian idealism is viewed by Kant as a doctrine which uses the indubitability of inner experience (self-consciousness *in time*) as a basis for calling into question the real existence of outer things. Dogmatic idealism, on the other hand, is said to deny the reality of outer things on the basis of certain intrinsic difficulties in the concept of space and the nature of outer appearances. (Kant says of Berkeley that he "did not consider" time.[27] The two positions, as Kant conceives them, have quite different starting points, and therefore require different answers.[28] In his discussion, Kemp Smith has not sufficiently observed these important distinctions. Contrary to what he implies, there is no obvious reason to doubt that what Kant intended as his real answer to dogmatic idealism is identical with his apparent answer, and has to do with his doctrine of space.[29]

The main strength of Kemp Smith's account is that it does provide an explanation of the change in Kant's treatment of Cartesian skepticism. Yet it is perfectly reasonable to suppose that the early charges of idealism or Berkeleyanism[30] affected Kant's later discussion of Descartes, without concluding that Kant himself would have viewed his earlier argument as a form of dogmatic idealism. Kant may have come to realize that his original reductionist argument

[27] *Prolegomena, loc. cit.* This remark might suggest an acquaintance with Berkeley's *De Motu*, where discussion is concentrated on the concept of absolute *space*. See n. 34.

[28] Because of this distinction, I believe commentators have erred in regarding Kant's reply to an idealist argument in A 36=B 53 ff. as directed against Berkeley and/or dogmatic idealism. (Cf. Kemp Smith, *op. cit.*, p. 157, and Arnulf Zweig's introduction to *Kant: Philosophical Correspondence, 1759-1799* [Chicago: University of Chicago Press], pp. 10-11, n. 11.) It is rather the distinct, "Cartesian" line of thought that Kant here has in mind.

[29] It might be objected that regardless of Kant's intentions he *in fact* needs the second edition argument to distinguish his position from (the historical) Berkeley's, so Kemp Smith is right on the one point of real philosophical significance. To this, there are two replies: (1) *Apart from* this argument Kant would have reasons to hold that his position provides a stronger defense of the reality of spatial appearances than Berkeley's (see sec. V, below); (2) the historical Berkeley does not deny that the natural world is lasting or enduring. Of course it might be possible to define *some* philosophical position that would be contradicted by the second edition refutation, but not by Kant's doctrine of space.

[30] The doctrine of the first analogy is linked with the enterprise of avoiding Berkeleyan implications in a letter written to Kant by his disciple J. S. Beck:

> [A man] becomes aware [of the proceedings of the understanding in accordance with the categories] when I ask him to suspend all the objects in space and, after the passing of 50 years, set up a world again. He will assert that both worlds go together and that no empty time has passed, that is, that he can only conceive of time in connection with something persisting. Attention must be paid to this, in order to lay the ghost of Berkeleian idealism. (Zweig, *op. cit.*, p. 228)

In an earlier letter Beck writes, à propos of the issue of "Berkeleyanism":

> Appearances are the objects of intuition, and they are what everybody means when he speaks of objects that surround us. But it is the reality of just these objects that Berkeley denies and that the *Critique*, on the other hand, defends. (*Ibid.*, p. 195)

James Beattie, with whose work Kant was familiar in translation, remarks that Berkeley's doctrine includes the position that things cease to exist as soon as they ceased to be perceived. (And Beattie makes no mention of the role of God in Berkeley's philosophy.) Cf. *Essay on the Nature and Immutability of Truth*, revised ed., *Essays*, vol. I, p. 49.

did suggest—contrary to his intentions—the reduction of all reality to the flux of inner sense. (This would help account for the emphasis placed on the concept of *permanence* in the second edition.) The dogmatic idealist, however, is said to argue that space and matter in space are impossible or illusory.

III

Colin Turbayne is even more impressed than Kemp-Smith with the "Berkeleyan" character of the first edition reply to Descartes. In his paper, "Kant's Refutation of Dogmatic Idealism," [31] Turbayne traces the "systematic similarity" between Kant's position and the "main argument of Berkeley's *Principles [of Human Knowledge]* and *[Three] Dialogues [Between Hylas and Philonous]*." [32] Kant's vindication of the reality of bodies in space, he maintains, parallels in its essential steps Berkeley's refutation of both causal realism and the skepticism or illusionism which this doctrine dialectically engenders. According to Turbayne, both Kant and Berkeley find the answer to skepticism in the repudiation of independent existence (existence outside the mind) for physical objects, and the affirmation of the reality of sensible appearances. Turbayne recognizes that in itself the similarity can support only the thesis that Berkeley anticipated Kant. He would like to claim, however, that the resemblance is a result of direct influence: that "Kant was thoroughly familiar with Berkeley's doctrine and learned from it." [33] He acknowledges that this supposition is in apparent conflict with Kant's various misrepresentations of Berkeley. However, he thinks he can show that, despite appearances, the textual evidence actually favors the view that Kant had a "sure comprehension" of Berkeley's philosophy. The misrepresentations must therefore be construed as "deliberate . . . perversions." [34]

Turbayne's case for this rather startling thesis rests partly on the observation (developed at some length) that Kant's remarks about Berkeley are not *wholly* inaccurate or hostile. While I think Turbayne somewhat overstates Kant's acknowl-

---

[31] *Philosophical Quarterly*, vol. 5 (1955), pp. 225-244.

[32] *Ibid.,* p. 229. Turbayne thinks this position is reflected in all Kant's anti-idealist passages except the second edition Refutation. However, throughout his paper he relies very heavily for citations on the first edition "Paralogisms," and eventually he admits that Kant is closer to Berkeley in this passage than anywhere else (p. 243).

[33] *Ibid.* Turbayne also contends that Kant does not attempt to refute Berkeley in the first edition because of the close similarity between their views (p. 243). Thus he accepts both (a) and (b) of the propositions listed on p. 263, above. Of the second edition argument Turbayne says only that Kant here utilizes "a method of proof of the external world" different from that of the other anti-idealist passages (p. 229).

[34] *Ibid.,* pp. 242-243. Turbayne maintains in particular that Kant had read the *Three Dialogues* and *De Motu.* He stresses that a German translation of the former work was available prior to the publication of the first edition of the *Critique,* contrary to a claim made by Kemp Smith. (The *Principles* would not have been accessible in German. It is generally believed that Kant did not read English.) Turbayne's observation that Kant could well have read *De Motu* is important; I have no quarrel with this suggestion (see sec. IV, below). My contention is only that Turbayne fails in his attempt to show that Kant manifests an accurate knowledge of Berkeley's general philosophical position, as elaborated in the *Dialogues* (but not, of course in *De Motu*).

edgement of affinity with Berkeley,[35] it does not seem necessary to deal with this part of his argument in detail. Even if every textual point in this part of Turbayne's paper were accepted, it would follow only that Kant's view of Berkeley is not unrelieved fantasy. It would not follow that Kant had sound first hand knowledge of Berkeley's writings, or that he secretly knew of Berkeley's own claims to empirical realism.

The key point in Turbayne's case however is his contention that Kant's attribution of illusionism to Berkeley can be seen on close inspection to reflect knowledge rather than ignorance. This paradoxical claim is supported ingeniously (but I think ultimately unconvincingly). First Turbayne points out that Kant customarily ascribes to other philosophers doctrines which *he* regards as logical consequences of their positions, rather than what he knows to be their real views.[36] Secondly, he alleges that close reading of Kant's main anti-Berkeley passage in the *Prolegomena* shows that this is exactly what is behind the ascription of illusionism. In this passage (which I have quoted in part above) Kant claims that Berkeley's "illusionism" derives from his purely empirical understanding of spatial concepts. After distinguishing his own a priorism from Berkeley's empiricism, Kant produces the following sentence:

It follows from this that, as truth rests on universal and necessary laws as its criteria, experience, according to Berkeley, can have no criteria of truth because its phenomena (according to him) have nothing *a priori* at their foundation, whence it follows that experience is nothing but sheer illusion; whereas with us, space and time (in conjunction with the pure concept of the understanding) prescribe their law to all possible experience *a priori* and, at the same time, afford the certain criterion for distinguishing truth from illusion therein.[37]

In his interpretation Turbayne focuses on the clause, "whence it follows that experience is nothing but sheer illusion." He comments (without argument):

Kant thus holds that illusion is a necessary consequence of Berkeley's view, not that it is Berkeley's view. This highly significant admission makes it more than likely that Kant's repeated assertions elsewhere to the effect that Berkeley actually believes in dogmatic idealism are instances of Kant's habit of ascribing to other philosophers what are, in fact, consequences drawn by Kant himself.[38]

---

[35] Turbayne claims that the two statements about Berkeley in the second edition of the *Critique* correctly ascribe Berkeley Kant's "own denial of transcendental realism" and "his own insight into the relation of transcendental realism and illusionism" (p. 241). But what Kant seems actually to ascribe to Berkeley in these passages (which have been quoted above) is a denial of the reality of space *based on a failure to comprehend the possibility of an alternative to transcendental realism*. Kant there seems unquestionably to view Berkeley as accepting the transcendental realist *conception* of space, but as denying that there *can exist* anything satisfying that conception.

[36] *Ibid.*, pp. 240 f. He supports this claim with a citation from Kemp Smith's *Commentary*, and some reference to Kant's treatment of Leibniz.

[37] *Op. cit.*, pp. 242 f. Turbayne seems to follow the Beck translation in his citations from the *Prolegomena*.

[38] *Ibid.*, p. 243. The sentence reads in German:

Hieraus folgt: daß, da Wahrheit auf allgemeinen und notwendigen Gesetzen als ihren

Now the proposition that Kant did not think Berkeley was a deliberate illusionist is doubtless consistent with the rather erratic syntax of the *Prolegomena* sentence in question. It is certainly not accurate to say that Kant "admits" the point, however. To hold that illusionism is a necessary consequence of Berkeley's view (as Kant clearly does) of course does not *preclude* also believing that Berkeley drew that consequence himself. The passage is merely compatible with Turbayne's thesis; it surely does not provide the direct confirmation he requires.

Therefore, Turbayne's arguments that Kant deliberately and almost systematically misrepresented Berkeley's position seem to me quite tenuous. Turbayne somewhat mitigates the obstacles to assuming that Kant had a close familiarity with Berkeley's writings; but he is far from establishing that this assumption provides the "only adequate explanation"[39] of the facts pertaining to Kant's treatment of Berkeley. On the contrary, as I shall show in the next section of this paper, there is an alternative way of interpreting all the passages we have referred to, on the assumption that Kant did think of Berkeley as an avowed illusionist.

But what of the alleged similarities between Kant's reductionist argument and Berkeley's position? As I will explain below, I think Turbayne also overstates this aspect of his case.[40] On the other hand, there are without question some striking parallels. These could be wholly coincidental. Yet it should be observed that one does not have to choose between denying *any* influence and accepting a position as strong as Turbayne's (that Kant had detailed first hand knowledge of Berkeley's philosophy). Information need not be "direct" or fully accurate in order to be influential.

Recognition of a distinction between the historical Berkeley and Kant's Berkeley is helpful in several ways. First, it promotes a more accurate reading of Kant's statements about other idealisms. (This should be evident from our discussion of Kemp Smith.) Secondly, it completely eliminates a question which should have been troubling to both Kemp Smith and Turbayne (neither mentions it). Namely, assuming Kant does need an argument like the second edition refutation in order to answer Berkeley, why should he so austerely refrain from openly using this argument against Berkeley? Thirdly, this distinction prescribes a specific approach to a question that does trouble Turbayne: what can Kant have been thinking of in urging his doctrine of space against Berkeley?[41] (One must first form a picture of "Kant's Berkeley.") Finally, the distinction shows that evaluation of Kant's *philosophical* relation to the *actual* Berkeley may require a broader perspective than the explicitly anti-idealist passages provide. For these are apt to bear only obliquely on the arguments of the *Dialogues* and *Principles*.

Kriterien beruht, die Erfahrung bei Berkeley keine Kriterien der Wahrheit haben könne, weil den Erscheinungen derselben (von ihm) nichts *a priori* zum Grunde gelegt ward; woraus denn folgte, daß sie nichts als lauter Schein sei, dagegen bei uns Raum and Zeit (in Verbindung mit den reinen Verstandesbegriffen) *a priori* aller möglichen Erfahrung ihr Gesetz vorschreiben, welches zugleich das sichere Kriterium abgibt, in ihr Wahrheit von Schein zu unterscheiden. (Vorlander ed., p. 145)

[39] *Op. cit.*, p. 240.
[40] *Ibid.*, pp. 238, 243.
[41] See p. 22, and n. 48.

I will now try to explain in more detail Kant's conception of "the *dogmatic idealism* of Berkeley." [42]

IV

As a result of some interesting recent scholarship, it is now known that Berkeley was repeatedly characterized both as an illusionist and as a rationalist in the pre-Kantian literature of the eighteenth century.[43] Let us assume that Kant uncritically accepted these contemporary misrepresentations. We will then require two additional assumptions, neither of which seems especially bold: first, that Kant knew that Berkeley was one of the most outspoken critics of the Newtonian conception of space;[44] and second, that he had learned in some perhaps indirect manner that Berkeley reduced space and spatial appearances to "mere empirical representations." Let us also bear in mind that vindication of knowledge of the natural world was inseparably connected in Kant's thought with the possibility of knowing synthetic truths *a priori*. The possibility of establishing that there are necessary truths valid of outer experience was in turn regarded by Kant as dependent upon the doctrine that space is *a priori* and transcendentally ideal.

Now from these observations and assumptions we can develop a quite cohesive account of Kant's conception of "Berkeleyan" or dogmatic idealism. Kant credits Berkeley with the following views:

1. A real thing in space (or "matter") is properly conceived as an entity existing "outside the mind" in an independently and necessarily existing absolute space such as that conceived by Newton.

2. But there are contradictions and anomalies in the notion of such an entity.

3. Hence there are no real things in space.

4. There are of course representations or ideas of "outer things." (These constitute the data of the senses.)

5. As "mere empirical representations" with nothing *a priori* or rational or necessary at their foundation they must be classed as illusion.

On this interpretation it finally becomes clear how Kant could attribute an empiricist view of space to Berkeley, while at the same time characterizing him as a rationalist. If Berkeley was a rationalist, and if he held there was no rational basis for spatial representations (but merely a sensationalistic one), he would *naturally* hold that spatial appearances are mere illusion. Of course all this seems

---

[42] *Critique*, B 274.

[43] See Harry M. Bracken, *The Early Reception of Berkeley's Immaterialism: 1710-1733* (The Hague: Martinus Nijhoff, 1959, *passim*. Bracken traces the development of Berkeley's eighteenth century reputation as an idealist and a skeptic, as one who rejects the evidence of the senses and reduces bodies to "phantoms." He also notes that Jesuit writers of the period characterized Berkeley as a "Malbranchiste de bonne foi," who went beyond his master by actually denying the existence of matter. A sentence quoted by Bracken from one of their reviews reads in part: "Mr. Berkley (sic) continues to sustain obstinately *that there are no bodies and that the material world is only an intelligible world* . . ." (p. 17). Bracken himself tentatively suggests a link between Kant and Berkeley's early critics (see esp. pp. 87-88).

[44] As noted above, it seems possible that Kant was familiar with *De Motu*.

preposterous in relation to Berkeley's actual views,[45] but (as we have just noted) it is not out of conformity with his eighteenth century reputation, nor with Kant's own anti-empiricist patterns of thought.

We can also now see how Kant could consistently have believed both that Berkeley regarded space as "mere appearance" and that Berkeley suffered from transcendental realist preconceptions. What Berkeley, on Kant's view, failed to grasp is that a "real thing in space" could at the same time be "mere appearance"; that to affirm space and bodies cannot exist independently of the knowing subject is *not* equivalent to affirming that there is no such thing as spatial *reality*.

Kant's position, as he was himself at pains to point out, turns on the possibility of distinguishing "transcendental externality" (existence unconditioned by the knowing subject) from empirical externality or existence in space.[46] He seems to assume that Berkeley, together with Descartes and other transcendental realists, failed to grasp the cogency of such a distinction. As a result they failed to appreciate that denial of the possibility of subjectively unconditioned objects in space was not equivalent to denying the possibility of "real things in space." [47]

It remains true, even on this interpretation, that Kant gives slightly different versions of the logical basis of Berkeley's "illusionism" in the *Prolegomena* and in the second edition of the *Critique*. To hold that spatial appearances are illusory because there can be no transcendent causes in space outside the mind is not quite the same as to conclude spatial appearances are illusory because they have nothing a priori "at their foundation." These two positions do not seem to conflict with each other, however. For instance, Berkeley could be thought of as assuming that the existence of real things in space requires that *one* of the following propositions be true: either "spatial appearances have some basis in reason, some grounding in necessary truths," or "spatial appearances have cognitively unconditioned causes in space outside the mind." Other possibilities could be suggested. But there is really no need to speculate further on this question, nor need we assume that an intricately developed conception of the logic of "dogmatic idealism" dictated the details of Kant's treatments in the two works. I have been interested only in showing that the major apparent conflicts within and between these treatments can be resolved.

V

Now I would like to make two suggestions concerning the historical relevance of Kant's remarks about Berkeley. We have noted that Kant may have been influenced by contemporary misrepresentations of Berkeley as an illusionist and a

---

[45] The late work *Siris,* however, has sometimes been interpreted as Platonist. It certainly does exhibit a more "mystical and visionary" pattern of thought than Berkeley's early (and now better-known) books.

[46] *Critique,* A 370 (for instance).

[47] Or, in Descartes' case, that denial of immediate knowledge of such unconditioned objects is not equivalent to denial of immediate knowledge of real things in space.

rationalist to assume that Berkeley shared some of Kant's own antipathies to radical empiricism. To this extent his "replies" do not have the *ad hominem* effect that Kant presumably intended, for it is not true that Berkeley linked radical empiricism with illusionism. However, a first hand acquaintance with Berkeley's works would probably not have dissuaded Kant from holding that Berkeley's attempt at vindicating empirical realism is unworkable. For since *Kant does* hold the view that "truth requires something *a priori* at its foundation," an empiricist analysis of the external world—no matter how realist in intent—must be for him ultimately a philosophy of illusion. Hence, even if Kant had had a sound knowledge of Berkeley's intentions, his reply might not have been altogether different. The doctrine of the *a priori* status of space is not merely (as Turbayne says) a "legitimate difference" between Kant's philosophy and Berkeley's; it is from Kant's point of view a doctrine of absolutely fundamental importance for the vindication of external reality.[48] Whether Kant's position on this matter is justifiable to any degree is of course another, very complicated question—one that I shall not attempt to deal with in this context.

There is, however, a rather curious respect in which Kant's remarks about Berkeley's view of space do have significant *ad hominem* relevance. For there is one respect in which it is not entirely far-fetched to claim that Berkeley *was* an illusionist with respect to space. Consider the following well-known passage from the *Principles of Human Knowledge*:

. . . That we should in truth see external space, and bodies actually existing in it, some nearer, others farther off, seems to carry with it some opposition to what has been said of their existing nowhere without the mind. The consideration of this difficulty it was that gave birth to my *Essay Towards a New Theory of Vision*, which was published not long since, wherein it is shown that distance, or outness is neither immediately perceived by sight, nor yet apprehended or judged of by lines and angles, or anything that has a necessary connection with it; but that it is only suggested to our thoughts by certain visible ideas and sensations attending vision, which in their own nature

---

[48] Turbayne regards the doctrine of space as an *a priori* form of sensibility as essentially irrelevant to the defense of empirical realism. Hence, while this doctrine constitutes a genuine difference between Kant's position and Berkeley's, "Kant's appeal to it . . . as a guard against illusion, which Berkeley lacked . . . creates difficulties" (p. 243). The antidote to the illusionism generated by transcendental realist assumptions "is not the *a priori* nature of space, but its ideality or subjectivity" (*ibid.*).

Turbayne, however, points out himself that Kant (like Berkeley) appeals to the criterion of lawfulness or coherence to distinguish reality from illusion within experience. He seems further to acknowledge that on Kant's view the availability of such a criterion presupposes the validity of synthetic *a priori* judgements (*op. cit.*, pp. 237-238). But he regards this aspect of Kant's position as incidental to the "central argument" against skepticism or idealism allegedly shared with Berkeley (*ibid.*).

I find it difficult to determine precisely what Turbayne is claiming here. Surely the grounds for distinguishing reality from illusion cannot be incidental to a defense of empirical realism. On Kant's view the distinction depends on knowledge of universal laws; and this in turn presupposes synthetic *a priori* knowledge of objects of experience—which ultimately depends on the *a priori* character of space. It is highly dubious, then, that Kant shares Berkeley's "central argument" to the extent of endorsing a vindication of empirical realism that could function completely independently of the "*a priorist*" Critical framework. If this is Turbayne's position, I think it requires modification.

have no manner of similitude or relation either with distance or things placed at a distance. . . .[49]

Berkeley goes on to remark that the "ideas of sight and touch" are two distinct species, and that in his *Theory of Vision* the argument had been directed only to the former:

That the proper objects of sight neither exist without mind, nor are the images of external things, was shown even in that treatise.[50]

He acknowledges that the contrary was there supposed to hold of tangible objects, but indicates that this "vulgar error" was not disputed only because the point was irrelevant in a treatise on vision. He continues:

So that in strict truth the ideas of sight, *when we apprehended by them distance and things placed at a distance, do not suggest or mark out to us things actually existing at a distance,* but only admonish us what ideas of touch will be imprinted in our minds at such and such distances of time, in consequence of such and such actions.[51]

This passage, together with its correlate in the *Three Dialogues*, [52] suggests not only that we merely seem to perceive things "existing at a distance," but also that if the contrary were allowed, it might count against the doctrine that nothing exists outside the mind. And it is a notably accurate characterization of such a position to say that "space [or spatial distance] must be a property of things in themselves." That is, Berkeley's problem arises (at least partly) from what Kant would regard as a failure clearly to distinguish empirical or spatial externality from "transcendental externality," or existence altogether "outside the mind." Kant's reply would then be that his doctrine of space as an *a priori* form of intuition allows for the avoidance of transcendental realism (things exist "nowhere outside the mind"), without requiring an empiricist reduction of space to a purely temporal order among empirical representations.[53] (The transcendental ideality of space, Kant insists, does not entail that "bodies merely *seem* to exist outside me.")[54]

---

[49] § 43.
[50] § 44.
[51] *Ibid.* My emphasis.
[52] *The Works of George Berkeley Bishop of Cloyne*, ed. A. A. Luce and T. E. Jessop (Edinburgh: Nelson, 1948-1956), vol. II, p. 202 (First dialogue).
[53] Max Jammer has also seen in Berkeley's conception of space an "extreme subjective idealism . . . the final conclusion of an empiricistic approach," to which Kant's position provides a significant alternative. Cf. *Concepts of Space* (New York: Harper, 1960 [Harper Torchbook]), pp. 133-134. J. L. Borges is another who ascribes appropriate significance to Berkeley's reductionism with respect to space:

Hume noted for all time that Berkeley's arguments did not admit the slightest refutation nor did they cause the slightest conviction. This dictum is entirely correct in its application to the earth, but entirely false in Tlön. The nations of this planet are congenitally idealist. . . . The world for them is not a concourse of objects in space; it is a heterogeneous series of independent acts. It is successive and temporal, not spatial. ("Tlön, Uqbar, Orbis Tertius," trans. by J. E. Irby.)

[54] *Critique*, B 69.

In recent decades Berkeley's commentators have tended to dismiss as a strange aberration his notion that irreducible perceptions of spatial distance would somehow conflict with his "idealism" or immaterialism. To this extent they have evidently endorsed a central tenet of Kant's transcendental idealism: that existence "actually at a distance" is not incompatible with existence "in the mind" or "in us." [55] Certainly Berkeley's discussion of the issue reveals considerable confusion, and doubtless on more than one level. This need not mean, however, that his worry is completely without basis. It is not easy to deny *all* connection between spatial existence and what Kant would call transcendental externality—as philosophers other than Berkeley have sometimes observed. H. W. B. Joseph suggests that perception of space-relations is in some sense a sufficient condition for belief in a "real world outside the mind":

The relation of what we feel or hear to the feeling or hearing of it is not the same with that of what we see or touch to the seeing or touching it. Where the apprehension of figure and space-relation enters, there enters the thought of a difference between what is, and how it appears to us, which is immediate; this . . . is what presupposes the existence of 'things outside me'.
And there one is tempted to leave the matter, and say that these things are real and independent of mind, and that we come alone and get to know them.[56]

More recently, P. F. Strawson has contended that distance or some close analogue of distance is at least a necessary condition for our possessing the concept of independently existing objects.[57]

Perhaps, then, there is need for more thorough discussion of the problem (with a careful separation of logical and strictly genetic questions), before we conclude that Berkeley's intuitions are wholly spurious. It is possible that the notions of spatial externality and independent existence cannot be so sharply separated as Kant assumes. Such considerations could weigh against the cogency of grounding an empirical realism in a "transcendental idealism." On this point Kant's advantage over the historical Berkeley may not be as secure as it seems.

Conclusion

I have argued that Kant conceived of Berkeley as an illusionist, who denied the reality of bodies in space because he had discovered absurdities in the current

---

[55] Cf. Luce, *Berkeley's Immaterialism*, pp. 8, 119-120; D. M. Armstrong, *Berkeley's Theory of Vision* (Melbourne University Press, 1960), pp. 26 ff. Armstrong writes (p. 31):

Suppose we accept immaterialism. How must we modify the New Theory of Vision? It is clear that we must now deny that tangible objects exist independently of their being perceived, but we do not have to deny that these objects are at a distance from our bodies and set in circumbient space.

[56] "A Comparison of Kant's Idealism with That of Berkeley," *Proceedings of the British Academy*, vol. XV (1929, Henriette Hertz Trust Lecture). p. 22.
[57] See esp. *Individuals* (London: Methuen, 1959), p. 75.

(Newtonian) conception of space. Kant must have wrongly assumed that Berkeley's critique of Newton formed the basis for his metaphysical conclusions—which in the eighteenth century were widely reputed to be of an illusionist nature. Kant could thus represent his own doctrine of space, which he thought avoided the difficulties in the Newtonian view, as an answer to Berkeley. (I have tried to show that the "Berkeleyan" strategy Kant uses against Descartes in the first edition Paralogisms need not be taken to indicate a more accurate knowledge of his predecessor than is consistent with these errors.) I have also pointed out that there actually is an important difference between Kant and Berkeley with respect to the status of space. While Berkeley's philosophy may have been, in intent, as "realist" as Kant's, it must be acknowledged that Berkeley found it desirable to deny the reality of spatial distance in order to meet a possible objection to his metaphysical position. The thesis that Kant imagined to be the polemical essence of Berkeley's philosophy, derived from the critique of Newton, in fact emerges as a sort of defensive footnote unconnected with any claims about "absurdities" in the concept of space.

The Rockefeller University

Kant and Berkeley: The Alternative Theories

by George Miller, Cincinnati/Ohio

"The relation between Berkeley and Kant remains in part a mystery not yet fully solved. Whatever it is, it is complex and paradoxical."[1] So says Colin Turbayne, whose observation is supported by almost everyone who has discussed the relationship between the two philosophers. Although, as I will argue, the mystery is due largely to the commentators, Kant is not blameless. For even though Kant was extremely angered by the charge that the first edition of the *Critique of Pure Reason* was "Berkeleyan", a charge Kant claimed rested on an "unforgiveable and almost deliberate misunderstanding"[2], Kant has surprisingly little to say about the doctrinal differences between his position and Berkeley's in subsequent writings. And what little Kant said failed to satisfy his contemporary critics[3] and subsequent critics and commentators. Because of the striking doctrinal affinities between the two philosophers, and the paucity of Kant's account of the differences, it is hardly surprising that the commentators disagree about the relationship between Berkeley and Kant.

Colin Turbayne claims that an adequate theory about the relationship between Berkeley and Kant must account for the following facts: (1) Kant's many obvious misinterpretations of Berkeley; (2) Kant's denial that his position resembles Berkeley's; (3) Kant's extreme animus, reserved, amongst philosophers, for Berkeley alone; (4) the omission of any direct treatment of Berkeley in the first edition of the *Critique;* (5) Kant's first edition promise to deal with Berkeley and the failure to do so; and (6) the belated indication, in the *Prolegomena* and second edition of the *Critique,* that Berkeley had already been undermined in the

---

[1] "Editor's Introduction" to George Berkeley's *A Treatise Concerning the Principles of Human Knowledge.* Library of Liberal Arts, No. 53, New York: 1957, p. xix.

[2] I. Kant, *Prolegomena to any Future Metaphysics,* translated by P. G. Lucas, Manchester: Manchester University Press, 1953, p. 47. Akademie-Ausgabe, Bd. IV, p. 290.

[3] Despite the *Prolegomena* and second edition of the *Critique* claims that his position differed from Berkeley's, Kant's critics persisted in interpreting his position as "Berkeleyan". In a letter to Kant (Nov. 10, 1792) J. S. Beck, a student of Kant's, reported that Garve, in so far as he was willing to defend the *Critique,* was forced to admit that Kant's idealism was identical with Berkeley's. Arnulf Zweig, Kant's *Philosophical Correspondence,* Chicago: The University of Chicago Press, 1967, p. 195. In reply (Dec. 4, 1792), Kant says that Garve's remarks do not "deserve the slightest attention", *ibid.,* p. 198. No doubt this kind of reply on Kant's part tended to reinforce his critics in the belief that Kant was unable to distinguish his position from Berkeley's.

Aesthetic[4]. As far as I have been able to determine, there are two theories about the relationship between Berkeley and Kant[5]. I intend to show that: (a) each theory is unable to explain all of the facts; (b) each theory provides inconsistent explanations for some of them; and (c) the difficulties in each theory result from certain assumptions common to both of them. Part of what I intend to show is that as long as we make these assumptions, the relationship between Berkeley and Kant will remain a mystery which cannot be solved.

The purpose of this paper is not to explain the relationship between Berkeley and Kant; it is, through an examination of the two theories, to remove many of the difficulties which stand in the way of an adequate theory. I will examine first what has been called the traditional theory, and I will then consider a theory put forward by Colin Turbayne. The aim of my examination of the two theories is to isolate and expose a set of common dubious assumptions underlying both theories.

The Traditional Theory

Those who hold the traditional theory[6] claim that there are many passages in the *Critique*, notably in the first edition, that strongly invite comparison to Berkeley's views, and that there is an overall orientation in Kant's position which is reminiscent of Berkeley. Yet despite these similarities, it is evident from Kant's remarks about Berkeley that he not only opposed the position which he took Berkeley to be espousing, but that the position he attributed to Berkeley seems to be at variance with the position actually held by Berkeley. Kant accused Berkeley

---

[4] Colin Turbayne, *Kant's Refutation of Dogmatic Idealism*, The Philosophical Quarterly, V. 20 (July 1955), p. 240. Turbayne claims that there are four sets of facts to be explained. What I have distinguished as (5) and (6), he includes under (4).

[5] It has recently come to my attention that there is a third theory about the relationship between Kant and Berkeley. The theory is advanced by Margaret D. Wilson in her paper, *Kant and 'The Dogmatic Idealism of Berkeley'*, Journal of the History of Philosophy, IX, Number 4 (October, 1971), pp. 459—476. Although Wilson's theory consistently explains the facts that she deals with, the theory fails to explain all of the facts. In particular, Wilson provides no explanation for (4) and (5).

[6] All of the English commentators subscribe to the traditional theory. Among others, these include: Kemp Smith, *A Commentary to Kant's Critique of Pure Reason*, 2d ed. London: Macmillan, 1930, pp. 155 ff. and 298 ff. T. D. Weldon, *Kant's Critique of Pure Reason*, London: Oxford University Press, 1958, p. 10. A. C. Ewing, *A Short Commentary on Kant's Critique of Pure Reason*, London: Methuen, 1961, p. 182. H. J. Paton, *Kant's Metaphysics of Experience*, New York: Macmillan, 1951, II, p. 376. For the most succinct statement of the theory see W. H. Werkmeister, *Notes to an Interpretation of Berkeley*, New Studies in Berkeley's Philosophy, edited by Warren Steinkraus, New York: Holt, Rinehart and Winston, 1966, pp. 163—168.

of "degrading bodies to mere illusion"[7] and of regarding the "things in space as merely imaginary entities"[8]. He also attributed to Berkeley a "visionary idealism"[9] which embodies the doctrine that "all cognition through the senses is nothing but sheer illusion"[10]. A superficial acquaintance with Berkeley shows that he held none of these views, and, as Kemp Smith observes, "in order to make Kant's account of Berkeley's teaching really comprehensible, we seem compelled to assume that he had never himself actually read any of Berkeley's writings"[11]. A first-rate philosopher like Kant, who displayed keen insight into the views of Leibniz, Newton, and Hume, must have formed his opinion of Berkeley from distorted second-hand accounts of the Irish thinker. In short, the theory tells us that the "Berkeley" described and dismissed in Kant's writings was a straw-man whom Kant had uncritically accepted from the writings of those early critics of Berkeley who had attributes to Berkeley a variety of absurd beliefs and doctrines.

In support of this interpretation, the traditional theorists claim that Kant's knowledge of English was imperfect[12], and that none of Berkeley's writings appeared in German before 1781, the year of the publication of the first edition of the *Critique*. Subsequent to 1781, Kant could have read Berkeley's *Three Dialogues between Hylas and Philonous* in German translation[13]. Thus, Berkeley was available to Kant before he replied to his critics in the *Prolegomena* (1783) and the second edition of the *Critique* (1787). But, the theory continues, in light of Kant's remarks about Berkeley in these works, he had not bothered to read Berkeley[14].

---

[7] I. Kant, *Critique of Pure Reason*, translated by N. K. Smith, New York: Macmillan, 1958, B 71. Following the standard practice, references to the first and second editions will be by page numbers and the letters A and B respectively.

[8] B 275.

[9] *Prolegomena*, p. 51.

[10] *Ibid.*, p. 145.

[11] Kemp Smith, *Commentary*, p. 156.

[12] Kemp Smith claims that there is no evidence that Kant read a single English book. *Ibid.*, p. 156. Robert P. Wolff notes that Kant may have had a command of the language sufficient to read popular articles. *Kant's Debt to Hume via Beattie*, Journal of the History of Ideas, XXI, No. 1 (January—March 1960), p. 123.

[13] Kemp Smith, *Commentary*, p. 156. This was the first of Berkeley's writings to appear in German translation and, according to Kemp Smith and others, it was first published in Leipzig in 1781.

[14] The theorists assume that all of the extant accounts of Berkeley (whether French, German or English) distorted his position, that Kant was restricted to German translations of Berkeley's works, and that Kant's remarks about Berkeley indicate that he could not have read any of Berkeley's works. Robert P. Wolff points out that Kant understood French. *Kant's Debt to Hume*, p. 123. Thus, Kant could have read the following French translations of Berkeley's writings before 1781: *Alciphron* (translated in 1734), *Siris* (translated in 1745), and the *Three Dialogues* (translated in 1750). A. C. Fraser, *The Works of George Berkeley*, Oxford: Oxford University Press, 1901, Vol. III, p. 404. Harry Bracken also notes that Berkeley's *Dialogues* was the subject of

As to the indirect sources of Kant's knowledge of Berkeley, the traditional theorists are not in total agreement. A. C. Ewing suggests that Kant may have gotten his Berkeley from "quoted extracts"[15], and Kemp Smith says that Kant may have formed some of his impressions of Berkeley from Hume's *Inquiry*[16] and from Kant's German neighbor, J. G. Hamann[17]. But of those who have considered the matter most carefully, the consensus is that Kant's chief source was most probably the highly defective account of Berkeley in James Beattie's *Essay on Truth*[18]. The *Essay* was translated into German in 1772, and a copy was available in the University of Königsberg Library. Kant's *Prolegomena* references to Beattie's views on Hume indicate that Kant had read the *Essay* with care[19].

The traditional theory easily explains four of the six facts, for if Kant's "Berkeley" came from Beattie and/or similar sources, we can account for: (1) the misinterpretations of Berkeley; (2) the denial that his position resembles Berkeley's; and (3) the animus for Berkeley. As to (4), or the omission of any direct

one excellent piece of criticism — a review which appeared in a French journal, *Journal-Literaire*, May—June, 1713. According to Bracken, "unlike the vast majority of criticism published during Berkeley's life, this took him seriously, raised philosophical questions, and avoided ridicule". *The Early Reception of Berkeley's Immaterialism: (1710—1733)*, Martinus Nijhoff, The Hague, 1959, p. 12. The German commentator, Ernst Cassirer, holds that while Kant's remarks about Berkeley indicate that Kant had not read the *Principles* or *Dialogues*, he suggests that Kant could have gotten his views of Berkeley from *Siris*. He cites both the 1745 French translation and a 1745 German translation. *Das Erkenntnisproblem in der Philosophie und Wissenschaft der neueren Zeit*, Band 2. Berlin, 1911, p. 327.

[15] *Short Commentary*, p. 182. Ewing fails to cite any works which Kant was or could have been familiar with which contain quoted extracts from Berkeley's writings.

[16] David Hume, *An Inquiry Concerning Human Understanding*, edited by Charles Hendel, New York: Library of Liberal Arts, No. 49, 1955, pp. 163—64. Although Kemp Smith maintains that Kant could have gotten some of his impressions of Berkeley's views on space from the *Inquiry*, Hume does not mention or discuss Berkeley's views on space in this work.

[17] Kemp Smith, *Commentary*, p. 157. L. W. Beck suggests that Kant may have gotten some of his "stranger judgments about Berkeley" from Hamann, who, according to Beck, "fancied himself an expert on all things British". *Early German Philosophy*, Cambridge: Harvard University Press, 1969, p. 476, Note 130.

[18] The full title is: *An Essay on the Nature and Immutability of Truth, in opposition to Sophistry and Scepticism*. References in this paper are to the Hopkins and Earle edition, published in Philadelphia in 1809. For an accurate summary of Beattie's position and his criticisms of Berkeley, see Werkmeister, *Notes*, pp. 164—168.

[19] *Prolegomena*, pp. 7—8. Akademie-Ausgabe, Bd. IV, p. 258. A number of commentators consider the *Essay* to be of considerable importance in Kant's philosophical development. Robert P. Wolff maintains that Kant probably first learned of Hume's analysis of the causal maxim and his equally important discussion of the self from the *Essay. Kant's Debt to Hume*, p. 117. As I will attempt to show, what Wolff takes as the basis of Kant's knowledge of Hume's views provides us with grounds for questioning the important assumption of the traditional theory that Kant accepted Beattie's account of Berkeley as accurate.

treatment of Berkeley in the first edition, the theory suggests that Kant thought it unnecessary to discuss a position which, given Beattie's account of it, was so obviously absurd. However, the theory has trouble with (5) and (6), and, as I will attempt to show, these difficulties provide reasons for not only questioning the consistency of the explanations provided for (1) and (4), and (5), but also for questioning whether (1) is a fact at all.

Because of the explanations for (1) and (4), the theory has trouble with (5), or Kant's failure to keep the first edition promise to deal with Berkeley. It is interesting to note that although Berkeley is not mentioned by name anywhere in the first edition, the traditional theorists assume that Kant's *Fourth Paralogism* reference to dogmatic idealism and his promise to deal with it is a reference to and a promise to deal with Berkeley[20]. Most of the traditional theorists make no attempt to explain why Kant made no attempt to redeem his promise, but those who do claim that Kant either knew or came to realize that he could not keep the promise without refuting himself. Kemp Smith maintains that however unwilling Kant was to admit it, his position, "especially in the *Dialectic*, frequently coincides with that of Berkeley"[21]. In particular, Smith claims that in the *Fourth Paralogism* Kant attempts to refute Descartes "by virtually accepting the . . . position of Berkeley"[22]. Hence, Smith concludes, Kant was "bound to fail in his promise to refute . . . dogmatic idealism [Berkeley]. Fortunately he never attempts to do so"[23].

Did Kant, in the *Fourth Paralogism* and throughout the *Dialectic*, use views and doctrines espoused by Berkeley or did he use views and doctrines which Beattie and others had attributed to Berkeley? All of the commentators, including the traditional theorists, agree that Kant used views and doctrines espoused by Berkeley. If this is true, then the traditional theorists are correct in claiming that Kant could not keep his promise to deal with Berkeley. However, the traditional theorists tell us, in their explanations for (1) and (4), that the Berkeley that Kant knew was not the historical Berkeley but the "Berkeley" of James Beattie. Let us consider some of the views and doctrines which Beattie's "Berkeley" holds. Beattie's "Berkeley" claims that a horse which a man sees "coming toward him at full gallop, [is] an idea in his mind, and nothing else"[24], and, therefore, the man should be unconcerned about getting out of the path of this "mental" horse. In addition, "Berkeley" holds or is logically bound to hold (Beattie never makes it clear whether he is reporting Berkeley's views or what Beattie considers to be the consequences of them) that "external objects (that is, the things we take for external objects) *are in every respect different from what they appear to be*"[25].

[20] A 377.
[21] Kemp Smith, *Commentary*, p. 157.
[22] *Ibid.*, p. 305.
[23] *Ibid.*, p. 305.
[24] Beattie, *Essay on Truth*, p. 148.
[25] *Ibid.*, p. 277. Italics mine.

"Berkeley" must therefore admit that the candle one sees "hath not one of those qualities it appears to have: it is not white, nor luminous, nor round, nor divisible, nor extended..."[26]. For all we know, it "may be an Egyptian pyramid, the king of Prussia, a mad dog, or nothing at all"[27]. Now if this is the "Berkeley" Kant knew and had promised to deal with, then it is difficult to understand why Kant or, for that matter, Berkeley would have had any difficulty in dealing with him. It would seem that if we are to assume that the first edition dogmatic idealist is Berkeley, we are forced to admit that the Berkeley Kant knew was a much more formidable opponent than the philosopher of the well-known misinterpretations[28].

Before we consider the problems which the theory has with (6), I would like to call attention to (a) a very important difference in the way in which Beattie expounded and discussed the views of Berkeley and Hume, and (b) Kant's *Prolegomena* evaluation of Beattie as an expositor of the views of Hume. It seems to me that when we take due note of both (a) and (b), we have additional reasons for questioning the assumption that Kant uncritically accepted Beattie's account of Berkeley as accurate.

With respect to (a), I want to call attention to Robert P. Wolff's claim about Beattie[29]:

Whatever Beattie's philosophical faults, he was an exhaustive and accurate reporter. His more than forty quotations, paraphrases, and summaries of passages from the *Treatise* contained several important arguments which Hume had omitted from the later *Enquiry*.

Although Wolff notes that Beattie's attacks on Hume were, more often than not, irrelevant, Wolff claims that "in the course of his attack, Beattie quoted from the *Treatise* again and again" which had "the happy result that Kant was... brough up against Hume's criticisms of *a priori* knowledge"[30]. Wolff is clearly correct about Beattie's discussion of Hume, but a careful reading of the *Essay* shows just the opposite is true in Beattie's discussion of Berkeley. While in his discussion of Hume, Beattie provides the reader with numerous quotations from and accurate paraphrases of passages from the *Treatise*, quotations and paraphrases which, according to Wolff, allowed Kant to distinguish Hume from Beattie's "Hume", Beattie, in his discussion of Berkeley, neither quoted from nor paraphrased passages of Berkeley's writings. Hence, although Beattie provided Kant with the basis for distinguishing Hume from "Hume", he failed to provide Kant with the basis for distinguishing Berkeley from "Berkeley".

---

[26] *Ibid.*, p. 277.
[27] *Ibid.*, p. 277.
[28] Margaret Wilson also notes that Kemp Smith's account of the relationship between Berkeley and Kant "involves a much more positive view of Kant's understanding of Berkeleyan doctrine" than Smith admits. She observes that Kemp Smith "seems unaware of this apparent inconsistency in his interpretation". *Kant and 'The Dogmatic Idealism of Berkeley'*, p. 464.
[29] Wolff, *Kant's Debt to Hume*, p. 117.
[30] *Ibid.*, p. 118.

In addition, in his discussion of the "modern sceptics and sophists", Beattie treated Hume's position either as if it were identical with or merely a consequence of Berkeley's[31]. Indeed, he raised the same sorts of objections against both positions. Even though he made the interesting admission that he was unable to combat their subtle philosophical arguments, Beattie nevertheless dismissed their views because they were inconsistent with the plain dictates of common sense and because of the supposed devastating practical consequences which would follow if their teachings were to become generally accepted. If, Beattie reasoned, men were to accept Berkeley's teachings, then "in less than a month after, there could not, without another miracle, be one human creature alive on the face of the earth"[32].

In the *Prolegomena*, Kant not only acknowledges his debt to the "sagacious" Hume, but he also makes it clear that he thought that Beattie had utterly failed to understand Hume's position on the causal maxim and other important issues. It is also evident from his remarks that Kant did not regard Beattie highly, either as a philosopher or, more importantly, as an expositor of the problem which Hume was concerned with. He says of Beattie, "it is positively painful to see how utterly Beattie missed the point of [Hume's] problem"[33]. And, further, "I should think that Hume might fairly have laid as much claim to common sense as Beattie, and in addition to a critical reason (such as the latter did not possess), which keeps common sense in check"[34]. If Kant had reservations about Beattie as an expositor of Hume, then what sort of impression would he have formed of Beattie as an expositor of Berkeley? It seems much more reasonable to assume that Kant *did not* rather than that Kant *did* accept Beattie's account of Berkeley as accurate.

As far as (6) is concerned, or Kant's belated indication, in the *Prolegomena* and in the second edition of the *Critique,* that Berkeley had already been undermined in the *Aesthetic,* the traditional theory provides no explanation at all. It is important to note both that Berkeley is first mentioned by name in these works, and that *all* of the well-known and often cited "misinterpretations" occur in these works. Because they assume that all of Kant's remarks about Berkeley are in fact misinterpretations, the traditional theorists simply ignore Kant's claim that Berkeley's position has been "undermined . . . in the Transcendental Aesthetic"[35].

It is evident that whatever plausibility the traditional theory has rests on the crucial assumption that Kant's remarks about Berkeley are in fact misinterpretations. I will now attempt to challenge this assumption by selecting one of the most well-known and often cited "misinterpretations" and show how, when the remark is considered in the context of the passage as a whole, that it turns out not

[31] Beattie, *Essay on Truth*, p. 50 and pp. 211—212.
[32] *Ibid.*, p. 273.
[33] *Prolegomena*, p. 7. Akademie-Ausgabe, Bd. IV, S. 258.
[34] *Prolegomena*, p. 8. Akademie-Ausgabe, Bd. IV, S. 259.
[35] B 275.

to be a misinterpretation at all but an accurate statement of certain views actually held by Berkeley.

One remark cited by every traditional theorist as clear evidence that Kant did not understand Berkeley is the *Refutation of Idealism* claim that Berkeley "regards the things in space as merely imaginary entities"[36]. If attention is restricted to the remark alone, then we must agree with Copleston that "Berkeley did not hold that all external objects are mere products of the imagination in the sense which would naturally be given to this description"[37], i. e., that Kant misinterpreted Berkeley. But if we consider the remark in terms of the passage as a whole and in relation to the reasons Kant gives for making the claim, then the appropriate conclusion is that Kant had sure knowledge of at least some of Berkeley's views. He says that "Berkeley ... maintains that space, with all the things of which it is the inseparable condition, is something which is *in itself* impossible; and he therefore regards the things in space as merely imaginary entities"[38]. It seems to me that what Kant is claiming is that Berkeley not only rejected the Newtonian view that space is something which exists in itself independent of all things and of our sensibility, a view which Kant also rejected, but that Berkeley also claimed that any supposed occupants of this real space are products of our imagination. In the *Essay on Motion*, Berkeley says[39]

> From absolute space then let us take away now the words of the name, and nothing will remain in sense, imagination, or intellect. Nothing else then is denoted by those words than pure privation or negation, i. e., mere nothing.

And throughout his writings, Berkeley maintained that any supposed occupants of this "real" space are little more than imaginary entities. It seems to me that an analysis of those other passages where the "misinterpretations" occur indicate that Kant had a sure knowledge of Berkeley's position. But if these remarks by Kant about Berkeley are accurate statements of views actually held by Berkeley, then we must take seriously Kant's claim that Berkeley's position has been undermined in the *Aesthetic*.

Those who hold the traditional theory do little more than assume that Kant's remarks about Berkeley are "misinterpretations". This assumption in turn forces them to make a host of additional assumptions to explain the "misinterpretations". After ruling out the possibility that Kant could have read Berkeley, a distorted second-hand account of Berkeley is produced which Kant either did or could have read. If we then assume that Kant accepted the account as accurate, we can explain (1) the misinterpretations, (2) Kant's animus for Berkeley, and (3)

---

[36] B 275.
[37] *A History of Modern Philosophy.* Vol. 6, Part II, New York: Image Books, 1964, p. 66.
[38] B 275. Italics mine.
[39] *The Works of George Berkeley*, Vol. IV, edited by A. A. Luce, New York: Thomas Nelson and Sons, 1951, No. 53.

his denial that his position resembles Berkeley's. But as I have attempted to show, a careful examination of the principal claims and assumptions of the theory reveals a lack of consistency in explaining some of the six facts. While (4), or the omission of any direct treatment of Berkeley in the first edition, is accounted for by assuming that the "Berkeley" Kant knew was a straw-man that he had un-critically accepted from distorted accounts of Berkeley's position, and, accordingly, a philosopher not to be taken seriously, (5), or Kant's failure to keep his first edition promise to deal with Berkeley, is explained by the supposed similarity between Kant's views and those of the "real" Berkeley and Kant's presumed realization that he could not refute the "real" Berkeley. In short, (4) is explained by assuming that Kant did not know the "real" Berkeley, and (5) is accounted for by assuming that he did. I have also attempted to show that a careful examination of the entire passage in which one of the well-known "misinterpreta-tions" occurs reveals that Kant's remark is not a misinterpretation at all but an accurate statement of some of Berkeley's views. Although there is more that can be said against the traditional theory, I believe that I have shown that: (a) the theory fails to explain all of the facts; (b) it provides inconsistent explanations for some of them; and (c) there are reasons for questioning whether some of the alleged facts are facts and whether some of the assumptions underlying the theory are legitimate.

Turbayne's Theory

In opposition to the traditional theory is one advanced by Colin Turbayne. Although Turbayne assumes that the six facts are facts, he rejects the traditional theory explanation for most of them, claiming that[40]:

All the evidence, both internal and external, indicates that Kant probably studied Berkeley carefully, understood him better than most of his modern critics, and adopted many of Berkeley's insights and made them his own.

Turbayne argues that: (a) Kant could have read two of Berkeley's important works before publishing the first edition of the *Critique;* (b) that a careful analy-sis of Kant's writings indicate that Kant used Berkeleyan arguments against tran scendental realism, a position which is similar to, if not identical with, what Ber-keley called materialism; (c) that a careful examination of those passages in Kant's writings where Berkeley is mentioned reveal that Kant understood Berkeley; and (d) that Kant hid his debt to Berkeley by deliberately misinterpreting his account of the Irish philosopher. Turbayne's theory is an interesting one, and it is impor-tant to get clear about its principal claims and the assumptions underlying many of them.

---

[40] "Editor's Introduction" to *Berkeley's Principles, Dialogues and Philosophical Corres-pondence,* New York: Library of Liberal Arts, No. 208, 1965, p. xxxi.

Against the claim that Kant could not have read any of Berkeley's writings before 1781, Turbayne notes that Kant could have read Berkeley's Latin treatise, *De Motu* (published in 1721), and, more importantly, the *Three Dialogues*. Turbayne calls attention to the fact, noted by other scholars but missed by almost all of the traditional theorists, that the *Dialogues* was available in German translation in 1756, or some twenty years before the publication of the *Critique*. This translation, brought out by C. E. Eschenbach[41], was included in a larger work which also contains a translation of Arthur Collier's *Clavis Universalis* and Eschenbach's attempted refutation of Berkeley and Collier[42].

Of the eight passages in Kant's writings which are directly relevant to understanding Kant's relationship to Berkeley, Turbayne selects the following as most important[43]: (1) the *Fourth Paralogism* (A 366—A 380); (2) *Prolegomena*, No. 13, Notes II and III; (3) *Prolegomena*, Appendix, Second Part; (4) *Aesthetic* (B 69—B 71); and (5) *Refutation of Idealism* (B 274—B 279). Although, Turbayne claims, the commentators have tended to interpret these passages as exclusively concerned with the views of Descartes and/or Berkeley, Turbayne argues that if the passages are studied in the order in which they were written, one finds an underlying central argument directed against the basic assumptions underlying most of the philosophical thinking of Kant's day. The argument begins by outlining a set of assumptions common to most of the 17th and 18th Century metaphysicians and natural philosophers; assumptions which constitute a basic outlook which Turbayne calls the "Newtonian World-View". Turbayne claims that

---

[41] Eschenbach was a professor of philosophy at Rostock, and the teacher of Tetens. There is no evidence that Kant was familiar with Eschenbach's writings. However, Kant studied the writings of Tetens with great care. L. W. Beck, *Early German Philosophy*, p. 476, note 130.

[42] The work was entitled: *Samlung der vornehmsten Schriftsteller die Würklichkeit ihres Körpers und der ganzen Körperwelt läugnen. Enthaltend des Berkeleys Gespräche zwischen Hylas und Philonous und des Colliers Allgemeinen Schlüssel. Übersetzt und mit wiederlegenden Anmerkungen versehen nebst einem Anhang worin die Würklichkeit der Körper erwiesen wird von Joh. Eschenbach, Prof. Philos. zu Rostock* (Rostock bey Unton). Most of those who mention the work have been more interested in Kant's relationship to Collier than in his relationship to Berkeley. Arthur Lovejoy refers to the work and calls attention to important affinities between Collier and Kant. He does not claim, however, that Kant made secret use of Collier's doctrines. *Kant and the English Platonists, Essays Philosophical and Psychological in Honor of William James*, New York: Longmans, Green, and Co., 1908, p. 289 ff. H. B. Acton, who holds an interesting variation of the traditional theory, also refers to the Eschenbach translation and suggests that "Kant's . . . interpretation of Berkeley is so completely at fault that it seems possible that he made use of Eschenbach's book and confused Collier's arguments with those of Berkeley". *Idealism, Encyclopedia of Philosophy*, New York: The Macmillan Company, 1967, Vol. IV, p. 113.

[43] The remaining passages are: (1) *Aesthetic* (A 37—41/B 54—55), (2) Section 6, *The Antinomy of Pure Reason* (A 491—497/B 519—525), and (3) *Prolegomena*, No. 49. I will attempt to show that (2), or the *Antinomy* passage, can be used to call into question the consistency of Turbayne's theory.

Kant's argument against this outlook has "a systematic similarity, in its principle features, with the main argument of Berkeley's *Principles* and *Dialogues*"[44]. In those works, Berkeley was concerned to expose the fallacies inherent in a way of thinking about the world, a way of thinking which led to a position which Berkeley called "materialism", which, in turn, inevitably gives way to a cheerless scepticism. Although Berkeley allied himself with the sceptics to explicate the consequences of the "Newtonian World-View", Turbayne maintains that Berkeley turned the argument of the sceptics against them to provide a unique proof of the external world. Turbayne claims that a strikingly similar argument is found in Kant's writings, particularly in the *Fourth Paralogism*, and he sees this as strong internal evidence that Kant, employing different terms, used Berkeley's arguments to undermine and replace a way of thinking about the world which Berkeley had undermined and replaced some seventy years before.

It is necessary to provide a brief statement of the argument in order to clarify some of the interesting doctrinal affinities between Berkeley and Kant, and to make clear some of the important assumptions underlying Turbayne's theory. However, before I outline the argument, I want to call attention to the fact that Turbayne assumes both that what Berkeley calls "materialism" Kant calls "transcendental realism"[45], and that "materialism" and "realism" are but two different names for a common position which Turbayne calls the "Newtonian World-View"[46].

The realist assumes the absolute reality of space and time, and he holds that material objects exist by themselves, as occupants of real space and in an absolute time order, independent of our sensible awareness of them. The realist distinguishes between the primary and secondary qualities of bodies[47]. The former, e. g., extension and shape, really characterize bodies, while the latter, e. g., heat and color, belong only to appearance and have no existence apart from minds.

Berkeley and Kant claim that the realist is deluded in thinking that the human mind can transcend experience and know reality[48], and this delusion, which prompts the realist to distinguish real things from sensible objects, ends in scepticism. Throughout his writings, Kant opposes empirical idealism, which, Turbayne claims, Kant sub-divides into sceptical idealism (which doubts) and dogmatic idealism (which denies) the existence of bodies in space outside us or, as Turbayne interprets this claim, "the reality of the sensible world"[49]. Kant noted that once

[44] Turbayne, *Kant's Refutation*, p. 229.
[45] For the sake of brevity, I will use "realism" to stand for both "transcendental realism" and for "materialism".
[46] Turbayne, *Kant's Refutation*, p. 230.
[47] Turbayne ignores the fact that Kant also distinguishes between primary and secondary qualities, a distinction which Berkeley consistently argued against.
[48] Turbayne ignores the fact that Berkeley was also a victim of this illusion. It would seem that Berkeley's thinking was far more infected by the realist assumptions than Turbayne is willing to admit.
[49] Turbayne, *Kant's Refutation*, p. 231.

we adopt realism, sceptical idealism is inevitable and dogmatic idealism unavoidable. Berkeley anticipated Kant's insight, for, in the *Three Dialogues*, Hylas, who begins as a realist, is led first to doubt and then to deny the reality of the external world[50].

Having reduced realism to scepticism, Berkeley and Kant turn the tables on the sceptics. The first step in their attempted refutation is to call attention to a truth acknowledged by the realists, namely that the *esse* of sensible things is their *percipi*[51]. The realists had used this doctrine in correcting the common man who mistakenly believes that sensible things exist unperceived. By making full use of the doctrine, both philosophers assimilate the external things of the realist into the realm of ideas or appearances[52]. Because they accept and use this doctrine, Berkeley and Kant seem to accept the conclusions of the sceptics. Both deny that this is so, breaking with the sceptics by insisting on the reality of the sensible things. This final step constitutes both their refutation of scepticism and their proof of the external world[53]. There are, of course, difficulties in such a proof, the chief one concerning perceptual error or illusion, for, if bodies are reduced to appearances, it would seem that the external world cannot be distinguished from a dream. Both philosophers deny that this follows, insisting that the distinction between reality and illusion retains full force. The criterion for the real is coherence within experience; there are no illusions of sense but only delusions of the understanding.

If Turbayne is correct that Kant and Berkeley used a common argument to reduce realism to scepticism and to undercut the sceptics, then why does Kant claim that Berkeley is a dogmatic idealist? Despite the interesting similarities between the two, it would seem that Kant failed to understand Berkeley[54]. Although Turbayne admits that Kant's remarks about Berkeley are misinterpretations, he nevertheless denies that Kant was ignorant of Berkeley's position. He argues that an awareness of Kant's "customary procedure in discussing the views of other philosophers"[55], and a careful examination of those passages in which Berkeley is mentioned indicate that Kant had accurate knowledge of Berkeley, and that the misinterpretations represent Kant's attempt to hide his debt to Berkeley.

Turbayne claims that when Kant discussed the views of other philosophers, he would present "not their real views, but rather the consequences he considers to be entailed by them"[56]. The consequences drawn by Kant are then ascribed to the philosophers as views actually held by the philosopher. In support of this claim,

[50] *Ibid.*, p. 232.
[51] *Ibid.*, p. 234.
[52] Turbayne translates Kant's important technical term *Vorstellung* as "idea" rather than as "representation". *Ibid.*, p. 230, Note 12.
[53] *Ibid.*, p. 235.
[54] *Ibid.*, p. 240.
[55] *Ibid.*, p. 240.
[56] *Ibid.*, p. 240.

Turbayne says that although Kant knew Leibniz's views, he nevertheless ascribed to Leibniz views which Leibniz never held. Hence, had Kant studied Berkeley as carefully as he studied Leibniz, it is possible that his account of Berkeley would be distorted[57]. Having muted the objection that Kant's misinterpretations are incompatible with knowing Berkeley, Turbayne examines three important passages where Berkeley is mentioned by name, passages which Turbayne claims "secrete Kant's real view of Berkeley"[58].

Turbayne begins with the *Refutation of Idealism* passage where Kant claims that[59]:

> Berkeley maintains that space, with all the things of which it is the inseparable condition, is something which is in itself impossible; and he therefore regards the things in space as merely imaginary entities. Dogmatic idealism is unavoidable if space is interpreted as a property that must belong to things in themselves. For in that case space, and everything to which it serves as condition, is a non-entity. The ground on which this idealism rests has already been undermined by us in the *Transcendental Aesthetic*.

Turbayne claims that in this passage Kant correctly ascribes to Berkeley Kant's own denial of the absolute reality of space and its occupants, and he also (correctly) claims that Berkeley had explicated the consequence of the realist position, *viz.*, absolute scepticism, "with its denial not only of the reality of absolute space, but the reality of the whole sensible world"[60]. When the passage is properly understood, Turbayne insists that it shows that Kant explicitly acknowledges that Berkeley had shown that dogmatic idealism is the unavoidable consequence of realism. In short, it supports Turbayne's claim that Kant had accurate knowledge of Berkeley's position.

Turbayne considers next the second edition *Aesthetic* passage where Berkeley is mentioned by name[61], a passage in which Kant attempts to meet the objection that his own doctrine of the ideality of space entails illusion. Kant maintains that the contrary is true, that it is only if we follow the realists and ascribe absolute reality to space that it becomes impossible to avoid dogmatic idealism. As Kant puts it, if we ascribe absolute reality to space, then "we cannot blame the good Berkeley for degrading bodies to mere illusion"[62]. Here again Kant indicates a clear understanding of Berkeley's analysis of realism, and since Kant claims that dogmatic

---

[57] Turbayne appeals to Kemp Smith for support. Kemp Smith claims: "Kant, following his usual method in the discussion of opposing systems, is stating what he regards as being the logical consequence of certain of Leibniz's tenets, rather than his avowed position." *Commentary*, p. 140, note 6. However, it would seem that Kemp Smith can be cited against Turbayne, for on p. 605 he notes: "Kant's first-hand knowledge of Leibniz's teachings was very limited. He was acquainted with it chiefly through the inadequate channel of Wolff's somewhat commonplace exposition of its *principles*."

[58] Turbayne, *Kant's Refutation*, p. 241.

[59] B 275.

[60] Turbayne, *Kant's Refutation*, p. 241.

[61] B 69—B 72.

[62] B 71.

idealism is avoidable if one does not ascribe absolute reality to space, he indicates that he and Berkeley, but not the realists, can avoid dogmatic idealism.

In the final important passage, the Appendix to the *Prolegomena*, Kant correctly says that Berkeley held that space and its contents are ideal, and Kant openly acknowledges that he and Berkeley are one on this point. Kant further correctly observes that Berkeley regarded space as an empirical idea which, like the things it contains, is known to us only by means of perception[63]. Kant then claims that it is because of the different ways in which he and Berkeley conceive space, that Kant, but not Berkeley, can avoid dogmatic idealism. Kant claims that space must be interpreted as an *a priori* form of sensible intuition to provide a sure distinction between reality and illusion, and, therefore, to avoid dogmatic idealism.

Turbayne claims that since Berkeley neither held nor intended to hold that bodies are imaginary entities, that "Kant's assertion that he does is a misinterpretation"[64]. What Kant actually means when he says that Berkeley is a dogmatic idealist, is that dogmatic idealism is an unavoidable consequence of Berkeley's views. According to Turbayne, Kant's repeated assertions that Berkeley is a dogmatic idealist are to be understood as instances of Kant's habit of ascribing to a philosopher what are, in fact, consequences drawn by Kant. Turbayne goes on to claim that since Kant knew Berkeley's position, the misinterpretations should be "more properly called 'perversions'"[65], i. e., deliberate misinterpretations.

As to why Kant distorted his account of Berkeley, Turbayne tells us that it was to hide his debt to the Irish thinker. And Kant wished to hide his debt because he deplored what he took to be some of Berkeley's conclusions, thinking that Berkeley was committed to a mystical and visionary system, and also because of the uninformed opinion of Berkeley as a "befooled enthusiast who sought notoriety by his paradoxes"[66]. Presumably, Kant could not "acknowledge debt to such a man, or even to admit affinity"[67].

Unlike the traditional theory, Turbayne claims that he can explain all of the facts. (1) and (2), or the misinterpretations and Kant's denial that his position resembles Berkeley's, are accounted for by the "perversion thesis". (3), or Kant's animus for Berkeley, is explained in part by the "perversion thesis", but more fully by Kant's attempt to inform his readers that he opposes any position which even hints at being mystical and visionary. (4), or the omission of any direct treatment of Berkeley in the first edition, is accounted for by Kant's attempt to hide his debt to Berkeley. It is interesting to note that Turbayne's explanation of (5) is identical with that provided by the traditional theory. According to Tur-

---

[63] *Prolegomena*, p. 145. Akademie-Ausgabe, Bd. IV, p. 374.
[64] Turbayne, *Kant's Refutation*, p. 242.
[65] *Ibid.*, p. 243.
[66] *Ibid.*, p. 244.
[67] *Ibid.*, p. 244.

bayne, since Kant's position in the *Fourth Paralogism* most closely resembles Berkeley's, Turbayne claims that had Kant tried to keep his promise and "sought to refute Berkeley ... he must have ended in hopeless confusion, for he would have been refuting himself. He therefore did not even try"[68]. Finally, Turbayne explains (6) in terms of the impact of the critical reviews of the first edition of the *Critique*. The critics smoked Kant out on his relationship to Berkeley, thus making it imperative for him to distinguish his own position from Berkeley's.

The merit of Turbayne's theory is that it examines many of the interesting doctrinal affinities between the two philosophers. He is correct in calling attention to the similar ways in which the two explicated the sceptical consequences of modern philosophy, and the strikingly similar ways in which they attempted to reply to scepticism. Nevertheless, there are serious difficulties in Turbayne's theory. While some of the difficulties result from what Turbayne either fails to make clear or to discuss, other difficulties are attributable to various assumptions and claims which Turbayne makes. I will consider first those difficulties which are the result of omissions, and I will then take up those which arise from claims and assumptions which Turbayne makes. As with my examination of the traditional theory, my primary aim is to explicate those assumptions which stand in the way of an adequate explanation of the relationship between Berkeley and Kant.

The most obvious difficulty in Turbayne's theory is the "perversion thesis", which he resorts to because he wants to hold both that Kant knew Berkeley, and that Kant misinterpreted Berkeley's position. Apart from the fact that the thesis is highly unflattering to Kant, Turbayne never really explains why, nor, more importantly, how Kant perverted his account. As to why, Turbayne says that Kant wished to hide his debt. Though deeply indebted to Berkeley, Kant could not openly admit this for fear of having his own position linked with Berkeley's. Kant may have believed that as long as he was seen as Berkeley's satellite, his position would not receive serious consideration. By resorting to misinterpretation, he may have hoped to keep the albatross of the vulgar characterization of Berkeley from being draped about his own neck.

Although the account was deliberately distorted, Turbayne tells us that Kant does reveal his debt to Berkeley, particularly in the passages where Berkeley is mentioned by name. The passages contain two messages: "although *they seem* to indicate misconceptions ... they *secrete* Kant's real view of Berkeley"[69]. Turbayne suggests that while the misconceptions are planted to ward off those who are unable to appreciate the subtle similarities and differences between the two philosophers, the similarities and differences are there for the discerning reader, along with Kant's tribute to Berkeley. Kant can therefore be seen as having both an understandable personal motive and possibly a laudable motive for his treatment of Berkeley. There are, however, other things which Turbayne

[68] *Ibid.*, p. 243.
[69] *Ibid.*, p. 241. Italics mine.

says which indicate that these are not the reasons he believes that Kant distorted his account of Berkeley.

To get at Turbayne's reasons, we must consider how, according to Turbayne, Kant distorted his account. For Turbayne, two things must be established to claim that Kant perverted his account of a philosopher. It must be shown that Kant had an accurate understanding of the philosopher, and that Kant consistently ascribed to the philosopher views which are actually Kantian-drawn consequences of the philosopher's views. Turbayne believes that he has shown both with respect to Kant's discussion of Berkeley, and, therefore, Kant perverted his account. But on these criteria and Turbayne's own claims about the way in which Kant discussed Leibniz, Newton and other philosophers, we would have to say that Kant perverted his account of Leibniz, Newton and the others as well. Turbayne is aware of this consequence, and, in a footnote, he hedges the application of the "perversion thesis" to Kant's discussion of Leibniz and Newton. Turbayne says: "In the case of Newton and Leibniz . . . Kant is usually more careful. For them he uses phrases such as 'They have to admit', and 'They are obliged to deny'"[70]. But if these phrases hedge the application of the thesis to Kant's discussion of Leibniz and Newton, then it can also be shown, from Kant's own words, that the thesis does not apply to Kant's discussion of Berkeley in an unqualified way.

For Turbayne, the one passage in Kant's writings which contains the most sustained discussion of Berkeley's views and, more importantly, contains Kant's attempt to distinguish his position from Berkeley's is the Appendix to the *Prolegomena*. Kant says there[71]:

> Berkeley regarded space as a mere empirical representation which, like the appearances in it, only becomes known to us, together with all its determinations, by means of experience or perception; I on the contrary first show that space (and likewise time, to which Berkeley paid no attention) with all its determinations can be known by us *a priori* because it, as well as time, is present in us before all perception or experience as pure form of our sensibility, and makes possible all intuition of sensibility, and hence all appearances. *From this it follows:* that as truth rests on universal and necessary laws as its criteria, experience with Berkeley can have no criteria of truth because nothing was laid (by him) *a priori* at the ground of appearance in it, *from which it then followed* that they are nothing but illusion; whereas for us space and time (in conjunction with the pure concepts of the understanding) prescribe their laws *a priori* to all possible experience, and this yields at the same time the sure criterion for distinguishing truth in it from illusion.

In this passage Kant does not ascribe to Berkeley directly what he takes to be the consequences of Berkeley's position; on the contrary, as the phrases "from this it follows" and "from which it then followed" make clear, Kant claims that dogmatic idealism is a consequence of Berkeley's position and not a position actually held by Berkeley. Turbayne must therefore admit that Kant does not pervert his account of Berkeley. However, I don't think that the so-called common practice of ascribing to philosophers what are Kantian-drawn consequences

[70] *Ibid.*, p. 243, Note No. 37.
[71] *Prolegomena*, pp. 145—146. Italics added. Akademie-Ausgabe, Bd. IV, p. 374—375.

of their views is the reason Turbayne believes that Kant perverted his account of Berkeley.

The reason emerges near the end of the paper[72] where Turbayne claims that Kant's appeal to his doctrine of space as an *a priori* form of intuition, while a legitimate difference between Berkeley and Kant, is irrelevant to whether Berkeley can or cannot avoid dogmatic idealism. According to Turbayne, the crucial step in avoiding dogmatic idealism is the insistence upon the ideality of space, and not its *a priori* character. Turbayne further suggests that Kant was aware of this, for, according to Turbayne, throughout the various refutations of the realist position, Kant had claimed that realism reduces to dogmatic idealism because it distinguishes things from sensible objects, and not because it fails to make the assumption that space is a condition for all experience. And, Turbayne continues, the Kantian antidote to dogmatic idealism "is not the *a priori* nature of space, but its ideality or subjectivity, which assimilates space and its contents into the realm of ideas, and thus *prevents* illusion"[73]. In an accompanying footnote[74], Turbayne claims that Kant's doctrine of space as an *a priori* form is advanced to account for the apodeictic certainty of geometry. It is, in short, irrelevant to Kant's attempt to avoid dogmatic idealism. Turbayne is therefore claiming both that Berkeley's position does not entail dogmatic idealism, and, more importantly, that Kant was well aware that it did not. If this is true, then Kant clearly perverted his account of Berkeley by attributing to Berkeley a view which he did not hold and which Kant knew did not follow from any views held by him. What is crucial for Turbayne to show is that the Kantian doctrine of space as an *a priori* form is not relevant to the dogmatic idealism issue, and that Kant knew that it was not relevant. He makes no attempt to show either; he is content to claim that this Kantian doctrine is not relevant and that Kant knew this. Like the traditional theorists, Turbayne also fails to take seriously Kant's claim that Berkeley's position is undermined by the *Aesthetic*.

Although in this paper I cannot undertake a discussion of Kant's views on space and how they relate to Berkeley, I would like to call attention to a couple of features of Kant's views which, I think, provide good reasons for questioning Turbayne's assumptions and claims. Turbayne assumes both that (a) Kant's doctrine of space as an *a priori* form is not relevant to dogmatic idealism, and (b) that Kant's primary reason for advancing the doctrine was to explain the apodeictic certainty of geometry. (b) suggests that Kant's sole argument for space as an *a priori* form is that this is necessary to account for the apodeictic certainty of geometry. This, however, is clearly not the case, for in both editions of the *Aesthetic* Kant claims that[75]:

[72] Turbayne, *Kant's Refutation*, p. 243.
[73] *Ibid.*, p. 243.
[74] *Ibid.*, p. 243, Note 39.
[75] A 24/B 39.

Space is not an empirical concept which has been derived from outer experiences. For in order that certain sensations be referred to something outside me (that is, to something in another region of space from that in which I find myself), and similarly in order that I may be able to represent them as outside and alongside one another, and accordingly as not only different but as in different places, the representation of space must be presupposed. The representation of space cannot, therefore, be empirically obtained from the relations of outer appearances. On the contrary, this outer experience is itself possible at all only through that representation.

Whatever we may think of the above argument, it seems clear that Kant is arguing that space is an *a priori* form because it cannot be derived from experience. On the contrary, experience presupposes space. As to (a), it seems that Kant believed that what is crucial for avoiding dogmatic idealism is to show that we do in fact experience bodies in space. As Kant says in the *Refutation of Idealism*, the crucial question is "whether we have an inner sense only, and no outer sense, but merely an outer imagination"[76]. Kant was of the view that in order to avoid dogmatic idealism, we must show that we do have an outer sense or that we do experience bodies in space. It seems to me that what Kant was objecting to in Berkeley's position is that, in so far as Berkeley treats space as an empirical idea derived from experience, Berkeley is committed to the position that we only seem to see bodies in space, and that in reality all that we are aware of is a succession of non-spatial sensations and impressions. And because Kant treats space as an *a priori* form, he can claim that we actually do see bodies in space outside ourselves.

Another difficulty in Turbayne's theory, which is related to the above, is that he ignores the *Refutation of Idealism*. Turbayne claims that the commentators failed to see that Kant's eight refutations of idealism are not so much directed against Descartes and/or Berkeley as that they constitute a central argument against realism and its ramifications, sceptical and dogmatic idealism. Although the central argument is put most clearly in the *Fourth Paralogism*, Turbayne holds that it is discernible in all of the others, with the exception of the *Refutation of Idealism*. The sole reason Turbayne gives to support his claim is that "Kant uses a method of proof of the external world different from that of the preceding seven"[77]. He therefore says that he will "ignore the *Refutation* ... except in so far as it presents Kant's views on Berkeley"[78], i. e., views which Kant ascribes to Berkeley. Turbayne means what he says, and reference is made to the passage only in so far as it sheds light on doctrines which Kant ascribes to Berkeley. Now it hardly follows from the fact that Kant uses a method of proof in the *Refutation* different from the previous passages, that the passage is therefore unrelated to the central argument against both realism and, more importantly, sceptical and dogmatic idealism. A number of traditional theorists claim, with justification, that if the argument of the *Refutation* is sound, then, although it is explicitly

---

[76] B 277 a.
[77] Turbayne, *Kant's Refutation*, p. 229.
[78] *Ibid.*, p. 229.

directed against Descartes, it "constitutes a no less complete refutation of Berkeley"[79]. If the traditional theorists are correct, it would seem that Kant has, in addition to his criticisms of Berkeley's views on space, additional reasons for claiming that Berkeley is unable to avoid dogmatic idealism. It would seem that it would be important for Turbayne to evaluate the claims of the traditional theorists concerning the *Refutation of Idealism*. He makes no attempt to do so.

While the above difficulties are due to what Turbayne fails to discuss and/or make clear, his theory also has difficulties because of the claims and assumptions which he makes. One crucial assumption is that what Berkeley calls "materialism" Kant calls "transcendental realism", and that "materialism" and "transcendental realism" are but two names for the "Newtonian World-View". According to Turbayne, the materialist or realist holds "the absolute reality of space and external bodies in it"[80]. Among the materialists or realists, Turbayne includes "Newton, Leibniz. More, Clarke ... Locke ... Descartes ... Malebranche"[81]. And, for Turbayne, all of them supposedly subscribe to the doctrine that space is a "prior condition of all experience"[82]. Although Kant's writings support the claim that Kant regarded all of these philosophers as transcendental realists, it seems to me that Kant's writings indicate that Kant did not believe that they all subscribed to the views that (a) space is absolutely real, (b) that the real things are material objects, and (c) that space is a prior condition of all experience. It is clear from the *Critique* and Kant's other writings that Kant took Leibniz to be a transcendental realist, although Kant explicitly acknowledges that Leibniz held none of the above views[83]. My point is that Turbayne is mistaken in assuming that Kant took transcendental realism to be identical with what Berkeley called "materialism". It seems to me that it would be more accurate to say that Kant considered what Berkeley called "materialism" to be but one of the possible transcendental realist positions. Rather than defining transcendental realism in terms of the explicit doctrines of several philosophers, it seems that Kant characterized the position in terms of certain very general assumptions and beliefs held by many philosophers, e. g., that the human mind can know reality. If this is the case, then it weakens Turbayne's claim that Kant, some seventy years later, made secret use of Berkeley's arguments to refute the same position which Berkeley had already refuted.

While the above difficulties indicate that Turbayne's theory does not explain all that it sets out to explain, his theory is also open to the charge that it lacks consistency. As with the traditional theory, it is interesting to note that Turbayne's

---

[79] Kemp Smith, *Commentary*, p. 313.
[80] Turbayne, *Kant's Refutation*, p. 241.
[81] *Ibid.*, p. 241.
[82] *Ibid.*, p. 243.
[83] See, for example, A 40, B 57, A 277 and B 333. Also, see George Miller's *Kant's First Edition Refutation of Dogmatic Idealism*, Kant-Studien, Heft 3, 1971, pp. 298—318.

theory is not consistent in the explanations for (4) and (5). While Turbayne accounts for (4), or the omission of any direct treatment of Berkeley in the first edition, by Kant's attempt to hide his debt to Berkeley, Turbayne then tells us, in his account of (5), that Kant nevertheless promises to refute Berkeley and then makes no attempt to do so. But if Kant were intent on hiding his debt to Berkeley, then why would Kant, by making a promise which he makes no attempt to redeem, call the reader's attention to Berkeley? In addition, if Kant supposedly had a sure knowledge of Berkeley's position before he published the first edition of the *Critique*, then either he knew that he could or he knew that he could not refute Berkeley. If he knew that he could, why didn't he carry out his promise? If he knew that he could not, then why did he promise to do so? It is doubtful that Turbayne can resolve any of these problems.

A final difficulty concerns Turbayne's important claim that Kant had a sure knowledge of Berkeley's position. Turbayne says that Kant sub-divides empirical idealism into sceptical idealism and dogmatic idealism. What he fails to note or even to mention is that the two sub-divisions are mentioned and discussed not only in the *Fourth Paralogism*, but in *Section 6* of the *Antinomy* as well. Note, however, what Kant says about the two-subdivisions of empirical idealism[84]:

> It would be unjust to ascribe to us that long-decried empirical idealism, which, while it admits the *genuine reality of space* denies the existence of extended beings in it, or at least considers their existence doubtful.

In this passage, which appears in both editions of the *Critique,* Kant claims that the idealist who doubts the existence of extended beings (the sceptical idealist) and the idealist who "denies the existence of extended beings" (the dogmatic idealist) both admit that space is real. But, as we have seen, Turbayne tells us that Kant was well aware that Berkeley was not a realist on space. If we assume, as Turbayne does, that the dogmatic idealist of both editions is Berkeley, then the passage is clear evidence against Turbayne's claim that Kant had sure knowledge of Berkeley.

If the fundamental weakness of the traditional theory is the failure to go beyond Kant's remarks about Berkeley to a careful examination of the passages in which they occur, the major weakness in Turbayne's theory is that it makes more of the affinities between Berkeley and Kant than Kant's writings permit. Turbayne pushes the affinities and ignores the differences to the point where Kant is seen as doing little more than using Berkeley's arguments to refute a position which Berkeley had already refuted. In reply to the traditional theorist Werkmeister's question as to why "Kant did not make use of Berkeley's arguments?"[85], Turbayne tells us that they are the only arguments that he did use. It is not clear whether Turbayne sees Berkeley as a pre-critical Kant or Kant as a post-critical

---

[84] A 491/B 519. Italics mine.
[85] Werkmeister, *Notes,* p. 164.

Berkeley. But as Turbayne never discusses nor even mentions the salient features of the critical standpoint, it seems that he simply interprets Kant's position as Berkeley's restated[86].

The primary intent of this paper has not been to demonstrate the inadequacies of two theories about the relationship between Berkeley and Kant, but to show that the inadequacies result from two assumptions common to the theories. The first assumption is that Berkeley is the first edition dogmatic idealist Kant promised to but was unable to refute. As we have seen, this assumption requires the exponents of the traditional theory to provide an explanation for this presumed fact which is inconsistent with the explanations provided for Kant's obvious misinterpretations of Berkeley and the omission of any direct treatment of Berkeley in the first edition. The assumption also causes problems for Turbayne. As we have seen, Turbayne explains the omission of any direct treatment of Berkeley in the first edition in terms of Kant's attempt to hide his debt to Berkeley. Yet, by promising to refute Berkeley and then making no attempt to do so, Kant calls the reader's attention to Berkeley. Turbayne is also faced with a related difficulty in that he tells us that even though Kant had a sure knowledge of Berkeley's position, he did not know whether he could or could not refute Berkeley[87]. The second assumption common to the two theories is that Kant misinterprets Berkeley's position[88]. Because of this assumption, the exponents of the traditional theory simply ignore Kant's claim that Berkeley's position has been undermined in the *Transcendental Aesthetic*. Although Turbayne claims that many of Kant's remarks about Berkeley are not misinterpretations, e. g., Kant's claim that Berkeley held that space is ideal, and Kant's claim that Berkeley had explicated the sceptical consequences of transcendental realism, Turbayne nevertheless concludes that Kant's repeated characterization of Berkeley's position is in fact a misinterpretation. As a consequence, Turbayne, like the exponents of the traditional theory, ignores Kant's claim that Berkeley's position has been undermined in the *Transcendental Aesthetic*. Because of these assumptions, the two theories not only fail to provide an adequate explanation of the relationship between the two philosophers, but the explanations that they do provide seem to lack consistency. It would seem that if these assumptions give rise to insurmountable difficulties, then the first step in developing an adequate theory would be to question the assumptions which cause the problems, regardless of however plausible these assumptions may appear to be.

---

[86] Margaret Wilson raises a similar objection against Turbayne. *Kant and 'The Dogmatic Idealism of Berkeley'*, p. 472, Note 48.

[87] For an explanation of Kant's first edition promise to refute dogmatic idealism which is free of these difficulties, see my paper, *Kant's First Edition Refutation of Dogmatic Idealism*.

[88] It is interesting to note that Margaret Wilson's theory also requires the assumption that many of Kant's remarks about Berkeley are in fact misinterpretations. *Kant and 'The Dogmatic Idealism of Berkeley'*, p. 470.

Kant's Critique of Berkeley

HENRY E. ALLISON

THE CLAIM THAT KANT'S IDEALISM, or at least certain strands of it, is essentially identical to that of Berkeley has a long and distinguished history. It was first voiced by several of Kant's contemporaries such as Mendelssohn, Herder, Hamann, Pistorius and Eberhard who attacked the alleged subjectivism of the *Critique of Pure Reason*.[1] This viewpoint found its sharpest contemporary expression in the notorious Garve-Feder review to which Kant responded at length in the *Prolegomena*. In subsequent times it has been championed by Schopenhauer, and most nineteenth century German commentators on the relation between the two philosophers.[2] In addition, it has been, and continues to be, the prevailing view of the vast majority of British writers on Kant, including, with significant qualifications, Norman Kemp Smith.[3]

This tradition continues despite the fact that Kant specifically, and in no uncertain terms, repudiated this identification in the *Prolegomena* and the second edition of the *Critique*. In both works he responds to the charges of subjectivism, and in so doing distinguishes his position from that of Berkeley, who in the eighteenth century was commonly regarded as a solipsist and denier of the "external world."[4] In contra-distinction to Kant's own critical or transcendental idealism, which explains the possibility of synthetic *a priori* knowledge within the realm of possible experience, Berkeley is characterized as a "dogmatic" or "visionary idealist." He is judged guilty of "degrading bodies to mere illusion" (B69), of regarding things in space as "merely imaginary entities" (B274), and of holding with all "genuine idealists" that: "all knowledge through the senses and experience is

---

[1] Cf. Hans Vaihinger, *Commentar zu Kant's Kritik der Reinen Vernunft* (Stuttgart, Berlin, Leipzig, 1892), II, 494-505.
[2] Cf. Friederich Fredericks, *Der Phainomenale Idealismus Berkeley's und Kant's* (Berlin, 1871); Robert Zimmerman, "Über Kant's Widerlegung des Idealismus von Berkeley" (*Sitzungsberichte der Akademie der Wissenschaften, Vienna, Philos.-hist. Kl.*), LXVIII (1871); Gustav Dieckert, *Über das Verhältnis des Berkeleyschen Idealismus zu Kantischen Vernunftkritik* (Konitz, 1888).
[3] This is a consequence of the general British tendency to view Kant in phenomenalist terms. A typical recent example is found in P. F. Strawson, *The Bounds of Sense* (London, 1966). Kemp Smith in his *Commentary to Kant's* Critique of Pure Reason (2nd ed., rev., 1923) takes great pains to distinguish between the subjectivist strand in Kant's thought, which is essentially identical to Berkeley's position, and the genuine critical doctrine which stands side by side with it in the text.
[4] Cf. H. M. Bracken, *The Early Reception of Berkeley's Materialism 1710-1733*, rev. ed. (The Hague: Martinus Nijhoff, 1965).

[43]

nothing but sheer illusion, and only in the ideas of pure understanding is there truth" (374).[5]

One of the chief reasons for the continuation of the Kant-Berkeley tradition is that these, and similar statements about Berkeley, which we find in these works and in Kant's correspondence with Beck, have not been taken very seriously by Kant's critics. They are usually dismissed as obvious misinterpretations, due to Kant's ignorance of Berkeley's actual writings, and of his reliance upon distorted second and third hand accounts of Berkeley's thought such as is to be found in Beattie. Furthermore, this view is often supported by the philological reflection that Kant did not read English, and that Berkeley's writings were not yet available in German translation.[6]

The philological argument, however, loses much of its force when we consider that there was indeed a German translation of Berkeley's *Dialogues*, which although apparently unknown to nineteenth century scholars, was readily accessible to Kant. This is to be found, together with a translation of Collier's *Clavis Universalis* and critical analyses, in a work by the professor of philosophy at Rostock, Johann Christian Eschenbach, entitled: *Samlung der vornehmsten Schriftsteller die die Wirklichkeit ihres eignen Körpers und der ganzen Körperwelt leugnen* (Rostock, 1756). Furthermore, in addition to this work, which was probably known to Kant, there is Berkeley's important Latin work, *De Motu* (1721), as well as French translations of many of Berkeley's other writings, which Kant was perfectly capable of reading. The existence of these works does not, of course, prove that Kant actually read them. In view, however, of Kant's great interest in both British philosophers and *Schwarmerei*, it seems highly probable that Kant had at least some first-hand acquaintance with Berkeley's thought.[7]

The recognition of this probability renders necessary a reexamination of the whole question of Kant's relation to Berkeley. This has been undertaken by a recent critic, Colin Turbayne, who combines this recognition with the reaffirmation of the essentially Berkeleian nature of Kant's thought. Basing his analysis largely upon the fourth *Paralogism* of the first edition, Turbayne shows in detail not only that Kant and Berkeley raised substantially similar objections against the sceptical implications of the Cartesian theory of ideas, but also argues that they overcame this scepticism by the identical device of equating ideas or appearances with "real things." Taken by itself this is nothing more than a careful restatement

---

[5] References to the *Critique of Pure Reason* will be to the first (A) and second (B) edition pagination. Quotations will be from the Norman Kemp Smith Translation. References from *Prolegomena* will be to the *Akademie Ausgabe*, and quotations from the Lewis White Beck translation.

[6] The most detailed statement of this view is found in J. Janitsch, *Kant's Urteil über Berkeley*, Diss. (Strassburg, 1879).

[7] A contrary view is offered by Eugen Stabler in his *George Berkeley's Auffassung und Wirkung in der Deutschen Philosophie bis Hegel*, Inaugural Dissertation (Tübingen, 1935), pp. 39-56. Stabler argues specifically against the claim that Kant was familiar with the Eschenbach translation on the grounds that his criticisms of Berkeley suggest a lack of first hand acquaintance. He, however, fails to discuss *De Motu*. The contrary was maintained by Lewis Robinson, "Contributions à l'Histoire de l'Evolution Philosophique de Kant," *Revue de Métaphysique et de Morale*, 31 (1924), 205-268. Here Robinson argues specifically for the influence of the Eschenbach translation of Collier's *Clavis Universalis* on the formation of the doctrine of the antinomies.

of the subjectivistic reading of the *Critique*, but when combined with the acknowledgement of Kant's first hand knowledge of Berkeley, it leads to the intriguing thesis that Kant's derogatory comments about Berkeley are the results of a deliberate attempt to deceive the learned world. "Since the misrepresentation stem from accurate knowledge," Turbayne writes, "they are deliberate, and are, therefore, more accurately called perversions." [8] This willful misinterpretation is held to be the result of Kant's animus towards all things mystical, and of his desire to disarm his critics of the inevitable charges of idealism, and thus, to pave the way for a more favorable reception for the *Critique*.

Quite obviously, the ultimate basis for this serious attack on both Kant's philosophical significance and personal integrity is the affirmation of the essentially Berkeleian nature of his argument. If this be denied it becomes possible to view Kant's remarks about Berkeley in a more favorable light. Furthermore, highly relevant in this context is Turbayne's admission that Kant's criticism of Berkeley, like his comments upon other philosophers, are to be construed as analyses of the consequences which the position in question entails, rather than as direct reports of what it explicitly states.[9] It is, therefore, only to be expected that when judged in accordance with the canons of historical scholarship, Kant's treatment of other philosophers often appears to be unfair and distorted. The task of this paper is thus to show that despite the superficial similarities to which Turbayne and others point, Kant's transcendental standpoint differs fundamentally from Berkeley's position, and that Kant's criticisms are a legitimate and philosophically significant expression of this difference.

Since Kant viewed Berkeley's "dogmatic idealism" as a logical development of Cartesianism, this task can best be accomplished by means of an analysis of that portion of the *Critique* wherein Kant most fully defines his transcendental idealism in opposition to the Cartesian theory of ideas, viz. the fourth *Paralogism* in the first edition. We shall endeavor to show that, when understood in light of Kant's conception of transcendental ideality, this section of the *Critique*, which is generally counted amongst its most subjectivistic portions, and in which, according to Kemp Smith: "Kant refutes the problematic idealism of Descartes by means of the more subjective idealism of Berkeley," [10] does indeed contain a valid statement of the distinctively Kantian idealism. This idealism will then be briefly compared with Berkeley's position by means of an analysis of their respective treatments of the crucial primary-secondary quality distinction. Finally, in light of these considerations we shall examine Kant's specific criticisms of Berkeley.

I

The argument of the fourth *Paralogism*: "Of Ideality," constitutes the first version of the "Refutation of Idealism," and was completely recast in the second

---

[8] Colin Turbayne, "Kant's Refutation of Dogmatic Idealism," *The Philosophical Quarterly*, 5 (1955), 243.
[9] *Ibid.*, p. 240.
[10] Kemp Smith, *op. cit.*, p. 305.

edition. It is directed specifically against the "empirical idealism" of Descartes, which Kant later came to call "material, or problematic idealism." Kant informs us that the term idealist in this context is not to be understood as referring to those who deny the existence of external sensible objects (the "dogmatic idealist"), "but only to those who do not admit that their existence is known through immediate perception, and who therefore conclude that we can never, by any possible experience, be completely certain as to their reality" (A368).

This idealism, with its conception of the problematic status of the external world, is seen to be a consequence of the Cartesian doctrine of the primacy of the *cogito*. The decisive feature of this doctrine is the epistemic priority which it grants to inner over outer experience. My own existence and conscious states are held to be the sole objects of direct acquaintance, and the existence of external objects is only ascertainable by means of a process of causal inference. However, in that "the inference from a given effect to a determinate cause is always uncertain, since the effect may be due to more than one cause," Kant concludes:

it always remains doubtful whether the cause be internal or external; whether, that is to say, all the so-called outer perceptions are not a mere play of our inner sense, or whether they stand in relation to actual external objects as their cause. (A368)

This is a classic formulation of the "problem of the external world," and Kant's aim is to show that it is in reality a pseudo-problem, which only arises from the tacit acceptance of a false metaphysical assumption. Kant calls this assumption or standpoint transcendental realism, and he opposes it to his own transcendental idealism. The defining characteristic of transcendental realism is its confusion of appearances with things in themselves. Proponents of this position regard "time and space as something given in themselves, independently of our sensibility" (A369). As a result of this erroneous conception of space and time they inevitably treat "appearances" or "mere modifications of our sensibility," i.e. objects in space and time, as things in themselves. Although taken in the broadest sense, this may be said to refer to all non-critical standpoints,[11] it most clearly characterizes the metaphysical position of the philosophers of modern natural science from Descartes to Newton. This view of space and time gave rise in these thinkers to a conception of "reality" or nature as composed of bodies containing only "primary qualities," e.g. extension, figure, weight, motion and solidity, while the so-called "secondary qualities," e.g. colors, sounds and smells, which are equally pervasive features of our everyday experience, were dismissed as subjective, as "mere ideas in the mind" or "sensations," caused, in some manner or other, by the inter-action between the "real," mathematically described external world, and the human organism.

Kant's main contention in this section is that it is this misguided realism which gives rise to the equally misguided idealism of the Cartesian school. This is because on the assumption that physical objects exist independently of the mind, the

---

[11] I argue for this view in my "Transcendental Idealism and Descriptive Metaphysics," *Kant-Studien*, Heft 2 (1969), 216-233.

transcendental realist "finds that, judged from this point of view all our sensuous representations are inadequate to establish their reality" (A369). Here Kant reveals a keen insight into the connection between the metaphysical conception of nature developed by the "new science" and the Cartesian-Lockean theory of ideas, viz. the theory that ideas or sensations are the immediate objects of consciousness. His claim is, in effect, that this standpoint, which presupposes the truth of the mathematical conception of nature, is not able to account for its own possibility. The transcendental realist defines nature or reality in such a way that it remains totally inaccessible to consciousness. He thus is unable to justify the validity of his conception. This leads inevitably to an empirical idealism wherein that which is in fact accessible to consciousness are only its own private and subjective modifications, viz. Cartesian ideas and sensations. It is no doubt with this in mind that Kant concludes:

If we treat outer objects as things in themselves, it is quite impossible to understand how we could arrive at a knowledge of their reality outside us, since we have to rely merely on the representation which is in us. (A378)

In opposition to this view, and to the scepticism which it entails, Kant offers his doctrine of transcendental idealism, which he claims to have established in the *Transcendental Aesthetic.* This is defined as "the doctrine that appearances are to be regarded as being, one and all, representations only, not things in themselves" (A369). Unlike transcendental realism this is held to be consonant with an empirical realism, that is to say, with the view that we have genuine experience of bodies in space, and that these bodies are real, public entities rather than private ideas or sensations. Such a conception of experience would seem to be a necessary presupposition of any natural science, but according to Kant, such a conception can only be justified if we regard the bodies in space, of whose existence we are assured by experience, as mere appearances, and hence as "nothing but a species of my representations, the objects of which are something only through these representations" (A370).

Thus, Kant resolves the problem of knowledge of the external world by showing that the world in question is not, in fact, external in the sense in which transcendental realism believed. In sharp contrast to the empirical idealist, the transcendental idealist has no difficulty in "accepting the existence of matter on the unaided testimony of mere self-consciousness, or of declaring it to be thereby proved in the same manner as the existence of myself as a thinking substance" (A370). He can therefore maintain that his experience of a world of bodies in space is as immediate and veridical as the experience of his own subjective states. This, however, is only because he regards space and time as forms of human sensibility rather than as things in themselves, so that both they, and the things in them are not external in the "transcendental sense."

As this brief recapitulation of Kant's argument suggests. and as Kant explicitly tells us (A372-373), the whole debate between him and the Cartesians, or between transcendental and empirical idealism turns on the meaning of external or *"ausser uns."* According to Kant this term has two distinct meanings, and the confusion between appearances and things in themselves, and the ensuing sub-jectivism and scepticism is due largely to the failure to properly distinguish between them. From an empirical or commonsense standpoint bodies are *"ausser uns"* in the sense that they are located in space, not in the mind. It is also possible, however, to take *"ausser uns"* in a "transcendental" or "intellectual sense" "in conformity with the pure concepts of the understanding," and this is the sense in which, according to Kant, it is understood by the transcendental realist. Kant is not explicit as to precisely what he means by this latter sense, but the reference to the pure concepts of the understanding suggest that it involves regarding an exernal body, or nature itself, as the totality of bodies, as a distinct substance, which therefore stands in ontological independence from our minds. But, Kant argues, to regard, as the Cartesians obviously do, the external world of bodies in space as a distinct substance or collection of distinct substances, is to confuse the transcen-dental with the empirical sense of *"ausser uns,"* and therefore not only to con-fuse appearances with things in themselves, but to create in the process an un-bridgeable gulf between the private, "inner world" of thought, and the public, objective world of mathematical natural science.

Given this distinction, however, Cartesian subjectivism and scepticism can be avoided and empirical realism maintained. Bodies or matter can now be adjudged external in the empirical sense, viz. they are in space, and as such they are directly apprehended by the mind in sense experience. But since space itself is a form of sensibility these bodies are at the same time appearances, which in the transcendental sense are ideal, or in the mind. Yet Kant concludes, this ideality does not prevent us from admitting that "something which may be (in the transcendental sense) outside us, is the cause of our outer intuitions." The point to be kept in mind, however, is that this is not the empirical object, i.e. the object of scientific investigation with which we are here concerned. This latter object, which Kant, in contrast to the empirical object, calls the "transcendental object," and which is here equivalent to the thing in itself, is not apprehended in experience, but is merely "a ground (to us unknown) of the appearances . . ." (A379-380).

Now, it must be admitted that, apart from this last reference to the mysterious transcendental object,[12] which at first glance seems at odds with the main thrust of Kant's argument, the basic line of reasoning which Kant adopts here is in many ways similar to what we find in Berkeley's *Principles* and *Dialogues*. What Kant calls transcendental realism includes, although it is far broader than, what Berkeley calls materialism. Moreover, both philosophers address themselves to the Cartesian tradition, and both attack the sceptical implications of the dualism which characterizes this tradition. It is, therefore, indeed tempting to see not merely an anticipation, but an actual influence on Kant when Berkeley writes:

for so long as men thought that real things subsisted without the mind, and that their knowledge was only so far forth *real* as it was conformable to *real things*, it follows,

---

[12] Cf. my "Kant's Concept of the Transcendental Object," *Kant-Studien,* Heft 2 (1968), 165-186.

they could not be certain that they had any real knowledge at all. For how can it be known, that the things which are perceived, are conformable to those which are not perceived, or exist without the mind? (*Principles* 86)

Furthermore, this similarity extends not only to the diagnosis of the disease, but also to the prescription of the remedy. For both philosophers this remedy is idealism, understood as the identification of the empirically real with the contents of consciousness. Thus, both hold against the Cartesians that we are immediately aware of "real things," and both claim that this can only be justified on the assumption that these "real things" are in some sense mental. Kant calls them appearances or "representations in us" and Berkeley calls them ideas or sensations, whose *esse* is *percipi*. However, despite these terminological differences, their positions are substantially identical.[13]

Nevertheless, it remains the case that Kant was quite insistent upon distinguishing his transcendental or critical idealism from Berkeley's dogmatic idealism. The key to this distinction is obviously the allegedly transcendental or non-empirical nature of Kant's idealism. His claim is that the thesis of the ideality of bodies, their status as appearances, or "mere representations in us," is to be understood in the transcendental, and not in the empirical sense. It is because Berkeley does not understand ideality in this sense that he, in effect, "degrades bodies to mere illusion." Hence, if this is to be rendered intelligible, and Kant's position distinguished from Berkeley's, it will be necessary to determine more precisely the meaning and justification of this claim.

II

Kant's most explicit discussion of the transcendental-empirical distinction is to be found in a passage at the beginning of the *Transcendental Logic*. This passage is worth quoting at length since Kant himself tells us that "it extends its influence over all that follows":

Not every kind of knowledge *a priori* should be called transcendental, but that only by which we know that—and how—certain representations (intuitions or concepts) can be employed or are possible purely *a priori*. The term 'transcendental', that is to say, signifies such knowledge as concerns the *a priori* possibility of knowledge, or its *a priori* employment. Neither space nor any *a priori* geometrical determination of it is a transcendental representation; what can alone be entitled transcendental is the knowledge that these representations are not of empirical origin, and the possibility that they can yet relate *a priori* to objects of experience. The application of space to objects in general would likewise be transcendental, but, if restricted solely to objects of sense, it is empirical. The distinction between the transcendental and the empirical belongs therefore only to the critique of knowledge; it does not concern the relation of that knowledge to its objects. (A56-B80-81)

---

[13] Cf. Turbayne, *op. cit.*, pp. 229-239.

The main import of this passage lies in its substitution of the "critical" conception of the relation between the transcendental and the empirical for the traditional rational-empirical dichotomy. Thus, instead of a super, trans-empirical science of "Being," the transcendental emerges as a kind of second order knowledge of knowledge, a reflection on the nature, conditions and limits of our *a priori* knowledge.[14] As a consequence the transcendental-empirical distinction is denied any ontological significance. This is the point of the remark that the distinction "belongs only to the critique of knowledge, it does not concern the relation of that knowledge to its object." Hence, while within the critical perspective it is both possible and necessary to distinguish between our first order, empirical knowledge, and our transcendental or philosophical reflection on the necessary conditions of such knowledge, we cannot venture outside this perspective and lay claim to any "transcendental knowledge" of any transcendental or non-empirical objects, i.e. "objects in general," as opposed to objects of the senses. In Kant's own terms it means that "the proud name of Ontology . . . give place to the modest title of a mere analytic of the pure understanding" (A247-B303).

This passage also implies, however, that there is an *a priori* or rational element in our knowledge of empirical objects. This is, of course, the main brunt of the argument of both the *Transcendental Aesthetic* and the *Transcendental Analytic,* which show respectively that there are *a priori* intuitions and concepts which relate necessarily to all objects of experience. Thus, although pure reason is denied its transcendent or metaphysical pretentions, it is given an immanent role within experience, which is to be distinguished both from its practical use, and its strictly philosophical function of determining the necessary conditions and limits of empirical knowledge.

As Hermann Cohen has suggested, the key to this critical standpoint, the feature which most sharply distinguishes it from both rationalism and empiricism, is the affirmation of an *a priori* element in sensibility.[15] This is the theme of the "metaphysical expositions" of the concepts of space and time. Here Kant argues for the *a priority* of both space and time, and consequently, their status as forms of sensibility, on the grounds that they are conditions of possible appearances rather than determinations dependent upon, or empirical representations derived from these appearances. This is accomplished by means of the demonstration of the inevitable circularity of any attempt to account for our conceptions of space and time in a purely empirical or psychological manner. Reduced to its simplest terms, Kant's main point is that we cannot hold with the empiricists that these conceptions are derived from our prior experience of externality and succession, because they are necessarily presupposed in any such experience. Thus, rather than abstractions from the concrete relations between things, space and time must be affirmed to have a logical or conceptual priority over these things, as they provide the framework in which alone we can experience these relations This priority is what Kant means by *a priority,* and it is also the basis for the ideality of space and time. This latter point is a direct consequence of the basic Kantian principle

---

[14] Cf. Graham Bird, *Kant's Theory of Knowledge* (London, 1962), p. 38.
[15] Hermann Cohen, *Kant's Theorie der Erfahrung,* 2nd rev. ed. (Berlin, 1885), p. 606.

which underlies the entire argument of the *Critique*: "We can know *a priori* of things only what we ourselves put into them" (BXVIII). As *a priori* space and time must have their source in the subjective constitution of the human mind. Thus, they only serve to determine the relations of appearances and not things in themselves.

Space and time, however, are not merely forms of sensibility or intuition, but they are also themselves pure intuitions. As such they can function as the source of the synthetic *a priori* propositions found in both pure and applied mathematics. This is the point of the "Transcendental Exposition" of space and time. Here Kant argues that if we view space and time as empirical concepts, abstracted from experience, then mathematics would be a merely empirical science, and as such, lacking in necessity. If, on the other hand, we view space and time as *a priori* concepts, either clear or confused, rather than intuitions, then mathematics becomes a merely analytical science and its application to nature rendered inexplicable. It is, therefore, only on the assumption that space and time are *a priori* forms of intuition and themselves pure intuitions that the possibility of mathematics and a mathematical science of nature can be explained.

It is here that we find the ultimate basis both for Kant's empirical realism and his critique of transcendental realism. As we have already seen, Kant defines empirical realism as the doctrine that we are as immediately aware of bodies in space as ourselves in time. Consequently, our judgments about such bodies are exempt from the sceptical difficulties imagined by the Cartesians. But these judgments are for Kant, as for Descartes, essentially those of the mathematical physicist. Thus, the justification of such a realism is equivalent to the justification of the possibility of a mathematical science of nature. This, however, requires the recognition of the *a priori* character of the forms of sensibility, and hence its distinction from the understanding. If this distinction be lost sight of, then bodies in space will inevitably be regarded as transcendentally real, i.e. things in themselves, with the result that such bodies will be held to be either un-knowable (sceptical idealism) or non-existent (dogmatic idealism). The recognition, however, of the *a priori* nature of the forms of sensibility, and the transcendental ideality of the objects of experience which it entails, not only provides the means for understanding the error of the Cartesian position, but also for justifying an empirical realism, and consequently, explaining the possibility of a mathematical science of nature.

The ideality which characterizes the objects of experience can be regarded as transcendental in a two-fold sense. First of all, it is arrived at by means of a critical reflection on the necessary conditions of our *a priori* knowledge rather than by a metaphysical reflection on the nature of being. In this regard it stands in sharp contrast with the demonstration of the impossibility of matter, which according to Kant constitutes the basic claim of "dogmatic idealism" (A377). Moreover, this difference in method also results in a fundamentally different conception of ideality. The basic characteristic of the empirical or dogmatic idealism which Kant attacks is the essentially private nature of the objects of awareness. These objects are ideal or subjective in the sense that they are private sense data, standing in temporal, but not spatial relations. This is why they are characterized as ideas or sensations. The claim that they exist in the mind is consequently of an empirical nature, and is supported by factual arguments such as the appeal to perceptual illusion and the famous example of the pain which is felt in the amputated limb.

In contradistinction to the Cartesian theory of ideas, the basic feature of Kant's transcendental idealism is its affirmation of the public or objective nature of the objects of "outer experience." These objects are bodies in space rather than Cartesian ideas or sensations. It is true that the bodies are appearances, and as such, "representations in us." Nevertheless, it is equally clear that Kantian appearances are not "in us" in the same sense as Cartesian ideas, or Berkeleian sensible things. The latter, as is befitting their private status, are properly located in the empirical or individual consciousness. As "transcendentally ideal," however, Kantian appearances are referred to what he calls in the *Critique*: "transcendental consciousness," and in the *Prolegomena*: "consciousness in general."

This transcendental consciousness, and its equivalent, transcendental apperception is not to be construed as either an individual or super-individual mind. Kant defines it quite simply as "the bare representation I" (A117 note) which constitutes the logical form of all knowledge. It is thus a logical principle, which much like a Platonic archetype, provides the form of unity to which every empirical, i.e. individual consciousness, must conform if it is to yield consciousness of a public, objective world. To say, therefore, with Kant that appearances are representations in the mind is not to make either a psychological or an ontological claim, but merely to point to the subjective sources of the *a priori* conditions to which every object of experience must conform. These subjective conditions (both sensible and intellectual) are not the ground of the being of objects of experience, but of their being known, and these objects of experience are called appearances because they can only be known in relation to these subjective conditions, and hence, not as they are in themselves. The claim is of a completely different order than Berkeley's contention that sensible things are "collections of ideas," understood in the Cartesian sense as contents of an individual consciousness. Both, it is true, were designed to overcome Cartesian scepticism, but while Berkeley does so by dismissing one of the members of the duality, viz. matter or *res extensa*, Kant does so by putting the whole problem in a radically new perspective.[16]

III

The fundamental difference between the idealisms of Berkeley and Kant can be seen in a more concrete fashion by means of a brief consideration of their respective treatments of the primary-secondary quality distinction. Both rejected this distinction in its traditional form, but their criticisms move in two radically divergent directions.

---

[16] *Ibid.*, p. 134.

Berkeley's criticisms of this distinction are well known. He quite correctly regarded it as one of the basic expressions of the materialism which he was attacking, and he discusses it at length in both the *Principles* and the *Dialogues.* Many of the objections which he raises against it are not particularly original, being taken largely from the sceptical literature, and especially from Bayle. These basically involve the claim that the arguments for the subjectivity of the secondary qualities, e.g., the relativity of our perception of color and sound, apply equally to the primary qualities. His central criticism, however, does seem to be original with him.[17] This takes the form of an application of the more general critique of the doctrine of representative perception to the distinction in question:

But it is evident from what we have already shown, that extension, figure and motion are only ideas existing in the mind, and that an idea can be like nothing but another idea, and that consequently neither they nor their archetypes can exist in an un-perceiving substance. Hence it is plain, that the very notion of what is called *matter* or *corporeal substance,* involves a contradiction in it. (*Principles* 9)

Thus, the privileged position which the mathematical physicists give to the spatial characteristics of body is denied. Primary and secondary qualities have precisely the same ontological status. Both are ideas in the mind whose *esse* is *percipi.* Moreover, since these qualities exhaust what we mean by a body or a sensible thing, such things can be defined as "collections of ideas," and as such, have no existence apart from a mind perceiving them. Hence, in repudiating the distinction between primary and secondary qualities, Berkeley is *eo ipso* repudiat-ing the notion of matter or corporeal substance as the alleged support of these qualities. Since all qualities have the same status which was formerly granted only to secondary qualities, the notion of matter becomes completely superfluous.

This leads inevitably to the repudiation of the mechanistic world view which is so intimately connected with this distinction. Since all the qualities of body are nothing but ideas or sensations, all are held to be "visibly inactive." This, Berkeley tells us, is because: "The very being of an idea implies passiveness or inertness in it" (*Principles* 25). Thus, not only is the conception of the interaction of mind and matter as the cause of our ideas rejected, but the whole notion of mechanical causality is banished from a nature which is composed solely of inert, inactive ideas.

Mechanistic causality is replaced by the activity of the divine will, and the rela-tion of cause and effect by the relation of sign and thing signified. The divine will imprints those ideas which constitute the system of nature upon the minds of finite spirits in an orderly and uniform manner, and the principles of this uniformity are the laws of nature. Hence, although one idea cannot, strictly speaking, be the cause of another, it can function as its sign; so that the appearance of the one will lead the mind to expect the advent of the other. Since the principles of this uniformity are dependent upon the divine will, they can be learned only by expe-

---

[17] Turbayne, *op. cit.,* p. 234.

rience. Nevertheless, such experience, Berkeley contends, "gives us a sort of fore-sight, which enables us to regulate our actions for the benefit of life" (Principles 31).

Berkeley's attitude towards Newtonian science must be understood in light of this essentially religious, and from Kant's point of view, dogmatic and mystical standpoint. Berkeley presents himself, both in the *Principles* and *De Motu*, with which as we have suggested, Kant was probably familiar, not as an enemy of science, but merely as a critic of its false metaphysical assumptions. These include the doctrine of matter and its infinite divisibility, and the conceptions of absolute space, time and motion. His claim is that by ridding science of these vacuous abstractions, he is not only disposing of excess baggage, but also avoiding the atheistic and sceptical implications of the Newtonian world view. In point of fact, however, Berkeley only grants a strictly pragmatic value to science. Its legitimate function is not to uncover causes, this being defined as the task of metaphysics, or "first philosophy," but merely to discover analogies and regularities, which, since they depend upon the will of God, have no inherent necessity, and thus, cannot be known *a priori*. Knowledge of these regularities are indeed necessary for the conduct of life. Nevertheless, their discovery, and the formation of "mathematical hypotheses" in terms of which they are described, should not be confused with genuine, i.e. philosophical insight into the true nature and cause of things. This viewpoint can already be found in the *Principles*, but it is much more explicit in *De Motu*, where after describing the nature and purpose of scientific explanation, Berkeley concludes:

Only by meditation and reasoning can truly active causes be rescued from the surrounding darkness and be to some extent known. To deal with them is the business of first philosophy or metaphysics. Allot to each science its own province; assign its bounds; accurately distinguish the principles and objects belonging to each. Thus it will be possible to treat them with greater ease and clarity. (72)

Kant likewise rejected the primary-secondary quality distinction in the form in which it is found in thinkers such as Descartes and Newton. He did so because he saw it as a reflection of that transcendental realism which is based upon a failure to distinguish between empirical and transcendental externality, and which leads inevitably to empirical idealism and scepticism. Thus, Kant like Berkeley rejects the Newtonian metaphysical scheme wherein absolute space and time are conceived as two transcendentally real, infinite containers, within which bodies, composed of primary qualities, move and are located, while the sensible qualities, motion and place of the objects of our daily experience are regarded as subjective or "apparent." Unlike Berkeley, however, Kant re-interprets rather than repudiates this distinction and the mechanistic conception of nature with which it is entwined.

Kant's reinterpretation of this distinction is a direct consequence of his more basic distinction between transcendental and empirical subjectivity. This is not apparent in the brief discussion in the *Prolegomena* (289-290), where Kant does indeed sound very much like Berkeley. It is, however, quite clear in the *Critique* and especially in the central discussion at the end of the treatment of space

(A28-30-B44-45). Here Kant explicitly distinguishes between the subjectivity of space, and *a fortiori* of the primary or spatial qualities of objects, and the subjectivity of the secondary qualities. The basis for this distinction lies in the fact that "with the sole exception of space there is no subjective representation, referring to something outer, which could be entitled objective."

This point is developed somewhat differently in the two editions. In the first version Kant distinguishes between spatial and secondary qualities on the grounds that in contradistinction to the latter, which do not belong to the object, even regarded as appearance, but to the "special constitution of sense in the subject," space and its determinations, "as a condition of outer objects, necessarily belongs to their appearance or intuition." As in the traditional view, spatial characteristics are regarded as inseparable from body, while the so-called secondary qualities are "connected with the appearances only as effects accidentally added by the particular constitution of the sense organs." This is essentially the Cartesian, Lockean, Newtonian doctrine, now viewed as holding within the phenomenal realm. Understood in this sense, secondary qualities are empirically subjective, while primary qualities are empirically real and defining characteristics of appearances.[18] Finally, Kant adds, almost as an afterthought, that although no one can have *a priori* representations of colors and tastes, since they are merely sensations in the mind, "all kinds and determinations of space can and must be represented *a priori*, if concepts of figures and of their relations are to arise" (A30).

In the second edition it is precisely the *a priori* character of space, and its function as the source of synthetic *a priori* knowledge which bears the brunt of the argument. There is, Kant here claims, no other subjective representation from which we can derive *a priori* synthetic propositions as we can from intuition in space (B44). Hence, although other representations are indeed subjective, they "strictly speaking" have no ideality. Rather than being sources of *a priori* knowledge, they merely belong to the subjective constitution of our manner of sensibility. As "mere sensations" or private data of the individual consciousness, they do not have any cognitive function, i.e. they do not serve to determine an object.

This provides us with a clear expression of the transcendental character of Kant's idealism. All representations are subjective, or "in the mind," but only those which function as sources of *a priori* knowledge are deemed "ideal." Ideality is here used in an essentially Leibnizian sense to refer to a level of reality which is less than the noumenal or monadological, but more than merely private or empirically subjective. Furthermore, the distinction between empirical and transcendental subjectivity or ideality is formulated in terms of the presence or absence of a cognitive function. Secondary qualities thus keep their traditional status as sensations in the mind which do not represent anything in *rerum natura*. The primary or spatial qualities, on the other hand, are objective in that they are, as

---

[18] Cf. Erich Adickes, *Kant's Lehre von der Doppelten Affektion unseres Ich als Schlüssel zu seiner Erkenntnistheorie* (Tübinben, 1929), esp. pp. 47-59 where Adickes discusses the development of this doctrine in the *Opus Postumum*. This is shown to be clearly connected with his dynamic theory of matter, and his conception of the object qua composed of primary qualities as "*Erscheinung an sich.*"

science teaches, the essential properties of body or matter. To be sure, space together with its determinations are ideal, but this ideality must be understood in the transcendental sense, and so regarded

is a critical reminder that nothing intuited in space is a thing in itself, that space is not a form inhering in things in themselves as their intrinsic property, that objects in themselves are quite unknown to us, and that what we call outer objects are nothing but mere representations of our sensibility, the form of which is space. The true correlate of sensibility, the thing in itself, is not known, and cannot be known, through these representations; and in experience no question is ever asked in regard to it. (A30-B45)

Now although it may seem somewhat paradoxical, it is clear that when viewed from Kant's transcendental standpoint, Berkeley's idealism can be regarded as an offshoot of transcendental realism.[19] Certainly in his critique of materialism Berkeley did not arrive at the Kantian conception of transcendental subjectivity. All of the ideas or sensations which together constitute the sensible world are, for Berkeley, in the mind in precisely the same sense as the ideas of secondary qualities are for the Cartesians. This, as we have seen, was the whole point of his critique of the primary-secondary quality distinction. Unlike Kant, Berkeley never really breaks with the Cartesian theory of ideas. He assumes from the beginning that the immediate objects of consciousness are ideas, and in rejecting the other half of the Cartesian dualism proceeds to identify these ideas with "real things." Such a move, however, will simply not work. Cartesian ideas are in their very nature private objects of the individual consciousness. As such their significance is determined by their contrast to "real things" or *rerum natura*. This was the point of Kant's reflection that empirical idealism is merely the reverse side of a transcendental realism. Thus, to identify these ideas with "real things" is indeed to commit oneself to a radical subjectivism, which leads ultimately to the denial of the distinction between truth and illusion.

Berkeley, of course, did not see this, and he did not see it because he was still a captive of the Cartesian principles which he attacked. His polemic with "materialism" is carried on from beginning to end within the old categories: *rerum natura* must be either transcendentally real (a distinct substance or collection thereof) or empirically ideal (a collection of ideas in individual consciousness). He saw quite clearly the difficulties of the former view, and in this regard he may be said to have anticipated Kant. Envisioning, however, no third alternative, he had no choice but to opt for the latter view despite its even greater absurdities. The result is a position which Kant defined as dogmatic idealism. Since it is a development of the Cartesian position, Kant's refutation of the former applies *a fortiori* to the

---

[19] Although Kant never explicitly accuses Berkeley of identifying sensible things with things in themselves, it is noteworthy that in one place (*Critique of Practical Reason*, 53) he accuses Hume, who is certainly generally regarded as a phenomenalist, of taking the objects of experience as things in themselves, and suggests that this is the reason why he is unable to explain the possibility of *a priori* knowledge. For a discussion of this passage see Lewis White Beck, *A Commentary on Kant's Critique of Practical Reason* (Chicago: The University of Chicago Press, 1966), pp. 181-182.

latter, and this in general seems to have been the way in which Kant regarded the matter. Nevertheless, in response to certain criticisms of his own position he was forced to deal specifically with Berkeley, and it is to these specific criticisms that we now turn.

IV

The earliest references to Berkeley are to be found in the *Prolegomena*. The first are in the *Anmerkungen* to § 13, wherein Kant defines his transcendental "or better critical idealism" in relation to other forms of idealism, including Berkeley's. *Anmerkung I* contains a reiteration of the familiar claim that the doctrine of the transcendental ideality of space is the only possible basis for the justification of the objective validity of geometry. In *Anmerkung II* Kant proceeds to distinguish his position from idealism on the grounds that real idealism asserts "that there are none but thinking beings," and consequently denies the existence of things in themselves external to the thinking subject. In opposition to this Kant declares:

I, on the contrary, say that things as objects of our senses existing outside us are given, but we know nothing of what they may be in themselves, knowing only their appearances, that is, the representations which they cause in us by affecting our senses. Consequently I grant by all means that there are bodies without us, that is, things which, though quite unknown to us as to what they are in themselves, we yet know by the representations which their influence on our sensibility procures us. These representations we call "bodies," a term signifying merely the appearance of the being which is unknown to us, but not therefore less actual. Can this be termed idealism? It is the very contrary. (288-289)

In *Anmerkung III* this view is developed specifically in reference to the "visionary idealism of Berkeley" which is alleged to "convert actual things [*wirkliche Sachen*] (not appearances) into mere representations." In regard to this Kant proclaims:

My idealism concerns not the existence of things (the doubting of which, however, constitutes idealism in the ordinary sense), since it never came into my head to doubt it, but it concerns the sensuous representation of things to which space and time especially belong. (293)

Moreover, we find Kant making essentially the same point in a letter to Beck of December 4, 1792. The latter, who did not really know what to make of the thing in itself, had written to Kant on November 10th, telling about the contentions of Eberhard and Garve that Kant's idealism was identical to Berkeley's. Beck naturally rejected this, but his concern was to separate the question of Kant's relation to Berkeley from any discussion of the thing in itself. "Even if we assume that the *Critique* should not even have mentioned the distinction between things-in-themselves, and appearances," he writes, "we would still have to recall that one must pay attention to the conditions under which something is an object." These objects, he continues, are appearances, and "it is the reality of just these objects that Berkeley denies and the *Critique* defends.[20] Thus, Beck sees the weakness of the Berkeleian position to lie in its denial of the empirically real objects of experience, rather than the thing in itself, and this is further seen to be a result of the failure to recognize the *a priori* element in experience.

In his response however, Kant essentially re-affirms the claim which he had previously made in the *Prolegomena*:

Messrs. Eberhards' and Garves' opinion that Berkeley's idealism is the same as that of the critical philosophy (which I would better call the principle of the ideality of space and time) does not deserve the slightest attention. For I speak of ideality in reference to the *form of representations*: but they interpret this to mean ideality with respect to the *matter*, that is, the ideality of the *object*, and its very existence.[21]

This appeal to the existence of things in themselves in the characterization of his idealism is generally regarded as an evasion by Kant's critics. Thus Turbayne asserts quite flatly: "This recourse is completely out of line with the other 'refutations,' and indeed with the critical philosophy."[22] Such a reading, however, not only fails to notice the continuity of Kant's thought on this point, but it also reveals a failure to comprehend the critical meaning of the thing in itself as the "true correlate of sensibility." Kantian appearances, like Cartesian ideas, require a correlate. Their status is only adequately defined in contrast to something which is transcendentally real, or "real *per se*." Unlike Cartesian ideas, however, they are not empirically ideal, i.e. they are not the private data of an individual consciousness. This is because the thing in itself, unlike the Cartesian *res extensa*, is not another sort of entity, ontologically distinct from the appearances in the mind. Rather it is one and the same thing regarded in a different manner, i.e. as existing independently of the subjective forms of sensibility through which it is given to the human mind. It is because sensibility has *a priori* forms (space and time), in terms of which the "matter of experience" is necessarily given to the mind, that the objects of experience are deemed phenomenal or ideal. But this whole account is only intelligible if one assumes a thing in itself which is received by the mind under these subjective conditions. To deny the existence of the thing in itself is thus to deny the Kantian conception of sensibility, and hence of appearance. It is indeed to be guilty of that confusion of appearances and things in themselves which is characteristic of transcendental realism. Thus, we can conclude that in a sense Beck is right. Kant's real quarrel with idealism concerns the reality of bodies in space, i.e. appearances. Nevertheless, for Kant, the denial of the thing in itself is *eo ipso* a denial of the reality of such bodies because it entails a denial

---

[20] *Kant's Philosophical Correspondence 1759-1799*, ed. and trans., Arnulf Zweig (Chicago, 1967), 195.
[21] *Ibid.*, p. 198.
[22] Turbayne, *op. cit.*, p. 238.

of the appearance-thing in itself distinction, in light of which alone the objectivity or reality of such bodies can be demonstrated.

The second reference to Berkeley in the *Prolegomena* is in the portion of the appendix which is specifically directed against the Garve-Feder review. Kant's purpose is once again to distinguish his idealism from Berkeley's, and it is in this connection that he writes:

The dictum of all genuine idealists, from the Eleatic school to Bishop Berkeley, is contained in this formula: "All knowledge through the senses and experience is nothing but sheer illusion, and only in the ideas of the pure understanding and reason is there truth."

The principle that throughout dominates and determines my idealism, is on the contrary: "All knowledge of things merely from pure understanding or pure reason is nothing but sheer illusion, and only in experience is there truth." (324)

It is perhaps this passage more than any other which has given rise to the charge that Kant's criticisms of Berkeley were the product of ignorance. How, after all, can one otherwise explain the inclusion of this empiricist and critic of abstraction in the Eleatic tradition which denies the evidence of the senses? This is especially incomprehensible in light of Berkeley's explicit and frequent affirmation of the veracity of sense experience.

One possible explanation is that Kant's characterization of Berkeley's position refers not to the *Principles* and *Dialogues,* but to the *Siris,* which can be justly described in these terms. This has been suggested by Cassirer, who points out that there was a German translation of the first half of the work (dealing with the medicinal value of tar water) published in 1745, and that a French translation of the whole work appeared in the same year.[23] However, although serious doubts can be raised against the claim that Kant was actually familiar with the French translation, and thus with the specifically philosophical portion of the *Siris,*[24] this assumption is not really necessary to explain the above passage. This can be understood on the assumption that Kant was acquainted with the much more accessible *De Motu,* wherein the Platonizing tendencies which became explicit in the *Siris,* are already clearly present, especially when viewed from Kant's critical standpoint. Here the decisive factor is the essentially pragmatic value which Berkeley gives to science, and hence to sense experience, and which he contrasts with the value of metaphysics or first philosophy. It would indeed be quite natural for Kant to view this claim as a variation on Malebranche's thesis that "the senses were not given us for knowledge of things as they are in their own nature, but only for the preservation of our own body."[25]

One could argue that this way of viewing the matter is not an accurate assessment of Berkeley's intent. Nevertheless, the important point is that it is perfectly

---

[23] Ernst Cassirer, *Das Erkenntnisproblem in der Philosophie und Wissenschaft der neuern Zeit* (Berlin, 1911), II, 327.
[24] This is argued by Stabler, *op. cit.,* pp. 56-58.
[25] Malebranche, *De la Recherche de la Vérité,* Book I, Chapter V.

consistent with Kant's conception of sensibility as a source of knowledge with *a priori* forms. The affirmation of the reality of sense experience is, for Kant, equivalent to the affirmation of the ideality of space and time as *a priori* forms or conditions of experience. If this be denied, then understanding or reason becomes the sole source of truth, and this leads either to the Leibnizian conception of sense experience as a confused anticipation of reason, or to the Cartesian-Malebranchian (and to Kant's mind Berkeleian) view of it as of merely pragmatic significance.

Kant makes this quite clear in his subsequent explanation of what he knew to be a paradoxical sounding claim. He begins by acknowledging a partial agreement with the "above idealists." This agreement concerns the status of space and time "together with all they contain" as appearances rather than things in themselves. However, Kant continues:

But these, and among them more particularly Berkeley, regarded space as a mere empirical representation that, like the appearances it contains, is, together with its determinations, known to us only by means of experience or perception. I, on the contrary, prove in the first place that space (and also time, which Berkeley did not consider) and all its *a priori* determinations can be known by us, because, no less than time, it inheres in us as a pure form of our sensibility before all perception or experience and makes all intuition of the forms, and therefore all appearances, possible. It follows from this that, as truth rests on universal and necessary laws as its criteria, experience, according to Berkeley, can have no criteria of truth because its phenomena (according to him) have nothing *a priori* at their foundation, whence it follows that experience is nothing but sheer illusion; whereas with us, space and time (in conjunction with the pure concept of the understanding) prescribe their law to all possible experience *a priori* and, at the same time, afford the certain criterion for distinguishing truth from illusion therein. (374-375)

The key point here is the contention that space is for Berkeley "a mere empirical representation." This not only suggests a firsthand knowledge of Berkeley's writings, but also serves to underline the crucial Kantian distinction between empirical and transcendental ideality. It thus shows why Kant identified Berkeley's doctrine with the former and hence with illusionism. We have already seen that, as a Newtonian, Kant regards spatiality as a defining characteristic of body. He justifies this on the idealistic grounds that space is an *a priori* form of sensibility rather than a self-subsistent, infinite container, and he thus claims that it is both empirically real and transcendentally ideal. If, however, space be viewed with Berkeley as an empirical representation, the genesis of which is explained by a psychological analysis, then its role as a form or condition of experience is denied. It becomes simply another item of consciousness, dependent upon the pre-given sensations from which it is abstracted. But if this be the case then, according to Kant, we cannot explain the possibility of our experience of a public objective world, not to mention a mathematical science of such a world, and, Kant reasons: "whence it follows that experience is nothing but illusion." This, to be sure, is not Berkeley's thesis. He does not hold that experience is illusion or illusory; quite the contrary. Kant, however does not claim that this is Berkeley's view. What he does claim, is that this is a necessary consequence of Berkeley's view, and this, we can see, is because his merely empirical conception of space results in a collapse of the distinction between transcendental and empirical ideality.[26]

Finally, in reference to the discussion of Berkeley in the *Prolegomena*, a passage is worthy of note which although not found in the published version, was appended to an earlier and substantially identical draft of the above argument:

> Berkeley found nothing constant, and so could find nothing which the understanding conceives according to *a priori* principles. He therefore had to look for another intuition, namely the mystical one of God's ideas, which required a two-fold understanding, one which connected appearances in experience, and another which knew things in themselves. I need only one sensibility and one understanding.[27]

This passage, which seems to have been completely ignored by all of the commentators on Kant's relation to Berkeley, is important not only because it provides us with some additional insight into the grounds for Kant's characterization of Berkeley's idealism as mystical, but more basically because the reference to the distinction between the divine and human mind is perhaps the strongest philological indication which we have that Kant was indeed familiar with Berkeley's *Dialogues* in which the notion of the archetypal divine intellect plays such a large role. This is one crucial aspect of Berkeley's thought which appears to have been completely ignored by those secondhand accounts which are alleged to have been the sole source of Kant's knowledge of Berkeley's philosophy. In fact, Eugen Stabler, who has undertaken what is by far the most detailed discussion of this historical question, justifies his claim that Kant was unfamiliar with the Eschenbach translation largely on the grounds that his discussion completely ignores this distinction.[28] To be sure, the translation of Berkeley's distinction into a Kantian framework can be viewed as a distortion of Berkeley's intent, but it nevertheless remains the case that Kant was aware of this distinction, and thus greatly increases the probability that Kant had a firsthand knowledge of the *Dialogues*.

The two criticisms of Berkeley added in the second edition of the *Critique* are developments of the arguments already sketched in the *Prolegomena*. The first is to be found in an addition to the *Aesthetic*, wherein Kant distinguishes between *Erscheinung* and mere *Schein*. The main point is the familiar claim that far from confusing appearance and illusion, the doctrine of transcendental ideality is the only basis for distinguishing between the two. This is because it is the only basis for establishing the empirical reality of the objects of experience. Thus, in discussing the transcendental ideality of space and time, Kant writes:

---

[26] The same argument naturally applies, *mutatis mutandis* to time. It is noteworthy, however, that Kant refers to the fact that Berkeley does not dicuss time. This suggests that his knowledge of Berkeley was limited to the *Dialogues* and *De Motu*, cf. Turbayne, *op. cit.*, p. 242.

[27] *Kant's Gesammelte Schriften*, ed. Deutsche Akademie der Wissenschaften zu Berlin, XXIII (1955), 58.

[28] Stabler, *op. cit.*

It is only if we ascribe *objective reality* to these forms of representation, that it becomes impossible for us to prevent everything being thereby transformed into mere *illusion*. For if we regard space and time as properties which, if they are to be possible at all, must be found in things in themselves, and if we reflect on the absurdities in which we are then involved, in that two infinite things, which are not substances, nor anything actually inhering in substances, must yet have existence, nay, must be the necessary condition of the existence of all things, and moreover must continue to exist, even although all existing things be removed,—we cannot blame the good Berkeley for degrading bodies to mere illusion. (B70)

The second reference to Berkeley is contained in the "Refutation of Idealism." As in the first edition, Kant's main concern is with Descartes, but he does add a brief discussion of Berkeley's "dogmatic idealism." Here idealism, now called "material idealism," is defined as the theory "which declares the existence of objects in space outside us either to be merely doubtful and undemonstrable or to be false and impossible." The former is held to be the problematic idealism of Descartes, and the latter the "dogmatic idealism of Berkeley." In reference to Berkeley, Kant writes:

He maintains that space, with all the things of which it is the inseparable condition, is something which is in itself impossible; and he therefore regards the things in space as merely imaginary entities. Dogmatic idealism is unavoidable, if space be interpreted as a property that must belong to things in themselves. For in that case space, and everything to which it serves as condition, is a non-entity. The ground on which this idealism rests has already been undermined by us in the Transcendental Aesthetic. (B274)

Like the criticisms in the *Prolegomena*, these passages are intended to show the consequences of Berkeley's views and not to describe them. Moreover, here, as in the second criticism in the *Prolegomena*, we see that Kant locates the primary source of Berkeley's difficulty in his conception of space. This criticism presupposes the doctrine which Kant shares with the Newtonians, viz. space is a condition of bodies or the objects of outer experience. Thus, to deny the objective reality of space is *eo ipso* to deny the empirical reality of body, and this is what Kant means by "degrading bodies to mere illusion." This is, once again, the inevitable result of the confusion of transcendental with empirical ideality. Berkeley, of course, does not argue in precisely the way that Kant suggests. He does not assert that since space and time are unreal, bodies are merely imaginary. He does, however, criticize the Newtonian conception of absolute space and time in the *Principles*, and in *De Motu* (53) he claims that Newtonian absolute space is a "mere nothing." Thus, Kant is simply pointing to the logical connection between Berkeley's critique of the doctrine of absolute space and his conception of sensible things as empirically ideal "collections of ideas."

In so doing he is also granting a sort of historical justification to Berkeley's position as the inevitable outcome of transcendental realism. Berkeley is credited with anticipating the critical philosophy in seeing the absurdities to which the Newtonian conception of space and time as infinite non-entities leads. He is also judged correct in holding that such non-entities cannot be regarded as objectively real, and hence as the condition of bodies. Thus, Kant is in effect saying that given the assumption with which Berkeley started, viz. that if space and time are viewed as conditions of objects of experience, they must have the kind of reality which Newton ascribes to them, that Berkeley is perfectly correct in rejecting such non-entities, and consequently, in concluding that the objects of experience are merely collections of ideas which have no existence apart from a mind perceiving them. Berkeley's problem, however, as seen from Kant's perspective, is that his whole polemic with "materialism," of which the Newtonian conception of absolute space is the supreme expression, is carried on within the old transcendentally real-empirically ideal framework which he was trying to criticize. Thus, space, time and the whole of *rerum natura* must be either "transcendentally real" (a distinct substance or collection thereof) or empirically ideal (a collection of ideas in an individual mind). He saw quite clearly the absurdities in the former view, and in this regard he may be legitimately said to have anticipated Kant. In rejecting the former, however, he fell into the even greater absurdity of identifying *rerum natura* with the latter, or what is perhaps even worse from Kant's standpoint, with the contents of the divine mind. This is the inevitable result of his failure to consider a third alternative, that which is offered by the critical philosophy, wherein space, time and all things in them are held to be transcendentally rather than empirically ideal.

Thus construed, Kant's criticisms of Berkeley not only hang together in a fairly coherent manner, but also make a good deal more sense than is generally assumed. Their condescending tone ("the good Berkeley") and emotionally charged language, as well as some of the specific criticisms are indeed reminiscent of the kind of standard and uncomprehending criticisms of Berkeley which are found in the philosophic literature of the eighteenth century. A good deal of this can be explained in terms of the polemical context in which Kant offered these criticisms, a context in which Berkeley's position was assumed to be absurd, and in which he was therefore forced to emphasize the differences in their philosophies as strongly as possible. Under different circumstances it is entirely possible that Kant might have offered a much more conciliatory critique, although it must be continually kept in mind that Kant tended to view all philosophers in light of his own categories and concerns. Nevertheless, these considerations should not prevent us from realizing that Kant's idealism is fundamentally different from Berkeley's; that his criticisms of Berkeley point to these differences and suggest a firsthand acquaintance with his thought; and above all that a critical examination of a philosophy from one's own perspective is quite a different thing from a deliberate falsification of that philosophy.

University of Florida

On Kant's Analysis of Berkeley

by Gale D. Justin, Chicago

Kant explicitly discusses Berkeley in two passages of the second edition of the *Critique*[1]. Most commentators have taken the view that Kant's treatment there either misrepresents or is irrelevant to Berkeley[2]. This in turn has made it difficult to evaluate Kant's disclaimer that his enterprise resists association with Berkeley. In this paper I argue that Kant provides a fair, even incisive analysis of Berkeley's doctrine. The success of this account should remove a traditionally persistent obstacle to clarification of Kant's relation to Berkeley[3].

[1] References will be to Immanuel Kant, *Critique of Pure Reason*, tr. Norman Kemp Smith (London 1929).

[2] See, for example, H. J. Paton, *Kant's Metaphysics of Experience*, II (London 1936), 376—377; Norman Kemp Smith, *A Commentary to Kant's Critique of Pure Reason* (London 1923), pp. 155—161; T. D. Weldon, *Introduction to Kant's Critique of Pure Reason* (Oxford 1945), pp. 8—10; Colin M. Turbayne, *Kant's Relation to Berkeley*, in: Kant Studies Today, ed. Lewis White Beck (La Salle, Ill., 1969), pp. 88—116; originally published in Philosophical Quarterly, 5 (1955), under the title *Kant's Refutation of Dogmatic Idealism*; and, to a lesser extent, Margaret D. Wilson, *Kant and the Dogmatic Idealism of Berkeley*, Journal of the History of Philosophy, IX (1971), 459—475.

[3] The theory that Kant misrepresents Berkeley figures centrally in Colin M. Turbayne's influential but, I believe, ultimately unsatisfactory interpretation of Kant's relation to Berkeley. Turbayne asserts not merely doctrinal kinship but also Kant's indebtedness to Berkeley. Indeed, Kant's apparent misinterpretations (in B 70—71 and B 274) are construed as misrepresentations designed to conceal the debt. Stress is placed on the "Fourth Paralogism" where Kant argues against transcendental realism in a fashion reminiscent of Berkeley's arguments against Lockeian materialism. Impressed by the apparent parallel (here and elsewhere), Turbayne claims that Kant is in fact a practitioner of Berkeley's doctrine. Aside from the possibility that Kant may not have even had Berkeley in mind when writing the "Fourth Paralogism" (see footnote immediately below), there is the fact that sceptical arguments against materialism were anything but novel (Locke, for instance, was aware he had to meet them). More important, however, is that the allegation of purposive misrepresentation turns, I think, on a wrong analysis of B 70—71 and B 274. Turbayne's view is that these passages attribute to Kant the "ultimate logical consequence" of transcendental realism, a view Kant knew Berkeley to reject. Hence, the thesis of misrepresentation. First, there is a problem with the logic of this interpretation for, as is well known, transcendental realism leads to scepticism; but dogmatic idealism (*denial* of spatial objects) simply does not *follow* from scepticism (*doubt* of spatial objects). Dogmatic idealism ensues only if one wants to embrace transcendental realism and simultaneously *avoid* scepticism. Second, I hope to show that Kant's objection to Berkeley turns rather on quite far reaching difficulties in the latter's views on space. And if Kant's analysis in B 70—71 and B 274 proves both more sophisticated and more accurate than Turbayne allows, then his general interpretation calls for some reappraisal. (There will be no space to provide that here.)

The passages in question are B 274 in the "Refutation of Idealism":

> He [Berkeley] maintains that space, with all the things of which it is the inseparable condition, is something which is in itself impossible; and he therefore regards the things in space as merely imaginary entities. Dogmatic idealism is unavoidable, if space be interpreted as a property that must belong to things in themselves. For in that case space, and everything to which it serves as condition, is a non-entity.

and B 70—71[4]:

> If we regard space and time as properties which, if they are to be possible at all, must be found in things in themselves, and if we reflect on the absurdities in which we are then involved, ... we cannot blame the good Berkeley for degrading bodies to mere illusion.

These passages suggest that for Kant the crucial features of Berkeley's doctrine are affirmation of the thesis ("TR") that space, if possible, must be a property of things in themselves and denial of the thesis ("TS") that space is a property of things in themselves. For from TR and the falsity of TS follows the impossibility of space and, thus, of objects in space. Hence, Berkeley is forced to dogmatic idealism, scouting objects in space as "mere illusion" and "imaginary entities".

The brevity of Kant's account leaves much unexplained as well as the impression that it applies loosely at best to Berkeley's stated doctrine. Indeed, a first glance at the salient features of Berkeley's philosophy shows little, if any connection with denial of TS and commentators have accordingly dismissed our passages as misrepresentation. It will be prudent, however, to delay agreement on the point, heeding Kant's own dictum that "It is by no means unusual ... to find that we understand him [another philosopher] better than he has understood himself"[5]. In this spirit we should look to Kant's concern with the logic rather than the letter of Berkeley's position. And on this score I hope to show that he emerges quite favorably.

To begin with, Kant is maintaining the incoherence of the *objective* reality of space (whether subsistent or inherent) and, at the same time, affirming Berkeley's acumen in rejecting such a view (TS). Moreover, by supplementing B 70—71 with Kant's commentary on transcendental realism (in the "Fourth Paralogism") TS is further faulted on the grounds that, *were* it coherent, the doctrine incorporating it is nonetheless hopelessly sceptical. And Kant attributes this insight to Berkeley as well.

TS is incoherent because it precludes saying what sort of thing space is. The inherence view, that space is a property of objects, founders on the requirement

---

[4] There is a first edition reference (A 377) to dogmatic idealism, the doctrine explicitly attributed to Berkeley in the second edition's "Refutation of Idealism" (B 274). However, George W. Miller argues (*Kant's First Edition Refutation of Dogmatic Idealism*, Kant-Studien, 62 (1971), pp. 298—318) that A 377 is aimed at Leibniz. If so, this serves our purpose insofar as our interpretation is restricted to just those second edition passages explicitly mentioning Berkeley plus a similar passage from the *Prolegomena*.

[5] *Critique*, A 314/B 370.

that space "continue to exist, even although all existing things be removed"[6]. For how can a property of objects remain, failing the objects? On the other hand, the subsistence view, that space is a thing in its own right, fares no better. For space is held to exist only in order to contain all *things*. Hence, space both is a thing (namely, space) and is not a thing insofar as it is not something in space. Thus, both interpretations of TS harbor incoherencies and the thesis itself must be rejected.

Berkeley's rejection of the objective reality of space is unambiguously stated in *De Motu* which argues specifically against the Newtonian concept of absolute space on the grounds that we are able neither to experience nor to form a coherent conception of such space[7]. Extension is its only conceivable positive feature which, says Berkeley, implies that absolute space can be measured, divided, touched, etc. But as it lacks these features, so must absolute space lack extension. Hence, the notion itself is meaningless, for extension was supposed its defining criterion. And *a fortiori* the assertion of its existence is meaningless. Kant is clearly aware of Berkeley's accord on this point, for B 71 states that Berkeley is *not to be blamed* for rejecting TS. (Although Kant actually says that Berkeley is not to be blamed for degrading objects to mere illusion, since this is a consequence of rejecting the objective reality of space we may assume him cleared on the former count as well.) In this respect at least, then, Kant surely has Berkeley's doctrine correct.

Besides the objective reality of space Kant also understands Berkeley to reject the assumption that objects exist independently of the senses in that they are not immediately perceivable but must be inferred (to exist) from representations. This amounts to the traditional dualistic assumption. Kant treats both as aspects of the doctrine he entitles "transcendental realism".

While B 70—71 does not state Berkeley's rejection of both TS and the dualistic assumption, Kant's attribution elsewhere[8] to Berkeley of a non-dualist position and his insistence on distinguishing between dogmatic and problematic idealism show awareness of Berkeley's joint rejection. The contention that Kant took Berkeley to reject dualism outright rather than merely to espouse a qualified form of it is enhanced by the similarity between Kant's criticism of dualism and Berkeley's objection to "Lockeian" materialism. Kant's main complaint is that limiting perception to representations of objects renders the veracity of perception systematically uncertain:

If we regard outer appearances as representations produced in us by their objects, and if these objects be things existing in themselves outside us, it is indeed impossible to see

---

[6] *Critique*, B. 71.
[7] George Berkeley, *De Motu sive De Motus Principio & Natura, et de Causa Commicationis Motuum*, in *The Works of George Berkeley*, ed. A. A. Luce and T. E. Jessop, IV (London 1951) sec. 53, p. 45.
[8] *Critique*, B 274.

how we can come to know the existence of the objects otherwise than by inference from the effect to the cause; and this being so, it must always remain doubtful whether the cause in question be in us or outside us[9].

Berkeley offers a similar criticism of "Lockeian" materialism which also incorporates the dualistic assumption[10].

This much goes smoothly and reflects considerable grasp of Berkeley's doctrine. On the other hand, certain of Kant's remarks seem not to fit this result. In particular, what are we to make of Kant's assertion that Berkeley degrades "bodies to mere illusion"[11] or his charge that for Berkeley objects in space are "merely imaginary entities"[12].

At first sight these are puzzling remarks, since for Berkeley we perceive real and not imaginary items. But it is also true that Berkeley gives rather different significance to the phrase "real thing". For Berkeley real things are minds and ideas in them. His denial of the existence (reality) of non-mental substances in space is aptly reflected in the following remark:

> It is indeed an opinion strangely prevailing amongst men, that houses, mountains, rivers, and in a word all sensible objects have an existence natural or real, distinct from their being perceived by the understanding. But with how great an assurance and acquiesence soever this principle may be entertained in the world; yet whoever shall find in his heart to call it in question, may, if I mistake not, perceive it to involve a manifest contradiction. For what are the forementioned objects but the things we perceive by sense, and what do we perceive besides our own ideas or sensations; and is it not plainly repugnant that any one of these or any combination of them should exist unperceived[13].

Berkeley is here objecting to the *independent* existence of objects in space. Holding both that sensible objects are perceived and that whatever is perceived is an idea, he concludes that sensible objects are ideas. There is, then, a contradiction in saying that sensible objects exist unperceived, since ideas just are the (internal) objects of perception. The argument could be halted by faulting the second premise, that we perceive only ideas, for Berkeley's conclusion requires identification of sensible objects and ideas. On the other hand, Kant's objection to Berkeley does not turn on this identification. Indeed, Kant evidently thought it unworthy of refutation, since he groups Berkeley's "visionary idealism" (that which "turns

---

[9] *Critique,* A 372.
[10] George Berkeley, *A Treatise Concerning the Principles of Human Knowledge,* in *The Works,* II (London 1949), sec. 86, p. 78: "So long as men thought that real things subsisted without the mind, and that their knowledge was only so far forth *real* as it was conformable to *real things,* it follows, they could not be certain that they had any real knowledge at all. For how can it be known, that the things which are perceived, are conformable to those which are not perceived, or exist without the mind?" Cf. *Principles,* secs. 18, 87, 101.
[11] *Critique,* B 71.
[12] *Critique,* B 274.
[13] *Principles,* sec. 4, p. 42.

real things ... into mere representations") with those doctrines labeled "chimeras of the brain"[14]. In any case, Kant shows little interest in the identification.

Instead, B 70—71 and B 274 emphasize that Berkeley makes space an impossible concept by assuming TR and is thereby compelled to deny the existence of spatial objects (which for Berkeley would have to be things in themselves). It is still unclear exactly how denial of objects "follows from" denial of objectively real space. Kant clearly thinks the two are connected:

> If space be interpreted as a property that must belong to things in themselves ... [then] space and everything to which it serves as condition, is a non-entity[15].

There are at least two interpretations of this remark. First, it may mean that the container view of space is incoherent and, hence, implies denial of whatever the container contains (namely, objects). Vaihinger favors this interpretation. He takes both this passage and B 70—71 to argue the emptiness of the concept of absolute space because it lacks a coherent object[16]. And the rejection of absolute space entails rejection of objects existing in space, since the *raison d'être of* the former is containment of the latter.

An obvious difficulty with this account is that it applies, if at all, only to the subsistence view of objectively real space. Yet both B 70—71 and B 274 are concerned *generally* with the objective reality of space. In B 274 illusionism or denial of objects is unavoidable if "space be interpreted as a property that must belong to things in themselves". Similarly, B 70 says "it becomes impossible for us to prevent everything being ... transformed into mere *illusion* ... if we regard space and time as properties which, if they are to be possible at all, must be found in things in themselves". Now space can be interpreted as a property or characteristic of things in themselves either as something subsistent (existing in its own right) or as something inherent in things in themselves[17]. Hence, the first interpretation is inadequate, since it covers only the subsistence view of space while the argument is clearly meant to cover the inherence view as well.

Moreover, the argument of B 70—71 and B 274 is not obviously compelling against just the subsistence view of space. Failing some account of the connection between objects and absolute space, the argument does not adequately show rejection of the former to follow rejection of the latter. Certainly, Vaihinger's interpretation is no help on this score. For rejection of a *container* (whether space or otherwise) is of itself no warrant for rejection of the items allegedly contained. In view of these difficulties prudence recommends seeking an alternative.

[14] Immanuel Kant, *Prolegomena to Any Future Metaphysics*, tr. Peter G. Lucas (Manchester 1953), pp. 50—51.
[15] *Critique*, B 274.
[16] See Hans Vaihinger, *Commentar zu Kants Kritik der reinen Vernunft*, II (Stuttgart 1892), 493.
[17] *Critique*, A 39/B 56.

A more fruitful interpretation is provided by reflection on Kant's statement that the view under attack makes space a property of *things in themselves.* On this view the concept of an object is supposed related to the concept of objectively real space such that denial of the latter entails denial of the former. We are, therefore, obliged to clarify just how the concept of a thing in itself might presuppose the concept of objectively real space.

Sometimes Kant understands by things in themselves objects which are alleged knowable "in themselves" or, alternatively, apart from reference to other objects[18]. Such objects are not those known perceptually, since a perceptual object is known always relative to other objects. We know or identify an item as occupying a certain spatial region by, say, the resistance we meet in encountering it or by its relation to other items in its vicinity. Nevertheless, we can, according to Kant, at least conceive of objects as capable of individuation apart from such reference. If we now want to conceive such objects as existing in space, we might do so in two ways[19]. First, we may locate the objects in question in absolute space. Every such object can then be individuated at any moment without reference to other objects merely by its determinate position in absolute space. Since points in absolute space are not a function of the objects comprising space but are absolutely and uniquely determined, reference to other objects does not figure in this account of individuation. We achieve this solely in terms of the object's location(s) in absolute space.

Second, we may assume that an object's spatial location *vis-à-vis all other* objects in space is an *internal* property of the object[20]. This view construes space itself either as a property of objects taken together or as a property of any one of them — since a property of each object is its spatial relation(s) to all others. To pick out or individuate an object we need only a complete description of the object in question, since part of the description will be a uniquely individuating property, namely, its comprehensive spatial location. And since this "ideal" description is internal to the object, reference of other objects is not involved. Thus, this view diverges from the first which secured individuation apart from reference to other objects by excluding all relations to other objects. While preserving such relations, the second view manages the same result by rendering them

---

[18] Cf. *Critique*, B 67: "A thing in itself cannot be known through mere relations; and ... since outer sense gives us nothing but mere relations, this sense ... [cannot contain] the inner properties of the object in itself."

[19] This should not be thought to counter Kant's standard thesis that things in themselves (should there by any) are not in space or time. We are merely trying to provide some sense to the supposition that space and time might be properties of things in themselves.

[20] Talk of internal properties is notoriously vague. Roughly, I have in mind here a property which could be ascertained from the object alone or the concept of the object. Leibniz evidently held something like this in regard to all properties (see, for instance, *Discourse on Method*, VIII & IX). The full view is ultimately untenable because it entails the reducibility of relational propositions to subject-predicate propositions.

wholly internal properties of the object. Thus, listing of properties entails no reference to other objects.

There are, then, two senses in which the concept of a thing in itself might be logically related to the concept of objectively real space such that meaningfulness of the former presupposes the latter. The incoherence of both the underlying views of space would infect as well any conception of objects presupposing either. In this light B 70—71 and B 274 amount to the following: Construing objects as things in themselves (as capable of individuation apart from reference to other objects) requires, if they are conceived to exist in space, that space be either subsistent or inherent. But on neither view can we say what sort of thing space is. Hence, both are empty notions. But then things in themselves drop out because their existence presupposes either of two empty conceptions of space. Therefore, both B 70—71 and B 274 appear to attribute Berkeley's idealism to his rejection of the related assumptions that spatial objects must be things in themselves and that space, if possible at all, is objectively real.

The objection that this analysis differs greatly from Berkeley's presentation can be met by simply granting that Kant nowhere deals explicitly with Berkeley's actual arguments. This by no means discredits Kant's analysis for his main point is surely correct. Berkeley rejects what Kant takes to be the basic assumptions of dualism: (1) that space is objectively real and (2) that objects are things in themselves existing independently of us in this space. Further, even more than absolute (Newtonian) space, Berkeley is set on refuting the concept of a causally effective material substance existing in absolute (Newtonian) space. Of course, when Kant argues that rejection of (1) entails rejection of (2) because (1) is a necessary condition of (2), he is not reporting Berkeley's actual argument. Rather, he is unpacking the logic of Berkeley's doctrine. Kant shows that, other arguments notwithstanding, denial of (1) entails and, hence, commits Berkeley to denial of (2).

Kant proceeds in B 274 to state the effectiveness of the "Transcendental Aesthetic" as preventive medicine against dogmatic idealism: "The ground on which this [dogmatic] idealism rests has already been undermined by us in the Transcendental Aesthetic." The "Aesthetic's" remedy is to provide a conception of space (and time) alternative to *objectively* real space (and time). For Kant it is Berkeley's (unwise) affirmation of something like TR which, with rejection of TS, eliminates the possibility of a general theory of space. The "Aesthetic's" theory of space as *a priori* but ideal (or subjectively real) enables Kant to deny TR without denying spatial objects. This altogether different conception of space provides (for Kant) sufficient distinction of his position from Berkeley's. (We shall not consider here the final success of Kant's positive view.)

Kant's awareness of the categorical nature of Berkeley's rejection of real space is quite unambiguous. The Berkeley of the *Prolegomena*, for instance, is made a practitioner of the view that "space" refers just to particular (perceptual) spaces:

Berkeley regarded space as a mere empirical representation which, like the appearances in it, only becomes known to us, together with all its determinations, by means of experience or perception[21].

I take the passage to assert that the concept space is an empirical concept for Berkeley, gotten by somehow "abstracting out" particular perceptual spaces and ignoring the spatial occupants simultaneously given in perception. Kant raises a special objection to such a conception of space, namely, that it renders geometry a purely empirical science for loss of universality of the concept[22]. In addition, he has a general objection to abstracting the concept at all. Even granting that spaces are independently given in perception, abstracting the concept space pre-supposes that we think of the perceived spaces as parts of a single space. But parts of space are not empirically given as parts of space. Hence, to suppose them such is to presuppose the very concept of space itself. The concept, rather than abstracted from perceptions, is itself presupposed by such an activity[23].

One might suggest that by "empirical representation" Kant means to impute to Berkeley a relational theory of space[24]. Kant's choice of the expression *Vorstellung* ("representation") might better support the above interpretation insofar as the expression may frequently be rendered "concept" (cf. A 68/B 93 & A 69/ B 94). But as Berkeley seems agreeable to either view, let us suppose Kant to here furnish him with a relational theory of space. What sense can then be made of the claim that Berkeley makes the concept of space impossible? The claim holds, indeed it emerges from an argument which is Kantian, in spirit at least. For Berkeley may now be taken to hold that the concept of a system of relations between existents is "built up" from particular such systems. The problem is that specification of the particular systems ultimately presupposes a single, comprehensive system. Clearly, any two particular systems of relations may be qualitatively identical, yet numerically distinct. For given a system xRyR'z, if R and R' are genuine relations, then different sets of qualitatively identical objects can exhibit these relations. If so, such systems would be distinguishable *only* in terms of a wider system of relations of which they are part. Hence, short of sacrificing the distinction between numerical and qualitative identity of systems, the concept of a single system of relations between objects is indispensable. It is presupposed by the notion of particular such systems.

So on either interpretation of what Kant means by "empirical representation", Berkeley's conception of space presupposes the concept of a single space or a

---

[21] *Prolegomena*, p. 145. Immediately following, Kant underscores Berkeley's neglect of time. As Turbayne notes (p. 112) the remark is understandable on the (likely) assumption that Kant had read only *Three Dialogues* and *De Motu*.

[22] *Critique*, A 40/B 57.

[23] Cf. *Critique*, A 25/B 39: "These parts [of space] cannot precede the one all-embracing space, as being, as it were, constituents out of which it can be composed; on the contrary, they [the parts] can be thought only [as parts] *in* it."

[24] Miller takes this interpretation, p. 316.

single system of spatial relations. It follows that Berkeley's denial of the possibility of a general theory or concept of space entails, even if unwittingly, denial of his own particularistic view of space. Such an account, if at all accurate, would indeed vindicate Kant's charge that Berkeley makes space impossible.

Thus, B 70—71 and B 274 retail consequences of Berkeley's assumption of TR, that space, if possible at all, must be a property of things in themselves (i. e., must be objectively real); while the *Prolegomena* passage underscores Berkeley's lack of an alternative account of space.

Kant's preoccupation with Berkeley's rejection of space is puzzling, as is his reluctance to turn the argument of the "Refutation of Idealism" against Berkeley as well as Descartes. One reason for the latter is the argument's orientation against dualism, in particular the assumption that we are immediately aware of our mental states but must infer the existence of spatial objects. Kant correctly recognizes Berkeley's distaste for this assumption as well as for the objective reality of space. Hence, Berkeley merits independent analysis in view of his divergence from Descartes.

Kant's preoccupation with Berkeley's rejection of space is self-serving. By indicating how Berkeley's "illusionism" follows from TR and rejection of TS, Kant provides further support for his own view of space and time as forms of intuition. Not only did Berkeley (with Kant's blessing) announce the incoherence of both the subsistence and inherence views of space and time but also these views preclude a satisfactory account of objects. And since this is due to certain realist assumptions about space and time, the realist position is undermined — leaving the field to Kant's alternative. Thus, Kant's analysis of Berkeleian illusionism vindicates his own view of the ideality of space and time. The rhetorical impact of this is clear, for it was mainly Kant's view of space and time as forms of intuition which had led critics to class him with Berkeley.

While the *Critique* focuses on Berkeley's rejection of space and objects in space, the *Prolegomena* makes a different but related point. Here rejection of any *a priori* features of experience makes impossible universal rules or principles of the sort required for distinguishing objective experience from subjective awareness:

> As truth rests on universal and necessary laws as its criteria, experience with *Berkeley* can have no criteria of truth because nothing was laid (by him) *a priori* at the ground of appearances in it, from which it then followed that they are nothing but illusion; whereas for us space und time (in conjunction with the pure concepts of the understanding) prescribe their law *a priori* to all possible experience, and this yields at the same time the sure criterion for distinguishing truth in it from illusion[25].

According to Kant, Berkeley's inability to provide for objective experience breeds inability to distinguish merely subjective awareness from actual perception. This is due at least partly to his rejection of any *a priori* features of experience. For it is then incumbent upon Berkeley to provide for objective experience solely

[25] *Prolegomena*, p. 146.

in terms of mental contents because only minds and their ideas are real. But this is no mean task, since the mental content of objective experience differs from that of subjective awareness neither in kind nor in quality. They do not differ in kind, for imagined as well as perceived objects and events are particulars (as opposed to concepts or universals). We cannot imagine (hallucinate or dream) a white rabbit or a traffic accident in general. Likewise, we cannot imagine *numbers*, although we may imagine, say, a certain numeral "3" or three things. Further, appeal to clarity, vividness or specificity is merely wistful. A hallucination of a white rabbit may be clearer or more vivid than the corresponding perception should the latter occur in adverse circumstances (say, in foggy weather). Similarly, the alleged lack of specificity in imagination, dreams, etc., does not distinguish them from perception. The superior describability of actually perceived objects is less a function of object specificity than of the possibility of re-examination. Of course, Berkeley is barred appeal anyway to the latter because he denies repeated perception of the same thing, at least of the same spatial object. Moreover, he apparently extends such denial to perception of the same idea as well[26]. At any rate detail of description fails of itself to distinguish objective from subjective experience. For I may be unable to report the eye-color of a fog bound white rabbit just as I may not have enriched my imaginary white rabbit so as to include its eye-color. Hence, neither in kind nor quality does the object of imagination adequately contrast with the object of actual perception. Thus, Kant's above remarks in effect deny Berkeley a conception of objective experience fashioned merely by inspection of mental contents.

Unsurprisingly, Berkeley's strategy for securing objectivity invokes coherence:

The ideas of sense are more strong, lively, and distinct than those of the imagination; they have likewise a steadiness, order and coherence, and are not excited at random, as those which are the effects of human wills often are, but in a regular train or series[27].

In addition to (1) the quality of the idea and (2) its contingency on the will, (3) its internal coherence or fitting together with other ideas also distinguishes objective from merely subjective experience. But (1), as we have seen, provides no criterion of objectivity and (2), though perhaps sufficient to distinguish imagination from perception, will not do for distinguishing hallucinations or illusions from perceptions. Finally, (3) presupposes the specifiability of what counts as "fitting together". Failing some prior notion of perceptual coherence, it is undecidable whether a given perception is veridical or not.

Suppose the test perception that of a man before a barn. Now for Berkeley a satisfactory account of the veracity of this perception need include appeal only to facts like the following. Not only do I seem to see the man standing before the barn but also audio and kinematic tests would result in my seeming to hear or

---

[26] George Berkeley, *Three Dialogues Between Hylas and Philonus*, in *The Works*, II (London 1949), 247.
[27] Berkeley, *Principles*, sec. 30, p. 53.

touch him. And the man's position before the barn is not relinquished simply at the closing and opening of the eyes. Further, past experience makes it sensible (or not) to perceive a man standing before rather than flying above a barn. But without an independent showing that veridical perceptions just are those subjective awarenesses exhibiting such features, the perceptual facts themselves do not secure veracity of perceptions. Initially, nothing demands that the object of perception endure through a measurable period of time; nor is it obvious that a perception which "makes sense" in terms of past awareness is veridical. Past experience of white swans is no warrant for judging perception of a black swan illusory. Thus, failing some independently justifiable principles which determine a precise sense of what counts as experiential cohering, Berkeley's appeal to coherence is vacuous. And in this sense Kant's charge that Berkeley is unable to distinguish reality from illusion is appropriate.

In this same *Prolegomena* passage, Kant claims to provide an account of objective experience and so to sustain the distinction between merely subjective awareness, on the one hand, and experience of an objective world, on the other hand. With the concepts of space and time, the categories provide rules constitutive of objective experience. They thus enable meaningful use of the concept of coherence by determining a precise sense of what may count as experiential cohering. For example, according to Kant, we know *a priori* that objective experience (as opposed to dreams, imaginings, hallucinations, etc.) consists of measurable objects in a single space and time. Moreover, such objects exhibit causal and reciprocal relations to one another. These features provide grounds for asserting when experiences cohere and when not. That Kant considers this sufficient for the distinction is clear from A 376:

> From perceptions knowledge of objects can be generated, either by mere play of imagination or by way of experience; and in the process there may, no doubt, arise illusory representations to which the objects do not correspond... To avoid such deceptive illusion, we have to proceed according to the rule: *Whatever is connected with a perception according to empirical laws, is actual.*

We need not here determine the adequacy of this account of objectivity. Of note is just that Kant was keenly aware of the importance of his divergence from Berkeley on this point[28].

---

[28] Turbayne has claimed that the categories and space provide two points of distinction between Kant and Berkeley. His further claim (p. 107) that the former were "never directly developed" against Berkeley is plainly answered by the passage at hand as well as the passage cited in footnote 30. His attitude on the second point is quite puzzling. On the one hand, Turbayne grants that the *a priori* character of space provides Kant with "an additional criterion of reality" (though it surely does more than this) but, on the other hand, he claims its use in this passage "as a guard against illusion, which Berkeley lacked ... creates difficulties" (114). It is quite unclear both what these difficulties are and what Turbayne's exact point is.

Kant contends that, ultimately, the cost of objectivity for Berkeley is appeal to an intuition of God and his ideas. That certain concepts provide for knowledge of an objective sort is justified not by examination of the conditions of knowledge but by appeal to an intuition of God. Coherence, order and regularity function as objectivity criteria only because God guarantees the possibility of objective experience[29]. Kant's expression of this point is unambiguous:

> Berkeley found nothing constant, and could neither find anything which the understanding conceived according to *a priori* principles, thus he had to seek still another intuition, namely the mystical intuition of God's ideas[30].

Mere inspection of mental contents cannot provide for the universal rules or principles presupposed by objective experience. Consequently, the touchstone of his justification of objective experience is an entirely *ad hoc* or extra-logical consideration — appeal to God and his ideas.

Kant, on the other hand, eschews uncritical appeal to intellectual intuition as part of an account of objectivity. This alone would secure the distinctive character of his brand of idealism:

> My so-called (properly critical) idealism is thus of a quite peculiar kind, namely in that it reverses the usual idealism, and through my idealism all knowledge *a priori*, even that of geometry, first receives objective reality, which could not be asserted even by the most zealous realist without this my proved ideality of space and time[31].

> In fact, a quite crucial point is at stake here. According to Kant, we know *a priori* that objects knowable for us must be in space and time. (This is the significance of space and time as *a priori* forms of intuition.) From this can be generated other conditions on knowable objects which in turn provide a conception of objective experience. We may say, for instance, that any knowable object must satisfy those conditions required for determining spatiotemporal position because knowing (individuating) an object requires, in principle, determination of its position in space and time. So whatever is required for spatiotemporal determination is equally required for knowledge of objects. Moreover, such conditions constitute a conception or theory of objective experience, since we know *a priori* that any knowable object must satisfy them. Hence, Kant's doctrine of the *a priori* nature of space is central to his account of objectivity. The final success of his doctrine is a complicated question, not to be dealt with here.

[29] See Berkeley, *Principles*, secs. 30 & 32, pp. 53—54.
[30] *Kant's gesammelte Schriften*, ed. Berlin Academy, XXIII (Berlin 1955), p. 58. I include here as well the immediately preceding text which gives considerable substantiation to the main claims of this paper. "Space and time are not objects in their own right nor characteristics inhering in objects; they lie only in the senses. So far I am in agreement with all idealists. But space and time are not impressions of my senses which we learn through experience, nor are they empirical forms. Rather they are forms of sensibility which precede *a priori* all experience and make objects of experience possible as appearances. Herein my system diverges from that of Berkeley and others and thereby also ceases to be idealistic; for I can understand how I am able to judge of objects of the senses *a priori* and with apodictic certainty and the extent to which my sensible representations exhibit truth, i. e., connection according to laws known *a priori*" (pp. 57—58).
[31] *Prolegomena*, p. 146.

Kant's so-called critical idealism "reverses the usual idealism" by securing the objectivity of experience through an analysis of a *fact* of experience — intuition of objects in space and time. Ordinary idealism, on the other hand, secures facts of experience through appeal to a rational intuition[32]. To overlook this reversal is to make the very mistake which so misled the early (and some later) critics of Kant[33].

We may conclude, then, that Kant betrays a keen grasp of Berkeley's doctrine. Both characterizing Berkeley as rejecting objectively real space and objects in space and committing him to rendering objects mere illusion are justified. For Berkeley does reject absolute (Newtonian) space as well as the notion of material substance as a causally efficacious something existing in absolute space. Further, Kant correctly contends that Berkeley's restriction of reality to minds and ideas precludes a trouble-free account of objectivity. Indeed, the cost of objectivity for Berkeley seems to be severence of his doctrine from the sort of account provided by Kant. So the view that Kant's remarks are irrelevant to Berkeley and that he unwittingly practices the same philosophical doctrine has considerable ground to make up.

---

[32] *Prolegomena*, p. 146n states the general thesis that idealism gets objectivity at the cost of non-sensible or rational intuition: "Visionary idealism ... (as already can be seen from *Plato*) inferred from our knowledge *a priori* (even that of geometry) another intuition than that of the senses (namely intellectual intuition), because it never occurred to anyone that the senses should also intuit *a priori*." Some commentators have puzzled over Kant's classifying Berkeley as a rationalist. But the account of this passage, that rationalism was the price of objectivity for Berkeley, is quite straight forward and historically close. This balances Margaret Wilson's view that the rationalist label is likely due to Berkeley's "eighteenth century reputation" (p. 471).

[33] See especially Garve-Feder's initial review of the *Critique* in the *Zugabe zu den Göttingischen Anzeigen von Gelehrten Sachen*, January 19, 1782.

Kant's Refutation of Idealism

MYRON GOCHNAUER

IN THE SECOND EDITION of the *Critique of Pure Reason* Kant inserted a refutation of idealism in the examination of the "Postulates of Empirical Thought." This is one of the most condensed sections of the *Critique*, but because of the nature of its subject it is also one of the most important. It is the most direct attempt to set the Kantian position off from Berkeley and more particularly from Descartes. In spite of the evident importance Kant placed on these passages the argument is marred by subtle shifts of terminology so that the casual reader is likely to misunderstand the position which is being upheld. Indeed, as we shall see, this terminological difficulty is to be found in the very formulation of the thesis to be proved in the section. It is the purpose of this paper to draw out, or perhaps to reconstruct, the main argument of the refutation and in the process clarify exactly what is and what is not being proved. The argument as it will be reconstructed is not found explicitly in the section under consideration, but then it can hardly be expected that what is essentially a one-paragraph argument can adequately spell out all that it involves, particularly when the literary style is a good illustration of all the negative comments which have been leveled against the German metaphysical writings.

In the section which Kant labels the "Refutation of Idealism" he proposes to deal with what he calls "material idealism." This is defined as the "theory which declares the existence of objects in space outside us either to be merely doubtful and indemonstrable or to be false and impossible" (B 274).[1] The former is dubbed problematic idealism and the latter dogmatic idealism. The problematic type is best illustrated, according to Kant, by Descartes, and the dogmatic type by Berkeley.

There seems to be considerable agreement among commentators that many of the changes in the second edition, including the addition of this refutation, were attempts to correct misunderstandings and misinterpretations of the first edition which resulted in, among other things, Kant being identified with some form of idealism, presumably close to a Berkelean position.[2] If the motive behind this section was a concise and unquestionable refutation of, and hence differentiation from, Berkeley, then it is a failure, for it deals in cursory fashion with the position of Berkeley, merely reaffirming that there is a difference between the *Critique's* position and the dogmatic idealist, and referring the reader back to the arguments of the "Aesthetic."

Kant takes dogmatic idealism to be based primarily on the proposition that the existence of things in space is impossible, and that this impossibility stems from the impossibility of space itself (B 274). This position results, he says, from holding that space and time are properties of things in themselves. If we hold this view then we are

---

[1] All references to the *Critique* are from the Norman Kemp Smith translation (Macmillan, 1929).

[2] See, for example, H. J. Paton, *Kant's Metaphysics of Experience* (George Allen and Unwin, 1936), II, 376, and T. D. Weldon, *Kant's Critique of Pure Reason* (Oxford, 1958), p. 81 and p. 189.

[195]

committed to the absurdities that "two infinite things, which are not substances, nor anything actually inhering in substance, must yet have existence, nay, must be the necessary condition of the existence of all things, and moreover must continue to exist, even although all existing things be removed" (B 70–71). This view was discussed in the "Aesthetic" and supposedly refuted there by showing that space and time are not absolute in the sense of being somehow associated with things in themselves, but rather are the forms of sensible intuition. The argument of the "Aesthetic," then, undermines the dogmatic idealist by showing that space is *not* impossible. It is beyond the scope of this paper to examine this argument, for it would involve a careful examination of the "Aesthetic" as a whole. Without making any judgment on the soundness of the "Aesthetic" we can, however, see that it does not do all that Kant would require of it in establishing the conclusion of the "Refutation." There are at least three positions which Kant should rule out, but which this argument does not even touch.

First of all, it does not rule out the position which holds that space does not in fact exist even though it is not, strictly speaking, impossible. It might be pointed out here in favor of Kant that it is not at all clear just what sorts of argument could be advanced in favor of this kind of position, so it may be that Kant did not consider it worthy of refutation, since it has nothing to support it.

Secondly, Kant's argument has not touched the position which holds that although objects in space are not strictly impossible they do not as a matter of fact exist. It is presumably the task of the "Analytic" to show how such objects of knowledge are possible, but as a whole the *Critique* is not designed to show that we *do* have experience or objective knowledge, but rather what the presuppositions of such knowledge are. With this view of the *Critique* it is apparent that some additional argumentation would be required to refute the claim that objects in space do not exist even though they are possible. Once again it can be said in favor of Kant that it is not clear what sorts of argument could be advanced in favor of such a position.

Thirdly, his argument does not show that the existence of things we think are in space is not impossible. An idealist could well admit that space is not impossible, but that things existing in such a space *are* impossible. Indeed, Berkeley takes this very line in his *Three Dialogues Between Hylas and Philonous*. In these dialogues he nowhere bases his position on the impossibility of space, but rather on the impossibility of unperceived objects. As he says in both the *Dialogues* and *A Treatise Concerning the Principles of Human Knowledge* he is content to let his entire case rest on this impossibility of unperceived objects. The "idealist argument," if there is one, is basically the challenge to produce an unperceived object; the manifest impossibility of this is taken to prove the idealist's case.[3] Nowhere does this sort of argument even mention, let alone rely on, the impossibility of space, so any idealist who bases his position on the argument completely escapes this part of Kant's refutation. It might be noted that this type of idealism *is* in need of refutation, for its basic argument does have sufficient appeal that others have accepted it.[4] In addition, the idealist's argument would lend itself, if rigorously maintained, to a position which would deny the very possibility of truly objective knowledge; and however non-commital the *Critique* may be, it cannot allow that it merely states the presuppositions, if there be such things, of something which is impos-

---

3 In the *Principles* Berkeley is willing to "readily give up the cause" if the challenge can be met (section 22), and in the *Dialogues* he prefaces the challenge by saying, "I am content to put the whole upon this issue" (Dialogue I).

4 See, for example, F. H. Bradley, *Appearance and Reality* (Oxford, 1930), pp. 127–128.

sible. If objects in space are impossible, as the idealist might be interpreted as maintaining, then knowledge of them does not merely not exist, but is actually impossible; and if knowledge is impossible, then the question "What are the presuppositions of knowledge of things in space?" is either senseless or has no answer. Indeed, if Berkeley is correct and "unperceived object" is a manifest repugnancy as he claims, and if the objects in space are to be identified as unperceived objects (or objects which can exist unperceived), then any claim that someone *knows* something about such objects will be in some sense contradictory since what he supposedly knows cannot be true. And then the *Critique* becomes trivial since a contradiction can take any statement or set of statements as presuppositions.

In the end we can conclude of this section that *if* some idealist bases his position on the impossibility of space, and *if* the arguments of the "Aesthetic" are correct, then Kant has refuted that position. Since Berkeley does not use this basis for his idealism he escapes Kant's refutation.

The more substantial and subtle argument in the "Refutation" is directed against the problematic form of idealism, that supposedly held by Descartes or other representationalists. Problematic idealism, it will be recalled, is that type which holds the existence of objects in space outside us to be doubtful and indemonstrable. Now, in refuting this Kant begins with what he takes to be a basic position of the idealists and attempts to show that this position makes necessary his own thesis. The premise he chooses is that we have inner experience, or knowledge of inner states. The task he sets himself is that of showing that "inner experience, which for Descartes is indubitable, is possible only on the assumption of outer experience" (B 275). This is the announced intent of the proof.

Before the proof begins, however, he finds it necessary to modify the starting premise somewhat. Instead of taking the premise merely that we have inner experience, he uses the more particular claim that we have knowledge of our inner states *as temporally determined*. He thus states the thesis he is attempting to prove as follows: "The mere, but empirically determined, consciousness of my own existence proves the existence of objects in space outside me" (B 275). That "empirically determined" is equivalent in this context to "temporally determined" can easily be seen from the first sentence of the proof: "I am conscious of my own existence as determined in time" (B 275).

When we keep in mind the general outlines of what Kant is doing, namely showing that inner experience is possible only if there is outer experience, the following sort of interpretation of the argument suggests itself. Knowledge of inner states or occurrences is parasitic upon, or depends upon, our having knowledge of things in the world or in space. It is not simply the existence of myself, or the existence of certain of my inner states which requires that we have outer experiences. It seems very possible to have some kind of lively mental life without there even existing things in space; indeed, this fact supplies much of the plausibility of the position Kant is attempting to refute. If we knew that we could not have the inner states that we do unless there were an outer world, then the problem would be solved, since no one is prepared to deny that we do have *some* mental states. Kant could well admit that we can have mental occurrences without there being an external world, but the statement of the problem suggests that he is dealing with more than this. He is concerned with knowledge of mental states, and the claim is that while we might be said to have some sort of knowledge (in a minimal sense) of our representations without having knowledge of the world, we cannot have knowledge of these mental events as determined *in time* or as holding a determinate time without also having knowledge of things in space. In short, we know ourselves as beings in time, as beings who have had certain experiences at certain times, or as having histories. Now this, Kant claims, is impossible without outer experience.

The reasoning used to back up this claim is confusing at best, and confused at worst, owing in no small part to the terminology used. There are two apparent interpretations of the section possible. We could, on the first approach, pay particular attention to the wording of the thesis and the summary. In these Kant speaks of *consciousness of* my existence in time. The thesis has been quoted above, and the summary of the argument holds that "the consciousness of my existence is at the same time an immediate consciousness of the existence of other things outside me" (B 276). The addition of the word "immediate" lends emphasis to this consciousness element of the argument. If we are struck by these uses of "consciousness" we are likely to take the argument in a sort of phenomenological way; if there were not things in space I could not even be *aware* of my own existence in time. We might call this the phenomenological approach.

Norman Kemp Smith takes this line, although perhaps without full awareness, in his commentary on the *Critique*. He says, for example, in commenting on the relation of inner and outer experience, that "inner experience, consciousness of the flux of inner states, is only possible in and through experience of independent material bodies in space,"[5] and along similar lines, in discussing B 277-8, he claims that Kant "is now asserting that consciousness of both space and motion is necessary to the consciousness of time."[6] Kemp Smith is certainly taking the passage in terms of consciousness and it is equally clear that he takes "conscious" as akin to "aware." Indeed, he uses the terms interchangeably in the introduction while discussing the nature of consciousness for Kant. He says that Kant's position "amounts to the assertion that *consciousness is in all cases awareness of meaning,*" and immediately goes on to say, "There is no *awareness,* however rudimentary or primitive, that does not involve the apprehension of meaning. Meaning and awareness are correlative terms."[7] This approach imposes a psychological or at best a phenomenological interpretation on the section. On this line we can observe, or we are aware of, various representations, sensations, or whatever the immediate data of consciousness are called, and among the things of which we are conscious is the temporal location of certain of these representations. I am aware that a particular representation precedes or follows another, and that there is a constant flux of these representations. Now, if I were not aware of certain things in space I simply could not be aware of this temporal flow or the temporal location of the representations; I would have no awareness of things being in time. On this view I could not even have the *illusion* that things were temporally ordered, for that would in itself be an awareness of things being temporally ordered even though I may be mistaken as to the "correct" order.

This interpretation is supported by much of the text, particularly a note in the "Preface." Kant says, for example, that "this consciousness of my existence in time is bound up in the way of identity with the consciousness of a relation to something outside me, and it is therefore experience not invention, sense not imagination, which inseparably connects this outside something with my inner sense" (B xl, note a). Here again the emphasis is on merely being conscious of something, and this is clearly a matter of aware-

---

[5] Norman Kemp Smith, *A Commentary to Kant's Critique of Pure Reason* (Macmillan, 1923), p. 313.

[6] *Ibid.,* p. 311.

[7] *Ibid.,* p. xli. The emphasis in the second of these quotes is mine.

ness which may be mistaken, rather than knowledge or experience. Kant says, of course, that it is experience, but this is the conclusion of the argument, while the reasons are given solely in terms of consciousness. The very same note makes clear that for Kant, to be conscious of something is not the same as to experience it or have objective knowledg of it. In the note he explicitly mentions being conscious of representations, and representations are by their natures subjective, although they may contribute toward gaining knowledge. Other examples can be found both in the note in the "Preface" and in the "Refutation" itself which lend credence to the phenomenological interpretation, but enough has already been said to indicate its initial plausibility.

There are two related weaknesses of this interpretation. If Kemp Smith is an adequate example of this approach then it seems to lead one to absurd positions on the nature of objects and representations, and (therefore) does not allow for a cogent argument in support of the Kantian thesis. If we take this phenomenological approach to the argument, the permanent in perception which Kant holds to be necessary for all determination of time (B 275) has no obvious interpretation. If it is necessary for the mere awareness of things being in time, then it must somehow be present to us in every awareness of every representation, in so far as every representation appears to us as temporally determined. There simply *is* no phenomenological permanent thing which could play this role. This is problem enough for this interpretation, but the next step in the argument presents a further difficulty. Kant claims that "perception of this permanent is possible only through a *thing* outside me and not through the mere *representation* of a thing outside me" (B 275). This leads Kemp Smith to claim, "The proof of the second edition . . . argues that though outer appearances are immediately apprehended they must be existences distinct from the subjective states through which the mind represents them."[8] Note that he says certain *appearances* are *existences* distinct from certain subjective states. Now, this is patently absurd, for an appearance by its very nature cannot be something which is different or distinct from the mental state which is a representation. It is simply nonsense to hold that some appearances are not mental. Admittedly this permanent of which Kant speaks cannot be subjective, but to identify it with an appearance, as the phenomenological interpretation seems committed to do, is to impose the most severe distortion on the very meanings of the terms; it is, in fact, flatly to contradict oneself. Kemp Smith makes a point of interpreting Kant without "distorting" the text to make it consistent, but if we allow such glaring contradictions as the one under discussion we relegate the "Refutation of Idealism" to the philosophical compost pile, for an inconsistent argument is no argument at all.

As can be seen from what has been said above, the phenomenological interpretation does not appear to allow the Kantian argument even the *possibility* of being cogent. In addition to this, there seems to be no good reason to suppose that the simple awareness of time or of things as existing in time requires some phenomenological object which is permanent and in relation to which things seem to change. As long as we are speaking merely of awareness or consciousness of time no permanent is necessary. I can be aware of a flux or of change and hence of time simply on the basis of differing representations and perhaps some degree of what we would normally call memory. In short, even if we can avoid the contradiction mentioned above, the argument of the "Refutation" is unsound, or at best not clearly sound, on the phenomenological interpretation. The crucial

---

[8] *Ibid.*, p. 312.

premise which Kant needs, that determination of time presupposes something permanent in perception, has no apparent support if taken in this way. There is nothing in the text which offers support to this premise, for the only likely candidate is the argument of the "First Analogy," and it only deals with mere appearances. *Appearances* cannot themselves be the things in space of which we have objective knowledge, and any attempt to make the identification involves us in the previously discussed absurdity of holding that some appearances are existences independent of subjective states.

So in the end we can say of this first interpretation of the argument of the "Refutation" that at worst it involves us in outright contradiction and at best fails to offer support for the required premise.

The second interpretation of the argument emphasizes the experience element, as the first interpretation emphasized the consciousness element. It will be recalled that the task Kant set for himself was to show that inner *experience* was possible only on the assumption of outer *experience*. For Kant, experience is objective knowledge, so on the interpretation under consideration we are dealing with knowledge of oneself in time rather than simply awareness of oneself in time. Once we make the shift from mere awareness or consciousness to knowledge the argument of the "Refutation" begins to make sense, although it is still much too abbreviated.

The key premise is as before: "All determination of time presupposes something permanent in perception." How can we make sense of this claim? As we have seen, if we take it in the straight phenomenological sense it is either contradictory or groundless. Taking the cue from Jonathan Bennett[9] we might argue something as follows. In order to make temporal determinations or true temporal assertions we must have some criterion or criteria independent of the mere appearance of temporal ordering. If there were not this independent criterion then there would be no way to distinguish between being in a certain temporal order and merely seeming to be, a distinction which must be made if we are to have knowledge of time. Consider the example relevant here, that of temporal ordering of inner states. We are aware of a succession of appearances and the consciousness of our own existence which can accompany these appearances (B 277). It may seem that some awarenesses precede others or are located in a temporal sequence. How can the temporal sequence of the various self-awarenesses become part of our knowledge? How, for example, could I know that I started reading the *Critique* a week after I read *How to Do Things With Words,* or that I thought of a proof for a certain theorem before I began considering epistemic logic? If I can legitimately make such knowledge claims there must be some way of justifying them. We need something permanent in the sense that it does not depend on the appearances we are trying to check. It must be permanent to the extent that it is not merely another appearance of temporal sequence, for if it were it too would be in need of justification. One might look at it this way: we are attempting to justify subjective impressions of temporal order as a whole, so we must seek some justification which is other than this type of appearance. In this sense we can speak of that by which we justify the claim about time as "permanent." Not only must it be different, but it must also not require justification. In other words, we must have knowledge with regard to these independent checks. So the permanent of which Kant speaks is something outside of or other than subjective temporal appearance, and something of which we have objective knowledge.

---

[9] Jonathan Bennett, *Kant's Analytic* (Cambridge, 1966), chap. 14.

That this interpretation of the "permanent" is not a pure invention can be seen from the modification or clarification of the argument which Kant noted in the "Preface." He says that the permanent cannot be an intuition within me, and then goes on to justify the claim by observing that all of the data given of my existence is in the order of representations or appearance, and "representations themselves require a permanent distinct from them, in relation to which their change, and so my existence in time wherein they change, may be determined" (B xl, note a). In other words, representations may be *determined* as changing only if there is something independent to which they can be related or by which they can be checked. Now, since this is said of representations in general and not any specific group of them, it must be the case that the permanent is something other than a representation.

One possible type of object which is not a representation and yet is related to them is the noumenal object. But clearly this will not satisfy the requirements since noumena are by their natures unknown to us and hence cannot be the things by which the temporal order of representations is determined. There remains but one kind of thing to play this role, and that is the object of scientific knowledge, objects in space.

How are we to justify this claim that knowledge of *objects in space* is necessary to knowledge of the temporal order of our representations? As we saw above, knowledge claims about the temporal location of representations require justification, and this justification must be something other than more representations. This sort of position has been convincingly argued for by Wittgenstein by means of his example of buying several copies of the morning newspaper to make sure that the information we read in one was correct (although, of course, he used the example for a slightly different purpose). We need something independent, against which we can check our representations if we are to have knowledge. The only candidate for this something independent is objects which are interpersonal, namely objects in space, the objects of scientific knowledge. If we have knowledge of such independent, "public" objects, then we can justify knowledge claims about our own histories by checking the appearances of temporal order (including our memories) against the various common historical information sources, such as other people's memories, documents, artifacts, scientific retrodiction, and so on. These public sources provide us with the objective knowledge against which the changes of appearance can be determined with respect to time. My memory of having read the Austin book a week before having begun the *Critique* can be checked against the memories of my friends, bookstore receipts, notes, letters, etc., and thereby yield knowledge of the temporal order of two items of my consciousness. My memory regarding the theorem and epistemic logic is amenable to similar checks. Without such sources knowledge of these inner states as determined in time would be impossible. The most I could claim would be that I remember them in that order (or perhaps better, I *seem* to remember them in that order, if we take "remember" to be a success verb).

It might be noted in passing that the interpretation we are now considering parallels, on many points, the argument of the *Philosophical Investigations* against private language. Wittgenstein's argument goes farther, clearly, than Kant's, since he is concerned with the language itself while Kant is concerned only with knowledge, which may be expressed in a language. But both arguments rely on showing that a certain thing (correct ascription of sensations for Wittgenstein, and knowledge of myself in time for Kant) is impossible unless something else is the case. This form of argument is common enough, and it may therefore seem idle to point out that both of the arguments take this form.

However, the interesting and significant point is that they not only have this general form, but also are very similar in their ways of establishing the impossibility. Both claim that we need something *independent of* our awarenesses or impressions if we are to accomplish what we are interested in (correctly ascribing sensations, or knowing ourselves in time). Briefly, Wittgenstein asks how someone claiming to formulate a private language would define the terms to be used. The obvious answer is that he would do it by ostensive definition, by impressing on himself the connexion between the sign and the private entity or sensation. Unfortunately, this crucial connection between the sign and the sensation is not satisfactory, since "in the present case I have no criterion of correctness. One would like to say: whatever is going to seem right to me is right. And that only means that here we can't talk about 'right'."[10] In others words, in order to sensibly say that I have the connexion right I must have some criterion of correctness which establishes the difference between *being* right and *seeming* or appearing right. In short, we require a justification, and "justification consists in appealing to something independent."[11] There is more involved in Wittgenstein's discussion, but this is a rough outline of the major attack against private language. It can easily be seen that there is considerable similarity between this outline and Kant's argument on the second interpretation. In the Kantian argument we claim to know something about the temporal ordering of appearances, and when pushed for a justification the obvious answer is that we are *aware* of the ordering, just as the person in Wittgenstein's argument justifies ascription of private sensation terms by appeal to his *awareness* or impression of the connexion between the terms and the sensations. In both arguments it is shown that mere appearing or seeming is not enough, that it does not establish a difference between *seeming* to be right (about applying the term to the correct sensation, or about the correct order of the appearances) and actually *being* right. Both arguments go on from this point to claim that we must have a justification which consists in appeal to something independent of the impression or appearance, and finally both arguments identify these independent criteria as bound up with public observables. In each case it is argued that these independent sources are required, and not merely optional.

There is, of course, the obvious difference between the arguments that Wittgenstein extends it further and concludes that once we admit the "external" criteria the "inner" states simply drop out of the picture, while Kant is firmly, though on occasion uneasily, wedded to the phenomenological talk. But the point here is that there is a remarkable similarity between the general approaches in the two arguments. It is not the purpose of this paper to show that this type of argument, or the Kantian version of it, is sound, but what we can say of the second interpretation of the argument of the "Refutation" is that it results in an argument or the suggestion of an argument which has considerable plausibility, whatever the final verdict on it might be. The parallel with Wittgenstein's argument should be sufficient to show that it is a kind of argument which cannot be dismissed out of hand as obviously incoherent, and to this extent it is preferable to the first interpretation, the phenomenological one. Of the two most obvious interpretations of the argument of the "Refutation," then, the second is to be preferred to the first in so far as it can be given a coherent and perhaps even compelling form, while the phenomenological approach is either contradictory or without adequate grounds for its premises.

If we accept this second interpretation, however, we are faced with the consequence that at the very least the terminology of the section is confused, for the very statement of

---

[10] Ludwig Wittgenstein, *Philosophical Investigations* (Macmillan, 1953), #258.
[11] *Ibid.*, #265.

the thesis is in terms of consciousness, which is the sort of thing which can be mistaken, rather than knowledge. To make the argument coherent we must assume that wherever Kant speaks of consciousness he is using it as synonymous with experience or objective knowledge rather than with awareness as he seems to do in other places. This assumption is clearly preferable to the first interpretation which perhaps gives Kant credit for terminological consistency but transforms him into a fuzzy-thinking phenomenologist of sorts.

At this point it may be well to differentiate this interpretation of Kant's argument from another one which, superficially, appears much the same. In a highly provocative article in this journal (Volume VI, No. 1) Professor Skorpen argued for an interpretation which transformed the argument of the "Refutation" into one which establishes a realism of the Thomistic variety, and thereby refutes much of Kant's own position. This interpretation appears most clearly in a discussion of the meaning of "immediate" in Kant's claim that self-consciousness (self-knowledge) is immediate consciousness (knowledge) of the external world.

Professor Skorpen presents two major, closely related, points. He holds that knowledge of the self is also knowledge of the outside world, and second, that "self-knowledge is indeed 'immediate' knowledge of an outside world in the sense that any report on the former is analytically a report on the latter."[12] It should be clear that the first of these is at odds with the interpretation presented in this paper. My interpretation involves only that knowledge of the world is necessary for, or presupposed by, self-knowledge. Self-knowledge is not world-knowledge, although it implies it. Textual support can be found for both of these positions. The conclusion of Kant's proof lends credence to Skorpen's view: "The consciousness of my existence is at the same time an immediate consciousness of the existence of other things outside me" (B 276). A restatement of the conclusion in the first note, however, supports the alternate view: "In the above proof it has been shown that outer experience is really immediate, and that only by means of it is inner experience . . . possible" (B 276). Since this is the case there is no purpose in quibbling over the point, and we can be content with choosing that view which lends itself to the best interpretation of the argument as a whole.

This brings us to Skorpen's second major point, which outlines an interpretation of the Kantian argument different than the one developed above. Both Skorpen's and my interpretations reject the phenomenological approach discussed earlier. Although he is not too clear on the matter, his interpretation can be seen to rely on the experience or knowledge element, as does mine. It might be worthwhile to spell out his argument in some concise form:

    (1) I have knowledge of myself in time.

    (2) Any proposition specifying what I know about myself is true.

    (3) Any proposition specifying what I know about myself involves reference to an external world.

    (4) If the referent of any of the referring terms of a proposition does not, did not, and will not exist, then the proposition is not true.

Therefore (5) It is not the case that the referent of any of the referring terms of any proposition specifying what I know about myself does not, did not, and will not exist.

Therefore (6) The external world does, did, or will exist.

Skorpen does not, of course, present it in this form, but it seems to be a fair representa-

---

[12] Erling Skorpen, "Kant's Refutation of Idealism," *Journal of the History of Philosophy*, VI, 1 (January, 1968), 32.

tion of what he intended, and the premises he does not mention, (2) and (4), are not ones I would wish to dispute here. It should be obvious from this formulation that his interpretation, like my own, relies on the fact that we have *knowledge* of ourselves in time, not mere awareness or consciousness. If premises (1) and (3) are changed so as to be about awareness rather than knowledge, the argument will fail, for then there is no guarantee that the relevant propositions are ·true, and the truth of the propositions is essential to the argument.

The argument differs from the one developed in this paper, however, in relying on *reference* to the external world rather than dependence on such a world for justification or criteria of truth. Skorpen says self-knowledge implies world-knowledge because self-knowledge *refers to* the world; my position says that self-knowledge implies world-knowledge because the world provides the only possible justification for self-knowledge claims, or the only criterion of their truth. These are entirely distinct. A blood-sugar level of, say, 60 or less at a certain point in a glucose tolerance test may be the criterion for hypoglycemia, but to say that Hitler suffered from hypoglycemia is not to *refer to* such a test. A knowledge claim does not refer to its justification or the criterion for its truth.

Now, there are two major problems with Skorpen's version of the argument. The first is that it would unnecessarily limit the sorts of things we know about ourselves. For him all items of self-knowledge contain reference to the outer world, so if we come across any propositions about ourselves which do not make reference to the world we must conclude that we do not know them. Unfortunately, there are many such propositions. For example, "I felt sick before I thought of the solution to the equation $2x + 7 = 18$" may be such a proposition. It might, furthermore, be something I would want to claim I *knew*. If Skorpen is right I either cannot know this, or it makes some reference to the outer world. The latter possibility is clearly ruled out, so I am forced to conclude that I do not know the proposition. Skorpen guards himself against such examples by claiming, "even reports like 'I was hostile', 'I am hallucinating', etc., are elliptical for longer reports stating where, when, and under what circumstances."[13] This will not serve the purpose, however, for his examples are too restricted; they both contain predicates which presuppose some non-private world of objects or individuals. Hostility is the sort of thing directed at other people, and hallucination seems to rely on there being some sort of reality. The example of feeling sick and solving an equation does not rely on such presuppositions; I might feel sick and I might solve equations even if there were no external world. But what I could not do without an external world would be to *know* the temporal ordering of these two items of consciousness. There are innumerable examples like this where the questions of "where, when, and under what circumstances" need not be raised at all. Such examples point to nothing in the world, directly or otherwise. If Skorpen were correct we could not have knowledge in these cases. This is clearly too restrictive.

The second major problem with Skorpen's version of the argument is that it is not true to the intent of Kant's proof. Kant apparently took great satisfaction in turning the game played by idealism against itself (B 276). It is essential to the Kantian proof to start with an idealist premise. To begin with a disputed premise would be to produce an argument much weaker than the one Kant intended. Skorpen's version converts the argument into one which is based on just such a disputed premise. The premise in question is, of course, the claim that "I am conscious of my own existence as determined in time." On Skorpen's interpretation it turns out that the bits of knowledge which make up the knowledge

13 *Ibid.*, 33.

of my existence in time are bits which are *about the world* as well as myself since they refer to the world. That is, the examples which support the premise are about the world as well as myself. Now, clearly, a Cartesian would object to such a starting point, allowing as immediately known only those items which do not already refer to the world. A proposition like, "I am at my typewriter," would not be accepted by the Cartesian as immediately known, for knowing it would involve knowing something about the world outside my ideas, and this must be mediately known, if it is known at all. The very examples which Skorpen takes as backing for the premise, and which are necessary for his argument, are ones which the idealists would dispute—and they would dispute them because they are obviously *about the world* as well as the private individual. The interpretation I have suggested in this paper, however, works even if we throw out biographical propositions which refer to the world, and stick to such things as the temporal ordering of particular sensations. If we accept Skorpen's version, then, we weaken the Kantian argument by basing it on a disputed premise, while if we accept the version developed in this paper Kant's argument is seen to be based on a premise justified by appeal to examples indisputable to the idealists, as was Kant's apparent intention.

There remains one point on which Skorpen's argument and mine might be confused. It might seem that both versions argue for the existence of the same type of object, that my "objects in space" or "objects of scientific knowledge" are identical with Skorpen's Thomistic objects. Now, the first part of this seems substantially correct, but it is not as important as it might first appear. Both versions point only toward the existence of *non-private* objects, or objects open to public knowledge, but require nothing further about the nature of these objects. They might be Thomistic objects, or they might be objects "manufactured," as it were, by theory-relative observations within the context of the conceptual scheme of a scientific theory, or they might be something else; the only restriction is that they be public. If one were to make a case for the inconsistency of the "Refutation" with the rest of the *Critique* one would have to show that the objects of knowledge Kant deals with in the *Critique* as a whole are not public objects, for the public nature of the objects is all the "Refutation" establishes. This appears to be a rather unpromising task, but it is beyond the purpose of this paper to argue the point.

If we accept the argument in the form developed here, exactly what does it show? The conclusion of the argument is that *if* we have experience of inner states in time then we have experience of objects in space, that is, "outer" experience. This explicitly rules out a position such as Descartes' if we assume that Descartes would be willing to admit the starting point, that we have knowledge of our inner states in time. This is unobjectionable. But the argument has the obvious weakness that it will not touch any idealist who is willing to give up the claim that we have knowledge of our inner states in time. Although it is not perfectly clear what position Hume would take on this matter, it seems possible that one could develop a position consistent with the general outlines of Hume's position which would deny just the premise Kant needs for his refutation of idealism. One might hold that the only justification which could be given for a knowledge claim about, for example, the temporal relation of two awarenesses in the past would be some impression or image here and now; and since we have no way of checking to see whether the memory impression actually corresponds with the temporal ordering of the remembered experiences we can no more claim to *know* that the experiences occurred in that order than we can claim to know that our sensation of squareness corresponds with the actual primary qualities of some object in the world. There is simply no rational justification for such a claim, even though we may find it impossible to give up our beliefs regarding it. This can obviously be argued at considerable length, but a little thought should show that this line of reasoning is consistent with Hume's general position. This sort of position escapes Kant's refutation since it denies the original premise, that we have inner experience.

It might also be noted here that although Berkeley escaped the thrust of the argument Kant directed against him specifically, it seems that this second argument of the "Refutation" would hold against him as well as Descartes. It is unlikely that Berkeley would be willing to deny that we have knowledge of our inner states in time, and this is all that Kant requires. As is clear from Professor Turbayne's excellent article on the relation of Berkeley and Kant,[14] however, it may be that Berkeley would not be "refuted" by the conclusion of the Kantian argument. Turbayne convincingly argues that to a considerable degree the empirical realism Kant seeks to establish throughout all of the various refutations of idealism is the same as the realism which Berkeley ultimately held. If this is correct, then Berkeley may have *welcomed* the Kantian argument of the "Refutation" as new support for his position. At the very least we can say that Berkeley's position appears to be such that it allows the Kantian argument, whether or not that argument establishes a conclusion objectionable to Berkeley.

Of the two arguments of the "Refutation," then, we can conclude that the first, directed against Berkeley, simply misses the mark altogether and fails to establish what it claims to, while the second, if interpreted in the manner suggested, is a compelling argument against Descartes and perhaps Berkeley, although it fails to touch the complete skeptic who is not willing to allow that we have knowledge of inner states in time.

University of Western Ontario

---

[14] "Kant's Relation to Berkeley" in L. W. Beck, *Kant Studies Today* (Open Court, 1969), pp. 88–116.

Kant's Transcendental Idealism

by Wilfrid SELLARS,
University of Pittsburgh

I

1. When Kant mobilizes the position which he calls
'transcendental idealism' to resolve the antinomies, he describes it as
the doctrine that "everything intuited in space and time, and therefore
all objects of any experience possible to us, are nothing but appearances, that is, mere representations which, in the manner in which
they are represented, as extended beings or as series of alterations,
have no independent existence outside our thoughts." He contrasts
this thesis with that of the "realist, in the transcendental meaning of
the term" who "treats these modifications of our sensibility as self-
subsistant things, that is, treats *mere representations* as things in
themselves" (A 490-1; B 518-9).

2. Since Kant calls his idealism 'transcendental' in order to indicate that it enables him to account for the existence of synthetic
a priori knowledge concerning objects in space and time, he has,
strictly speaking, no use for the term 'transcendental realism.' since
on his account of synthetic *a priori* knowledge we could have no
such knowledge of spatio-temporal objects if they were things themselves. Nor did realists, as he sees it, claim that their realism accounted for the existence of such knowledge, although at least some of
them would have taken realism to be compatible with it.

3. The title of this essay is, of course, overly ambitious. In
particular, it seems to promise as much discussion of 'transcendental'
as of 'idealism.' My primary concern, however, is with the ontological aspects of Kant's idealism, and only incidentally (and by implication) with epistemological issues concerning synthetic *a priori*
knowledge. I note in passing, however, that since the ontological
aspects of Kant's idealism concern in large part the ontology of mental
states, and since, although epistemology is not psychology, it is
mental states which are the proper subjects of epistemic appraisal,
Kant's ontology of mental states is directly relevant to his epistemology and, consequently, to his transcendental philosophy.

■ 193 ■

4. I shall be primarily concerned with the views Kant expresses in the first edition. I am, however, in whole-hearted agreement with his claim that there is a fundamental identity between the views expressed in the two editions. In the *Preface* to the second edition (B xxxvii ff.) he explains the changes he has made as a matter of removing "difficulties and obscurity" which "not, perhaps, without my fault, may have given rise to misunderstandings," and of omitting or abridging, to make room for new material, "certain passages which, though not indeed essential to the completeness of the whole may yet be missed by many readers as otherwise helpful." He suggests that the "loss [...] can be remedied by consulting the first edition," thus implying that the deleted material coheres with the new material. As regards "the propositions themselves and their proofs," however, he claims that he has "found nothing to alter," a statement which he shortly repeats with even greater force by characterizing the new edition as "altering absolutely nothing in the fundamentals of the propositions put forward or even in their proofs," though he does grant that this [he hopes] more intelligent exposition [...] "here and there departs so far from the previous method of treatment that mere interpolations could not be made to suffice" (B xlii).

5. It is surely implied by these claims that in Kant's eyes the refutation of idealism which was added in the second edition is not only compatible with the teachings of the first, but is implied by them. I think this is correct. The 'new' refutation simply applies the content of the *Analytic of Principles,* and, in particular, the *Analogies* to the topic of idealism, an application which is present in, though not highlighted by, the first edition refutation. And when Kant explains why he has relocated the refutation in the *Postulates of Empirical Thought,* his reason is a good one rather than, as Bennett characterizes it, a "silly" one.[1] Anyone who studies the fourth Paralogism must feel the awkwardness involved not only in classifying the theses of Rational Psychology in terms of 'relation,' 'quality,' 'quantity' and 'modality,' but, in particular, the treatment of problematic idealism as the modal counterpart of the substantiality, simplicity and personal identity of the soul. The relation of our knowledge of material things to our perceptual experiences is far more at home in a section devoted to the thesis that "that which is bound up with the material conditions of experience, that is, with sensation, is actual." For this bound-up-ness, when one spells it out *does have* an inferential aspect and therefore does lead naturally to the Cartesian problem.

6. I shall not, therefore, discuss the second edition refutation as such, since I hope to convince you that its familiar claims are in-

[1] *Kant's Analytic,* p. 166.

deed contained in the first edition, indeed in the first edition refutation itself. For in spite of its 'subjectivist' flavor, the latter contains a reference to and, indeed, a summary of the answer to the
question "What is an object of representations?" raised first in the
introductory passages of the first edition Transcendental Deduction,
answered in highly schematic form, raised again in the Second
Analogy, and this time given a fleshed-out answer which is repeated
in the text of the second edition. And it is Kant's answer to *this*
question which is central to the contrast he draws between his
idealism and the idealisms he calls 'dogmatic' and 'problematic.'

II

7. In the passage from the *Dialectic* with which I began, transcendental idealism is characterized *directly* as the view that "everything intuited in space and time, and therefore all objects of any
experience possible to us, are nothing but appearances, that is mere
representations which [...] have no independent existence outside
our thoughts." It is characterized *indirectly* by its contrast with
realism "in the transcendental sense," according to which these
objects are "self-subsistant things," or "things in themselves." In a
key footnote which occurs in the fourth Paralogism (A 375n) Kant
writes

> We must give full credence to this paradoxical but correct proposition,
> that there is nothing in space save what is represented in it. For space is
> itself nothing but representation, and whatever is in it must therefore be
> contained in the representation. Nothing whatsoever is in space, save insofar
> as it is actually represented in it. It is a proposition which must indeed
> sound strange, that a thing can exist only in the representation of it, but
> in this case the objection falls, in as much as the things with which we
> are concerned are not things themselves, but appearances only, that is,
> representations.

Kant here does not use the contrast between existence 'inside' or 'outside' our 'thoughts,' but it is clear that he is treating the relevant
sense of 'representation' as equivalent to 'thought,' for he has just
written that while "something which may be (in the transcendental
sense) outside us" — i.e. which exists in itself — "is the
cause of our outer intuitions [...] this is not the object of which
we are *thinking* in the representations of matter and of corporeal
things; for these are merely appearances, that is mere kinds of representation, which can never be met with save in us..." (A 372). It is
clear that to 'represent' is here a case of to 'think' and that Kant,
who is elaborating the definition he has just given of 'transcendental
idealism' as

> the doctrine that appearances are to be regarded as being one and all
> representations only and not things in themselves (A 369)

is introducing in his comments on this definition the formula of the
later definition in the *Dialectic* according to which the objects of
intuition "have no independent existence outside our thoughts."

8.   Intuitions, in the relevant sense, are a species of 'thought'
and when Kant says that appearances are "mere kinds of representation", we certainly should not interpret this as meaning that appearances are mental acts of thinking. They are items which exist 'in' our
thoughts, i.e. which are, in an appropriate sense, represented*s* rather
than acts of represent*ing*. And when he adds that "appearances are
not to be met with save in us" this must, of course, be construed in
terms of his distinction between the 'empirical' and the "transcendental' senses of 'in us' and 'outside us.'

9.   Now mental acts which are intuitings are not, of course
judgings. But they are nevertheless *thoughts*. In the important classification of representations (*vorstellungen*) which Kant gives in an
introductory passage of the *Dialectic* (A 319; B 376) Kant includes
sensations as well as intuitions as representations. A sensation however is a "mere modification of the mind," whereas an intuition
(though not a *general* concept) is an "*erkenntnis*" ("*Cognitio*"). Its
distinctive feature is that although, like a general concept, a *cognitio,*
it is a singular one and does not refer to an object "mediately by
means of a feature which several things may have in common" as do
general concepts.

10.   Kant holds the interesting and important view which I have
explored elsewhere,[2] that an 'intuition of a manifold' as contrasted
with a sheer 'manifold of intuition' is an 'erkenntnis' which presents
us much as does an Aristotelian 'phantasm' (*tode-ti*) *as* a this-such,
though it is not a judgment of the form '(this) is (such).'[3] In a
paragraph (A 79; B 105) of the Metaphysical Deduction of the
Categories, which can almost be described as the Transcendental
Deduction and the Schematism in embryo, Kant tells us, in effect,
that intuitions of manifolds contain the very categories which can
be found in the general concepts which we apply to these intuitions
(and which we have, indeed, by "analytic thinking", derived from
them) (A 78-9).

> The same function which gives unity to the various representations *in*
> *a judgment* also gives unity to the mere synthesis of various representations
> *in an intuition;* and this unity, in its most general expression, we entitle
> the pure concept of the understanding. The same understanding through
> the same operations by which in concepts, by means of analytical unity,

---

[2] *Science and Metaphysics*, London and New York, 1968, Chapter I.
[3] One should also bear in mind Ockham's concept of a perceptual intuition,
and his claim that God could bring it about that the object intuited not exist.

it produced the logical form of a judgment, also introduces a transcendental content into its representations, by means of the synthetic unity of the manifold in intuition in general. On this account we are entitled to call these representations pure concepts of the understanding, and to regard them as applying *a priori* to objects — a conclusion which general logic is not in a position to establish.

Thus singular judgments which express basic perceptions have the form

(This-such) is *so and so*

and the categories which are implicit in the general concept *so-and-so* can be true of the subject of the judgment, i.e. the object intuited, because the intuition of the *this-such* also contains the categories.

11. It is essential to see that intuition is a species of *thought,* for any sense-datum like approach makes essential features of Kant's theory of knowledge unintelligible, e.g. the *Schematism.* Thus the categories apply to intuitions, because, although the content of *sensations* does not contain the categories, the content of *intuitions* (of manifolds) does. *This* is the point of Kant's problem about homogeneity and of his solution.

III

12. Let us take seriously, then, the thesis that intuitions of manifolds are thoughts. And let us apply to them the ontological categories which the Cartesian tradition, rooted in scholastic tradition had applied to thoughts. An adequate discussion would call for a whole cluster of distinctions in which themes from Husserl, the early Brentano, Meinong, and the later Brentano would be inextricably involved. I shall use a bare minimum of distinctions and resolutely avoid probing into the deeper metaphysical issues involved.

13. Descartes distinguishes between the act and the content aspects of thoughts. The content, of course, 'exists in' the act. And, of course, contents *as contents* exist only 'in' acts. On the other hand, there is a sense in which something which 'exists in' an act can also exist, to use Kant's phrase, 'outside' the act. In Descartes terminology, that which exists 'in' the act as its 'content' can have 'formal reality' in the world.[4]

14. The concept of 'existence in thought' is, of course, a metaphor. So, of course, is the idea that a thought is *true* if its content

---

[4] I have avoided Descartes' use of the phrase 'objective reality' in connection with contents, since it has, of course, a quite different meaning in Kant and in contemporary philosophy.

'corresponds' to something actual in the world. In the Cartesian tradition, this account of truth holds both of thoughts of individuals and thoughts of states of affairs. Thus a thought of an individual is true if there 'corresponds' to it an actual individual, i.e. if the individual exists not only 'in the thought' as its content, but in the actual world. Similarly, the thought of a state of affairs is true if there 'corresponds' to it an actual state of affairs, i.e. if the state of affairs which exists in the thought as its content, also exists in the actual world.

15. I have spoken of *actuality* where Descartes speaks of 'formal reality.' In Kant's terminology what Descartes means by 'formal reality,' and which Cartesians would *equate* with actuality, is 'existence in itself' or, to use the latinate term of the *Prolegomena,* existence *'per se.'* Kant clearly accepts the Cartesian contrast between 'existence in thought' and 'existence *per se,'* — so much so that he takes it for granted, as did most of his predecessors.[5]

16. One final terminological point: The *content* of the thought of an individual was considered to be, in an important sense, an *object* of the thought. Indeed the thought would have in this sense an object even if nothing in the actual world corresponded to it. Later philosophers drew tidy distinctions between 'immanent objects' and 'transcendent objects,' and we are all familiar with the intuitive appeal of these metaphors. Philosophical terminology consists largely of metaphor added to metaphor in the hope that the mixture will crystalize out into clear and distinct categories.

17. For Kant, then, an act of intuiting a manifold is a thinking of a this-such in space and/or time. The this-such is something that exists 'in' the act. The problem with which Kant is dealing can be characterized initially as that of whether individuals in space and/or time also have existence *per se.* Kant's answer, to anticipate, is that these intuited items exist *only* 'in' acts of intuition.[6] That is, no items in space and/or time exists *per se.* He will nevertheless insist that some items which exist in acts of intuition are *actual.* This obviously requires a distinction between *actuality* and *existence per se,* which were conflated by his predecessors.

---

[5] Including the British Empiricists who, in the process of muddling through to important philosophical insights, muddied many classical distinctions.
[6] A more complete discussion of this point would have to comment on those passages in which Kant allows that things in themselves are objects of perceptual intuitions. After all, if the latter contain the pure categories, and if the latter constitute 'the pure concept' of an 'object' ["The pure concept of this transcendental object which... (concept) in all our knowledge is always one and the same (A 109)], then things in themselves would 'correspond' (in the Cartesian sense) to intuitions, though not *qua* intuitions of spatio-temporal items. See A 490-1; B 518-9 quoted in the first paragraph; see also *Science and Metaphysics,* pp. 42 ff

IV

18.   It will be useful to connect Kant's concept of the intuition of a manifold' with that strand of contemporary perception theory which operates with fairly traditional concepts of intentionality. A familiar notion is that of a perceptual taking. Perceptual takings are, so to speak, thinkings which are evoked in our minds by our environment or, in limiting cases, by abnormal states of our nervous system. Perceptual takings are usually thought to have propositional form. One takes *this is a cat*. One takes *there is a cat on that mat*. I suggest that what is taken is best expressed by a *referring* expression, thus 'this cat on this mat.' We should think of perceptual takings as providing *subjects* for propositional thought, rather than already having full-fledged propositional form.

19. · Again, if we think of a taking as a special case of a *believing*, it is best to think of it as a 'believing in' rather than a 'believing that.' In a perceptual taking one believes in *this cat on this mat*, and may believe, for example, that *this cat on this mat* is a siamese. Thus construed, perceptual takings are in many respects the counterparts of Kant's 'intuitions of manifolds.' They represent this-suchs; and it is worth noting that although they are not explicitly propositional in form, they obviously *contain* propositional form in the sense in which 'that green table is broken' contains 'that table is green.'

V

20.   Little needs to be said at this stage of the argument about the 'problematic idealism' Kant attributes to Descartes. Problematic idealism regards the claim that material things and processes exist *per se* as a coherent one, but one which can be established only by an inference from our perceptual states; an inference from effect to cause. Mental states have a privileged position in that they not only *can* have existence *per se*, but it is known, indeed 'directly' known, that some mental state exist *per se*.

21.   Before looking at Kant's refutation of problematic idealism, it is worth pausing to ask: If this is 'problematic' idealism, what might 'dogmatic' idealism be? One would expect it to be the view that material objects in space and time *could not* have existence *per se*, i.e. that there was an absurdity or contradiction in the idea of the existence *per se* of material objects. Berkeley certainly held this position, a fact which might strengthen the temptation to interpret dogmatic idealism along these lines.

22.   It is also worth noting that Berkeley did not deny that in a sense we (and a *fortiori* God) can conceive of material objects in space and time, where by the phrase 'material objects' I mean, so to speak, Lockean objects and *not* patterns of actual and counterfactual perceptual experiences.[7] Berkeley can be construed as holding that our actual and counterfactual perceptual experiences are grounded in God's plan to cause us to have those experiences we would have if (a metaphysical counterfactual) there *were* material objects including human bodies with sense organs, and minds and bodies were able to interact. In less theological terms, this can be formulated as the view that what exists *per se* other than our minds is the causal ground of our actual and counterfactual perceptual experiences.

23.   To return to the main line of argument it is only too clear that if we mean by 'dogmatic idealism' with respect to material objects the view that they cannot have existence *per se*, then Kant is a dogmatic idealist of the first water. Indeed, as we have seen, Kant makes dogmatic idealism *in this sense* the very corner stone of his transcendental idealism.

24.   What, then, does Kant mean by dogmatic idealism? And is any such view to be found in Berkeley? It should be clear that the only answer to the first question which satisfies the requirements of the argument to date is that Kant means by dogmatic idealism the view that nothing spatial can be *actual*, where actual does not mean 'exists *per se*.' Indeed Kant's own idealism, while denying that material objects exist *per se*, nevertheless insists that some at least of the spatial objects which exist 'in our thoughts' and, in particular, in our acts and intuitions, or perceptual takings, are, in the critical sense, *actual*.

25.   But what of the second question? To what extent is Kant justified in attributing to Berkeley the view which he (Kant) would express by saying that no spatial items are actual?[8] After all, *if*, as is often claimed, Kant in the first edition and on occasion in the second edition construes physical objects in terms of actual and counterfactual perceptual experiences, is he not in essential agreement with Berkeley?[9]

---

[7] I deliberately use this vaguer expression 'perceptual experiences' instead of 'perceptual takings,' since one of the essential differences between Kant and Berkeley concerns the analysis of what it is to be a perceptual experience.
[8] Notice that to pinpoint the issue I have retreated from the phrase 'material object' to 'spatial item.'
[9] Notice once again that I deliberately used the vaguer phrase 'perceptual experience.' for in the last analysis everything will hinge on how this phrase is interpreted.

VI

26.   At this point we must retrace our steps in order to advance. My discussion of Descartes' ontology of mental acts was not only schematic but radically incomplete.   For Descartes had *two* paradigms of what it is to be a mental state. Let me begin with the one I have neglected. Sensation is a mental state, though one in which the body is intimately involved, and his paradigm of a sensation is a feeling of pain.[10] To us, the obvious feature of a feeling of pain is that a feeling of pain simply *is* a pain. The existence of a feeling of pain is identical with the existence of a pain. Much more would need to be said to nail this point down,[11] but after all the analytic work has been done, the fact remains that a pain is a kind of feeling. If we put this by saying that a pain is a 'content' or 'object' of feeling, this should be regarded simply as a (misleading) paraphrase of the above. The danger arises from the fact that this usage would tend to assimilate feelings of pain to Descartes' second paradigm, the clear distinct *thought* of an object. It is in connection with the latter that he elaborates the distinctions which were inherited by Kant.

27.   It was obvious to Descartes that the mental state of thinking of a cube is not (at least in any ordinary sense of 'is') a cube. Thus, whereas a feeling of pain is a pain, a thinking of a cube is not a cube. Now in his systematic account of sensation, Descartes construes visual sensation on the model of pain. In terms of this paradigm, a sensation of red would be a case of red as a feeling of pain is a case of pain.   His construal, however, as Gassendi saw,[12] confronted Descartes with a problem. Surely the colors we experience have shape. But if the colors we experience have shape, then, if they are sensations construed on the model of pain, mental states can have shape. To get experienced color and shape together, Descartes, it seems, must either

(a)   give experienced colors the same status as shapes (deny that either can be a modification of the mind);

(b)   give the shapes of experienced colors the same status as colors (admit that modifications of the mind can have shape, as Gassendi thought we should).

[10] Another paradigm is to be found in his use of 'sensation' in connection with *seeming to see* in the second meditation. But while there is clearly a close connection between sensing and seeming to see an object, they are not identical, nor does Descartes equate them in his developed philosophy of mind.

[11] I have discussed this topic in "Metaphysics and the Concept of a Person," in *The Logical Way of Doing Things*, edited by Karel Lambert, New Haven, 1969 (reprinted as chapter XI in *Essays in Philosophy and its History* published by Reidel, Dordrecht, Holland, 1974).

[12] *Philosophical Works of Descartes*, eds. Haldane and Ross, Dover, 1934. Vol. II, pp. 196-7.

28.   Descartes gives no clear account of the matter. His official account is that while the sensation of red as such is unextended, the shape we perceive, and which has existence 'in thought', is confusedly believed to be the shape of something which *resembles* the sensation of red. Such beliefs date from early childhood. They are confused, because nothing can be like a sensation of red without being a sensation of red, and hence a modification of the mind[13]. In effect, Descartes gives perceived red the status of *believed in* red, and by doing so gives it the existence 'in thought' which the shape also has. This move requires a distinction between the sensed red which we introspect, and which is not extended, and the perceived shaped red, which is a *content* rather than a *modification* of the mind.

29.   Now Berkeley, as is well known, also assimilated color to pain. What, then, of shaped colors? When one feels a pain, there is an actual case of pain. When one senses a color, there is an actual case of color. But when the mind senses a triangle of red, is there an actual case of shape? When *directly* confronted with this question,[14] Berkeley's answer is *no*. The shape exists only 'by way of idea,' and it is clear that *here* the operative conception is a Cartesian *cogitatio* of which the shape is a *content* in a sense which does not entail that a mental state has a shape. But though Berkeley gives this answer, he is simply not clear about the status of shapes, and what stands out is his assimilation of the status of shape to that of color and, ultimately, to that of pain.[15]

30.   Now if Berkeley had consistently held that perceived shapes are not features of mental states, but have existence only 'in our thoughts' (in the Cartesian sense) he could nevertheless have argued (perhaps on proto-Kantian grounds) that no shapes have existence *per se*. Shapes would not exist 'outside the mind' in what Kant called the transcendental sense. They would exist only 'in' the mind, not as features of its states but as immanent objects. Berkeley, however, because of the slippery slope pain-color-shape, makes the quite different claim that shapes can not exist 'outside the mind' in the sense in which *pains* can not exist outside the mind. Even though he is not prepared to say in so many words that shapes are essentially features of mental states, he actually commits himself to this position.

---

[13] *Principles of Philosophy*, LXVII-LXX.

[14] *Principles of Human Knowledge*, section 49 (Fifth Objection).

[15] A more penetrating account would demonstrate that Berkeley initially conceived of all 'perceptions' as in the 'understanding' a move which, by taking thoughts as the paradigm of mental states, constituted exactly that blurring of the distinction between sensibility and understanding so obviously present in Spinoza, Leibnitz and the Wolffians — which Kant was to regard as a key philosophical error.

31. Thus it is not unfair on Kant's part to attribute to Berkeley the view that the concept of shaped items which are not mental states is an incoherent one, as incoherent as would be the concept of a pain which was not a mental state.

32. Now it is as evident to Kant as it was to Descartes that neither space itself nor any spatial object can be a modification of the mind or of a mental state. Thus, while Kant denies that either space or any spatial object has existence *per se*, and argues that the idea that they do is an incoherent one, he *also* argues that the idea of shapes which are not features of mental states is itself a coherent one. Thus, if shapes which are not features of mental states do not exist *per se* it is not because shapes are essentially features of mental states, but because shapes belong in space, and neither space nor anything in space can exist in itself.

33. We can now begin to appreciate why in Kant's sense of the term Berkeley was a 'dogmatic idealist,' and to interpret the following passage:

> Berkeley [...] maintains that space, with all the things of which it is the inseparable condition, is in itself impossible and he therefore regards the things in space as merely imaginary entities (B 274).

Given that Kant is clearly aware that on his own view neither space nor objects in space can exist in themselves, the *gravamen* of the charge against Berkeley must be that the latter's *reason* for holding this is such as to require, as his (Kant's) reasons do not, that "things in space are merely imaginary entities." For, once again, Kant clearly has up his sleeve the view that material things, though they necessarily lack existence *per se*, which was the *traditional* concept of actuality, can in the *critical* sense be actual. On my interpretation Kant would be recognizing that Berkeley's *reason* for rejecting the existence *per se* of space and spatial objects would be that shape and extension are essentially features of mental states. The concept of spatial items which are not mental states would be a figment of the *philosophical* imagination. They would be radically imaginary, not just imaginary in the empirical sense.

34. Kant obscures the justice of his characterization of Berkeley's position in the remark which follows, in which he claims that

> Dogmatic idealism is unavoidable if space be interpreted as a property that belongs to things in themselves. For in that case, space and everything to which it serves as a condition, is a non-entity (B 274).

Here the direct connection with Berkeley is lost. But that is as it should be, for Kant is merely pointing out that one can arrive at the conclusion that the concept of actual spatial items other than mental states is incoherent by a route other than Berkeley's. For if space is a property which must belong to things in themselves, then, Kant has argued, there can be no such thing. Hence, given the classical interpretation of actuality as existence *per se*, it would follow that the concept of an *actual* spatial object is incoherent. And if the only alternative to holding that space is a property of things in themselves were, as Berkeley thought it was, the view that spatial items are features of mental states, then the concept of actual spatial items which are not features of mental states would *also* be incoherent. We would be faced by a dilemma.

> *Either* space is by nature a thing in itself or a property of things in themselves *or* the spatial items which underlie our concepts of space and spatial items are (features of) mental states (sensations). On either alternative the concept of actual spatial items which are not mental states is incoherent.

Kant has prepared the way for an escape through the horns of this dilemma. He points out that the argument of the *Æsthetic* enables him to avoid the view that space is either a thing in itself or a property of things in themselves without agreeing with Berkeley that the concept of spatial items which are not mental states is incoherent.

35.   Yet even after he has established to his own satisfaction that the concept of an *actual* spatial item which is not a mental state is coherent, he still has to make the essential point that the concept of *actuality* does not coincide, as it traditionally did, with that of existence *per se*.

36.   I take it to be clear, then, that Kant holds that no spatial item (notice the cautious use of the term 'item' as contrasted with the richer term 'object') is a mental state. It can, however, be argued that in the first edition and on occasion in the second edition Kant held that material *objects* are, to use an anachronistic turn of phrase, logical constructions out of mental states which, though not spatial, are *representations of* spatial *items* — i.e. of which spatial items are the *content* or immanent objects. After all, he *does* write that

> In our system, on the other hand, these external things, namely matter, are in all their configurations and alterations nothing but mere appearances, that is, representations in us, of the reality of which we are immediately conscious (A 371-2).

I think that this interpretation is a mistake, though it must be confessed that because of his failure to make it clear when he is using 'representation' (and, in particular, 'intuition') in the sense of *act* of representing, and when he is using these terms in the sense of *content* represented, it has some initial plausibility.

37.   The crux of the matter as Kant clearly saw is his account of what it is to be an object of acts of representing. He formulates this account schematically in a passage (A 104) which prepares the

way for the first edition Transcendental Deduction, and develops it in a more full-bodied way in a key passage in the Second Analogy which occurs in both editions.[16]

38.   Our primary concern is with *perceptual* acts or takings. But in the first passage referred to above, Kant makes his key point in a way which abstracts, as the passage in the Second Analogy does not, from essential aspects of perceptual takings. Nevertheless, the concepts for which Kant is preparing the way is that of *rules for generating perceptual takings.*[17]

39.   The term 'rule' is a dangerous one, for its suggests deliberate activity or, at least, activity which would be deliberate if it weren't so *hasty* and, in the ordinary sense, thoughtless. Actually the most useful concept is that of a sequence of acts of representing which can reflectively be classified as conforming to a rule which is (at least in principle) graspable by thought. The rules in question must, according to Kant, be available, if one is to recognize that one's acts of representing belong together as an intelligible sequence.[18]

40.   Now it might be thought that by introducing the concept of a rule-governed sequence of perceptual representings, i.e. acts of perceptual taking, I am giving hostages to the view that material objects consist of rule-conforming sequences of perceptual takings. That I am *not* is implied by the fact (which I hope to make clear) that even the most tough-minded transcendental realist grants that veridical perceptual takings have the coherence which Kant is attempting to clarify by the concept of rule-conforming sequences. Roughly, Kant's transcendental realist thinks of the perceiver as deriving these rules by induction from experience, whereas Kant thinks that induction itself presupposes an antecedent grasp of these rules.

VII

41.   We can now turn our attention to Kant's initial explanation of what it is to be an 'object of representations.' He asks us to consider the intuitive representation of a triangle. Here the rich impli-

---

[16] I have in mind the passage (A 190; B 235) introduced as follows: "... it is a question for deeper inquiry that the word 'object' ought to signify in respect of appearances when these are viewed not in so far as they are (as representations) objects, but only in so far as they stand for an object."
[17] It might be helpful, here, to think of rules for generating sequences of acts of *imagining* which would be the counterparts of perceptual takings, if they had their source in outer sense.
[18] An elaboration of this theme would require an exploration in detail of Kant's conception of the transcendental unity of apperception as a necessary correlate of the intuition of objects.

cations of the concept of a perceptual taking are laid aside, for the
moment, and we are given an explanation which could concern a
construction in pure geometry. For the essential point he wants to
make is that while the object of the intuitive representing is indeed
a *triangle*, the triangle is not an existent *per se*, and that although
the content *triangle* specifies sequences of representing which count
as *coming to represent a triangle*, the object of the representing of
a triangle is *not* the sequence of representings which culminate in
the representing of the triangle. A triangle is neither a mental act of
representing a triangle, nor is it a sequence of mental acts each of
which represents a part of a triangle.

42. Before turning to the passage in the Second Analogy
which is essentially a development of the passage on which I have
been commenting but one which does take into account the specific
character of perceptual takings, let me elaborate briefly on the
triangle example in a way which will make for a smooth and easy
transition. After all, Kant's account of 'drawing figures in thought'
i.e. in pure intuition, is an idealized version, ascribed to the mind,
of drawing figures on paper. Now if we take seriously the three-
dimensionality of space, it strikes us that to represent a triangle in
space is always to represent it *from a point of view*. Thus, what we
represent is

  this equilateral triangle facing me straight-on
or
  this equilateral triangle at such and such an angle to my (metaphorical)
  line of sight.

43. Now it is by no means an original idea on my part that
intuitive representings of figures in three-dimensional space are essentially point-of-viewish. But its importance has been underestimat-
ed. For it means that we must distinguish between the figures —
which are *not* point-of-viewish — and the *total* content of the representing of the figure, which *total* content is point-of-viewish, thus

  equilateral triangle facing me straight on.

Let me repeat. Equilateral triangles are not point of viewish, but
they are, so to speak, intuited in perspective. The representing has
a content which specifies a point of view.

44. Thus, the *object* of a representing of an equilateral triangle
from a certain point of view is simply the equilateral triangle. But,
according to Kant's position, according to which we 'construct' or
'draw' figures in space, the concept of an equilateral triangle must
specify not only a sequence of representings in which we represent
one line, then, continuing to represent that line represent another line
at a sixty degree angle, then, continuing to represent these we rep-

resent the third side. It must also specify in an intelligible way what it means for two representings to be representings of an equilateral triangle from different points of view, i.e. representings which have the contents

equilateral triangle face-on

equilateral triangle at such and such an angle to my 'line of sight'

45. The notion of representings which have contents of this form obviously builds on pervasive features of perceptual takings. I do not simply perceptually accept a house; the content of my perceptual acceptance is something like

this house over there facing me left-edge-of-front-wise.

46. The point I am making is simple, but it is so essentially a part of a larger story that I shall have to disguise the torn edges to put it across. When, in the Second Analogy, Kant says (A 191; B 236) that "the object is *that* in the appearance which contains the condition of this necessary rule of apprehension," he is commenting on the example of a house which he has just introduced:

...immediately I unfold the transcendental meaning of my concepts of an object, I realize that the house is not a thing in itself but only an appearance, that is a representation ... (A 190-1; B 236).

Here it is clear that he means by 'representation' something *represented* i.e. a content or immanent object of an act of representing.

47. Nevertheless, although he calls the house an appearance, where this clearly does not mean that the house is an act of *representing*, he does say that

The appearance ... is nothing but the sum of these representations (of apprehension)

and it might be thought that Kant is characterizing the house as a sum of *acts* of representing. It is therefore important to note that he characterized the representations in question as "*that which lies in the successive apprehension.*" (A 191; B 236, emphasis mine) This must surely be his way of warning us that 'representation' here means *represented* rather than *representing*, i.e. Kant is relating the content *house* to the *contents* of successive *acts* of apprehension.

48. Kant is answering the question 'in what sense is the house the *object* of successive acts of apprehension.' His negative answer is that it is not *qua* house in itself. The actuality of the house *qua* object is not its existence *per se*. What is his positive answer? As I see it, he is telling us that the house *qua* object is that aspect of the content of the perceptual takings which explains (together with certain other factors) the belonging together *as state of the perceiver* of

certain perceptual takings (apprehendings). *But that aspect of the content of these perceptual takings is simply the content house which they share, thus*

```
house over there left-front-edgewise to me
house over there facing me
left side of house over there facing me
etc., etc.
```

49.   As in the geometrical example, all the representings are representings of a non-point-of-viewish object — the house — from a point of view, i.e. representings of house-from-a-certain-point-of-view. It is, in this sense, that the house is the sum of the point of viewish appearances. But if the total content of a perceptual act is point-of-viewish, it is *because* it is the content of a *perceptual* act. Thus, while the content *house* is not a point-of-viewish content, it explains (together with certain other factors) why such and such perceptual represent*ings* with contents which can be subsumed under the rubric

```
house-from-such-and-such-a-point-of-view
```

take place. Thus, the concept of a house as a perceptible object essentially involves a reference to perceptual acts, i.e. to the perceptual takings of a perceiver.

50.   Nevertheless the concept of a house as perceptible object is not the concept of the sequences of perceptual takings (actual and counterfactual) which (together with other factors) it explains. To pull my points together in one sentence,

> The object of a perceptual representing of a house is the non-perspectival content *house;* yet as the sort of item that can be the object of a perceptual representing, it must provide rules for explaining (together with other factors) why such and such sequences of perceptual takings with perspectival contents were necessary.

51.   It will have been noticed that I have written in several passages above that the content *house* is the source of rules which explain *together with other factors* why such and such sequences of perceptual takings were necessary. What do I mean by 'other factors'? The answer should be obvious, and peeks out from almost every page of the *Analogies. House* by itself can generate no explanation of the occurrence of a sequence of perceptual takings. It is only *house in such and such relations to a perceiver* which can do this. And this, obviously, means to a perceiver's body, and, of course his sense organs. The essential structure of the content of perceptual takings is not just

```
house from a certain geometrical point of view
```

but, to make a complicated point in a simple way

house in front ot my *sightful eyes*
ship in water moving to the left of *my sightful·eyes.*

In my argument I have thinned out this mutual involvement of object, circumstances and embodied perceiver into a ghostly 'object from a point of view.' But Kant took seriously the fact that perceivers are embedded in a spatio-temporal system of interacting substances. In other words the doctrine of the double affection of the self, far from being a problematic feature of Kant's critical idealism, is an essential feature of it, and is present in and, indeed, an essential feature of the argument of the Second Analogy.[19]

52. Kant denies that material things and processes exist *per se*, but he holds that in the critical sense they can be *actual* as contents which make an essential contribution to the explanation of the patterns in which perceptual experiences occur. But the deeper thrust of Kant's transcendental idealism is the thesis that the core of the knowable self is the self *as perceiver of material things and events.* And if it is relatively easy to see that the distinction between actual and non-actual material things and events is tied to the concept of an *actual* sequence of perceptual takings, it has (until recently) proved less easy to see that the distinction between actual and non-actual sequences of perceptual takings. i.e. between perceptual takings which are correctly and those which are incorrectly taken to have occurred in one's mental history, is tied to the concept of actual material things and events.

53. Kant saw that the concept of an *object* of perception contains a reference to the perceptual takings which are the criteria for its actuality. He *also* saw that the concept of a perceptual taking, as the taking of an *object,* contains a reference to material things and events which, if actual, would imply its own actuality. The actuality of perceptual takings and the actuality of material things and processes are not logically independent. And since, for Kant, the concept of matter-of-factual truth concerns the agreement of what we represent with what is, *in the critical sense,* actual, rather than, as traditionally, with what exists *per se,* he can pay his respects to what he calls "the nominal definition of truth" while giving it a radically new interpretation.

---

[19] As noted above (paragraph 22) even Berkeley came to see that the intelligibility of the patterns in which perceptual experiences occur involves the concept of embodied perceivers in a material world. However, since he was convinced that material objects could not exist *per se,* he gave them existence in God's Understanding and Providence as essential features of his plan for causing us to have the experiences we do.

KANT'S PHENOMENALISM

RICHARD E. AQUILA

I want to state as clearly as I can the sense in which Kant is, and the sense in which he is not, a phenomenalist. And I also want to state the argument which Kant presents, in the Transcendental Deduction, for his particular version of phenomenalism. Since that doctrine has been stated by Kant himself as the view that we have knowledge of "appearances" only, and not of things in themselves, or that material objects are nothing but a species of our "representations," it will of course be part of my task in this paper to deal with these fundamental notions. Some recent works on Kant have completely misinterpreted these notions, and because of this they have failed to capture the peculiar character of Kant's phenomenalism. Jonathan Bennett, for example, interprets Kant's claim that "objects are nothing but representations" as the claim that "statements about objects must be translatable into statements about intuitions."[1] I shall call such a view a reductive phenomenalism and argue in this paper that Kant is not a reductive phenomenalist. But Kant is, all the same, a phenomenalist. I shall call him an existential phenomenalist. The difference is this: Kant does not maintain, as Bennett claims, that all propositions which assert or presuppose the existence of objects must be translatable into statements which refer to intuitions alone, but he does hold that all such propositions are translatable into statements about the *existence* of intuitions alone. When Kant tells us, therefore, that objects are mere "appearances," he is not offering a theory about what empirical objects *are* (e.g., collections of sense-data) or about what we are really *referring* to when we refer to such objects, but he is offering a theory about the sense in which any empirical objects can meaningfully be said to exist. The significance of the distinction between reductive and existential phenomenalism is great.

[1] Jonathan Bennett, *Kant's Analytic* (Cambridge: Cambridge University Press, 1966), p. 127.

For it both allows Kant to do justice to those considerations which appear to lead to idealism or phenomenalism, while it does not at the same time require him to deny that the level at which we speak of material bodies and states is, and must be, a basic level of our conceptual framework. It cannot be one which is itself built upon, or constructed out of, some more basic level, e.g., out of talk about sense-data or sensory states. The uniqueness of Kant's phenomenalism lies precisely at this point.

I

The mistaken identification of Kant as a phenomenalist in the reductive sense is closely connected with a misinterpretation of the notion of intuition in Kant. If it is assumed that an intuition is a sensory state, for example, or a state of awareness of some sensory data or content, and that this is what is meant by the claim that it is an intuition of "appearances" only, then it is possible to maintain the Kantian claim that we have a direct knowledge of material bodies only so long as our judgments about such bodies are in some sense constructed out of judgments about sensory states. The assumption that Kant is a reductive phenomenalist has generally been based upon such an interpretation of the notion of intuition. Thus Bennett simply identifies an intuition with a sensory state in Kant and maintains that "Kant thinks that statements about phenomena are not merely supported by, but are equivalent to, statements about actual and possible sensory states."[2] But an intuition for Kant is not a sensory state, though if it is a sensory intuition it will of course be *connected* with some sensory state or states. Kant distinguishes two species of *Vorstellungen* which involve an essential reference to objects: intuitions are mental states which consist in a direct or "immediate" reference to some individual or individuals, while concepts are mental states which consist in a merely mediate reference to individuals, which refer, that is, to individuals only in the sense that they refer to some general feature or property *of* individuals (B33/A19).[3] Sensory or empirical intuition is intuition which involves sensation or

[2] *Ibid.*, pp. 22 and 55.
[3] References to Kant's *Critique of Pure Reason* appear in standard form. Translations are those of Norman Kemp Smith.

sensory states. But a sensory state is not itself a case of intuition: it is not a state which refers to objects, but only a state *through which* an intuition refers to, or is the awareness of, some object. Kant calls the object of an empirical intuition an "appearance" *(Erscheinung)*. Though no literal part of such an object is itself a sensation, each appearance does contain a part or aspect which *corresponds* to sensation, and Kant calls this the "matter" of the intuition (B34/A20). But an appearance does not consist of matter alone. It consists of matter organized by a certain formal structure, and Kant argues in the Transcendental Aesthetic that this formal structure is, in the case of outer intuition, that of three-dimensional Euclidean space. It follows that the proper object of an outer intuition is nothing other than a material body, i.e., matter which occupies some region of three-dimensional space. If propositions about material bodies, therefore, are to be analyzed in terms of propositions about outer intuitions, then any analysis of a proposition about material bodies would be circular. For it would be an analysis in terms of propositions about mental states defined as states which refer to material bodies. Thus one could not, on pain of a vicious circularity, interpret Kant as a reductive phenomenalist.

It might be thought that the sort of argument which I have just presented against the possibility of construing material object talk as logically secondary to talk about intuitions simply fails to notice what Robert Paul Wolff has called the "double role" which is played by representations in Kant. As Wolff points out, there does indeed seem to be something contradictory in the position which Kant defends. For while on the one hand Kant distinguishes a material object from our representations *of* that object, yet on the other hand he seems committed to *identifying* such an object with our representations of it. According to Wolff, the solution to the problem is this: considered in one way, a representation is simply a literal constituent or content of the mind; but when a representation is considered as a representation *of* some empirical object, then it is considered in a very different way. The difference is that in the latter case, a representation is no longer considered merely as a constituent of the mind, but as *organized* in a certain way with other representations. In other words, if the phenomenal object cannot be something distinct from our representations of it, then "the object must be simply a *special way of organizing the* representations."[4] This would appear to solve Kant's problem. For while there is a sense in which a way of organizing representations is nothing apart from those representations themselves, there is also a sense in which it is something distinct from any of the *particular* representations which are organized by it. Now strictly speaking, Wolff cannot literally mean that an object is simply a way of organizing representations. For a material object is presumably some sort of *entity,* and it is hardly clear how a "way of organizing" entities could itself be a genuine entity. But we may preserve the force of Wolff's point, I think, if we interpret Kant's claim not as the claim that phenomenal objects are just certain ways of organizing representations, but rather that material objects are nothing but representations themselves, insofar as the latter are organized in a certain way. Representations, then, would have a "double role" in the sense that they would be both literal contents of the mind, and yet also, when considered in another context, constituents of material objects and events. But even when the point is put in this way, it states a position which Kant clearly does not hold. For as Kant himself frequently reminds us, anything which is a literal constituent or content of the mind is subject to the formal conditions of time alone, and not of space. But a material object, as an object of outer intuition, is subject to the formal conditions of three-dimensional space, and it makes no sense at all to speak of inherently spatial objects as being nothing but certain nonspatial entities organized in a certain way.[5] To be sure, Kant does use the word *"Vorstellung"* with some ambiguity. At times it refers to a mental act of representing some object, and at times to the object which is represented by some act. But to admit that the word *"Vorstellung"* has such a double use as this is not to admit that there is a single sort of entity which functions in one context as an item in inner sense (a "mental content") and in another as an object of outer sense. There seems neither to be intelligibility to this Berkeleian suggestion, nor reason to think that Kant held the view. There is, then, no sense in which Kant

---

[4] Robert Paul Wolff, *Kant's Theory of Mental Activity* (Cambridge: Harvard University Press, 1963), pp. 262-63.

[5] That synthesis for Kant is the generation or construction of a material object out of inherently mental items, i.e., sensations, is taken for granted by, e.g., Harmon Chapman, in *Sensations and Phenomenology* (Bloomington: Indiana University Press, 1966), pp. 85-94.

could be taken to hold that material objects are only representations (in the sense of "mental contents") organized in a certain way. Perhaps, however, our account of Kant may be modified in the following manner. Perhaps Kant is not saying that a material object literally *is* a collection of representations, but only that all propositions *about* material objects are translatable into statements about representations. But I have already argued that such representations, being outer intuitions, are themselves describably only as representations of material objects in the first place. Thus when Kant argues that an empirical object is nothing but an appearance, or that it is merely a species of my own representations, he simply cannot be taken as offering a theory about what sort of entity or entities we are referring to when we refer to material objects. All that can be said on this score is that we are referring to matter which is organized into three-dimensional bodies which are located in Euclidean space. There is no more basic way of describing our talk about such entities.[6]

But what then *is* the point of Kant's insistence that the objects of intuition are mere appearances, or merely a species of our representations, if it is not to claim that propositions about such objects are reducible to propositions about intuitions? Recent works on Kant which have rightly resisted a reductive interpretation of Kant's views have nevertheless failed to provide a satisfying answer to this question. Some, for example, appear to claim that the word *"Erscheinung"* is simply a general term which is intended to cover all the possible objects presented as objects to the senses. The only point to saying that the objects of human knowledge are merely appearances is then to emphasize that we do have intuition, and hence knowledge, of objects only through the senses.[7] Strawson has succeeded, it is true, both in avoiding a reductive interpretation of Kant and yet nevertheless in recognizing the radically idealistic

[6] This would also seem to be a point which Wolff himself appreciates when he claims that Kant is not concerned with a question about objects, but rather with a question about objectivity (*op. cit.*, p. 264). But in that case it is not clear why we need to talk about a "double role" for representations in the first place. The only need for such a double role is presumably to explain how it could be mental contents to which we are referring when we refer to material objects.

[7] Graham Bird, *Kant's Theory of Knowledge* (New York: Humanities Press, 1962), pp. 44-46; D. P. Dryer, *Kant's Solution for Verification in Metaphysics* (Toronto: University of Toronto Press, 1966), pp. 504-07.

character of his claims. But the latter form part of a metaphysical apparatus which, according to Strawson, stands in no essential connection with the main arguments of the Transcendental Deduction or the Analogies of Experience.[8] Strawson thus formulates Kant's Transcendental Idealism only in the context of the notorious doctrine of "double affection," according to which all of our intuitions of bodies are themselves the result of a transempirical causality exercised by noumenal objects upon a noumenal ego. Certainly this is a fundamental context for an understanding of Kant's idealism. But it is also possible to formulate a doctrine which is sufficiently radical to be called a phenomenalism in the context of the sorts of purely *epistemological* considerations in which Kant engages in the Transcendental Deduction. This is what I shall attempt to do in the following sections. We are not forced to choose, therefore, between the claim that Kant is really not a phenomenalist in any significant sense at all, and the claim that his phenomenalism rests entirely upon a metaphysics of obviously dubious worth.

II

Any interpretation of Kant's epistemology must begin with the distinction between intuition and judgment. All cases of reference to objects, or of awareness of some object (as opposed to the mere *properties* of objects), count as intuitions for Kant. We are concerned with the special case in which our reference to an object is intended as a reference to something presented in sensory experience. Judgment will consist, in such a case, in the subsumption of the object under a general concept. There are, of course, judgments which do not contain any referring expressions at all, e.g., the judgment that "all bodies are divisible." Such a judgment would appear to contain only the two *concepts* "body" and "divisible." But I understand these concepts, as any concepts, only insofar as I know what sort of objects would count in intuition as instances of these concepts. That is, concepts without intuitions are empty (B75/A51). Thus it follows that even a purely general statement represents individual objects at least "mediately" (B93/A69), and it also follows that the primary form of knowledge consists in judgments in which a concept is applied to something presented in

[8] P. F. Strawson, *The Bounds of Sense* (London: Methuen & Co., 1966), p. 257.

empirical intuition, i.e., to something of which we are directly aware in experience. But Kant also holds another view about the relation between concepts and intuitions which appears to pose a difficulty for any interpretation of the Transcendental Deduction. This is the principle which Kant offers as a counterpart to the one to which I have just appealed: "intuitions without concepts are blind." What it would seem to express is the unobjectionable claim that there can be no reference to or awareness of an object simply as a bare "this." Any reference to an object must *already* involve the application of certain concepts, and, hence, in the case of sense perception, the recognition of that object as of a certain discriminable sort. But if we take Kant's task in the Transcendental Deduction to be the providing of an answer to the question, What is involved in predicating concepts of objects?, then it appears impossible to suppose that Kant is primarily concerned with the case in which concepts are applied to objects presented in empirical intuition. For the mere admission of empirical intuitions would presuppose precisely what Kant is trying to explain, i.e., how a concept can be applied to an object in the first place. Thus my argument in the preceding section that outer intuition is always intuition of some material body or of some state of empirically given matter may appear irrelevant to the issue whether Kant is a reductive phenomenalist. For if Kant is trying to explain what is involved in the application of concepts in experience, then empirical intuitions themselves would stand in need of an explanation. And if all such application involves a "synthesis of representations," then empirical intuition itself is possible only through a synthesis of representations. But, on the other hand, this does not seem possible as an interpretation of Kant's view either. For Kant is perfectly clear that intuitions and concepts exhaust the class of representations providing a reference to objects. Hence there is just nothing at all out of which empirical intuitions themselves could be synthesized. Some commentators have taken the ultimate elements of synthesis to be sensations, but I have already argued that this is a thoroughly non-Kantian view. We thus seem to be faced with a dilemma.

The solution to the difficulty is, I think, this. It is simply a mistake to suppose that the Transcendental Deduction is concerned to answer the general question, What is involved in applying a concept to objects? It is rather concerned with the more specific question, What is involved in applying a concept to an object in the special case where the object is assumed to be a *really existent* thing, and not, e.g., an object of mere imagination or hallucination? One reason for making this distinction is that it seems to provide the only possible ground for a distinction between the Transcendental Aesthetic and the Transcendental Analytic. Kant was concerned in the Transcendental Aesthetic with the possibility of geometrical knowledge. But geometrical knowledge surely involves the employment of certain concepts. What, however, distinguishes the geometer's employment of concepts from that which is investigated in the Analytic is that the former does not depend upon any assumption concerning the real existence of objects, e.g., of real triangles or circles. To be sure, Kant himself sometimes puts this point by saying that the pure geometer is not concerned with objects at all. But by this Kant appears to mean that the geometer is not concerned with real objects (B196/A157). For certainly Kant does want to say in the Aesthetic that the geometer is occupied with *something* which is given to him in pure intuition, and he applies certain predicates to this something. The point is only that no such predication amounts to or presupposes any existential judgment. A second reason for supposing that Kant is dealing only with the special conditions involved in asserting the existence of some phenomenal object, and not with the concept of a phenomenal object in general, is that Kant himself emphasizes that objects may appear to intuition which are not subject to the categories at all (B122/A89). Now Kant is concerned in the Transcendental Deduction only with that function of the understanding which presupposes the application of categories to objects. It follows, therefore, that Kant is not concerned with every possible intuition, but only with a certain subset of intuitions. But every intuition involves the concept of an object of some sort. Hence, Kant is not concerned with a general question about the concept of phenomenal object, but only with a special case of this question.

One way, of course, to avoid this conclusion would be to construe the passage to which I have just referred as expressing merely precritical thoughts. But this would seem implausible inasmuch as the passage in question appears in both editions of the *Critique*. Furthermore, the claim made in the passage is a perfectly harmless one which Kant should hardly have been required to deny. For it simply amounts to the admission that we find ourselves often in mental states in which a certain sort of object is presented to us, even though we would not want to say that the presented object exists. Reproductive imagination is, after all, a form of empirical intuition for Kant, and we are capable of imagining all sorts of unreal objects. Hallucination would appear to provide a similar case. What is more, it seems perfectly possible to imagine objects which do not conform to the Analogies of Experience (though not, as I shall argue presently, which fail to conform to the "mathematical" categories). Kant seems to be perfectly correct, therefore, in granting that subsumption of an object under the categories (or at least under the "dynamical" categories) is not a necessary condition for that object being *given* to us in intuition. As Kant puts the point, it is a necessary condition only for an object being *thought* by us. But what, then, can be intended by the case in which an object is not only given, but also thought? Kant cannot simply have in mind the employment of a concept in connection with our intuition. For it is clear that I need to employ the concept of a unicorn even in order to recognize that I am merely imagining or hallucinating a unicorn, though I need not at the same time be imagining or hallucinating it as conforming to the Analogies of Experience. It is clear that Kant is maintaining that I am committed to an employment of the dynamical categories only in case I go beyond the mere experience of my intuition, and beyond what can be provided by way of its description *qua* mere intuition, in order to judge the *reality* of the object of that intuition. If this is correct, then it would follow that Kant is not concerned in the Deduction with a general question about the concept of a phenomenal object. He is concerned only with a more specific question concerning the employment of concepts in order to express judgments which assert or presuppose the *existence* of the objects to which the concepts in question are applied. (It must be granted, of course, that I could not know that I am merely imagining a unicorn without also understanding what it would be like to assert the existence of a unicorn. But it does not follow from this that, if the dynamical categories are conditions of existential judgment, they must also be actually *applied* to a merely imagined unicorn.) The Transcendental Deduction, therefore, does not so much provide an elucidation of our reference to phenomenal objects as such, as it does an elucidation of the concept of phenomenal existence. And Kant's greatness lies, I shall argue, precisely in the insight that it is possible to provide a phenomenalistic account of empirical existence without committing oneself to a program of phenomenalistic reduction, that is, to assigning to the concept of a material body a merely derivative position without our conceptual framework.

The point which I have just argued receives confirmation from two other aspects of Kant's argument in the Transcendental Analytic. The first is the form which Kant's argument takes in the second edition Deduction. There, when he raises the issue of the "logical form of all judgments," Kant makes the claim that the function of the copula "is" in a judgment is to distinguish a claim with merely subjective validity from a claim which would be objectively valid for all (B141-42). The example which he gives is the distinction between my judgment that something *feels* heavy (to me) and my judgment that it really *is* heavy. A parallel distinction would presumably be one between a description of my imaginings as reports of the objects of my own mental life and a description of certain objects which are available for inspection by everyone. The fundamental issue, in other words, does not concern *what* the objects of intuition are (an imagined unicorn and a real unicorn would both be the same thing, namely, a unicorn), but rather what it means to say *that* they really are. This is also confirmed by Kant's distinction between the mathematical and dynamical categories. It is clear enough in itself that only the latter really fulfill the program of the Transcendental Deduction. But Kant himself also tells us that mathematical principles are concerned only with those features which an object must be represented as possessing insofar as it is an object of intuition (B199/A160). Even an imagined unicorn, for example, must be imagined as possessing a certain size and shape. The mathematical concepts ought therefore to find their place in the Transcendental Aesthetic. The reason that they do not, I believe, is that Kant failed to perceive the fundamental difference between the kind of synthesis which they involve (e.g., in the generation of a geometrical shape) and the kind of synthesis which is involved in the Analogies of Experience. It is clear, on the one hand, that the Aesthetic did not in itself exclude a treatment of synthesis. For it too dealt with the generation of geometrical figures. And it is also clear that the kind of synthesis which is involved in such a case has little bearing on the paradigmatic problem of synthesis which Kant considers in the Deduction. It is reasonable, therefore, to look only to the dynamical categories for an expression of the problem of the Transcendental Analytic. But these categories, according to Kant, are not concerned with appearances in themselves, that is, with what is essential to an empirical phenomenon as a phenomenon. They are rather concerned with judgments about the *existence* of appearances (B220/A178). This is what it must mean to say, as some have, that Kant is not concerned with the phenomenal *object,* but only with the concept of phenomenal object*ivity.* It is not, of course, that Kant denies that there really are such things as empirical objects. The point is that he is not offering a theory about what we are really talking about when we talk about such objects. Thus he is not, *a fortiori,* telling us that any such object really is but a series of representations organized in a certain way, or that what we are really referring to, when we refer to material objects, are certain of our own intuitions. What we are referring to is an object situated in three-dimensional space, that is, matter organized by spatial form, and there is no way which is more basic than this in which we may describe such an object.

III

The concept of synthesis, and the role which it plays in Kant's argument, can be understood only in terms of the above conclusion. We may suppose the first premise of that argument to be that a condition for the intelligibility of any concept is that I know what would count in intuition as an instance of that concept. Now I may have intuitions, according to Kant, both of real and of imaginary or merely hallucinated entities (not to mention the pure geometrical structures which are objects of nonempirical intuition). But it is clearly a necessary condition of imagining some entity that I at least understand what it would be like to discover the *existence* of such an entity. Thus the basic functions of the understanding must be determined by considering the case of existential judgment. We must consider, therefore, what is involved in judging not only that I am having an intuition of a unicorn, but that I am really perceiving a unicorn. Kant's point about such a case is this:

whereas the mere judgment that I am having an intuition of a unicorn is the report of a given intuition, the judgment that I am actually perceiving a unicorn consists in going beyond my momentary intuition and connecting that intuition with others. If I am really perceiving a unicorn, then it must be possible to obtain *different* intuitions, connected in certain ways with the given one, which I would also count as intuitions of a unicorn (and, indeed, of *this* unicorn), and my judgment gives expression to this possibility. Thus in the basic case of employing a concept, the concept of an empirical object does not function by representing to the mind the content of any given intuition. It rather serves to unify for thought a potentially infinite *manifold* of intuitions, only one of which can in fact be given at any particular moment. This is what it means to say that a concept provides the unity for a "synthesis of representations." But it by no means follows from this that the *object* of my judgment is in such a case a unity constructed out of some manifold, or that my judgment really refers only to a manifold of representations. For the manifold is a manifold of intuitions, and each of the intuitions is itself describable only by reference to its object. The Transcendental Aesthetic has already established, in particular, that outer intuitions are to be described as intuitions of some matter possessing the form imposed by Euclidean space.

Thus any given intuition in the manifold of outer sense is the representation of a state of matter determined by a spatial form and appearing under some particular description. The problem of "synthesis" is then the problem concerning necessary conditions for asserting relations between the states of matter which appear to *different* intuitions. Is, for example, the object which appears to intuition at time t_1 the *same* object as one which appears at time t_2? Or does the first at least continue to exist at t_2 even though it is not identical with any object which appears at t_2? Or does it cease to exist altogether at t_2 when the intuition of it no longer exists? Any such question is always legitimate in the case of a genuine perception, though it is generally an inappropriate question in the case of imagination or mere hallucination. The Analogies of Experience, of course, deal with such questions. But the Transcendental Deduction argues that any such question, being one about objects *as they appear* under some description in sensory intuition, must be equivalent to a question about the connections which obtain

among our perceptions themselves. Thus it is clear that the main
conclusion of the Transcendental Deduction—that knowledge of
an object is the representation of a necessary connection among our
perceptions—is a claim which has a point and can be seen as
emerging from the central issues considered in the Deduction,
without our having to suppose the Deduction to be part of a program of reductive phenomenalism. It is not part of such a program,
I have argued, because the manifold of perceptions is never itself
describable without the aid of the concept of a material body or
state, that is, of matter presented and organized in space. But
there is another sense, nevertheless, in which the Kantian claim
is a strongly phenomenalistic one. For it is a claim about the only
legitimate sense in which material objects or states might be said
to exist. They exist in the sense that perceptions of them are ob-
tainable in accordance with certain rule-governed connections.
This is the force of Kant's insistence that "appearances are themselves nothing but sensible representations, which, as such and
in themselves, must not be taken as objects capable of existing
outside our power of representation" (A104). Such a claim cannot
mean that we have knowledge of objects only insofar as they appear
to our senses. That is far too weak an interpretation to be plausible.
But neither can it mean that an empirical object is nothing distinct
from representations, in the sense in which the latter are something
contained in the mind. That would be far too strong an interpretation.

It is in the light of these considerations that we must now try to
understand the famous passage in the Second Analogy which has
led Wolff and others to speak of the "double role" played by
representations in Kant, a role which both allows representations
to be viewed as contents of the mind, and yet allows that material
bodies are nothing distinct from representations.

> Everything, every representation even, in so far as we are
> conscious of it, may be entitled object. But it is a question for
> deeper enquiry what the word "object" ought to signify in
> respect of appearances when these are viewed not in so far as
> they are (as representations) objects, but only in so far as they
> stand for an object. The appearances, in so far as they are
> objects of consciousness simply in virtue of being representa-
> tions, are not in any way distinct from their apprehension. . . .

Now immediately I unfold the transcendental meaning of my concepts of an object, I realize that the house is not a thing in itself, but only an appearance, that is, a representation, the transcendental object of which is unknown. What, then, am I to understand by the question: how the manifold may be connected in the appearance itself, which yet is nothing in itself? That which lies in the successive apprehension is here viewed as representation, while the appearance which is given to me, not withstanding that it is nothing but the sum of these representations, is viewed as their object. . . . (A)ppearance, in contradistinction to the representations of apprehension, can be represented as an object distinct from them only if it stands under a rule which distinguishes it from every other apprehension and necessitates some one particular mode of connection of the manifold. The object is *that* in the appearance which contains the condition of this necessary rule of apprehension (B235-36/A190-91).

Kant appears to be telling us, in this passage, that we are aware of a manifold of "objects" or "appearances," each of which is in some sense not distinct from the apprehension of it, but that we are also aware of objects or appearances in a sense in which they *are* distinct from any particular apprehensions of them. In this latter sense, the object or appearance is nothing but the rule-generated "sum" of objects or appearances in the former sense. But in what sense can we suppose Kant to be talking about objects which are not something distinct from the awareness *of* those objects? That Kant refers to such "objects" as *"Vorstellungen"* should not be taken as any evidence at all that what he is talking about are literal contents of the mind. For Kant frequently uses the word *"Vorstellung,"* and the words for the species of *Vorstellung,* in an ambiguous manner, sometimes to refer to an awareness of something, and sometimes for that of which we are aware. Those cases, for example, in which he refers to space itself as an intuition or representation (B39/A25) make it clear that at least much of the time we have to deal with what is a double use of the word "representation" by Kant, and not a doctrine concerning some special role for a single referent of that word. As a literal content of the mind, after all, an intuition has no spatial features whatsoever, whereas every *object* of at least outer intuition does possess such features. We must suppose, therefore, that those objects or appearances which are not distinct from the apprehension of them cannot strictly be identified with any contents of the mind, i.e., with states of awareness. They must be objects *of* such states, which are nevertheless dependent upon them. This suggests some sort of doctrine of sense-data. For sense-data are supposed to possess precisely this special property of being both distinct from, yet dependent upon, acts of sensory intuition. But of course there is no doctrine of sense-data in Kant. For sense-data are presumably two-dimensional entities, while the form of all objects of outer intuition is provided by the structure of three-dimensional spatiality. If there is, then, any object which is nothing distinct from the apprehension of it, this would have to be some matter which is spatially organized and which appears in intuition, i.e., some material body or state. But this is presumably precisely the sort of object which *is* distinct from any apprehension of it. We thus appear to be landed in a contradiction.

There is a very simple way out of this difficulty, however. What, I would suggest, Kant is doing in this passage is using the word "appearance" in the first of its two senses to stand for something which is not really an *entity* at all. He is using it to refer neither to a sense-datum, nor to a material body or state as such, but rather to the way in which an entity of the latter sort appears in intuition, that is, to *an object as it appears.*[9] Though the object itself is certainly distinct from any apprehension of it, the object as it is apprehended at some moment is not, in a fairly clear sense, distinct from the apprehension of it. For my description of the object as it is apprehended does not require me to go beyond my intuition in order to connect or relate it with other intuitions. That I am aware of an object appearing under description D_1 at t_1, and an object appearing under description D_2 at t_2, is a report of the "content" of two individual experiences. In making such a report, I am not concerned with any question that requires me to go outside these experiences, such as the question whether the object under description D_1 is the *same* as that appearing under description D_2, or whether it even exists simultaneously with the latter. To seek to

---

[9] For a discussion of Kant's vacillations between a "language of appearances" and a "language of appearing," see S. F. Barker, "Appearing and Appearances in Kant," *The Monist*, vol. 51, no. 3 (July, 1967), pp. 426 ff.

"go beyond" a momentary intuition in this sense, and beyond any description of an object which it may provide, is to recognize that one and the same object may appear in a manifold of ways, and hence cannot be known or identified in terms of any one of the ways in which it appears. When we see this point, we are then ready to view the appearances of an object not as *themselves* objects, but as ways in which objects appear and hence "only in so far as they stand for an object." But if this is so, then in what sense could Kant be telling us that the word "appearance," in the sense in which it stands for some empirical object such as a house, or some empirical event such as a boat moving downstream, is "nothing but the sum" of appearances in the first sense? For surely a house is not a mere collection of the manifold ways in which it appears. The response to this question must be that Kant's assertion is not to be taken literally. An object is the sum of the ways in which it appears only in the sense that our concept of the object is just a concept of that sort of body which appears in those various ways. There is nothing in this claim which implies a reductive phenomenalism, since, as I have already argued, none of the ways in which an object appears can itself be identified purely by reference to certain sensations or sensory states. We must conclude, therefore, that in one crucial sense a phenomenal object is something distinct from any representations of it. For what any such object is cannot be specified merely by reference to contents of the mind. But there is another sense in which a phenomenal object is *not* distinct from the representations of it. This is the sense in which our commitment to that object is nothing more than a commitment to the existence of certain contents of the mind. It is this distinction between reference and existence which makes Kant's phenomenalism a thoroughly unique sort of phenomenalism.

IV

I have argued for a certain interpretation of Kant's phenomenalism in this paper. If I have been correct, then Kant's phenomenalism differs in a very radical way from the phenomenalism of a philosopher such as Berkeley, and in a way which has not been fully appreciated by most of the commentators on Kant. Indeed, unclarity concerning the precise character of Kant's phenomenalism has led many to the suspicion that Kant himself may not have been clear about, or perhaps not even directly acquainted with, the actual views of Berkeley.[10] For Kant refers to Berkeley as "degrading bodies to mere illusion" (B71), and he takes Berkeley as an example of the "dogmatic idealist," that is, of one who holds the existence of material objects to be "false and impossible" and who "regards the things in space as merely imaginary entities" (B274). But Berkeley in fact denied the existence of material objects only *in a certain sense,* i.e., as things existing apart from our perceptions of them, and this is a view which Kant himself seems to hold. On the other hand, commentators have been quick to point out that there *are* important differences between the views of Kant and Berkeley, though not quite the ones which Kant himself seems to emphasize. According to Wolff, for example, the reason Kant was so justifiably confident that his own view differed from Berkeley's lay not in the fact that Berkeley denied the existence of material objects, but rather in the fact that Berkeley failed to perceive that material objects do not just *happen* to exist, but necessarily must be supposed to exist by any being who is capable of self-consciousness and self-knowledge.[11] Though this is a genuine difference between Kant's position and Berkeley's, it is not the only, nor even the most important, such difference. Jonathan Bennett has suggested another difference between the two forms of phenomenalism. According to Bennett, Berkeley naively identified a material object with a collection of ideas or intuitions. Such an identification leads, of course, to difficulties. For if a material body *is* a collection of ideas, then it can exist only so long as those ideas exist, and the latter exist only as long as they are perceived. Thus Berkeley is led to posit God as the eternal perceiver of the physical world. Kant is not faced with such difficulties, on Bennett's reading, because when Kant said that "objects are nothing but representations" he did not mean that an object literally *is* a collection of mental states. He meant that any proposition about a material object is completely translatable into propositions which refer to mental states (actual *and* possible) but which do not refer to objects.[12]

[10] Norman Kemp Smith, *A Commentary to Kant's Critique of Pure Reason,* second edition (New York: Humanities Press, 1962; reprint), pp. 155 ff. and 307-08.
[11] Wolff, *op. cit.,* p. 200.
[12] Bennett, *op. cit.,* p. 127.

If I have been correct in my argument, then this view about Kant is completely mistaken. For while any proposition which asserts or presupposes the existence of objects is translatable, according to Kant, into propositions about actual and possible intuitions, each of these intuitions is itself identifiable only as the intuition *of an object* which appears in some particular way. Thus reference to objects is not eliminable in favor of reference to intuitions, although the *existence* of objects is eliminable, I have argued, insofar as that existence is taken for something over and above the existence of intuitions themselves. This formulation also indicates in what respect Kant could accuse Berkeley of "degrading bodies to mere illusion" without necessarily having misunderstood him. To degrade bodies to mere illusion might be to take all of our references to bodies as in principle eliminable in favor of reference to purely mental entities. Such a reductive phenomenalism rests upon the supposition that what we are immediately or "directly" aware of in perception can be described in a purely sensory language which contains no reference to material objects. Reference of the latter sort needs to be built up or "constructed" out of a very complex set of references to entities of the former sort, i.e., to ideas, sense-data, sensory contents, or however such entities are described. But it follows from this that any philosopher who takes himself to be directly aware of material objects, and not merely of some other entities out of which reference to such objects is constructed, could describe a position such as Berkeley's as one which substitutes for the world of objects which I perceive a world of purely mental entities. Thus in criticizing Berkeley, Kant can be taken as raising against the reductive phenomenalist just the sort of objection which, it might at first appear, could be raised only by a direct realist. Kant, however, is an idealist. For though we are indeed directly aware of material objects, in the sense that reports of the content of sense-perception cannot be translated so as to eliminate all reference to such objects, these nevertheless do not really exist, or at least they exist *only in a certain sense*. Kant, in other words, is a direct transcendental idealist, and his position must be distinguished both from the indirect realism of a philosopher such as Locke *and* from the merely indirect transcendental idealism of the reductive phenomenalist such as Berkeley. I have argued that the insight which allows Kant to formulate this unique version of phenomenalism is the discovery that a reduction of statements about material objects to statements about the existence of intuitions alone does not require that we reduce all references to such objects to *references* to intuitions alone.[13]

University of Tennessee, Knoxville

[13] It might be argued that if I have been correct in my interpretation of Kant, then Kant's position is plainly contradictory. For it consists of the two propositions (a) that reference to material objects is ineliminable from reports of outer intuition and (b) that material objects do not really exist. But it is clear that Kant does not deny that material objects exist *simpliciter*. He denies that they exist only in a certain sense, i.e., in any sense which does not involve a logical connection with the existence of perceptions.

Re-Relating Kant and Berkeley

by Gale D. Justin, Sacramento

A prominent English-language interpretation of Kant's relation to Berkeley is to be found in Colin M. Turbayne's *Kant's Relation to Berkeley*. Originally published under the title *Kant's Refutation of Dogmatic Idealism*, the article has been recently reprinted in Lewis White Beck's, *Kant Studies Today*[1]. Although Turbayne's thesis that Kant's philosophy bears crucial similarities to Berkeley's has recently been challenged, the evidence for his thesis has not been examined in detail nor has an alternative theory as to the relation between Kant and Berkeley been suggested[2]. In this paper, I examine Turbayne's similarity thesis, pointing

---

[1] Colin M. Turbayne, *Kant's Relation to Berkeley, Kant Studies Today*, ed. Lewis White Beck (La Salle, III., 1969), pp. 88—116; orginally in the Philosophical Quarterly, V (1955), 225—244, under the title *Kant's Refutation of Dogmatic Idealism*. References to this work will be to the latter publication.

[2] Margaret D. Wilson (*Kant and 'The Dogmatic Idealism of Berkeley'*, Journal of the History of Philosophy, IX (1971), 459—475) takes issue with some of Turbayne's claims, in particular, his contention that "Kant was thoroughly familiar with Berkeley's doctrine and learned from it", (Turbayne, p. 239) and that, therefore, his misrepresentations of Berkeley must be construed as deliberate "perversions" (Turbayne, p. 243). Wilson also suggests that Turbayne may be making more of the similarity between Kant and Berkeley than is warranted by the texts. Nevertheless, Wilson shares Turbayne's view that Kant misrepresents the "historical Berkeley" (Wilson, pp. 461, 462—464, 469). George Miller (*Kant and Berkeley: The Alternative Theories*, Kant-Studien, 64 (1973), 315—335) also takes issue with Turbayne for stressing "the affinities between Berkeley and Kant... and [ignoring] the differences" (p. 334). In addition, he points out a number of inconsistences in Turbayne's account as well as in what he calls "the traditional theory" held by Kemp Smith, Weldon, Paton, among others. Miller claims that both Turbayne and the traditional theorists share two assumptions which render their accounts inconsistent. The first assumption is that the unnamed dogmatic idealist of the first edition "Fourth Paralogism" (*Critique*, A 377) is Berkeley, the second that Kant misrepresents Berkeley's position in both the *Critique* and the *Prolegomena*.
Miller suggests, I think correctly, that both assumptions are mistaken. Leibniz, rather, appears to be Kant's first edition dogmatic idealist. (See Miller, *Kant's First Edition Refutation of Dogmatic Idealism*, Kant-Studien, 62 (1971), 298—318.) On *this* assumption, Kant fulfills the promise of the first edition "Fourth Paralogism" to refute dogmatic idealism, for the "Second Antinomy" argues that both the Leibnizian thesis that every composite is composed of (immaterial) simples and its opposite that every composite is infinitely divisible are defensible and, hence, that neither thesis is more reasonable than the other. On the second assumption that Kant misrepresents Berkeley's doctrine, see my *On Kant's Analysis of Berkeley*, Kant-Studien, 65 (1974),

out what seem to be serious difficulties with it, and I propose an alternative
account of the relationship between Kant and Berkeley which illuminates, in
particular, the unique character of Kant's so-called Transcendental Idealism.

                                        I

For Turbayne the salient feature of the relation between Kant and Berkeley
is the "systematic similarity" in their "main" argument against scepticism.
Precisely, Turbayne says "It is my view that the central argument of the
'Refutations' [by which Turbayne means seven sections of the *Critique*] has a
systematic similarity in its principal features with the main argument of Berkeley's
Principles and *Dialogues*"[3]. The sections Turbayne is referring to are the first
edition "Fourth Paralogism", the "Appendix" and two other sections in the
Prolegomena (sections 13 and 49); two sections in the "Aesthetic" and section 6
of the "Antinomy of Pure Reason". Curiously enough Turbayne concedes that
the second edition "Refutation of Idealism" does not contain the argument he
jointly attributes to Kant and Berkeley. But this is just where one would expect
to find Kant's final argument against scepticism. This aside, I think it can be
shown that even those sections Turbayne relies on do not contain the argument he
outlines. Turbayne is claiming that in certain texts of both Kant and Berkeley
there is a common argument against scepticism and that the premises of the
argument are accurately stated in these so-called steps. Following then is a
statement of Turbayne's six step argument, with the supporting passages from
Berkeley and Kant indicated by upper case "B" and "K" respectively.
      Step I: The philosophers assert the absolute reality of space and time, and hold
that external objects exist by themselves independently of our senses.

      B. [The philosophers assert] the being of an absolute space, distinct from that which
is perceived by sense (*Principles*, 116). (The hold) that there are certain objects really
existing without the mind, or having a subsistence distinct from being perceived
(*Principles*, 56) .
      K. [The transcendental realists] ... maintain the absolute reality of space and time,
whether as subsistent or only as inherent (*Critique*, A 39) ... wrongly supposing that
objects of the senses, if they are to be external, must have an existence by themselves,
and independently of the senses (*Critique*, A 369).

      Step II: This doctrine of the philosophers makes them victims of the common
delusion that the human mind can venture beyond all possible experience.

      B. When we do our utmost to conceive the existence of external bodies, we are all
the while only contemplating our own ideas. But the mind taking no notice of itself,
is deluded to think it can and doth conceive bodies existing unthought of or without the

---

20—32. I am pleased to note Miller's agreement on several points (*Kant and Berkeley:
The Alternative Theories*, pp. 322, 330—332).
[3] Turbayne, p. 229.

mind; though at the same time they are apprehended by or exist in itself (*Principles*, 23).

K. [Transcendental realism involves] the transcendental illusion, by which metaphysics has hitherto been deceived and led to the childish endeavour of catching at bubbles, because appearances, which are mere ideas, were taken for things in themselves (*Prolegomena*, 13. Cf. A 369, A 491).

Step III: The philosophers' distinction of things from ideas leads inevitably to scepticism.

B. All this scepticism follows from our supposing a difference between *things* and *ideas* ... So long as we attribute a real existence to unthinking things, distinct from their being perceived, it is not only impossible for us to know with evidence the nature of any real unthinking being, but even that it exists ... We see only the appearances, and not the real qualities of things (*Principles*, 87—88).

K. Transcendental realism inevitably falls into difficulties, and finds itself obliged to give way to empirical idealism, in that it regards the objects of outer sense as something distinct from the senses themselves (*Critique*, A 371). [On this view] it is quite impossible to understand how we could arrive at a knowledge of their reality outside us, since we have to rely merely on the idea which is in us (*Critique*, A 378. Cf. *Prolegomena*, 49).

Step IV: The remedy consists first, in pointing out to the philosophers a truth they already know, namely that the *esse* of ideas or appearances is *percipi*.

B. The philosophers ... being of the opinion that ... the things immediately perceived are ideas which exist only in the mind (*Third Dialogue*, p. 262)[4].

K. Sceptical idealism thus constrains us to have recourse to the only refuge still open, namely, the ideality of all appearances ... for we cannot be sentient of what is outside ourselves, but only of what is in us (*Critique*, A 378). All appearances are not in themselves *things:* they are nothing but ideas, and cannot exist outside our mind (*Critique*, A 492).

Step V: The remedy continues by assimilating the so-called external bodies of the philosophers into the realm of ideas or appearances.

B. As to what is said of the absolute existence of unthinking things without any relation to their being perceived, that seems perfectly unintelligible. Their *esse* is *percipi*, nor is it possible they should have any existence, out of the minds or thinking things which perceive them (*Principles*, 3).

K. External bodies are mere appearances, and are therefore nothing but a species of my ideas, the objects of which are something only through these ideas. Apart from them they are nothing (*Critique*, A 370. Cf. *Critique*, A 491, *Prolegomena*, 13).

Step VI: And all these appearances are real.

B. I am of a vulgar cast, simple enough to believe my senses, and leave things as I find them (*Third Dialogue*, p. 229). I might as well doubt of my own being, as of the being of those things I actually see and feel ... Those immediate objects of perception, which, according to you, are only appearances of things, I take to be the real things themselves (*Third Dialogue*, p. 230, p. 244).

---

[4] References to the "Third Dialogue" of *Three Dialogues Between Hylas and Philonus* are to *The Works of George Berkeley Bishop of Cloyne*, ed. by A. A. Luce and T. E. Jessop, II (London, 1949).

K. I leave things as we obtain them by the senses their reality (*Prolegomena*, 13). In order to arrive at the reality of outer objects, I have just as little need to resort to inference as I have in regard to the reality of the object of my inner sense... For in both cases alike the objects are nothing but ideas, the immediate perception of which is at the same time a sufficient proof of their reality (*Critique*, A 371). An empirical realist allows to matter, as appearance, a reality which does not permit of being inferred, but is immediately perceived (*Critique*, A 371).

It should be clear, I think, that these steps do not constitute what we would call an *argument* against scepticism, at least not in the technical sense of the word. However, by adding a number of premises, the steps might be reconstructed as part of a deductively valid argument. My reconstruction is as follows:

Turbayne's Argument Reconstructed

1. If Transcendental Realism and/or Materialism [hereafter, "TR/M"] is correct, then space and time are absolute and external objects exist mind independently such that we must infer their existence from the ideas they cause in us. [P]
1 a. If external objects exist mind independently such that we must infer their existence from the ideas they cause in us, then the immediate objects of perception are ideas. [P]
1 b. If the immediate objects of perception are ideas, then the claim to *know* that external objects exist corresponding to these ideas implies that we can have knowledge of things we cannot in principle perceive[s]. [P]

2. If TR/M is correct, then the claim to *know* objects exist corresponding to these ideas implies that we have knowledge of things we cannot in principle perceive. [1, 1 a, 1 b]
2 a. If TR/M is correct, then the immediate objects of perception are ideas. [1, 1 a]
2 b. If the immediate objects of perception are ideas, then the existence of external objects corresponding to these ideas is doubtful. [P]
2 c. If TR/M is correct, then the existence of external objects corresponding to these ideas is doubtful. [2 a, 2 b]
2 d. Scepticism $=_{df}$ the doubt of the existence of external objects. [P]

3. If TR/M is correct, then scepticism is true. [2 c, 2 d]

4. Ideas do not exist independently of being perceived. [P]
4 a. If something does not exist independently of being perceived, then if it is perceived, its existence cannot be doubted. [P]
4 b. If an idea is perceived, then its existence cannot be doubted. [4, 4 a]

5. So-called external objects are just collections of ideas. [P]

6. If a so-called external object is perceived, then its existence cannot be doubted. [4 b, 5]
6 a. So-called external objects are perceived. [P]

---

[s] It should perhaps be noted that (1 b) and (2) are not required for the conclusion of the argument. But as Turbayne includes (2) in his statement of the argument, I have done so as well.

6 b. Therefore, their existence cannot be doubted. [6, 6 a]
6 c. Therefore, scepticism is false. [2 d, 6 b]

Unfortunately, this reconstruction of Turbayne's argument is open to a very simple objection: there are good reasons to think Premise 5 false[6]. Therefore, the argument, at least in its present form, is unsound. Of course, it is possible that Turbayne could provide some interpretation of his six claims which would show the conclusion, that scepticism is false, to follow from true premises. But since he provides no hints as to precisely what those premises might be and since some premise like (5) seems indispensable, we have no choice but to reject the argument.

It might be objected to this procedure that, in spite of his introductory remarks, Turbayne did not consider his six steps as an argument conclusively refuting scepticism. Rather, the claims were meant merely to state a position central to both Kant and Berkeley. In order to test this hypothesis, I will now consider whether the position encapsulated in Turbayne's six claims can be legitimately ascribed to Kant. I shall argue that the Kant passages Turbayne invokes for the crucial Steps 4 and 5 bear only superficial verbal resemblance to Turbayne's statement of (4) and (5). If this is correct, then Turbayne has not established that Kant and Berkeley share a common argument against scepticism, however we construe the use of "argument" here.

II

At the start it should be said that Turbayne's *only* defense of the similarity thesis is his marshalling passages which allegedly commit each philosopher to the step in question. Turbayne asserts Kant's complicity in Steps 4 and 5, the crucial steps in the so-called argument, on the basis of passages (with one exception) from the first edition "Fourth Paralogism" and the "Antinomies". Both sections are of early origin and the "Fourth Paralogism" is an explicitly reworked section of the *Critique*[7]. Moreover, Turbayne acknowledges that the second edition "Refutation of Idealism" argues against scepticism in an entirely different way. But he seems to regard the additions and revisions in the second edition as an *ad hoc* maneuver on Kant's part to distinguish his position from Berkeley's[8].

---

[6] Even if (5) were true, its ascription to Kant is dubious at best. I speak to this below. And if (5) is taken as implying translatability of statements about objects into statements not mentioning objects, then the notorious failure of this program bodes ill for (5). Cf. W. V. Quine, *Word and Object* (Cambridge, Mass., 1964) pp. 2—3. See also, Roderick Chisholm, *Theory of Knowledge*, (Englewood Cliffs, New Jersey, 1966) p. 62 and Footnote 4 p. 62.
[7] See Norman Kemp Smith (*A Commentary to Kant's Critique of Pure Reason*, New York, 1962) on the early origin of both these sections, pp. 431—440 and p. 457.
[8] Turbayne, p. 243.

6*

I think it can be shown, however, that the first edition passages do not support the similarity thesis which Turbayne endorses and are, in fact, of a piece with Kant's second edition "Refutation of Idealism"[9].

Turbayne's case for the claim that Kant and Berkeley share a common argument against scepticism rests primarily on Steps 4 and 5 of the argument. The first three steps contain a statement of a view called transcendental realism by Kant and materialism by Berkeley (Step 1); a similar analysis of the mistake underlying this view (Step 2); and the implication that such a view with its attendent distinction between ideas and objects entails scepticism (Step 3).

With regard to the first step it should be noted that while Berkeley does argue against (a) the absolute reality of space and (b) the independent existence of external objects from perceiving subjects, it is not at all clear that he takes (a) and (b) to constitute a single doctrine; nor is it clear that Locke (with whom we usually associate Berkeley's discussion of materialism) endorses (a). In that section of his *Essay Concerning Human Understanding* where Locke discusses the idea of space he takes no stand on its status[10]. Furthermore, Turbayne's suggestion (in the second step) that Kant and Berkeley identically diagnose the error of transcendental realism and materialism seems wrong. Turbayne thinks Kant criticizes transcendental realists for treating ideas as things in themselves and Berkeley materialists for interpreting ideas as external bodies. Turbayne's account of the respective diagnoses is very cursory, containing little more than what I have given. But, in any case, Kant's analysis in the first edition "Fourth Paralogism" of the error underlying transcendental realism can be shown, I think, to be quite different from Berkeley's account of the error underlying materialism. There Kant explains that transcendental realists postulate two different kinds of objects, inner objects immediately knowable and outer objects whose existence must be inferred, *because* they mistake a "difference in the mode of representing objects... as a difference in the things themselves" (*Critique*, A 379). Kant is saying, I think, that because objects of certain sensory states are thought of (represented) as being in both space and time whereas the objects of other sensory states are thought of (represented) as being in time only, the transcendental realist mistakenly assumes that the former objects could not be known in the same way as the latter are known, that is, immediately. He is thus lead to conclude that the existence of spatial objects must be inferred from the ideas they cause in us, for only in this way can we account for the fact that these objects are thought of as being outside us, that is, as being in space.

While this may not be a historically accurate explanation of how Descartes and the empiricists arrived at the representative theory of perception, it is,

---

[9] In this paper I am concerned to argue only that Turbayne misinterprets the first edition passages he quotes in support of his similarity thesis.

[10] See John Locke, *An Essay Concerning Human Understanding*, annotated by A. C. Fraser, I, (New York, 1959), 218—238.

I think, Kant's view of their mistake. Furthermore, to see the contrast between Kant and Berkeley on this point, it is important to emphasize that Kant emphatically denies our ability to give any "deep" or informative account of "objects" in the strictly univocal sense of the word. He says (*Critique*, A 379)

> Though the 'I', as represented through inner sense in time and objects in space outside me, are specifically quite distinct appearances, they are not for that reason thought as being different things. Neither the *transcendental object* which underlies outer appearances nor that which underlies inner intuition, is in itself either matter or a thinking being, but a ground (to us unknown) of the appearances which supply to us the empirical concept of the former as well as the latter mode of existence.

Berkeley, on the other hand, faults the materialists for construing what are mental "objects" (ideas) as if they were material objects (bodies in space). Thus Berkeley and the materialists attempt to do just what Kant denies can be done: give an informative (metaphysical) account of what objects really are apart from how they are conceptualized. Materialists, for Berkeley, are merely mistaken about the real nature of objects while for Kant questions about the real nature of objects, which separate Berkeley from the materialists, cannot even be raised. And the mistake of the transcendental realists consists in inferring from a difference in how objects are conceptualized, a difference in their metaphysical status and in the certainty which we can have of their existence.

It does not seem necessary to deal with the first three steps in any further detail, for even if the textual evidence were conclusive, it would only show that Kant and Berkeley reject an identical view and similarly diagnose its error. The stronger claim that they *share* an alternative philosophical doctrine, turns on the support for Steps 4 and 5, for these pretend to exhibit a parallel in Kant's and Berkeley's positive doctrines. For Kant's and Berkeley's recognition that "the *esse* of ideas or appearances is *percipi*" (Turbayne's usage) or, alternatively, that ideas (appearances for Kant) do not exist independently of being perceived constitutes for Turbayne the first move in their joint remedy for scepticism (Step 4)[11]. The second move consists in "assimilating the so-called external bodies . . . into the realm of ideas or appearances", (Step 5)[12]. In other words, the second move consists in some reductive thesis to the effect that objects are just (collections of) ideas.

To establish joint acceptance of Step 4 Turbayne couples Kant's statement at A 492 that "appearances are not in themselves *things*; they are nothing but ideas *[Vorstellungen]* and cannot exist outside our mind" with Berkeley's assertion in the "Third Dialogue" that "the things immediately perceived are ideas which exist only in the mind", (p. 262). It cannot be denied that these passages exhibit strong similarity, especially given Turbayne's translation of Kant's "*Vorstellung*" as "idea". The usual English rendering "representation",

---

[11] Turbayne, p. 232.
[12] Turbayne, p. 233.

is, in fact, in accord with Kant's own comments on his terminology[13]. We may, however, grant this license in translation, for the question remains whether the similarity is more than superficial.

Kant's statement at A 492 that appearances are not themselves things but only a species of our representations is echoed in numerous other passages of the *Critique*. The first edition "Fourth Paralogism" repeatedly criticizes the transcendental realists for "treating mere appearances as self-subsistent beings, existing outside us"[14]. In the "Second Analogy" Kant states that a "house is not a thing in itself, but only an appearance, that is, a representation"[15]. And in the "Aesthetic" he asserts that "objects in themselves are quite unknown to us, and . . . what we call outer objects are nothing but mere representations of our sensibility"[16]. Obviously, understanding Kant's general position in the *Critique* as well as his relation to Berkeley requires determining what it means to say that appearances are not in themselves things but mere representations, items which are in us and nothing apart from us or our sensibility.

Prima facie Turbayne's interpretation is not without plausibility, for Kant could appear to be offering a reductive analysis of objects in terms of either sensory states or representations *qua* objects of sensory states[17]. However, I believe this interpretation seriously misrepresents Kant and, moreover, is responsible for the "similarity" account Turbayne gives of the relationship between Kant and Berkeley. It is also inconsistent with Kant's persistant disclaimer that his position is Berkeleian[18]. Turbayne recognizes this and suggests

[13] Immanuel Kant, *Critique of Pure Reason* (London, 1933), A 319 / B 376 — A 320 / B 377. All references to the *Critique* will be to this edition.

[14] Kant, *Critique*, A 371. See also *Critique*, A 369.

[15] Kant, *Critique*, A 190 / B 236 — A 191.

[16] Kant, *Critique*, A 30 / B 45.

[17] The difference between talk of sensory states of a subject and talk of representations (ideas) *qua* objects of these states lies primarily in the fact that the former commits us to concrete particulars only. The state itself, such as seeing a tree, is counted a property of a person. The latter requires our ontology to admit not only concrete particulars but representations or ideas of these particulars. The difference shows up when we express a statement like "John sees a tree" in canonical notation. In one case we have a non-relational statement attributing a sensory state to a person. In the second case, we have a relational statement whose relata are John and the idea of a tree. The difficulties in the second view are notorious: (1) it leads to scepticism; (2) it raises the problem of the ontological status of ideas or representations, especially when unperceived; (3) it suggests the unattractive doctrine that immediate experience should be describable in language devoid of reference to physical objects. For our purposes it is important to note that Turbayne seems concerned neither with this difference nor the difficulty of deciding which type of reductive analysis Berkeley is engaged in.

[18] Kant, *Critique*, B 69 — B 72; B 274 — B 276; Immanuel Kant, *Prolegomena to any Future Metaphysics*, trans. by Peter G. Lucas (Manchester, 1953), Section 13, Remarks II and III and the Appendix. See also Kant's "Letter to J. S. Beck, December 4, 1792", in *Philosophical Correspondence 1759—99*, trans. and ed. by Arnulf Zweig (Chicago, 1967).

that in his anti-Berkeleian passages Kant is not being quite honest[19]. But I think there is reason to take Kant at his word.

First, an important objection to the reductive interpretation is the fact that unlike Berkeley, Kant *distinguishes* perceptions (or sensory states) from objects of perception. For example, in the "Postulates", he says:

We are able ... under the guidance of the analogies to make the transition from the perception of the attracted iron filings we know of the existence of a magnetic matter prevading all bodies, although the constitution of our organs cuts us off from all immediate perception of the medium[20].

Here Kant uses the example of a magnetic field to illustrate his claim that something is actual only if it is perceivable or related to our perceptions in accordance with the principles of the "Analogies". In the B-edition "Refutation of Idealism" Kant also distinguishes sensory states from objects, arguing that we can order our perceptions in time *only if* there exist objects in space. And the following passage from the second edition "Transcendental Deduction" is also relevant:

The manifold representations, which are given in an intuition, would not be one and all *my* representation, if they did not all belong to one self-consciousness. As *my* representations (even if I am not conscious of them as such) they must conform to the condition under which alone they *can* stand together in one universal self-consciousness, because otherwise they would not all without exception belong to me. From this original combination many consequences follow[21].

It is the second sentence in the quotation which concerns us here. Its interpretation is difficult if only because it is unclear what sense to give the phrase "as such" in the parenthesized portion. Kemp Smith underscores the second occurrence of "my" thus suggesting that "as such" refers to "my". Hence, one is encouraged to read the parenthesized remark "even if I am not conscious of them [representations] as mine". But not all editions of the *Critique* emphasize the second occurrence of "my". The Berlin Academy edition, for one, does not[22]. Hence, we need not follow Kemp Smith's textual grounds for reading "as such" with "my". Moreover, there seem to be independent philosophic reasons for not reading the line in question in this way. For if Kant is claiming that I need not be conscious of representations as mine then he must also be willing to claim that I could be conscious of representations but not conscious of them as my representations. This, however, makes no sense, for what would it mean for me to be conscious of a *representation* but not as *my* representation? If I am conscious of a representation, then *ipso facto* I am conscious of the representation as mine.

[19] Turbayne, p. 243.
[20] Kant, *Critique*, A 226 / B 273.
[21] Kant, *Critique*, B 132.
[22] Immanuel Kant, *Kritik der reinen Vernunft*, in Kant's *Gesammelte Schriften*, III (Berlin, 1911), B 132.

Indeed, this conceptual connection works the other way round as well. If what I am conscious of is mine, then I must be conscious of a representation. For example, the tree I see on a certain occasion is not mine (at least in the relevant sense) but the seeing of the tree or the representation of the tree is most certainly mine. Thus I recommend reading the parenthesized remark as "even if I am not conscious of them [representations] as representations". In other words, Kant holds that in some cases I may be conscious of objects but not of representations of the objects[23].

These considerations make it reasonable, I think, to consider an alternative explanation of Kant's insistence that appearances are not themselves things. The alternative I suggest is this: Kant is mainly concerned to emphasize that appearances are not things in themselves. In A 492 and similar passages Kant focuses on the *contrast* between appearances and things in themselves. Indeed, his repeated claim that appearances are representations or are only "in us" is precisely a way of denying that appearances are things in themselves. And to deny that appearances are things in themselves is not to assert that appearances are subjective states of the subject. What is being denied is, first, that it makes sense to speak of objects as determinant items which are given antecedently to or independently of judging subjects, and, second, that what objects are like is completely independent of certain general features of these subjects' judgemental apparatus. Kant's point is that we simply cannot meaningfully speak about objects at all or ask what they are like apart from *our* conceptual scheme or linguistic framework. For questions about objects presuppose the very framework and *any* answer presupposes some framework.

My contention, then, is that Kant's remark "appearances are not in themselves *things;* they are nothing but ideas [representations] and cannot exist outside our mind" bears only verbal similarity to Berkeley's claim that "the things immediately perceived are ideas which exist only in the mind". In fact they express different philosophical doctrines and so do not constitute evidence of doctrinal similarity. Berkeley advances a form of reductionism, while Kant asserts the distinction, crucial to his philosophy, between appearances and things in themselves. This distinction Kant refers to as "transcendental"[24]. It is, I think, fair to characterize the transcendental distinction as holding between two different conceptions of an object: objects conceived of as essentially items of judgements and objects conceived of as items determinant independently of judgements. Kant refers to the former as "appearances" and to the latter as "things in themselves"[25]. Accordingly, the appearance-thing in itself distinction is not to be conceived as distinguishing between two *sets* of objects, for the notion of a thing in itself

[23] See also Kant, *Critique*, A 159 / B 195 where Kant distinguishes objects from representations of objects.
[24] Kant, *Critique*, A 45 / B 62 — B 63; A 258 / B 313 — B 314.
[25] For a similar view of Kant's appearance — thing in itself distinction see Arthur Melnick's *Kant's Analogies of Experience* (Chicago, 1973), especially, Chapter IV.

is not that of an object or set of objects with a determinate, though peculiar property (namely, unknowability) but rather the notion of something considered apart from conditions that render objects determinate and, so, knowable at all.

The nature of the transcendental distinction can be clarified by contrasting it, as Kant does in the "Aesthetic", with the strictly empirical distinction between purely subjective experience (e. g. misperceptions) and objective experiences (those that are intersubjectively valid). The sourness of good wine to the disaffected palate would be classified as merely subjective effect; the sweetness of the wine objective. For the latter is invariant over ordinary observers under ordinary conditions. While this is a case where what the thing (the wine) is like (sour) is clearly dependent upon the subject, the dependence is of a different order from that exhibited in the transcendental distinction. There the dependence on the subject is not based on peculiarities of the subject's sense organs but on general features of his conceptual scheme. In particular, it is based on the fact that failing subsumption under the (some) conceptual scheme one cannot meaningfully speak of objects at all. Kant makes this point in the "Aesthetic" at A 45 / B 62 where he says:

> We commonly distinguish in appearances that which is essentially inherent in their intuition and holds for sense in all human beings, from that which belongs to their intuition accidently only, and is valid not in relation to sensibility in general but only in relation to a particular standpoint or to a peculiarity of structure in this or that sense. The former kind of knowledge is then declared to represent the object in itself, the latter its appearance only. But this distinction is merely empirical. If, as generally happens, we stop short at this point, and do not proceed, as we ought, to treat the empirical intuition as itself mere appearance, in which nothing that belongs to a thing in itself can be found our transcendental distinction is lost ... The rainbow in a sunny shower may be called a mere appearance, and rain the thing in itself. This is correct, if the latter concept be taken in a merely physical sense. Rain will then be viewed only as that which, in all experience and in all its various positions relative to the senses, is determined thus, and not otherwise, in our intuition. But if we take this empirical object in its general character, and ask, without considering whether or not it is the same for all human sense, whether it represents an object in itself ... the question as to the relation of the representation to the object at once becomes transcendental. We then realize that not only are the drops of rain mere appearances, but that even their round shape, nay even the space in which they fall, are nothing in themselves, but merely modifications or fundamental forms of our sensible intuition, and that the transcendental object remains unknown to us.

Kant is saying, I think, that we commonly distinguish in our experience objective from merely subjective experiences. Objective experiences are those which are invarient for ordinary observers under ordinary conditions. In Kant's words they "hold for sense in all human beings". As an example of an objective experience Kant gives the perception of rain by ordinary observers under standard conditions. And as an example of a subjective experience: the sight of a rainbow, the observation of which is due to (in Kant's words) the particular standpoint of the observer. But this is merely an empirical distinction where we treat the rain as a thing in itself and the rainbow as an appearance. If we proceed to ask whether the rain is an object in itself, determinable independently of (judging) subjects, the question is transcendental and the answer, Kant suggests, is "No". That there are objects is a function of the fact that there are subjects who judge. Consequently, objects are "nothing in themselves"[26].

If correct at all, this interpretation shows the similarity between Kant and Berkeley to be verbal and superficial. Equally wanting, therefore, is the doctrinal kinship Turbayne imputes in Step 4, and *a fortiori* that claimed in Step 5. While it is true for Kant that appearances do not exist independently of us and that (as asserted in Step 5) physical objects (bodies) are appearances and, consequently, do not exist independently of us, the phrase "independently of us" must be read in light of Kant's transcendental distinction. Objects cannot be individuated and, so, *cannot* be known independently of our (some) conceptual scheme. This lack of independence is of a quite different order from that claimed by Berkeley at least on one reasonable interpretation, namely where so-called external objects submit to analysis in terms of sensory states.

Therefore, Turbayne's main claim that Kant and Berkeley *share* an alternative to scepticism is not confirmed by the passages he cites in support of (4) and (5). While (4) and (5) may well be congenial to Berkeley, they cannot be allied with Kant.

Conclusion

The relationship, then, between Kant and Berkeley might be summarized as follows. Berkeley, at least on one interpretation, offers a reductionist account of objects in terms of sensory states. On another interpretation, he offers a metaphysical account of reality in terms of minds, ideas and God. Kant, on the other hand, offers neither a reductionist account of objects nor a metaphysical account of reality *as such*. For Kant, questions about the real nature of objects cannot even be raised[27]; and calling objects of both inner and outer sensory states "appearances" is not a reductionist move but a critical reminder of the fact that the notion of an object is correlative with that of a subject. Knowledge of *objects*, Kant contends, depends both on a manifold which is given and on conceptual or linguistic abilities which determine or specify the given in one rather than another way[28]. Kant, then, contrasts appearances which are objects

---

[26] Kant also claims in this paragraph that "the transcendental object remains unknown to us". By this I take him to mean that we cannot give a metaphysical account of the active correlate of our passive (sensible) intuition. See Kant, *Critique*, A 379 — A 380.

[27] See above, p. 83 and footnote 26.

[28] Cf. Kant, *Critique*, B 129 — B 130, where he remarks: "The manifold of representations can be given in an intuition which is purely sensible, that is, nothing but receptivity ... But the combination of a manifold in general can never come to us through the senses ... It ... is an act of the understanding." It should perhaps be said that space and time (though classified by Kant as intuitions as opposed to concepts)

conceived of as objects of judgements with things in themselves which are objects supposedly determinant independently of subjects and their conceptualizations of them.

The view I attribute to Kant bears certain similarities to Quine's indeterminacy of translation doctrine. For both, sensory data is underdetermined and *talk about objects* requires introduction of linguistic devises (judgement forms) that exceed anything implicit in the data. Hence, for Quine translation is indeterminate or from our point of view reference inscrutable while Kant would say things in themselves are unknowable. An important difference, however, is Quine's aknowledgement and Kant's denial of the possibility of alternative conceptual schemes. Both, however, are one (against Berkeley) in recognizing the empirical slack in our language. Claiming, then, that objects are merely appearances is Kant's way of calling our attention to this fact.

play a role (as do the categories) in our individuation of objects. Indeed, for us, objects are ultimately individuated in terms of spatiotemporal location. It is not part of my project, however, to argue that or how space, time and the categories function to individuate objects nor to reconcile the intuitional status of space and time with their intellectual role in our individuation of objects. For a discussion of these points see Melnick, *Kant's Analogies of Experience*.

Berkeley's Immaterialism and Kant's Transcendental Idealism

M. R. AYERS

Introduction

Ever since its first publication critics of Kant's *Critique of Pure Reason* have been struck by certain strong formal resemblances between transcendental idealism and Berkeley's immaterialism. Both philosophers hold that the sensible world is mind-dependent, and that from this very mind-dependence we can draw a refutation of scepticism of the senses.

According to Berkeley, the scepticism which makes philosophy ridiculous 'vanishes if we annex a meaning to our words, and do not amuse ourselves with the terms *absolute, external, exist* and such like . . . I can as well doubt of my own being, as of the being of those things which I actually perceive by sense'.[1] Ideas of sense constitute 'real things': i.e. ideas caused in us by God in conformity with the principles or rules which we call the laws of nature. It is their evident external causal origin, their givenness, together with their regular association with other ideas in the order of nature, which constitute the criteria by which 'real' or 'external' things are to be distinguished from 'chimeras and illusions on the fancy'.[2]

According to Kant's Fourth Paralogism, which appeared only in the First Edition of the *Critique*, since space as the form of outer sense is 'in us', what is given in space by the senses is in us too, but it nevertheless constitutes physical reality. It can be distinguished from mere illusion because a condition of determinate location in space and time is conformity with law, so that we can employ as our criterion of reality the rule, 'Whatever is connected with a perception according to empirical laws is actual'.[3]

Both Berkeley and Kant distinguish two senses of 'external'. For Berkeley, the word may mean 'absolutely independent of mind', in which sense there are no external physical objects; or it may simply mean 'externally caused' or causally independent of us, like ideas of sense.[4] He attributes the error in the ordinary man's view of physical reality to the assumption that what is external in the second sense is external in the first.[5]

[1] *Principles of Human Knowledge*, I, 87-91.

[2] *Principles*, I, 30-34.

[3] *Critique of Pure Reason*, trans. N. Kemp Smith (New York: St Martin's Press, 1965), A376.

[4] *Principles*, I, 90.

[5] *Principles*, I, 56.

51

M. R. Ayers

Similarly for Kant, 'external' may denote, first, 'that which as thing in itself exists apart from us', in which transcendental sense 'external' objects are entirely unknown; or it may denote 'things which are to be found in space', in which empirical sense 'external' objects are indubitably experienced. The 'transcendental realist' opens the door to scepticism by assuming that what is external in the second sense is also external in the first: i.e. that objects in space are thereby independent of mind.[6] Scepticism of the senses Kant calls 'empirical idealism', to which the antidote is a combination of 'transcendental idealism' (i.e. recognition of mind-dependence) with 'empirical realism' (i.e. employment of determinate existence in space under law as the criterion of reality). Despite differences in their arguments, these and other parallels make it natural to suppose that Berkeley had a not insignificant influence on Kant's thought.

Kant's own later efforts to distinguish his theory from Berkeley's, however, have convinced many readers that there was not in fact any such influence. Paradoxically, that is not because of his success in clarifying the difference between them, but because of his supposed abysmal failure. The Second Edition of the *Critique* and the *Prolegomena to Any Future Metaphysics* contain such seemingly inept characterizations of immaterialism that generations of commentators have held that their author could not have read Berkeley's main works, a conclusion which has been supported by the claim that neither the *Principles* nor the *Three Dialogues Between Hylas and Philonous* was available in German translation until after the First Edition of the *Critique*.

This traditional view of the relationship between the two philosophers has been challenged by contributors to a discussion initiated some years ago by Colin Turbayne.[7] Turbayne points out that (as well as *Siris*) *De Motu* and Eschenbach's translation of the *Three Dialogues* were readily available while Kant formulated his own theory. He further argues that Kant's criticisms can all be read as intelligible attempts to bring out genuine differences from Berkeley, provided that we take them to be founded, not so much on explicit doctrines, as on what Kant sees as the inevitable consequences of explicit doctrines. For Kant, Berkeley *in effect* believes these things. But in Turbayne's view Kant's main argument against scepticism of the senses, the argument which explains the term 'transcendental idealism', is not importantly different from Berkeley's. He believes that from all Kant's criticisms only minor or else irrelevant differences emerge, the significance of which Kant disingenuously exaggerates in a disreputable perversion of Berkeley's doctrines. Other commen-

[6] *Critique*, A373.
[7] C. M. Turbayne, 'Kant's Refutation of Dogmatic Idealism', *Philosophical Quarterly* (1955); republished as 'Kant's Relation to Berkeley' in *Kant Studies Today*, L. W. Beck (ed.) (La Salle: Open Court, 1969).

tators, however (in particular Gale Justin and Henry Allison[8]), have since argued persuasively that Kant does locate a fundamental line of distinction between himself and Berkeley. At the same time it seems in general to be agreed that Kant's criticisms do distort their object. In this paper I want to support and extend Allison's general position, but I also want to look again at the question of distortion. Since in the first part of my paper points which others have made and the additional points and modifications which I should like to make myself are sometimes rather entwined, I shall not spend time surveying previous arguments in detail. In the second part of the paper I shall be more on my own.

Absolute Space and Reality

Let us start with two notorious passages in the Second Edition of the *Critique*. First, in the Transcendental Aesthetic,[9] Kant claims that, if we ascribe objective reality to the forms of outer and inner sense, then the world of experience is 'transformed into mere illusion'.

> For if we regard space and time as properties which, if they are to be possible at all, are to be found in things in themselves, and if we reflect on the absurdities in which we are then involved, in that two infinite things, which are not substances, nor anything actually inhering in substances, must yet have existence, nay, must be the necessary condition of the existence of all things, and moreover must continue to exist, even although all existing things be removed—we cannot blame the good Berkeley for degrading bodies to mere illusion.

Secondly, in the preamble to the Refutation of Idealism,[10] Kant distinguishes two forms of 'material' (i.e. empirical) idealism. The material idealist

> declares the existence of objects in space outside us either to be merely doubtful and indemonstrable or to be false and impossible. The former is the *problematic* idealism of Descartes, which holds that there is only one empirical assertion that is indubitably certain, namely, that 'I am'.

---

[8] G. D. Justin, 'On Kant's Analysis of Berkeley', *Kant Studien* (1974); H. E. Allison, 'Kant's Critique of Berkeley', *Journal of the History of Philosophy* (1973). Margaret Wilson, in 'Kant and the Dogmatic Idealism of Berkeley', *Journal of the History of Philosophy* (1971), had argued that Kant's criticisms do correspond to important differences from Berkeley but also indicate that Kant did not know Berkeley's theory well.

[9] *Critique*, B70f.

[10] *Critique*, B274f.

The latter is the *dogmatic* idealism of Berkeley. He maintains that space, with all the things of which it is the inseparable condition, is something which is in itself impossible; and he therefore regards the things in space as merely imaginary entities. Dogmatic idealism is unavoidable, if space be interpreted as a property that must belong to things in themselves. For in that case space, and everything to which it serves as condition, is a non-entity.

All this may seem clear enough evidence of distortion on Kant's part, whether deliberate or unwitting. Both passages suggest that Berkeley treats all objects of the senses as illusions, ignoring his distinction between illusion and reality. Together they imply that one of Berkeley's arguments is of the form: 'Absolute space is a condition of the existence of bodies. Absolute space is an absurdity. Therefore bodies do not exist.' It is true that Berkeley does attack absolute space, in the form in which it is maintained by Newton, in the *Principles*, in *De Motu*, in *Siris* and, briefly and directly, in the *First Dialogue*. But no modern reader of all these works would naturally suppose that this attack constitutes the chief ground of his rejection of independently existing bodies.

How then might Kant's account of Berkeley be justified or excused or even understood in other terms than ignorance or dishonesty? The chief lines of the argument which emerges from recent discussion are as follows. First, Kant may have known of Berkeley's reality/illusion distinction but refused to be put off by it. It is for him a mere sop provided by someone who does not grasp that the only explanation which can do justice to the empirical reality of bodies is in terms of their determinate existence in space and time. Thus Kant regarded critics who assimilated him to Berkeley as having utterly failed to grasp the logic of his own account of the concept of empirical reality. Secondly, it is said that Kant's one-sided reading of Berkeley, supposing that he approached him through *De Motu* and *Siris*, would have made the attack on space seem more important to the critique of matter than it is.

In support of this second point it might be mentioned that in one passage in *Siris* Berkeley hints at just the kind of argument which Kant ascribes to him: 'From the notion of absolute space springs that of absolute motion; and in these are ultimately founded the notions of external existence, independence, necessity and fate'.[11] Berkeley has just cited Plotinus with approval as 'affirming that the soul is not in the world, but the world in the soul'. He thus seems to be suggesting that the belief in mind-independent bodies arises because people think of space rather than mind as the receptacle or container of bodies. In his earlier works, however, he ascribes belief in the mind-independence of ideas of sense to their involuntariness. The rival to the soul as that in which sensible objects exist is there not

[11] *Siris*, 271.

space but material substance, which is postulated by those who see that sensible qualities need a support but who do not grasp that what 'supports and contains' the entire sensible world is perceiving spirit.[12] So although the diagnosis of our mistake which is proposed in *Siris* is in one way typical of Berkeley, in another way it does not seem to fit in with his earlier arguments at all well. To attribute the *general* belief in mind-independence to the *philosophical* doctrine of absolute space is, moreover, a bit odd. One might speculate that in *Siris* Berkeley was less interested in explaining that ordinary belief than in expressing his increasing conviction that Newtonian metaphysics represented the chief philosophical impediment to the acceptance of immaterialism.

It seems very possible that, after the criticism of the first edition of the *Critique*, Kant searched through translations of Berkeley for evidence of his misapprehension of the connection between the concepts of space and of empirical reality, hitting upon this passage from *Siris* as peculiarly revealing. One reason for thinking so lies in the apparent origin of another notorious characterization of Berkeley, that well-known 'British Empiricist', as driven by the principle that 'all knowledge through the senses and through experience is nothing but illusion, and only in the ideas of pure understanding and reason is truth'.[13] For this passage seems to be nothing but a mildly tendentious paraphrase of *Siris*, 264 (cf. 253 and 303f.). Berkeley's editor, T. E. Jessop, seems quite right to argue that all such denigration of the senses in *Siris* is entirely compatible with the arguments of the earlier works.[14] In all the works, after all, the objects of the senses are characterized as 'inert, fleeting, dependent beings'. In *Siris* he makes the point that the senses are incapable of carrying us beyond such low-grade objects to the principles of science, which call for a rational 'discursive faculty', or to the independent, permanent, substantial realities, spirit in general and God, which are grasped by pure intellect.[15] It is just this Platonic conception of pure intellect penetrating beyond the sensible to the immaterial and ultimately real which Kant rightly opposes to his own principles. But the present point is that Kant takes his characterizations of Berkeley from

[12] Cf. *Principles*, I, 7, 73f., etc.

[13] *Prolegomena to Any Future Metaphysics*, trans. P. G. Lucas (Manchester: Manchester University Press, 1962), 374. Numerical reference follows the pagination of the Berlin Academy edition of the Collected Works.

[14] *The Works of George Berkeley, Bishop of Cloyne*, A. Luce and T. Jessop (eds) (London: Nelson, 1953), V, 14ff.

[15] For explicit mention of 'pure intellect' in earlier works cf. *Three Dialogues between Hylas and Philonous*, I (*Works*, II, 153) and *De Motu*, 53. But the well-known theory of 'notions' is also endorsement of a quasi-Cartesian pure intellect (without innate ideas). Cf. *Principles*, I, 27f., 89, 140 and 142; *Three Dialogues*, III, 232f.

55

Berkeley's mature reflections upon his own theory. It is difficult to see how they could prove ignorance of that theory.

That having been said, both Kant's diagnostic characterization of dogmatic idealism in the Second Edition of the *Critique* and its possible original in *Siris* have a rather puzzling feature. For they seem to imply that transcendental realists, as such, believe in absolute space, in some strong sense of 'absolute', as an independent entity. Yet, as both Kant and Berkeley would very well know, some transcendental realists, such as Aristotle and Descartes himself, approached space in a reductionist spirit, explaining it as no more than an attribute of bodies in some way abstractly considered. For Descartes, 'the same extension which constitutes the nature of body likewise constitutes the nature of space'.[16] Body and the space it occupies are logically distinguishable as species from genus, but are not ontologically distinct. Consequently the notion of a vacuum is a contradiction. Movement, i.e. change of place, is defined relatively to surrounding bodies. The rival doctrine of absolute space as an entity achieved respectability as a consequence of powerful anti-Cartesian arguments. Hobbes did not go all the way in this respect. He poured scorn on the 'childish' *a priori* arguments against a vacuum, and argued that there is no difficulty in a conception of space empty of all bodies. Such a conception is an abstraction from our experiential conception of body: it is 'the phantasm of a thing existing without the mind simply'[17] equivalent to the idea of the *possibility* of external body. But it is distinct from the idea of body, and is required in order that body 'may be understood by reason, as well as perceived by sense'.[18] It enters into the definition of motion, for example, which is not merely relative. Yet Hobbes carefully emphasizes that space is not a thing, but is simply nothing. There is an empty space between two bodies precisely when there is nothing between two bodies which do not meet. Others, however, like Gassendi and Henry More, went much further in their rejection of the reductionist view. What can be computed cannot be nothing. Gassendi produces the principle that space and time are neither substance nor accident: consequently 'all being is substance or accident or place in which all substances and all accidents exist, or time, in which all substances and all accidents endure'.[19] He simply swallows the traditional objection that to treat space as real is to allow something other than God which is uncreated and infinite. The Cambridge Platonist, Henry More, avoids that problem by identifying space with the immensity of God, quoting what was to become Berkeley's

16 *Principles of Philosophy*, II, trans. E. Haldane and G. Ross (New York: Dover, 1955), 10f.

17 *Elements of Philosophy*, II, vii, 2.

18 *Elements*, II, viii, 1.

19 *Syntagma*, Second Part, I, ii, 1, as translated by C. Brush, *Selected Works of Pierre Gassendi* (New York: Johnson Reprint Corp., 1972).

favourite text, 'in whom we live, move and have our being'. He calls space a logical rather than physical entity, a necessary condition of existence of every particular thing whatsoever, body or spirit. Its necessity is an aspect of the necessity of God to the existence of finite beings.[20] Newton was writing in this tradition when he distinguished between sensible or relative space on the one hand, and real or absolute space on the other,[21] a distinction present in a slightly different form in Locke's *Essay Concerning Human Understanding*[22] and explicitly attacked by Berkeley.[23] Newton also supplied some famous physical arguments for accepting absolute motion (i.e. that absolute space has effects) as well as the suggestion in the *Optics* that space is, as it were, the sensorium of God.[24]

The difficulty, then, is this. Descartes certainly held that space and time, if they exist at all, are properties of things in themselves. But he did not accept the 'absurdities' in which, according to Kant, such a belief is involved. For these absurdities are simply explicit elements of *anti*-Cartesian doctrines. The only coherent interpretation of Kant's argument seems to be this: 'Transcendental realism implies the doctrine of absolute space as an independent entity, even if this not understood by all transcendental realists. It makes dogmatic idealism unavoidable for them logically, even if not psychologically.' The relation between Descartes and Berkeley would accordingly appear like this: 'Berkeley recognizes certain features of our conception of space which make it inappropriate to things in themselves, but Descartes fails to recognize these particular features. Consequently Descartes sees nothing objectionable in our conception of space— he simply does not analyse it accurately. *Qua* problematic idealist, however, he raises the question whether anything external corresponds to our conception. But Berkeley rejects our very conception of space, and with it our conception of empirical reality: i.e. he reduces all sensory representation to illusion.'

The Criteria of Reality in Berkeley and Kant

If this interpretation is right, then it must presumably have seemed irrelevant to Kant that Berkeley cobbled up his own accounts of space on the one hand and of reality on the other, arguing that they do justice to what matters in our ordinary conceptions. But the question remains why Kant should have taken such a dismissive line, rather than more sympathetically treating Berkeley as a transcendental idealist who has been driven into a

[20] Cf. *Divine Dialogues*, I.
[21] *Principia Mathematica*, Def. VIII Schol.
[22] Op. cit., II, xiii, 10.
[23] *Principles*, I, 110–116, etc.
[24] *Optics*, qu. 28.

57

wrong analysis of our ordinary, mind-dependent conception of space by a failure to see that mind-dependence explains and makes innocuous the otherwise 'absurd' attributes of absolute space. It can only be this question, if anything, which keeps alive accusations of dishonesty and lack of generosity on Kant's part.

Perhaps what makes the difference for Kant is that, unlike Descartes, Berkeley explicitly attacks the right, logically inescapable conception of space *at all points*, as the conception of an impossible object. For, as others have remarked, the properties mentioned in his direct criticisms of Berkeley are not the only properties of space which for Kant are inescapable but which Berkeley refuses to swallow. There are also its being the common object of the senses, its being infinitely divisible, and its being *a priori*, a property manifested in the possibility of the *a priori* science of geometry. All these properties are, of course, recognized, and swallowed, by Descartes. For Berkeley, on the other hand,

> experience can have no criteria of truth because its phenomena (according to him) have nothing *a priori* at their foundation, whence it follows that experience is nothing but sheer illusion; whereas with us, space and time (in conjunction with the pure concepts of the understanding) prescribe their law to all possible experience *a priori* and, at the same time, afford the certain criterion for distinguishing truth from illusion therein.[25]

Kant's claim that he is sharply distinguished from Berkeley by his ability to derive the criteria of reality *a priori* (first from the conditions of objective existence in space and time and ultimately from the necessary unity of apperception) has been well discussed by others, and I do not have much to add. I should, however, like to give further emphasis to the point that Kant's explanation of the paradoxical properties of space, like his explanation of reality, essentially involves transcendental otherness. Space is the way things in themselves impinge on us. Empirical externality is the mode of representation of transcendental externality. To take just one example, the paradox of the purely relational difference between isomorphic incongruent figures is explained as follows: 'There is no intrinsic difference between such figures, only a relational one. The understanding assures us that there cannot be things which differ only relationally, but this "can well be the case with mere appearances".'[26] Kant does not mean that there can be entities comparable to Berkeley's ideas which differ only relationally: he means that an absolute difference may *appear* as a merely relative difference. That is the proof that spatiality, which allows such merely relational differences, is a form of appearance. Kant's appearances are

---

[25] *Prolegomena*, 374f., quoted by Allison, 60.
[26] *Prolegomena*, 286.

therefore, as he continually says, necessarily appearances *of* something, whereas Berkeley's ideas have no such intrinsic intentionality.

This point may seem at odds with the most 'Berkeleyan' passages, such as the Fourth Paralogism, in which Kant seems to make a sharp separation between transcendental object and empirical object, as if we could concern ourselves with the existence of the latter without any reference at all to the former. But Kant is struggling with a notably difficult area in the topic of intentionality, as we may remind ourselves if we make the comparison ('altogether insufficient' as he says it is) with secondary qualities such as colours. If what typically causes the sensation of blue is (say) a certain micro-texture of the surface of objects, is it or is it not the case that we can perceive that surface micro-texture? In a way we can, since we see it as blue. Yet in a way we cannot see it at all, and it does not appear to the closest inspection. In a way blue is the appearance on the one hand, distinct from surface micro-texture, the reality, on the other. Yet in a way the blueness of an object just *is* a certain surface structure as it appears to sight. Locke had this trouble with secondary qualities, and Kant accordingly has it with bodies. Just as Locke is led to suggest that 'blue' has two meanings, for appearance and for reality, so Kant is led to talk as if he were giving 'body' two meanings in the same breath:

I do indeed admit that there are bodies outside us, i.e. things which, although wholly unknown to us as to what they may be in themselves, we know through the representations which their influence on our sensibility provides for us, and to which we give the name of bodies. This word therefore means the appearance of that for us unknown but none the less real object.[27]

Thus despite the famous dictum about sensations without concepts,[28] Kant's sensory ideas or representations essentially contain something which points beyond themselves: they are not wholly 'blind' effects. Their spatiality is what makes them intrinsically *capable* of truth and falsity. The concepts of the understanding come into play at the stage of distinguishing *between* truth and falsity. Testing for illusion is testing empirically, which of course means causally, that a part of space is for a time filled in such and such a way.

This admirable, profound connection of the intentionality of our sensations with their being sensations of things in space was not without antecedents. Hobbes, as we have seen, held that to form the idea of pure space just is to focus on the perceived externality or otherness of things. Very possibly it was Hobbes' view which stimulated Berkeley's concern to

---

[27] *Prologomena*, 289.

[28] *Critique*, A51 (B75). In Kemp Smith's translation, 'intuitions without concepts are blind'.

deny that distance from the perceiver, or 'outness', is immediately perceived. The perception of distance is explained by Berkeley as a hypotheti-
cal judgment about future sensations based on a regular association between ideas of the same or different senses in the past.[29] There is no other
sort of 'outness' than that. Spatial externality thus does have a certain,
rather accidental connection with his criteria of reality, but only because
of the role of constant conjunction between ideas in his account of both.
The sole theoretical basis for the connection is the notion of a divine
language through which God forewarns us of the future course of
experience.

It may help us to understand why space and reality should be so dis-
connected in Berkeley's system if we remember the influence on him in
particular of Locke's theory of perception. Locke holds that we have
immediate sensory knowledge of the *existence* of external objects, but
strictly limited sensory knowledge of their *nature*. In what he calls 'actual
sensation' we are immediately aware that 'exterior causes' are acting on
us through the senses, but in this 'sensitive knowledge' we conceive of
such causes or powers purely through their effects.[30] Locke does of course
believe that the external powers to cause sensory ideas belong to bodies in
space. He holds that ideas of space 'resemble' their causes, and distinguishes primary from secondary qualities in this respect. Yet he treats such
beliefs as subsequent hypotheses or reasonable physical speculations not
included in immediate perceptual knowledge itself. His general theory of
representation is purely causal: simple ideas represent in thought their
regular causes.[31] Such a theory treats sensations as blank data rather than
as intrinsically intentional states. More accurately, it treats sensations as if
the sole respect in which they are intrinsically intentional is causal. External
objects are presented in sensation solely as the possessors of powers to
cause sensory effects. Hence Berkeley can claim that those powers might as
well belong to a spirit, indeed that that is the only intelligible hypothesis.[32]
But Locke's theory of perception is inadequate. For all sensation is, as
such, sensation of things in space, whether of things distant from the body,
in contact with the body or, as in the case of pain and other bodily sensations, within the body itself. Unless 'external objects' were presented in

---

[29] *Essay towards a New Theory of Vision*, 45 *et passim*.

[30] Cf. *Essay*, IV, xi, 2, etc. I do not mean to imply that it is not also helpful towards understanding Berkeley to consider Descartes' rather different account of
perceptual beliefs, and in fact *Principles of Philosophy*, II, 1, seems to set the
scene rather neatly for the Berkeleyan theory. But Berkeley does allude specifically
to the features of Locke's account described here.

[31] Cf. *Essay*, II, xxx, 2; II, xxxi, 2; etc.

[32] Cf. *Three Dialogues*, III, 239; *Theory of Vision Vindicated*, 11ff.; *Philosophical
Commentaries*, 80, 112.

sensation not only as causes of sensations but as objects in space, no particular object could possibly be identified as the single possessor of a number of experienced qualities, or the cause of a number of sensations. The philosophical issue is obviously too large for the present context, but the necessary connection between the spatiality and the intentionality of sensation is one of the things which Kant offers to explain by the doctrine that space is the form of outer sense, but which goes unrecognized by Berkeley.

Infinite Divisibility in Berkeley and Kant

Kant, then, represents Berkeley as primarily a critic of objective space who thereby deprives himself of the material for a conception of objective reality. Obsessed with space in his destructive arguments, Kant's Berkeley unduly neglects it in his botched-up account of 'real things'. Is the first part of such a characterization as inept as it might, *prima facie*, seem? I shall argue that it in fact places Berkeley, not at all inappositely, within a tradition to which arguments about space were indeed of central importance, the tradition which, as Kant says, stretches from the Eleatic School.[33] Other members of that tradition, contemporary with Berkeley, were Pierre Bayle and Arthur Collier, both of whom attack our notion of objective space as vigorously as Zeno can seem to do himself. Bayle, who certainly influenced Berkeley, remarks with respect to pure space that 'an unmovable, indivisible and penetrable extension' is 'a nature of which we have no idea, and is besides repugnant to the clearest ideas of our mind'.[34] Collier's *Clavis Universalis* was, in its German translation, bound in with Berkeley's *Three Dialogues*[35] and significantly favours antinomies. One is to the effect that 'an external world, whose existence is absolute' would have to be 'both finite and infinite' in extent.[36] Both Collier and Bayle devote considerably more space to an argument even more characteristic of the tradition to which they belong. Objective extension would have to be infinitely divisible, which is absurd, and objective motion is by all our lights impossible.[37]

The topic of infinite divisibility was central to the topic of the objective determination or measurement of space and time. On the evidence of the *Principles* and *Three Dialogues*, however, one might think that it was a topic, like that of pure space, with no more than a minor role in Berkeley's argument. That appearance is misleading. Both in early and late works a

[33] *Prolegomena*, 374.
[34] Cf. *Historical and Critical Dictionary*, article 'Leucippus'.
[35] See Turbayne, 226.
[36] *Clavis Universalis*, II, iii.
[37] Bayle, *Dictionary*, article 'Zeno'; Collier, *Clavis*, II, iv.

concern with infinite divisibility constitutes a major preoccupation at the heart of his objections to Newtonianism.[38] But it also permeates one of his most famous arguments of all.

In the *First Dialogue* Berkeley finds contradictions arising from the conjunction of three propositions. First, the presupposition accepted by Hylas at this stage of the argument (while he represents the naive realist) that the real size of an object is the size it is perceived to be. Secondly, the ordinary assumption that when two observers of different sizes, such as a mite and a man, perceive the same object, then they both perceive its size. (The same goes for the two eyes of one observer, 'looking with one eye bare, the other through a microscope'.) And thirdly, the principle that an object's real size is at any one time single and determinate. Philonous concludes that all determinations of extension are sense-relative, and that independent material objects could not possess determinate size and shape. A similar point is made about motion, and a further argument demolishes the suggestion that an absolute extension and an absolute motion are abstractible in thought from their sense-relative determinations, great and small, swift and slow. Hylas is thus left to defend belief in a material substance to which not even extension and motion can be attributed.[39]

The structure of the *First Dialogue* can make it seem that Berkeley simply extends to primary qualities the mechanists' arguments about secondary qualities. 'Was it not admitted as a good argument', Philonous asks in direct, if unfair allusion to Locke, 'that neither heat nor cold was in the water, because it seemed warm to one hand and cold to another?'[40] Yet Philonous can only make this appeal because poor Hylas currently represents Berkeley's common man, who assumes, prior to argument, that whatever particular colour or size is immediately perceived is independently real. The corresponding argument in the *Principles* is less misleading in more than one respect. First, an extension of the mechanists' arguments against secondary qualities is there taken to prove only the sceptical conclusion that 'we do not know by sense which is the true extension or colour of the object'. Secondly, the analogy with secondary qualities is drawn only *after* an independent argument that determinates of extension and motion are sense-relative. This latter claim rather surprisingly receives as its sole credential the statement that it is 'allowed' by modern philosophers.[41] Now we might reasonably wonder how 'modern philosophers' could possibly both allow that size and speed are relative to perception and at the

[38] On the one hand, in the early notebooks known as *Philosophical Commentaries*; on the other, in *The Analyst* and *A Defence of Free-Thinking in Mathematics*.

[39] *Three Dialogues*, I, 188ff.

[40] *Three Dialogues*, I, 189. Cf. Locke, *Essay*, II, viii, 21.

[41] *Principles*, I, 11.

same time distinguish sense-independent primary qualities such as size and motion from sense-relative secondary ones. In fact what Berkeley is doing is placing two different arguments to be found in mechanist philosophers face to face in confrontation. The first has to do with the limitations of the senses and infinite divisibility. Even by itself, in Berkeley's view, it leads to absurd consequences.

The authors of the Port Royal *Logic*, while on the fashionable topic of the limitations of our faculties, invite us to boggle at the implications of matter's being infinitely divisible. A grain of wheat contains a whole universe, which may itself contain proportionately smaller grains of wheat, and so *ad infinitum*. We cannot even in thought identify 'any part, no matter how small, that does not have as many proportional parts as does the whole world'. Immediately before this sally against atomism we have been told that the senses cannot inform us of the 'true and natural' or 'absolute' size of a body, as the existence of lenses is evidence:

> Our very eyes are spectacles, and how do we know whether they diminish or magnify the objects we see or whether the artificial lenses believed to diminish or magnify objects may not on the contrary give their true size? Nor do we know whether others perceive an object to be the same size as we do. Two people agree that a given body measures only five feet, but each may have a different idea of a foot.[42]

These two lines of thought came to be combined by Malebranche in a single sceptical argument. Because of the infinite divisibility of matter, 'nothing but infinities are to be found everywhere'. Yet our ideas of objects are 'proportionate to the idea we have of the size of our body, although there are in these objects an infinite number of parts that they do not disclose to us'. We cannot, that is to say, indefinitely divide the immediate object of vision: 'As far as vision is concerned, a mite is only a mathematical point. It cannot be divided without being annihilated.' Microscopes, together with the thought that 'our own eyes are in effect only natural spectacles' and that there could be microscopically small perceivers, should convince us that 'we must not rely on the testimony of our eyes to make judgments about size'. Indeed, 'nothing is either large or small in itself'.[43]

Like Malebranche, Bayle combines the topics of size and infinite divisibility, including a long and elaborate exposition of geometrical paradoxes of infinity taken by themselves to prove the impossibility of extension. He returns to the 'spectacles' passage from the Port Royal *Logic*,

[42] Arnauld and Nicole, *Logic, or the Art of Thinking*, IV, i, as translated by J. Dickoff and P. James (Indianapolis 1964).
[43] *Search After Truth* I, vi, as translated by T. Lennon and P. Olscamp (Columbus: Ohio State University Press 1980).

63

making the very tendentious comment that it concedes outright that determinate size is relative to the senses in just the way in which, according to 'modern philosophers', colours, heat, cold and so forth are sense-relative.[44]

All these discussions make it easy to understand Berkeley's claim, as tendentious as Bayle's, that 'modern philosophers' allow that determinate size is relative, although the *Logic* and even Malebranche are in fact arguing something rather different. But very like Malebranche, if to different effect, Berkeley ties the relativity of sensible size together with the infinite divisibility of extension by imagining an infinitely variable sense by means of which the realist's infinity of worlds within worlds, parts within parts of matter, might be observed. From the doctrine of infinite divisibility,

> it follows, that there is an infinite number of parts in each particle of matter, which are not perceived by sense. The reason therefore, that any particular body seems to be of a finite magnitude, or exhibits only a finite number of parts to sense, is . . . because the sense is not acute enough to discern them. In proportion therefore as the sense is rendered more acute, it perceives a greater number of parts in the object, that is, the object appears greater, and its figure varies, those parts in its extremities which were before unperceivable, appearing now to bound it in very different lines and angles from those perceived by an obtuser sense. And at length, . . . when the sense becomes infinitely acute, the body shall seem infinite. During all which there is no alteration in the body, but only in the sense. Each body therefore considered in itself, is infinitely extended, and consequently void of all shape or figure.[45]

This argument is explicitly an elucidation of the earlier discussion of sense-relativity and primary and secondary qualities in §11. Consequently it irresistibly suggests that infinite divisibility is also in Berkeley's mind in the *First Dialogue*. Unlike Bayle, of course, Berkeley does not conclude baldly that extension does not exist. The absurdities and contradictions are supposed to attach only to *external* and *independent* extension, to the belief that each physical thing has a single determinate extent variously perceptible by various observers under a variety of conditions. Once it is recognized that what really has extension is each separate idea which goes to constitute the 'thing', the problems vanish. For the contrast between contradictory, independent extension and untroublesome, sense-dependent extension, the contrast which runs through all Berkeley's arguments against the former, involves in his mind a positive doctrine about the latter. That is the doctrine of *minima sensibilia*, which we may reasonably suppose

44 *Dictionary*, article 'Zeno'.
45 *Principles*, I, 47.

64

was inspired both by Malebranche and by Locke's suggestion that 'sensible points' are the ultimately 'simple' ideas of extension.[46] Berkeley concluded that the extension of an idea, or sensible extent, is not infinitely divisible, since it is composed of a finite number of *minima*. *Minima* are parts without parts—otherwise they would not be *minima*. Consequently the *minima* of mites and men are equal, and microscopes do not enable us to see more of them. Mites and men simply see different extensions, while the microscope 'presents us with a new scene of visible objects'.[47]

For Kant, on the other hand, as for orthodox Cartesians, infinite divisibility is mathematically proved and hence undeniable: 'the proofs are based upon insight into the constitution of space, in so far as space is . . . the formal condition of the possibility of all matter'.[48] Yet at the same time, it is necessary to conceive of the composition of substances as a composition of indivisible simples. The evident clash of these supposedly evident principles constitutes the Second Antinomy, the explanation of which, according to Kant, lies in the fact that external substances are necessarily experienced in a successive synthesis of spatial appearances. If matter is infinitely divisible then the conception of the *complete* appearance of a thing is impossible, since it is impossible to complete the task of conceiving the possible appearances of its separable parts: on the other hand, to deny infinite divisibility is to claim what is manifestly untrue, that that task could be so completed that every discernible part had actually been discerned in experience. Kant's solution seems to be that the interminable synthesis of possible appearances which is a necessary feature of experience of things in space does not correspond to a feature of things in themselves. To experience an infinitely divisible object in space is not to experience an object with an infinite number of parts—but it is not to experience an object with a finite number of parts either. The answer to the question whether an object in space has a finite or an infinite number of spatial parts is necessarily indeterminate, like a similar question about the size of the universe. The question is therefore meaningless.[49]

The difference between the two solutions is characteristic of both philosophers. Kant embraces the paradoxical property of objective extension which Berkeley, retreating to the supposedly unproblematic subjective impression, rejects outright. Yet Kant's discussion is obviously a kind of commentary on the sceptical tradition within which Berkeley wrote. One might conclude that Kant was better educated than most of us to understand the *First Dialogue*.

[46] *Essay*, II, xv, 9.
[47] *New Theory of Vision*, 85; cf. *Three Dialogues*, III, 245.
[48] *Critique*, A439 (B467).
[49] *Critique*, A487f. (B515f.) and A505 (B533).

65

M. R. Ayers

The Determination of Space and Time and the Refutation of Idealism

All these issues relate to a general problem about the measurement and objective determination of space and time, and so can bring us round to the topics of the Refutation of Idealism. One discussion which seems likely to have influenced Kant considerably here was Leibniz's commentary on Locke's *Essay*.

Locke, in his account of ideas of determinate size, employs a model very like that of the Port Royal *Logic*, although without the sceptical consequences. Thus 'Men for the use and by the custom of measuring, settle in their Minds the Ideas of certain stated lengths, such as an Inch, Foot, Yard', etc. Using these as elements, we can construct an idea of any distance whatsoever, even of a quasi-infinite or indefinite distance.[50] Leibniz protests, rather profoundly, that there cannot be a distinct idea corresponding to each precise 'stated length'. 'For no one can say or grasp in his mind what an inch or a foot is. The signification of these terms can be retained only by means of real standards of measure which are assumed to be unchanging, through which they can always be re-established.'[51]

Leibniz's further discussion might suggest that this assumption of immutability depends on the assumption of immutable laws. For example, he considers the suggestion that a universal relationship, such as the length of a pendulum whose swing would take exactly one second at a specified latitude, should be used as a dependable unit of length. And it is clear that any doubt whether a particular physical standard, such as the standard metre, has changed length would have to be resolved (and would in principle always be resolvable) by means of scientific theory. So to have the notion of a foot is roughly speaking (ignoring complications having to do with the 'division of linguistic labour'[52] and so forth) to know how to determine a certain unit of physical measurement. And the possibility of physical measurement presupposes that the world is law-governed; and that might imply, and would certainly in Leibniz's time have been taken to imply, that it is composed of a law-governed substance or substances. Since the existence of determinate extension seems to presuppose the possibility of physical measurement, and it seems that extension is necessarily determinate, it also seems that we have here a proof that an extended world is necessarily law-governed, consisting of law-governed substance.

This argument is not advanced by Kant, still less by Leibniz. But a roughly parallel argument relating to time does appear in the *Critique*, in

[50] *Essay*, II, xiii, 4.

[51] *New Essays on Human Understanding*, II, xiii, 4, trans. P. Remnant and J. Bennett (Cambridge: Cambridge University Press, 1981).

[52] Cf. H. Putnam, 'Meaning and Reference' in *Mind, Language and Reality* (Cambridge: Cambridge University Press, 1975).

66

the Analogies. The seeds of something like this argument already exist in the *Essay* because Locke sees it as a special problem about the measurement of time that 'we cannot keep by us any standing unvarying measure of Duration', as we can of extension. A convenient measure of time must be 'what has divided the whole length of its Duration into apparently equal Portions, by constantly repeated Periods'. He first argues, however, that the succession of ideas itself gives us the idea of determinate duration, and supplies us with our first sense of 'constantly repeated periods'. For unless that were so, it would never have occurred to us, for example, that one diurnal or annual revolution of the sun was equal to the next. 'The constant and regular Succession of Ideas in a waking Man is, as it were, the Measure and Standard of all other Successions.' The primitive unit of time, the period from one idea to the next, Locke calls an 'instant'. Yet he does recognize that subjective judgments of time can be checked against objective phenomena, and he also sees that, whatever regular motion we choose as our measure, the judgment that it does measure the 'one constant, equal, uniform Course' of 'Duration itself' relies upon the judgment that 'the Cause of that Motion which is unknown to us, shall always operate equally'. In other words, he recognizes that measurement of time ultimately presupposes immutable substances and laws of nature.[53]

Leibniz, as we should expect, protests against the notion of the primitive subjective clock: 'Changes in our perceptions prompt us to think of time, and we measure it by means of uniform changes'. He seems to mean that our primitive sense of time is not a determinate measure of time. We need for that something much closer, and more evidently closer, to the operation of basic laws. He also makes the point that yardsticks are only relatively unchanging, so that they do not after all represent a fundamental distinction between time and space.

These arguments supply some of the ingredients of the Analogies and the Refutation of Idealism. (Another ingredient, which I shall ignore, is the traditional Aristotelian derivation of the measurement of time from a primitive division of time into *before* and *after* by the point *now*.) In the First Analogy Kant argues that the objective determination of time requires something permanent: succession must be conceived as the permanent undergoing change in accordance with law. The Refutation adds roughly the following argument: If I am to think of myself as more than a bare logical subject, I must have experience of myself as a thing with determinate duration in time. In that case, as well as the succession of my ideas or states of consciousness, something permanent must be the object of my senses. Inner sense, however, perceives only states of consciousness— no permanent self is perceived. I can only locate my states in determinate time by relating them to those permanent material objects, changing or

[53] *Essay*, II, xiv.

moving relatively to one another as the sun moves in relation to the earth, which are perceived by outer sense. Only in this way can I think of the self or subject of my states as having determinate duration, with successive states objectively ordered in time. Hence to accept one's own existence in time as indubitably given but to doubt that of external motions and clocks is incoherent, for to do the latter is to doubt the very perceptions which make experience of a permanent self possible. The concept of an enduring substance cannot be empirically employed in relation to the self unless it is first employed in relation to physical objects.

We can easily see why this argument is directed against Descartes, for whom the concept of absolute duration is quite unproblematic. The duration of a substance, whether matter or spirit, is for him not distinct from its being. The concept of duration is, moreover, prior to the concept of measurable time, which is a creation of the mind.[54] But consideration of Leibniz on Locke may also help to illuminate Kant's intentions. For Locke holds that something merely subjective, the succession of ideas, can give us a measurement of duration. A sceptic of the senses who thinks of the self as a substance in time must adopt Descartes' and Locke's presuppositions. Kant in effect turns an endorsement of Leibniz's objection to Locke into an anti-sceptical argument: i.e. we must turn to matter and the laws of physics for the possibility of that measurement of duration without which the concepts of duration and of time, of substance and of change in a substance, are empty and inapplicable. The argument presupposes that there is no identifiable empirical nature of the soul as there is of matter. Nothing in psychology corresponds to Newtonian physics. In this reasonable view there are once again echoes of such earlier writers as Gassendi, Malebranche and Locke.[55]

Kant presents the Refutation of Idealism as a proof of the existence of external objects in response to the 'problematic idealism' of Descartes. Berkeley is first set on one side with the claim that his position has already been refuted in the Transcendental Aesthetic. But there are two reasons why the Refutation might in any case be supposed an inappropriate argument against Berkeley. For any argument will work only against those who accept what it presupposes as undisputed, and the Refutation makes two such presuppositions which Berkeley rejects. First, it assumes the *concept* of a material permanent undergoing change, a concept which is not impugned by Descartes' scepticism but which Berkeley finds unintelligible and self-contradictory. Secondly, it assumes that the sceptic, like Descartes, sees the self as a substance with objectively determined duration, its states being objectively determined in time. Yet, although for Berkeley the

---

[54] *Principles of Philosophy*, I, 55ff.
[55] Cf. Gassendi, *Objections to Descartes' Meditations*, II, 6, 9; Malebranche, *Search after Truth*, III, ii, 7; Locke, *Essay*, IV, iii, 16f.; IV, iii, 29; IV, vi, 14.

68

self is a substance, on his official view he does not allow it objective duration or see its states as objectively determined in time—any more than he sees sensible bodies as objectively determined in space.

It may not always seem that Berkeley does reject objective or absolute time. For example, in an argument against absolute motion or velocity he claims that it is 'possible ideas should succeed one another twice as fast in your mind as they do in mine'.[56] Yet this argument is dialectical and *ad hominem*. It appeals, for example, to the Lockean principle that time is measured by the succession of ideas, understood to mean merely that we measure or estimate time that way. Berkeley himself actually holds to this principle in a much stronger, ontological sense: each spirit has its own time, determined or constituted by the succession of its own ideas. There is a temporal *minimum*, the instant from one idea to the next, which is without duration: 'the duration of any finite spirit must be estimated by the number of ideas or actions succeeding each other in that same spirit or mind'.[57] It would follow that the speed of the succession of ideas cannot vary from one person to another, and the only relevant intersubjective comparison possible would be between the length of time (i.e. number of ideas) between two given ideas in one person with the time between two other ideas in another person. Consequently no question of intersubjective simultaneity would be meaningful. Berkeley cannot allow, for example, that when two observers perceive, as we say, the same physical event or object, they have the ideas in question at the same time (or, for that matter, at different times). If a Berkeleyan does allow that such questions could arise, then, as the briefest reflection reveals, he will be plunged into contradictions. Berkeley's intersubjective 'reality' is so disintegrated that even time does not bind together the ideas which are supposed to constitute a real thing.

Whether Kant knew of Berkeley's extreme and wildly implausible retreat into subjectivity in the case of the determinations of time (as I have suggested he very probably did recognize the parallel move in the case of determinations of extension) is perhaps doubtful enough. Nevertheless it is one of the features of Berkeley's system which would seem fully to justify, not only Berkeley's exclusion from the scope of the Refutation of Idealism, but the charge that, with whatever sophistication, he 'degrades bodies to mere illusion'.

---

[56] *Three Dialogues*, I, 190.
[57] *Principles*, I, 98.

Kant's Conception of Berkeley's Idealism

by G. J. Mattey, Davis/California

The extent to which Kant's criticisms of Berkeley are fair and accurate is an issue of continuing interest and frustration for Kant scholars. Kant's responses to the claim that transcendental idealism is fundamentally identical to the idealism of Berkeley seem quite inconsistent with the doctrines of the *Principles of Human Knowledge* and *Three Dialogues*. The numerous attempts to explain this *prima facie* discrepancy fall within the following range of alternatives: either Kant was ignorant of Berkeley's real position, or if he understood it, he either presented it fairly or distorted it. The first alternative has been most widely accepted since its first full presentation – by Janitsch in 1879 – particularly in view of its endorsement by Kemp Smith[1]. That Kant deliberately distorted Berkeley's position because of its resemblance to his own, a similarity he believed would discredit him, was more recently defended in an influential paper by Turbayne, which provoked a serious reassessment of the situation[2]. Recently there have appeared various defenses of the correctness of Kant's reconstruction of Berkeley and of the way he contrasted his own view with that of Berkeley[3].

Compounding the obvious difficulties inherent in speculation concerning the sources of Kant's account are two further factors. First, although commentators have tended to treat them as a unity, Kant's comments on Berkeley span a period of roughly thirty years, during which time they varied remarkably. In his lectures of 1762–4, Kant outlines a version of Berkeley which is readily recognizable as the doctrine of the *Dialogues*, while in the more celebrated passages from the *Critique* and *Prolegomena*,

---

[1] Julius Janitsch, *Kants Urteile über Berkeley* (Straßburg: 1879). Norman Kemp-Smith, *A Commentary to Kant's Critique of Pure Reason*, Second Edition (New York: 1962), pp. 155–161. Cf. Désirée Park, *Kant and Berkeley's 'Idealism,'* in: Studi internationali di Filosofia, II (1970), pp. 3–10, where further evidence of misleading contemporary accounts of Berkeley is adduced.

[2] Colin Turbayne, *Kant's Refutation of Dogmatic Idealism*, in: Philosophical Quarterly, V, No. 20 (Juli 1955), pp. 225–244.

[3] Henry Allison, *Kant's Critique of Berkeley*, in: Journal of the History of Philosophy, XI, No. 1 (January 1973), pp. 43–63. Also, *Kant's Refutation of Realism*, in: Dialectica, XXX, No. 2/3 (1976), pp. 223–253. Gail Justin, *On Kant's Analysis of Berkeley*, in: Kant-Studien, LXVIII (1977), pp. 77–88. George Miller, *Kant and Berkeley: the Alternative Theories*, in: Kant-Studien, LXIV (1973), pp. 315–335. Margaret Wilson, *Kant and the Dogmatic Idealism of Berkeley*, in: Journal of the History of Philosophy, IX (1971), pp. 459–475.

one finds the Berkeley of *Siris*[4]. Kant has been accused of charging Berkeley with solipsism, yet within a few years of that apparent accusation he seems to have conceded that Berkeley was not an idealist but merely expressed himself poorly[5]. Each of these phases will be examined in the sequel.

Implicit in this catalogue of interpretations is the second difficulty – that Berkeley's own position underwent a metamorphosis in the years following the publication of his philosophy of immaterialism. The idealism of the *Dialogues* was as much a vindication of common-sense beliefs about sensible objects as an argument for the existence of God; indeed the latter proceded *a posteriori* from the intelligibility of the sensible world. By the time he wrote *Siris*, Berkeley had changed his emphasis, indicting the senses for their deceit and holding open the possibility of a glimpse of the divine Ideas "abstracted from all things corporeal, sensible and imaginable[6]." The outcome of an examination of the several Kantian pronouncements on Berkeley will reveal that they relatively accurately capture the spirit of these quite different Berkeleyan doctrines.

It is generally conceded that Kant could have read any of three of Berkeley's treatises: the *Dialogues, De Motu* and *Siris*. That he did not avail himself of the German translations of the *Dialogues* has been argued on the basis of a number of theses in the published criticisms which conflict with its contents, most notably the argument that Berkeley denied the reality of bodies because he had no criterion of sensible reality, but rather found truth only through intellectual intuition. Thus Kemp Smith concluded that, "In order to make Kant's account of Berkeley's teaching really comprehensible, we seem compelled to assume that he had never himself read any of Berkeley's own writings[7]." Against this view, Turbayne has argued that the structural similarities between Kant's attack on sceptical idealism in the Fourth Paralogism and Berkeley's treatment of scepticism in the *Dialogues* indicate that in reading the latter, Kant "noted those insights which contributed to the solution of the problem of modern philosophy, and made them his own[8]." Yet others have attacked the preceding statement, claiming that it is through the criticisms of, not the resemblance to, Berkeley's philosophy that Kant's familiarity with the *Dialogues* can be seen, and that far from being "preverse," they are accurate and decisive[9].

[4] Immanuel Kant, *Kants gesammelte Schriften*, Akademie edition (Berlin: 1910–72), Vol. XXVIII, pp. 42–43. References to Kant's works will cite the volume and page numbers from the Akademie edition, with the exception of the *Critique of Pure Reason*, where the standard abbreviations will be used.
[5] Ak. XXVIII 770 (*Metaphysik K$_2$*). Translations from the lectures on metaphysics are my own.
[6] George Berkeley, *The Works of George Berkeley*, ed. A. A. Luce and T. E. Jessop (London: 1948–57), V, p. 154 (*Siris*, § 337). All references to *Siris* and *De Motu* will cite the original section numbers. All other references will cite the volume and page numbers from the *Works*.
[7] Kemp-Smith, 156.
[8] Turbayne, 244.
[9] Kemp-Smith (159) and Turbayne (243) agree that they are perverse. Allison, Justin, Miller, and Wilson attack this view.

Another controversy centers on Kant's knowledge of the later phase of Berkeley's philosophy as enunciated in *Siris*. While Kant's published criticisms strikingly mirror the contents of that work, it has been argued that he could not have read it[10]. This line of argument intersects the first, in that the views Kant ostensibly derived from *Siris* must be reconstructed from material found in the *Dialogues* or else from secondary sources on the hypotheses that Kant did not read Berkeley's later work. Given this tangle of conflicting interpretations, one might best proceed chronologically through Kant's various treatments of Berkeley, in order to examine their contents in light of the information available to Kant at a given time.

The fundamental thesis of this investigation is that from early in his pre-critical period until the last decade of his life, Kant maintained an active interest in Berkeley's work and continually availed himself of primary sources of it. It must be granted that there was a sizeable amount of misinformation about Berkeley in the literature of Kant's time, but the kind of reconstruction from such sources of the entire argument against Berkeley – the "traditional approach" of Janitsch and Kemp Smith – is quite unnecessary.

Kant first mentioned Berkeley in his metaphysics lectures of 1762–4, which followed the publication of the 1756 German translation of the *Dialogues*[11]. Ironically, the bulk of the attention devoted to this important document has centered on the implications of Kant's witticism that "Bishop Berkeley in the treatise on the uses of tarwater for our bodies, doubts whether there are bodies at all[12]." Speculation concerning which edition of *Siris* Kant had in mind – the German translation of only the medicinal part or the French translation of the entire book – obscures the fact that despite certain misconceptions, Kant had a detailed familiarity with the *Dialogues*[13].

Taking over the definition of idealism given in Baumgarten's *Metaphysica* (the textbook for the course), Kant ascribed to Berkeley the view that "there is only a spirit-world[14]." This ontological monism led to the conclusion "that all bodies are merely appearances [*Erscheinungen*] of bodies in our soul[15]." Despite the inelegance of this formulation in Herder's notes, it is clear that Kant understood Berkeley to categorically

[10] By Eugen Stäbler, *George Berkeleys Auffassung und Wirkung in der deutschen Philosophie bis Hegel*, Inaugural Dissertation (Tübingen: 1935), pp. 57–58.
[11] By J. C. Eschenbach, *Samlung der vornehmsten Schriftsteller die die Würklichkeit ihres eigenen Körpers und der ganzen Körperwelt leugnen* (Rostock: 1756). Park (p. 3) conjectured, perhaps because the Akademie edition of the metaphysics lectures had not yet appeared, that Kant was unaware of the Eschenbach translation. She does point out, however, that a 1781 translation of the *Dialogues*, George Berkeley, *Philosophische Werke, Erster Theil* (Leipzig: 1781), appears in a catalogue of books owned by Kant.
[12] Ak. XXVIII, 42 (*Metaphysik Herder*).
[13] Stäbler, 57.
[14] Ak. XXVIII, 42. Cf. Baumgarten's definition: „Solos in hoc mundo spiritus admittens est Idealista", *Metaphysica* (Halle, 1757), § 402.
[15] Ak. XXVIII, 42.

deny the reality of bodies: "an idealist ... sees nothing as bodies[16]." Thus from the very outset there existed a fundamental misconception of Berkeley's doctrines in Kant's mind.

There is a *prima facie* conflict between the two claims that have just been advanced, for it would seem that a detailed knowledge of the *Dialogues* should have led Kant to recognize Berkeley's doctrine of the reality of bodies. Examination of the translation available to Kant reveals the ground of this anomaly, and it absolves Kant from any charge of misrepresentation. Two factors are crucial here. First, the translator, Eschenbach, repeatedly insisted that Berkeley's own position forced him to deny the reality of bodies. Secondly, Eschenbach's translation has Philonous explicitly denying that bodies have reality.

Concerning the first point, it is important to note that Eschenbach, in his many critical footnotes and in his appendix, recognized Berkeley's assertion of the reality of bodies. But, he added, this realism is based on a systematic misuse of the term "reality" [Würklichkeit], which for Berkeley meant "reality in thoughts" [Würklichkeit in Gedanken] rather than the common usage of "reality," namely, "existence [Daseyn] outside the thoughts of all thinking beings[17]." This in itself is a reasonable interpretation of Berkeley. What is grossly misleading is the apparent acceptance by Berkeley himself of Eschenbach's interpretation, an appearance due to the pervasive mistranslation of "material substance" as "corporeal reality." Its pernicious consequences are seen clearly enough from the opening remarks of the First Dialogue.

Hyl. ... It is said that you believed that there were no corporeal things at all in the world.
Phi. In all seriousness I hold to the opinion that such things as the philosophers call bodies are not really there [nicht würklich da sind][18].

Thus, one can hardly criticize either the conclusion drawn by Kant in his lectures (that Berkeley denied the reality of bodies), or the sarcastic tone of the discussion of the same philosopher who, to all appearances, blatantly contradicted himself by attempting to uphold the reality of bodies.

---

[16] Ak. XXVIII, 43.
[17] Eschenbach's position is best stated in his appendix. [An idealist] grants, of course, that the visible world *is real* [würklich sey]. Sun, moon and stars, he says, I really see with my eyes ... all this *is there* [ist da]; what reasonable man would question the reality of these things? So says the idealist! But what does he mean by this? *All these things unquestionably have their reality;* but where? *in my thoughts;* outside me, in fact, all this is not there. One must thus distinguish well in the language of the idealist these words, *reality* [Würklichkeit], *existence* [Daseyn], and *outer reality* [außer Würklichkeit], *existence outside the thoughts of all thinking beings* [Daseyn außer den Gedanken aller denkenden Wesen]. And therefore one sees that the idealist abandons and misrepresents linguistic usage. For when one says in ordinary life: *bodies are real;* one understands thereby outer reality (Eschenbach, 471–2).
[18] Eschenbach, 7. Cf. Berkeley, *Works*, II, 172. On occasion, "matter" is translated "Materie oder das Körperliche" (*e. g.*, Eschenbach, 173). Another misleading translation is "Gedanke" for "idea" throughout. Eschenbach stated in his preface (page ii) that he did not have access to the English original, and therefore based his translation on a French translation published at Amsterdam in 1750 (Jean Paul de Gua de Malves, *Dialogues entre Hylas et Philonous*).

It is important to note that Kant did not simply reproduce the conclusions of Eschenbach, but instead gave an independent analysis of Berkeley's position. He began his account by citing the basic argument from the First Dialogue that sensations are not in bodies but in us. Curiously, his examples, beauty and ugliness, are not those of Berkeley; and the one Berkeleyan example he did cite, colors, did not touch on their subjectivity. Thus colors are "not in the bodies, but merely in the refractions of the light rays, as the prism shows;" precisely the same point is made by Philonous in the First Dialogue, in almost identical language[19].

Kant recognized that if bodies are reduced to appearances on the grounds that we know only our sensations, it is impossible to refute such a position. He mentions the "argument of the stick" (presumably that a stick proves its reality by striking the body), which proves nothing because the stick itself could be "lively appearances[20]." Not only is Berkeley's criterion of vivacity mentioned, but the more important role of coherence is also cited. Hylas was made to object that dreams are indistinguishable from real things if the latter are ideas, to which Philonous replied that although there may be dreams as vivid and realistic as perceptions, they are still distinguishable from them due to the coherence of life[21]. Kant recognized the inadequacy of this response due to the possibility of coherent dreams pointing out that "if dreams were mutual and congruous, who would not take them for things that have taken place[22]." Thus Kant seems to have held that the reduction of bodies to sensation precludes a criterion separating them from fancy, a view which has some important implications for Kant's assessment of Berkeley in the *Prolegomena*.

Another reason Kant believed Berkeley's idealism to be irrefutable is the futility of the Cartesian argument that a good God would not deceive us about the reality of mind-independent bodies. Berkeley had explicitly attacked this ploy in the Third Dialogue, pointing out that bodies would then be instruments for the fulfillment of the divine will, which contradicts God's omnipotence[23]. Kant asked rhetorically whether it would not have been a "more concise process" for God "to work through representations than through bodies[24]." Against this line of reasoning, Kant had nothing but

---

[19] *Works*, II, 186. "Add to these the experiment of a prism, which separating the heterogenous rays of light, alters the colour of any object... And now tell me, whether you are still of the opinion, that every body hath its true real colour inhering in it..."

[20] Ak. XXVIII, 42. The word is "Prügel," which connotes a striking action. Eschenbach, interestingly, translated Berkeley's example of the bent oar as "stock" or stick, but there is no question of vivacity there.

[21] *Works*, II, 235. "And though [visions of a dream] should happen to be ever so lively and natural, yet by their not being connected, and of a piece with the preceding and subsequent transactions of our lives, they might easily be distinguished from realities."

[22] Ak. XXVIII, 43.

[23] *Works*, II, 243, "I do not suppose God has deceived mankind at all." At 219 he states, "The will of an omnipotent spirit is no sooner exerted than executed, without the applications of means..."

[24] Ak. XXVIII, 43.

vague suggestions about the consensus of man, but it was a topic to which he would return again and again.

It is thus clear that Kant understood the fundamental argumentation of Berkeley's idealism and its logical power, basing his account on several passages taken almost verbatim from the *Dialogues*. This, in the absence of an explicit reference to the book's title, is the strongest evidence one could expect in favor of the hypothesis that Kant studied the Eschenbach translation of 1756. It should be noted that none of these arguments appear in *Siris*, the work Kant did cite, and thus there is no evidence that at this time he was familiar with the philosophical part of that book. Finally, it must be admitted that Kant failed to recognize that an idealist could allow the possibility that appearances can be real – the view he later adopted as his own.

In the documents from the years immediately preceding the publication of the *Critique*, as Kant struggled toward a formulation of his own idealism, one finds no mention of Berkeley; it is instead Leibniz who became the paradigmatic idealist. It is not the case that Kant dismissed the force of the sceptical arguments. In the *Pölitz lectures* in the late '70's he stated that "bodies are pure appearances," in response to the sceptical difficulty that "the senses could give no certainty to something outside me, for appearances could be the play of my imagination[25]." Although this is the same line of reasoning he earlier attributed to Berkeley, even the *Reflexionen* fail to acknowledge its source.

The reduction of bodies to appearances is in fact attributed to Leibniz, who was poised against the sceptical doubter of the existence of bodies, and called a dogmatic idealist. Idealism is supported dogmatically through an appeal to an intellectual intuition of an intelligible reality. "I acknowledge thinking beings of which I have intellectual intuition, thus [dogmatic idealism] is mystical[26]." Bodies *cannot* be real beings, because their nature conflicts with what is known to be characteristic of true reality, in this case, thinking monads. Appearances are merely confused representations in beings with the power of representing or *vis representativa*. Thus the nature of bodies as extended implies that they are infinitely divisible, which contradicts the simplicity of monads. The intellectual intuition of the monads is crucial to the argument, since there is no inherent conceptual absurdity in supposing matter to exist on the view of Leibniz expounded by Kant. For this reason the dogmatic conclusion about bodies rests on mystical premises, so that Kant could equate dogmatic and mystical idealism.

This kind of idealism may seem to agree with Kant's brand, in that both admit that bodies are appearances, but the similarity is merely verbal. Since the Leibnizian appearance is taken to be a confused picture of monadistic reality, Kant claimed in the *Critique* that "appearance was, on his view, the representation of the *thing in itself*[27]."

---

[25] Ak. XXVIII, 206–7 (*Metaphysik Pölitz*).
[26] Ak. XXVIII, 207.
[27] A270/B326. Translations from the *Critique of Pure Reason* are from Kemp Smith's edition (New York, 1929) and are numbered in the usual manner.

Transcendental idealism, on the other hand, required that appearances not be taken to represent things in themselves, and hence allowed that there is no logical confusion in them. Appearances could then have an empirical reality which is impossible from the standpoint of dogmatic idealism.

In the first edition of the *Critique* there is but one reference to the dogmatic idealist, who is now characterized as denying the existence of matter. He "must base his view on supposed contradictions in the possibility of there being such a thing as matter at all – a view with which we have not yet been called upon to deal[21]." Kant did deal with it in the Second Antinomy, concerning simples and composites, where the target was obviously Leibniz[29]. It has been maintained that Kant was promising to refute Berkeley but failed to do so because this would have undermined his own idealism[30]. There are, however, several reasons to reject this hypothesis. Berkeley was first termed a dogmatic idealist in the second edition of the *Critique,* and there is no evidence that Kant had anyone but Leibniz in mind when he mentioned dogmatic idealism in the first edition. The arguments he did attribute to Berkeley in the early lectures are more akin to the sceptical variety of idealism than the dogmatic. Further, Kant did not recognize that Berkeley was an empirical realist, nor that he could have been. Thus Kant would hardly have conceived that in refuting Berkeley he would be refuting himself.

Kant's benign neglect of Berkeley came to an abrupt end when the Göttingen review of the *Critique* claimed that the "higher" idealism of the latter was based on the same foundation as Berkeley's[31]. In response to this criticism, the *Prolegomena,* which appeared shortly thereafter, contained two attacks on Berkeleyan idealism, one from the side of ontology and the other from that of epistemology. In both, Berkeley is characterized as mystical or visionary – the same epithet reserved originally for Leibniz – and as denying the existence of bodies, which was Kant's earlier view of Berkeley.

The primarily ontological criticism occurs within the context of a general charge that transcendental idealism reduces the sensible world to illusion. Rather, Kant argued, critical idealism merely maintains the thesis that we cannot know things that appear as they are in themselves. The genuine idealist goes further, denying the existence of the object that appears, and so it is he who regards the sensible world as sham.

---

[21] A377.

[29] A Leibnizian argument had in fact already been presented in the Amphiboly: matter has no absolutely inward nature; real being has only inward determinations, *ergo,* matter is no real being (A277/B333). That the dogmatic idealist was Leibniz was proposed by George Miller, *Kant's First Edition Refutation of Dogmatic Idealism,* Kant-Studien, LXII (1973), 315–35. Miller based his argument wholly on published texts, thus missing the explicit connection made between Leibniz and dogmatic/mystical idealism in the metaphysics lectures.

[30] Kemp-Smith, 157; Turbayne, 243.

[31] Göttingen Gelehrten Anzeigen (January 19, 1782), reprinted in Karl Vorlander, ed., *Pro- legomena* (Hamburg, 1957), 167–74.

Idealism consists in the assertion that there are none but thinking beings, all other things which we think are perceived in intuition, being nothing but representations in the thinking beings, to which no object external to them in fact corresponds[32].

This is an elaboration of the definition Kant had used in his early lectures, and it in fact precisely captures the essence of Berkeley's ontology.

Although he did not explicity term it dogmatic, Kant distinguished this standpoint from what he took to be the merely sceptical idealism of Descartes, whom Kant interpreted as claiming that there is no satisfactory proof of the external world. The idealism of Berkeley is mystical, in that its method is "to convert actual things (not appearances) into mere representations[33]." Why is this a mystical viewpoint? Rather than adopting the Leibnizian view that appearances are confused representations of real beings (the original mystical idealism), Berkeley denied that they represent actual things at all. But to make this dogmatic claim, he required the same kind of insight into the essence of real beings as did Leibniz, namely, the knowledge that real things are simple thinking substances. And Kant claimed that this could be obtained only through an intellectual or mystical intuition into things in themselves.

Berkeley had made the transition from sceptical to dogmatic idealism in the *Dialogues*, after acknowledging that the sceptical argument leaves open the bare possibility of the existence of matter[34]. It is argued first that ideas do not conform to the materialists' own conception of matter, in that the latter is said to be fixed and constant, while ideas are fleeting and variable[35]. Then it is claimed that ideas in no wise represent spiritual substances, in that they are inactive and unthinking[36]. Hence ideas represent no reality at all, the very conclusion Kant attributed to Berkeley. Yet it is not clear that Kant had the *Dialogues* in mind in his description of Berkeley's idealism, since a similar argument appears in *Siris*. The intelligible world, which is unchangeable, is more real than "the fleeting, transient objects of sense, which, wanting stability, cannot be subjects of science, much less of intellectual knowledge[37]." In this case, unlike the first, the contrast is between ideas and Platonic forms, rather than between ideas and substances, be they material or spiritual.

The question thus arises as to which of these two accounts Kant had in mind when describing Berkeley's ontology: what arguments led him to his idealism? Kant reconstructed them in the Appendix to the *Prolegomena*, where Berkeley is explicitly linked to Plato and the Eleatics with respect to his epistemology.

---

[32] Ak. IV, 288. Translations from the *Prolegomena* are taken from Lewis White Beck's edition (Indianapolis, 1950).
[33] Ak. IV, 293.
[34] *Works*, II, 205.
[35] *Works*, II, 205.
[36] *Works*, II, 216.
[37] *Works*, V, § 335.

The dictum of all genuine idealists, from the Eleatric School to Bishop Berkeley, is contained in the formula: "All knowledge through the senses and experience is nothing but sheer illusion, and only in the ideas of the pure understanding and reason is there truth[38]."

Only the intelligible world has an *a priori* element, and the lack of a sensible *a priori* (a deficiency first remedied by Kant himself) prevented the idealists from allowing reality to the sensible world. Berkeley specifically regarded space as an appearance of things in themselves, reducing it to an empirical representation[39].

It follows from this that, as truth rests on universal and necessary laws as its criteria, experience, according to Berkeley, can have no criteria of truth because its appearances (according to him) have nothing *a priori* at their foundation, whence it follows that experience is nothing but sheer illusion[40].

The difficulty with this account is obviously that it has Berkeley denying the reality of the sensible world on the basis of the lack of a criterion of truth therein, whereas even Berkeley's arguments against material substance (translated by Eschenbach as "corporeal reality") do not employ the premises cited by Kant. Further, Berkeley's discussion of space (in the guise of "distance or outness") does not lead to the denial of a criterion.

Several suggestions have been made to explain the connection between Berkeley's doctrine of space and his idealism. Wilson has argued that Berkeley's purely semiotic theory of distance "suggests not only that we merely seem to perceive things 'existing at a distance,' but also that if the contrary were allowed, it might also count against the doctrine that nothing exists without the mind[41]." It is in fact the case that Berkeley raised this possibility, but he also rejected it: "allowing that distance was truly and immediately perceived by the mind, yet it would not thence follow it existed out of the mind," since what is immediately perceived is an idea, which exists in the mind[42]. So it cannot be held that Berkeley himself inferred from the unreality of distance to that of bodies, an inference which would have required the additional premise that bodies must exist outside the mind.

Wilson bases a more persuasive argument on the differences between Kant's and Berkeley's theories of the nature of space. For Kant, space is a three-dimensional manifold which is a necessary condition for the existence of bodies. In particular, it is the condition for bodies' existing outside one another, which in turn is part of the nature of body. Thus if the "outness" relation were taken away, bodies could not

---

[38] Ak. IV, 374. (*Prol.*, appendix)

[39] Ak. IV, 374. This statement may seem to conflict with the claim that Berkeley converts actual things into mere representations. But since Berkeley's idealism was seen as Platonic rather than Leibnizian, he would be interpreted as holding that "things in themselves" are not actual, but only representations (archetypes) in God's mind.

[40] Ak. IV, 375.

[41] Wilson, 473.

[42] *Works*, II, 202.

exist". What Berkeley called "space," on the other hand, is a one-dimensional succession of sensations, what Wilson calls "an empiricist reduction of space to a purely temporal order among empirical representations"." On this reconstruction, then, Berkeley is really being criticized for having an inadequate conception of space, which leads to his denial of the reality of bodies.

While the differences between Kant's and Berkeley's conceptions of space are indisputable, Wilson's line of argument cannot be accepted because it does not reflect the pattern of reasoning actually employed in Kant's criticism. It is not the lack of an *ontologically* adequate conception of space, but rather a more general *epistemological* inadequacy which leads to the denial of the reality of bodies, in Kant's view. That is, the problem does not hinge on the account of the nature of space, but failure on the part of Berkeley to discover an *a priori* element in sensibility. Kant reckoned that his insight that space and time are *a priori* forms of sensibility signalled the birth of a new form of idealism. Traditional idealism cannot discover truth in experience because it finds truth in forms that are accessible to intellectual intuition alone (for example, Plato relegated the objects of geometry to the realm of the Ideas)". Transcendental idealism begins with the premise that intrinsic to sensibility is a source of truth: "it never occurred to anyone that the senses themselves might intuit *a priori*."

What makes Kant's argument seem odd is that in his attempt to emphasize the sensible *a priori*, he made it appear that space is the source of the coherence of experience, whereas his real position was that the laws tying experience together spring from the understanding. This can be seen from his earlier draft of the section in question:

> Berkeley found nothing constant, and so could find nothing which the understanding conceives according to *a priori* principles. He therefore had to look for another intuition, namely the mystical one of God's ideas, which required a two-fold understanding, one which connected appearances in experience, and another which knew things in themselves".

While it is the case that the Berkeley of the *Dialogues* found nothing in experience which the understanding conceives *a priori*, this was of no consequence to him, content as he was to work within a strictly empiricist epistemology (with the one exception of the use of the principle of sufficient reason in the proof of the existence of God). Far from postulating an intellectual intuition of the divine Ideas, he explicitly repudiated the notion that we have direct knowledge of the contents of God's mind". We know only our own ideas, and our direct notional knowledge extends no further than inner intuition".

---

⁴³ A370.
⁴⁴ Wilson, 473.
⁴⁵ Ak. IV, 375 n (*Prol.*, Appendix).
⁴⁶ AK. IV, 375 n. (*Prol.*, Appendix).
⁴⁷ Ak. XXIII, 58. Kant crossed out "intellectuelle" in favor of "mystische."
⁴⁸ *Works*, II, 213.
⁴⁹ *Works*, II, 214.

Despite these discrepancies, Allison has argued that the passage in the *Vorarbeit* is "perhaps the best philological evidence which we have that Kant was indeed familiar with Berkeley's *Dialogues*, in which the notion of the divine intellect plays such a large role[50]." It has already been established that the lectures of the early 60's are the most powerful evidence for Kant's knowledge of the *Dialogues;* the question is whether the passage from the *Vorarbeit* reflects that knowledge. The only possible argument remaining is that in the *Dialogues*, Berkeley admitted "a twofold state of things, the one ectypal or nature, the other archetypal and eternal," which would require intellectual intuition[51]. But in keeping with the general empiricism of the book, Berkeley only inferred the existence of archetypes as necessary for the production and existence of ideas in finite minds. No direct, intuitive knowledge is claimed[52].

It has been shown that Kant's account of Berkeley's doctrine of space and the relation of the finite mind to the divine does not reflect the contents of the *Dialogues*. There is one further argument that has been given to show that Kant made a rather sweeping inference to the conclusion that experience is illusion based on the contents of that book. Again, the problem centers around the lack of an *a priori* element in experience, but this time it is claimed that this forces Berkeley into a subjectivism which is incapable of supporting a doctrine of the empirical reality of bodies. Allison argues that space, as well as all other properties of the corporeal world, are reduced by Berkeley to empirical representations whose psychological origin renders them incapable of being conditions of experience.

But if this is the case, according to Kant, we cannot explain the possibility of a public objective world, not to mention a mathematical science of such a world, and Kant reasons, "whence it follows that experience is nothing but illusion[53]".

It cannot be denied that this pattern of thinking reflects Kant's attitude toward subjective idealism, but the doctrines on which it is based were undeveloped at the time he lectured on Berkeley, and the evidence indicates that he did not apply it to the *Prolegomena* argument. There is in fact one reference there to the kind of subjectivism Allison describes, *i. e.*, one which "changes mere representations into things," which might be termed "dreaming idealism[54]." But this was put forward as the converse of Berkeley's mystical attempt to change things into mere representations. Further, in the passage in the second edition of the *Critique* where the very distinction Allison makes is clearly delineated, Berkeley is not mentioned at all[55]. Thus Allison's suggestion, which is indeed the line Kant ought to have taken, does not hold up as a description of his actual procedure.

---

[50] Allison, *Kant's Critique of Berkeley*, 61.
[51] *Works*, II, 254.
[52] *Works*, II, 253.
[53] Allison, *Critique*, 60.
[54] Ak. IV, 293. For a fuller account, see A392.
[55] B44.

Cassirer's hypothesis, that Kant had *Siris* in mind, solves all the difficulties that have been raised and provides a natural explanation which does not require that he arrived at his characterization of Berkeley by unwarranted inferences[36]. The general classification of Berkeley as a Platonic idealist is borne out by the extensive and admiring account of that position in *Siris*. Here there is no spirited defense of empirical realism, the most positive comment being that "bodies exist only in a secondary and dependent sense[37]." The sensible world is continually degraded; and although Berkeley did not abandon common sense altogether ("there is a certain analogy, constancy, and uniformity in the phenomena of nature, which are a foundation of general rules"), he gave the weight of emphasis to the instability of the sensible world[38]. There is a corresponding view of the cognitive role of the senses, which strictly speaking know nothing, and thus, in Kant's terms, could not contain an *a priori* element[39].

On the other hand, the intellect is held up as the only source of knowledge: "intellect and reason are alone sure guides to truth[40]." Besides discovering the uniformities of nature, the intellect searches out a more worthy object of inquiry, though its success is limited by its relation to a body. "The most refined human intellect, exerted to its utmost reach, can only seize some imperfect glimpses of the divine Ideas, abstracted from all things corporeal, sensible, and imaginable[41]." This is the stuff of mystical idealism, and it can obviously be interpreted as positing an intellectual intuition of the real.

We are led astray, Berkeley maintained, by an overly active imagination, which leads to the postulation of such "phantoms" of empirical abstraction as absolute space. If space is the only unchanging element in a world of perpetual flux, the denial that it is an intelligible object deprives the world of everything truly constant, though along with other sensible objects it is "thought by many the very first in existence and stability, and to embrace and comprehend all other beings[42]." Berkeley went so far as to suggest that the existence of the external world itself is dependent on that of absolute space: "From the notion of absolute space springs that of absolute motion; and in these are ultimately founded the notions of external existence, independence, necessity, and fate[43]." There could be no more striking vindication of Kant's otherwise mysterious insistence that the doctrine of space was crucial to Berkeley's idealism.

In general, all the outstanding problems of the *Prolegomena* account are solved by the hypothesis that it was based on *Siris*. The only extant argument against it is that had

[36] Ernst Cassirer, *Das Erkenntnisproblem in der Philosophie und Wissenschaft in der neueren Zeit*, 2nd. ed., Vol. II, 325 ff.
[37] *Works*, V, *Siris* § 266.
[38] *Works*, V, *Siris* § 252, Cf. § 254.
[39] *Works*, V, *Siris* §§ 253, 264, 294, 305, 330, 340.
[40] *Works*, V, *Siris* § 264.
[41] *Works*, V, *Siris* § 337.
[42] *Works*, V, *Siris* § 292.
[43] *Works*, V, *Siris* § 271. Stäbler overlooked this passage, and claimed that Kant's argument could not be explained by reference to *Siris*.

Kant sought a source book for the refutation of the charge that his idealism was identical with Berkeley's he would have encountered the *Dialogues* and read them instead⁴⁴. But he was already familiar with that work from some twenty years before, and he may well have sought out new material. Since *Siris* was a work of Berkeley's maturity, is it not likely that it would have been accepted as his final word, by a philosopher whose own chief work appeared relatively late in life?

The story does not end here, for Kant in the second edition of the *Critique* posed a new and quite different challenge to Berkeley's idealism. Now it is called "dogmatic" and the role of space made absolutely central. Kant claimed that Berkeley deemed the existence of space impossible, because of absurdities in its very conception⁴⁵. It follows that he could not allow the existence of bodies in space:

> He maintains that space, with all the things of which it is the inseparable condition, is something in itself impossible; and he therefore regards the things in space as purely imaginary entities⁴⁶.

It was not Kant's contention that the notion of space was incoherent in itself, but rather that the impossibility of space follows from the materialist's conception along with the assumption that space must be regarded as a thing in itself⁴⁷.

It was maintained that Berkeley discovered three absurdities in this transcendental realist view of space: (1) it is an existing thing which is neither substance, accident, nor something else, (2) it is a condition for the existence of all things, and (3) it is capable of existing apart from all bodies. Although none of these is more than hinted at in *Siris*, all three can be found stated rather clearly in *De Motu*. In § 57 of that work, Berkeley raised the first objection in nearly identical language, and in § 53 he noted that as a condition of all things, space must be a condition of God's existence, which is absurd. Finally, space in the absence of all bodies would be unimaginable if conceived positively as extension, and inconceivable through merely negative predicates such as infinitude, immobility, etc⁴⁸. The fact that Kant reproduced arguments which are stated nowhere else makes it safe to assume that he used the treatise on motion as a source.

Yet quite in line with his refusal to recognize Berkeley's realism, Kant overlooked certain statements which would have allowed a realist position to emerge despite the denial of absolute space. Berkeley in effect repudiated the assumption that space must be a property of things in themselves. He admitted the coherence of the concept of "space comprehended or defined by bodies, and therefore an object of sense, [which] is called relative, apparent, vulgar space⁴⁹." Not only can this conception be entertained, but it is adequate to the needs of the sciences, for "all the famous theorems of the mechanical philosophy by which the secrets of nature are unlocked, and by which the

---

⁴⁴ Stäbler, 57–8.
⁴⁵ B70–1.
⁴⁶ B274.
⁴⁷ B274.
⁴⁸ *Works*, IV, *De Motu* § 53.
⁴⁹ *Works*, IV, *De Motu* § 50.

system of the world is reduced to human calculation, will remain untouched" by the denial of absolute space[70].

Kant's oversight can only be explained by way of his preconception that Berkeley was not an empirical realist and could not have been one without a sensible *a priori*. Alloson has suggested that there is a link between *De Motu* and *Siris* – that the Platonizing tendencies of the latter are already to be found in the former[71]. "Here the decisive factor is the essentially pragmatic value which Berkeley gives to science, and hence to sense experience, and which he contrasts with the value of metaphysics or first philosophy[72]." Yet in Berkeley's defense it must be stated that his view was not so different from Kant's after all. Both placed a higher value on some "superior science." Kant merely argued that it is practical rather than theoretical in nature. While Berkeley held that metaphysical knowledge is ultimately of value in explaining the causes of physical phenomena, it has no place in physics; rather, we ought "to distinguish between the sciences as to confine each to its own bounds[73]." In this way, Berkeley could distinguish between immanent principles which concern only our knowledge of things, and transcendent principles dealing with their existence: "the principles of experimental philosophy are properly to be called foundations and springs, not of their existence, but of our knowledge of corporeal things[74]."

Had Kant not been blinded by the image of a mystical enthusiast he took from *Siris*, he might have recognized a very real attempt to divorce the principles of science from the kind of transcendental realism which spells their doom (on Kant's view). But this again would have required the acknowledgement of an empirical realism which he did not find in Berkeley. No doubt the lack of an *a priori* sensible foundation for the space in which bodies exist precluded Berkeley, in Kant's mind, from successfully building a world on a merely empirical basis. To this extent he would have had at least some justification for consigning the refutation of Berkeley to the Aesthetic. But the fact that Berkeley was not made a target of the Refutation of Idealism shows that Kant did not think Berkeley believed it possible for there to exist a world of bodies outside us.

The final group of Kant's statements about Berkeley may be briefly surveyed. Some time in the period 1788–91 he made the puzzling claim that as a dogmatic idealist, Berkeley "denies the existence of all things save that of the one who asserts it[75]." Kant had in the lectures of the midsixties called this position "egoism" and distinguished it from the idealism of Berkeley (though he believed them to be only a short step apart)[76].

---

[70] *Works*, IV, *De Motu* § 66.
[71] Allison, *Critique*, p. 59.
[72] Allison, *Critique*, p. 59.
[73] *Works*, IV, *De Motu* § 42.
[74] *Works*, IV, *De Motu* § 36.
[75] Ak. XXVIII, 610.
[76] Ak. XXVIII, 42. Cf. Ak. VIII, 207 (*Metaphysik Pölitz*), where egoism is attributed to Spinoza and distinguished from Leibniz's idealism.

But as Stäbler has pointed out, to accuse Berkeley of solipsism is not consistent with other remarks about him, particularly in the *Prolegomena*[77].

In a well-known letter to Beck, who had informed him of Eberhard's and Garve's view that transcendental and Berkeleyan idealism are the same, Kant replied that this opinion is unworthy of attention, on the same grounds he gave in Part One of the *Prolegomena*. "For I speak of ideality in reference to the *form of representations*, but they interpret this to mean ideality with respect to the *matter*, that is the ideality of the object and its very existence"[78]." Berkeley's idealism is dogmatic, in that its primary motivation is metaphysical; and thus it questions the existence of things that appear, rather than merely pointing out that we do not represent them as they are in themselves.

Yet at about the same time he wrote to Beck, Kant seems to have rectified his basic misconception about Berkeley's idealism. In his lectures of 1792–3, he again claimed that Berkeley denied the existence of bodies, this time with the qualifier "as such"[79]. In a set of lecture notes covering the same material, there is an even stronger statement: "Bodies as such are not things in themselves, Berkeley would say, but he expressed himself wrongly and thus appeared to be an idealist[80]." Here Berkeley's realism is finally acknowledged, and as has been shown in the discussion of Kant's lectures of the 60's, it was not Berkeley who expressed himself wrongly, but the translator who was responsible for the incorrectness of expression.

It is impossible to determine the effect upon Kant's criticisms of Berkeley had his acquaintance with that philosophers's work begun more auspiciously. Kant might have treated Berkeley with more respect and thus improved Berkeley's rather pathetic image as a thinker. More importantly, he might have been able to profit from Berkeley's discussions of existence "in the mind" as a precursor to transcendental idealism. A more detailed treatment of Berkeley would at least have brought to light some of the notorious ambiguities in the doctrine of appearances and things in themselves, particularly in the first edition of the *Critique*.

On the other hand, Kant's chief criticisms of Berkeley, which are more clearly revealed in the premises of his arguments than in the conclusion, are not affected by the concession of Berkeley's realism. The failure to recognize an *a priori* element in sensibility, the inadequate account of space as a relation among bodies, the dogmatic denial of the existence of things that appear, are all features of Berkeley's true position. Had Kant from the very beginning granted to Berkeley the title "realist," the details of his polemics would have been different, but the judgment no less severe.

---

[77] Stäbler, 61.

[78] Ak. XI, 395. December 4, 1792.

[79] Ak. XXVIII, 680 (*Metaphysik Dohna*). It is added that "Dies ist der transcendente Idealismus, ihm steht der psychologische entgegen." Kowalewski's edition has "transcendentale" for "transcendente," which is probably an error. Arnold Kowalewski, *Die philosophischen Hauptvorlesungen Immanuel Kants* (rpt., Hildesheim, 1965), 604.

[80] Ak. XXVIII, 770 (*Metaphysik K₂*).

V

The 'Phenomenalisms' of
Berkeley and Kant

Margaret D. Wilson

BERKELEY AND KANT

Of all the major modern philosophical systems the views of George Berkeley have probably met with the most resistance, ridicule, and distortion. Among Berkeley's many detractors and distorters was Kant, who represented Berkeley as a "dogmatic idealist" who "degraded bodies to mere illusions." $(B71)^1$ As has frequently been pointed out, however, Kant's few direct remarks about Berkeley are not unrelievedly negative. In the *Prolegomena* particularly, Kant acknowledges a limited affinity with Berkeley, pointing out that they agree in treating space as ideal.[2] Kant goes on to indicate that he differs from Berkeley in regarding space as a priori rather than merely empirical, and for this reason is able to avoid Berkeley's illusionism. In the second edition of the *Critique of Pure Reason* Kant also points to his doctrine of space as the answer to dogmatic idealism—though the logic of his claim there is at least superficially quite different from that in the *Prolegomena* (B274; cf. B69).[3]

---

[1] I use Kemp Smith's translation of the *Critique* but with some modifications.
[2] See the Appendix of the *Prolegomena*.
[3] I compare the *Critique* passages with the *Prolegomena* statement in my "Kant and 'the *Dogmatic* Idealism of Berkeley,'" cited in note 4.

157

Margaret D. Wilson

The historical and philosophical relations between Kant and Berkeley are topics of long debate among Kant scholars. It is generally acknowledged—at least by twentieth century critics—that Berkeley was far from considering himself an "illusionist." According to one strong tradition Kant's own position is in important respects quite close to Berkeley's *real* position.[4] Within this tradition one finds disagreement over whether Kant was simply ignorant of this fact, as a result of lacking firsthand knowledge of most of Berkeley's writings, or whether he deliberately misrepresented Berkeley's position to conceal an intellectual debt.[5] According to another, more recently developed, viewpoint Kant's empirical realism/transcendental idealism is in fact significantly different from Berkeley's position—and in approximately the ways Kant indicates that it is different.[6] Some commentators in arguing this viewpoint have presented rebuttals to their predecessors' claims that Berkeley's works would in general have been inaccessible to Kant, because he did not know English. (In fact, various works were available in Latin, French, and even German during Kant's lifetime.) Some recent writers further hold that Kant's system is philosophically superior to Berkeley's in at least some of the ways Kant took it to be.[7]

The earlier *and* the more recent critcs have tended to portray Kant and Berkeley as united by a common concern: that of vindicating the certainty of our knowledge of bodies in the wake of Cartesian doubt. Both philosophers, it is held, sought to achieve

---

[4]See Norman Kemp Smith's *A Commentary to Kant's Critique of Pure Reason* (New York, 1923), pp. 156–57; Colin M. Turbayne, "Kant's Refutation of Dogmatic Idealism," *Philosophical Quarterly* 5 (1955), 225–44. I critically discuss Kemp Smith's and Turbayne's views in "Kant and 'the *Dogmatic* Idealism of Berkeley,' " *Journal of the History of Philosophy* 9 (1971), 464–70.

[5]Kemp Smith maintains the former view, Turbayne the latter.

[6]See George Miller, "Kant and Berkeley: The Alternative Theories," *Kant-Studien* 64 (1973), 315–35; Henry E. Allison, "Kant's Critique of Berkeley," *Journal of the History of Philosophy* 11 (1973), 43–63; Richard E. Aquila, "Kant's Phenomenalism," *Idealistic Studies* 5 (1975), 108–126; G. D. Justin, "On Kant's Analysis of Berkeley," *Kant-Studien* 65 (1974), 20–32; and Wilson, "Kant and 'the *Dogmatic* Idealism of Berkeley.' " In "Berkeley's Immaterialism and Kant's Transcendental Idealism," M. R. Ayers defends and extends Allison's position (*Idealism—Past and Present*, ed. Godfrey Vesey [Cambridge, Eng., 1982], pp. 51–69). I have also seen unpublished work by William Harper on a similar theme.

[7]Aquila, "Kant's Phenomenalism," 125–26; Allison, "Kant's Critique of Berkeley," pp. 52 and 56; Miller, "Kant and Berkeley," 321–23; 334–35.

158

this result by denying the Cartesian (and Lockean) interpretation of physical objects as the mind-independent causes of our subjective perceptions. Berkeley responded with the theory that bodies *just are* sets of subjective sense-perceptions, which are presented in orderly fashion to human minds according to the well-disposed will of God. Therefore, our certain knowledge of our own subjective states in itself guarantees the certain knowledge of bodies: there is no need for a tenuous, extraexperiential causal inference that must inevitably succumb to skeptical challenge. Against the view that Kant's idealist solution to skepticism is essentially similar to Berkeley's, recent critics have held that Kant secures unproblematic knowledge of bodies while avoiding Berkeley's sensationalistic reductionism. Kant's position, in other words allows him to enjoy the sweets of phenomenalism without the bitters of subjectivism.[8] Kant's theory of space and time as a priori forms of intuition, together with the transcendental deduction of the categories (and the ensuing elaboration of the "principles" of causality and substance), allow him to hold that objects are as immediately known as the series of inner experiences. At the same time they allegedly allow him to preserve such essential features of objectivity as permanence, publicity, and the distinction between truth and illusion—results not achieved by Berkeley's cruder theory. It sometimes is also stressed that Kant's and Berkeley's idealisms have quite different implications for the interpretation of Newtonian science, and that the two philosophers do not take the same view of the primary–secondary quality distinction.[9]

In my opinion the earlier tradition that assimilated Berkeleyan and Kantian phenomenalism is clearly erroneous. Further, I grant that Kant's own view of his relation to Berkeley may be

---

[8] I use the term 'idealism' more or less alternatively to 'phenomenalism' to characterize Berkeley's system as well as Kant's. For expository purposes it is convenient to follow the practice of Kant and several of his commentators in this respect. I am aware that some Berkeley scholars vehemently oppose the characterization of his position as 'idealist', but I do not really accept their strictures, and in any case the issue is not crucial to the points I want to make.

[9] Allison, in particular, provides a perceptive discussion of these issues ("Kant's Critique of Berkeley").

159

accurately captured by some of the recent commentators. Nevertheless, the full difference between Kant's and Berkeley's position has still not been correctly expressed. For both Kant and his recent commentators (including myself) have tended to overlook a radical difference in the philosophical motivations of the two systems. It seems ot me that this difference of concern would give Berkeley good reason to regard Kant's position as alien to, rather than an improvement of, his own in a quite fundamental respect. It is therefore quite wrong to represent Berkeley as getting about halfway to a result that Kant finally achieved. Development of this idea leads me to touch on some features of Kant's theory of 'appearances' that I find rather strange. Without attempting to assess further the recent claims about Kant's philosophical superiority to Berkeley, I suggest that clarification of the differences between the two philosophers' goals is a necessary step towards such assessment.

BERKELEY ON THE REALITY OF SENSIBLE QUALITIES

The principal claim I want to defend is that Berkeley understood the challenge posed by Descartes's (and Locke's) transcendental realism very differently than did Kant. Berkeley's mission, at least in the great early works, was to vindicate the reality of the objects of ordinary sense experience, *as sensed*. The *primary* foe in this connection is not the historically somewhat fictitious position of "Cartesian skepticism." It is rather the historically quite real and (in modernized form) still current position of Cartesian scientific realism.[10] But Kant's empirical realism *is* a form of scientific realism. It is *not* a vindication of ordinary sense experience (or "common sense") as Berkeley conceived it. In other words, whatever Kant may have achieved in demonstrating the claims to reality of appearances as he understood them, he

---

[10] I defend this perspective on Cartesianism in my book, *Descartes* (London, 1978).

160

has not demonstrated (or tried to demonstrate) the reality of phenomena as Berkeley understood them. For Kant, what is empirically real is primarily the material world of the science of his time—a world that does not possess colors, tastes, and the like in any literal, irreducible sense.[11]

Berkeley, on the contrary, takes as empirically real the objects of ordinary sense experience, literally and richly endowed with colors, tastes, and the other 'secondary qualities'—and perhaps with aesthetic, religious, and emotive 'qualities,' too. This position of course leaves Berkeley with problems about how to accommodate the more esoteric concepts of contemporary mechanism, and the explanatory successes achieved through these concepts. Berkeley did make earnest efforts to confront these problems—at times taking refuge in instrumentalist accounts. I certainly do not claim that he was fully successful in these efforts. But the goal itself of vindicating the reality of the sensible world as concretely sensed and experienced, as against the "abstractions" of the scientists, is in my view a far from frivolous one. After citing some passages that show Berkeley doing just that, I shall consider a variety of passages from Kant's first *Critique* which seem to indicate the great difference between Berkeley's and Kant's position concerning the relations among real appearances, sensations, and the entities of science.

Consider the opening of Berkeley's first *Dialogue*. Berkeley's spokesman Philonous is in a garden, where he encounters his prospective antagonist, Hylas. Hylas has endured a night of intellectual unrest; and as a result he has risen early. In what superficially appears to be mere indulgence in scene setting, Philonous is made to respond with the following effusion:

It happened well, to let you see what innocent and agreeable pleasures you lose every morning. Can there be a pleasanter time of the day, or a more delightful season of the year? That purple sky, those wild but sweet notes of birds, the fragrant bloom upon the trees and flowers, the gentle influence of the rising sun, these and a thou-

---

[11]This use of the term 'literal' is borrowed from John Mackie, *Problems from Locke* (Oxford, 1976), pp. 14–15.

Margaret D. Wilson

sand nameless beauties of nature inspire the soul with secret transports.[12]

But the passage is far from being as intellectually innocuous as the casual reader may suppose. Berkeley's citation of the beauties of nature (those, presumably, that are not "nameless") systematically touches on each of the commonly mentioned traditional 'secondary qualities,' omitting only taste. Thus we encounter in the garden color ("that purple sky"), sound ("those wild but sweet notes'), odor ("fragrant bloom"), and warmth ("gentle influence") of the rising sun. The emotive or affective aspects of the sensuously experienced natural scene are also lightly stressed.

Later, when the antagonist Hylas has been driven to concede that sensible objects have no reality "without the mind," and has thence concluded that there is no certain reality in nature, Philonous counters: "Look! are not the fields covered with a delightful verdure? Is there not something in the woods and groves, in the rivers and clear springs, that soothes, that delights, that transports the soul?"[13] And so on, at length. The speech concludes: "What treatment, then, do those philosophers deserve, who would deprive these noble and delightful scenes of all *reality*? How should those Principles be entertained that lead us to think all the visible beauty of the creation a false imaginary glare"?[14]

Elsewhere, in somewhat similar circumstances, Philonous emphasizes that the reality of the full range of the sensed qualities of a cherry is all that matters to us:

Hyl. . . . But, after all, Philonous, when I consider the substance of what you advance against *Scepticism*, it amounts to no more than this:—We are sure that we really see, hear, feel; in a word, that we are affected with sensible impressions.

Phil. And how are *we* concerned any farther? I see this cherry, I feel it, I taste it: and I am sure *nothing* cannot be seen, or felt, or tasted: it is therefore *real*. *Take away the sensations of softness, moisture, redness,*

[12]*Works of George Berkeley,* ed. A. A. Luce and T. E. Jessop, 9 vols. (London, 1948–51), vol. 2, p. 171.
[13]*Works,* vol. 2, p. 210.
[14]*Works,* vol. 2, p. 211.

162

■284■

tartness, and you take away the cherry, since it is not a being distinct from sensations. A cherry, I say, is nothing but a congeries of sensible impressions, or ideas perceived by various senses: which ideas are united into one thing (or have one name given them) by the mind, because they are observed to attend each other. Thus, when the palate is affected with such a particular taste, the sight is affected with a red colour, the touch with roundness, softness, [etc.]. Hence, when I see, and feel, and taste, in sundry certain manners, I am sure the cherry exists, or is real; its reality being in my opinion nothing abstracted from those sensations. But if by the word *cherry* you mean an unknown nature, distinct from *all those sensible qualities*, and by its *existence* something distinct from its being perceived; then, indeed, I own, neither you nor I, nor any one else, can be sure it exists.[15]

According to the common interpretation I have sketched, Berkeley is driven into empiricistic reductionism, and hence (unfortunately) into subjectivism, just because he supposes this is the only way to avoid the external world skepticism that is virtually built into Cartesian or Lockean scientific realism. I agree that there is clear evidence of this concern—for example at the end of the passage just quoted. Yet the several passages quoted indicate that Berkeley was not merely interested in affirming the reality of sensible appearances or qualities as a *means* to making a case for the reality of body in some form or other. It was precisely the reality of the world of experience, as experienced, that he was concerned to establish. Even if the Cartesian inference to *res extensa*, or the Lockean inference to (epistemologically indeterminate) real essences of physical substances were certain above all skeptical challenge, too much of reality as we conceive and experience it in ordinary life would have to be construed as "false imaginary glare." This at least is the reading I propose.

One further issue about Berkeley's conception of the reality of the world as we experience it is worth mentioning. Frequently in the *Dialogues* Hylas attempts the move of distinguishing the "real" sound or color or other quality (as the scientist understands it) from the mere sensation, with the aim of maintaining that the former at least is not simply "in the mind." Philonous

---

[15]*Works*, vol. 2, p. 249. Italics added.

Margaret D. Wilson

in turn makes fun of the idea that real colors are unseen, real sounds unheard, and so forth. The following passage is representative.

Hyl. I own myself entirely satisfied, that [colors] are all equally apparent, and that there is no such thing as colour really inhering in external bodies, but that it is altogether in the light. And what confirms me in this opinion is, in proportion to the light colours are still more or less vivid; and if there be no light, then are no colours perceived. ... It is immediately some contiguous substance, which, operating on the eye, occasions a perception of colours: and such is light.

Phil. How! Is light then a substance?

Hyl I tell you, Philonous, external light is nothing but a thin fluid substance, whose minute particles being agitated with a brisk motion, and in various manners reflected from the different surfaces of outward objects to the eyes, communicate different motions to the optic nerves; which, being propagated to the brain, cause therein various impressions; and these are attended with the sensations of red, blue, yellow, [etc.].

Phil. It seems then the light doth no more than shake the optic nerves.

Hyl. Nothing Else.

Phil. And consequent to each particular motion of the nerves, the mind is affected with a sensation, which is some particular colour.

Hyl. Right.

Phil. And these sensations have no existence without the mind.

Hyl. They have not.

Phil. How then do you affirm that colours are in the light: since by *light* you understand a corporeal substance external to the mind?

Hyl. Light and colours, as immediately perceived by us, I grant cannot exist without the mind. But in themselves they are only the motions and configurations of certain insensible particles of matter.

Phil. Colours, then, in the vulgar sense, or taken for the immediate objects of sight, cannot agree to any but a perceiving substance.

Having received Hylas's acquiescence in this restatement, Philonous concludes:

Phil. Well then, since you give up the point as to those sensible qualities which are alone thought colours by all mankind beside, you may hold what you please with regard to those invisible ones of the philosohers.

164

It is not my business to dispute about *them*; only I would advise you to bethink yourself, whether, considering the inquiry we are upon, it be prudent for you to affirm—*the red and blue which we see are not real colours, but certain unknown motions and figures which no man ever did or can see are truly so.* Are not these shocking notions, and are not they subject to as many ridiculous inferences, as those you were obliged to renounce before in the case of sounds?[16]

Viewed in one way, this passage of course shows Berkeley making a case for his general position that sensible objects have no existence without the mind. Roughly stated, a *sensible* color is a color as consciously experienced—not a stream of minute particles of which no one is directly aware in ordinary seeing. And Hylas admits that the *former* exists only in the mind. But at the same time, I suggest, the passage shows Berkeley insisting on the point that a *real color is* a color as consciously experienced—and that colors as consciously experienced are real colors, colors of things. Kant's position about perceptual reality is quite different, as we shall see.

KANT'S POSITION CONCERNING SENSIBLE QUALITIES

Throughout the first *Critique* Kant consistently seems to distinguish objects of experience or appearances (*Erscheinungen*) from sensations (*Empfindungen*). Sensations are the mere subjective results of the effects of "the real in appearances" on our peculiar organs of sense. The secondary qualities are assimilated by Kant to sensations. According to this complicated theory, then, bodies in space are transcendentally ideal because space is only the form of our sensibility, but their primary qualities are empirically real. Their perceived colors, odors, tastes, and so forth are not even *empirically* real.

Other commentators have pointed to this feature of Kant's

[16]*Works*, vol. 2, pp. 186–87.

165

position as an important difference between his idealism and Berkeley's.[17] I believe, however, that its profound significance for the difference in motivation and concern between the two philosophers has not yet been sufficiently appreciated.[18] Further, the attempt to affirm the primary–secondary quality distinction within an idealist or phenomenalist philosophy of body raises a perplexing issue about Kant's concept of appearance—an issue that surely deserves more consideration than it has received. Before articulating the problem I have in mind, I shall cite some relevant passages from three different parts of the *Critique of Pure Reason*: the Aesthetic, the Anticipations of Perception, and the Fourth Paralogism in the first edition (which has often been construed as an *especially* Berkeleyan passage.)

In *B44–45* of the Transcendental Aesthetic Kant writes:

> With the sole exception of space there is no subjective representation, referring to something *outer*, which could be entitled objective *a priori*. For there is no other subjective representation from which we can derive *a priori* synthetic propositions, as we can from intuition in space. . . . Strictly speaking, therefore, these other representations have no ideality, although they agree with the representation of space in this respect, that they belong merely to the subjective constitution of our manner of sensibility, for instance, of sight, hearing, touch, as in the case of sensations of colors, sounds, and heat, which, since they are mere sensations and not intuitions, do not of themselves yield knowledge of any object, least of all any *a priori* knowledge.
>
> The above remark is intended only to guard anyone from supposing that the ideality of space as here asserted can be illustrated by examples so altogether insufficient as colors, taste, etc. For these cannot rightly be regarded as properties of things, but only as changes in the subject, changes which may, indeed, be different for different men.[19]

---

[17]Cf. Allison, "*Kant's Critique of Berkeley*," pp. 52ff.

[18]I am aware of one important exception. In his Ph.D. thesis, "The Idealism of Kant and Berkeley" (University of Pittsburgh, 1979), George John Mattey stresses that Kant and Berkeley held quite different views on the primary–secondary quality distinction, and emphasizes the significance of this difference in comparing their idealisms.

[19]Allison also cites and discusses this passage and its predecessor in A ("Kant's Critique of Berkeley," pp. 56–56).

166

Part of the passage just quoted (toward the beginning) replaced a perhaps even more committed statement in the *A* edition, which includes the following sentences:

> The taste of a wine does not belong to the objective determinations of the wine, not even if by the wine as an object we mean the wine as appearance, but to the special constitution of sense in the subject that tastes it. Colors are not properties of the bodies to the intuition of which they are attached, but only modifications of the sense of sight, which is affected in a certain manner by light.[A28–29]

It may be noted that in this last passage Kant seems to agree with Berkeley that colors *are* sensations—not properties of light or nonsensational surfaces. But Kant is clearly distinguishing, in a most un-Berkeley-like way, between mere subjective effects of bodies, and objective properties of the bodies, considered as appearances.

In the Anticipations of Perception Kant's theory of perception comes through even more clearly. He reiterates the view that "sensation is not in itself an objective representation." (*A*166/*B*208). Appearances, however, besides intuition contain "the real of sensation as merely subjective representation, which gives us only the consciousness that the subject is affected, and which we relate to an object in general" (*A*166/*B*207–208). All sensation possesses intensity or degree, however, and this may be in turn taken to correspond to the "degree of influence on the sense." As Kant also says, "what corresponds in empirical intuition to sensation is reality [*realitas phaenomenon*]" (*A*168/*B*209). He continues:

> If this reality is viewed as cause, either of sensation or of some other reality in the appearance, such as change, the degree of the reality as cause is then entitled a moment, e.g., the moment of gravity. . . .
> Every sensation, therefore, and likewise every reality in the appearances, however small it may be, has a degree, that is, an intensive magnitude which can always be diminished. [A168–69/B210–11]

According to Kant's theory, then, physical causes (as understood by the scientist, such as gravity) affect our senses, giving rise to

167

sensations which, while not resembling properties of the object, nevertheless bear some correspondence to the latter, owing to the proportionality of cause and effect.

The Fourth Paralogism of the first edition is a passage that has been cited by commentators as showing Kant at his most Berkleyan. Some have been held that Kant abandoned the argument of this passage in the second edition *because it was too Berkeleyan.*[20] There are in fact a few phrases in the passage that seem a bit discordant with Kant's distinction elsewhere between sensation on the one hand, and the real in space that gives rise to sensation on the other hand. We find, for example, the following statement: "All outer perception thus directly proves something real in space, *or is rather the real itself* . . ." (*A*375, italics added). But this very sentence continues; ". . . and in this way is empirical realism thus beyond doubt, i.e. *there corresponds to our outer intuitions something real in space*" (*A*373, italics added).[21] And other statements in the Paralogism in *A* seem completely consonant with the account of perception we have noted in the Aesthetic and the Anticipations of Perception. For instance, Kant writes:

Space and time are indeed *a priori* representations, which dwell in us as forms of our sensible intuition, before a real object has determined our sense through sensation, so as to represent the object under those sensible relations. Only this material or real, this something that is to be intuited in space, necessarily presupposes perception, and can not independently of it, which indicates (*anzeigt*) the reality of something in space, be composed and produced by any power of imagination. . . . It is unquestionably certain that whether one takes the sensations of pleasure and pain, or even the outer ones, such as colors, heat, etc., perception is that through which the stuff to think objects of sensible intuition must first be given. This perception thus represents . . . something real in space. [*A*373–7]

[20]Kemp Smith, for instance. See my discussion in "Kant and 'the *Dogmatic Idealism* of Berkeley,'" pp. 463ff. On the alleged "Berkeleyanism" of the Fourth Paralogism, see Allison, "Kant's Critique of Berkeley," pp. 45ff.
[21]Kemp Smith introduces a sentence break that is not in the German.

168

Here again the theory Kant is propounding appears to be a causal one, for all the "noninferential" or "direct" knowledge perception is said to afford us of "something real in space." Perception and sensation have a necessary dependence on such reality, which is not itself reducible to the mere *forms* of sensible intuition. The ideality of the forms assures that 'the real in space' will itself count as mind dependent, however. Kant seems to suppose that this fact is sufficient to counter the challenge of problematic idealism.

I will not attempt to assess here how strong a response to "external world skepticism" this theory really is. (Kant himself, as noted, did not stick by it.) What I do want to stress is that it is not a Berkeleyan response. The "something real in space" (*etwas Wirkliches im Raume*) is not in the least the same thing as, for instance, Philonous's cherry, *comprised of* the sensations of softness, moisture, redness, tartness. It is rather merely the *cause of* such sensations, shaking the optic and the other sensory nerves.

It follows, I think, that Kant's theory of the relation of perceptual experience and reality is much closer to Descartes's than it is to Berkeley's. Unlike Descartes, Kant thought that space had to be construed as ideal or mind–dependent, if we are to evade the skeptic's challenge concerning the reality of 'outer objects.'[22] And unlike Descartes *and* Berkeley, Kant seems completely untroubled by the discrepancy between the subjective world of 'sensation' (colors, tastes, warmth, and so on) and the world of bare matter (or forces) portrayed by scientific theory.[23] But like Descartes, and unlike Berkeley, Kant construes the world of science, and not the world of sensation, as empirically real. Like Descartes, and unlike Berkeley, Kant holds that our experiences

[22]Cf. A27–28. Amazingly, some commentators seem to take the view that Descartes's conception of material substance as mind-independent *logically bars* him from holding that we can have knowledge of matter: see, in this connection, Allison, "Kant's Critique of Berkeley," p. 47. As far as I can tell, this interpretation completely overlooks the theory of innate ideas and the "divine guarantee."

[23]In *Descartes* I argue that this discrepancy was a serious concern of Descartes's, relating closely to his preoccupations with the problem of God's veracity, and the respects in which the senses can be said to "deceive."

169

of colors, tastes, and so on are mere "subjective sensations" that do nothing to "determine an object."[24]

If my remarks on Kant's theory of perception are correct, Kant is a very peculiar sort of 'phenomenalist' indeed. He cannot think that things just are the way they appear in ordinary sense experience, for the secondary qualities with which they appear to be endowed are only subjective sensations, sensations caused by the objects. The "something real in space" must, it seems, retain its mystery until its true nature is revealed by sophisticated scientific–philosophical inquiry. The reality of this sensorily remote, mysterious 'matter' is, of course, just what Berkeley would want to deny. Granted, for Kant the fundamental concepts of scientific understanding of this matter are also implicit in the ordinary experiential ordering of the world. This concession does not affect the fact that Kant—like Descartes and Locke before him and numerous "scientific realists" after him, and very *unlike* Berkeley—is a *critic* of what might be called the naive empiricist world view. Kant can be styled a phenomenalist not because he accords 'reality' to the ordinary 'image,' but only because the scientist's sophisticated reductive explanation of that image is, on Kant's view, elaborated within the framework of merely ideal 'forms of intuition.'

Thus, it may be that from one point of view Kant offers us the sweets of idealism without the bitters of subjectivism. From another point of view, I suggest, Kantianism yields the bitters of idealism, without the sweets of Berkeley's commonsense empiricism. In the Critical philosophy, as in the more naive materialism that Berkeley was attacking, a significant portion of our ordinary sense–world is rendered, in Berkeley's poignant expression, a false imaginary glare.

A corollary of this reading of Kant is that his conception of what constitutes 'experience' has to be, at best, somewhat recon-

---

[24]Cf. Descartes's discussion in *Principles of Philosophy*, part 2, 3–4; part 4, 197–9, in *Oeuvres de Descartes*, ed. Charles Adam and Paul Tannery, 12 vols. (Paris, 1957–), vol. 8–1, pp. 41–42; 320–23.

Here I assume the point of view argued earlier: that Berkeley was not merely concerned to refute the transcendental reality of matter, and correlatively to answer "Cartesian skepticism," but also to reinstate the reality of the sensible world as we experience it in ordinary life.

170

dite. The most interesting recent English–language commentaries—the works of P.F. Strawson and Jonathan Bennett—seem to me to go wrong in completely overlooking this important complexity.[25] Defense of this point would require, however, a far more detailed discussion than is appropriate here.

CONCLUSION

If my interpretation is right, Berkeley and Kant are very far apart in their views about physical reality, in relation to sense experience and science. I would like to point out, though, one widely overlooked point of apparent communality between the two 'phenomenalists'; namely, their respective concepts of a *non-human* apprehension. Both Berkeley and Kant stress the passivity of human sense experience, and contrast this way of experiencing objects with the wholly active, "archetypal" intelligence that can be attributed to God.[26] Of course both philosophers introduce the latter notion in a quite sketchy way, and there is much room for uncertainty about the exact nature of their views and speculation about disanalogies between them. For example, it

[25] See Jonathan Bennett, *Kant's Analytic* (Cambridge, Eng., 1966), pp. 22; and P. F. Strawson, *The Bounds of Sense* (London, 1966), p. 32. In the latter passage I take Strawson to be interpreting Kantian phenomena in terms of "ordinary reports" and "ordinary descriptions" of "what we see, feel, hear." On pp. 40–41 of *The Bounds of Sense* Strawson rather startlingly *contrasts* Kant with "the scientifically-minded philosopher"!

[26] Berkeley discusses the archetypal-sensible distinction in *Works*, vol. 2, pp. 241, 254, and in his 1729–30 correspondence with Samuel Johnson (*Works*, vol. 2, pp. 271–94). See also Russell A. Lascola,"Ideas and Archetypes: Appearances and Reality in Berkeley's Philosophy," *The Personalist*, 54 (1973), 42–59 (especially pp. 52ff) and George H. Thomas, "Berkeley's God Does Not Perceive," *Journal of the History of Philosophy* 14 (1976), 163–68. At B72 Kant contrasts our sensible intuition, to which objects have to be *given*, with "original" intuition, "which so far as we can judge, can belong only to the primordial being." Elsewhere, notably in Phenomena and Noumena, Kant does claim that we cannot even comprehend the possibility of an original intuition. (If Thomas's thesis as stated in his title is correct, then Berkeley's "to be is to be perceived (or to perceive)" thesis seems to require fundamental rephrasing. For it is surely Berkeley's view that both God and the archetypes in his mind have being.)

171

will immediately be noted that Berkeley is dogmatically assertive where Kant is critically circumspect in observations about the relation between God's mind and its 'objects'. Further, Berkeley succumbs to the temptation to appeal to archetypal intelligence as a basis for resolving objectivity problems that arise within his phenomenalist account of things: the problem of their continuous existence in particular. (Things are always in God's mind, even though human perceptions are intermittent.)[27]

Kant, on the contrary, evidently construes the resolution of such problems as an essential and integral requirement of the phenomenalist enterprise itself. All the same, Kant notoriously does hint that the appearances which for us constitute "empirical reality" are in some sense grounded in the things in themselves—where the latter may be at least speculatively identified with the objects of (God's) nonsensible intuition (See Bxxvi–vii). On the other hand, Berkeley's casual attempt to *integrate* the flow of human sense perceptions with the divine archetypal apprehension is surely undercut by his acknowledgment of the radical discrepancy between the two modes of apprehension.[28] To this extent, it seems, Berkeley as well as Kant must be attributed a qualified empiricism: a position that ultimately acknowledges

---

[27]Berkeley, in his youthful works, tried to use God's archetypes to ground the permanence and perhaps the "publicity" of the objects of outer sense: see *Works*, vol. 2, pp. 212; 230–31. Perhaps he later gave up on this idea. He makes hardly any reply to Samuel Johnson's queries about archetypes—especially in relation to the issue of permanence—even though Johnson expresses his questions clearly and rather persistently (*Works*, vol. 2, pp. 274–76; 285–86). (Berkeley does reply appositely to most of Johnson's other inquiries.) Allison, "Kant's Critique of Berkeley," p. 61, quotes a striking, often overlooked passage in Kant's *Gesammelte Schriften* in which Kant comments on Berkeley's recourse to "the mystical [intuition] of God's ideas." Although the passage is obscure, I take Kant to be saying that he, unlike Berkeley, does not need to call on the divine understanding to provide for the connection of appearances. The passage is also cited by Graham Bird in a different connection in *Kant's Theory of Knowledge* (New York, 1962), p. 37.

[28]According to Berkeley, "God perceives nothing by sense as we do" (*Works*, vol. 2, p. 241, and Thomas, "Berkeley's God Does Not Perceive," p. 166). Of course, the assimilation of Berkeleyan archetypes to nonsensible *intuitions* (in the Kantian sense) will not hold fully if the former are understood platonically, as universal forms—as Johnson *may* be understanding them in section 1 of his second letter (Berkeley's *Works*, vol. 2, pp. 285–86). I conjecture God's archetypes must be particulars for Berkeley's purposes in the early works—from which it would follow that their relation to our ideas is not one of form to instances.

172

that ordinary human sense perception is not the very last authority on the truth about things. And both philosophers, by introducing at least the possibility of a strictly active apprehension, leave room for the relative "mereness" of appearances to us.[29]

[29]This paper was completed under a grant from the American Council of Learned Societies, through a program funded by the National Endowment for the Humanities.

173

CHAPTER 6

IDEALISM: KANT AND BERKELEY

R. C. S. WALKER

KANT has often been compared to Berkeley.[1] His description of his own position as a kind of idealism inevitably suggests that he had much in common with Berkeley, but he repudiates this very firmly, and dismisses Berkeley as 'degrading bodies to mere illusion' (B 71).[2] Many writers on Kant have held that this dismissal shows how little he understood what Berkeley was saying; had he done so, in their view, he would have seen how similar Berkeley's idealism was to his own. But others, especially in recent years, have argued that he understood Berkeley quite well, and had an effective argument against him. If so, the argument is obscurely stated, and requires reconstruction.

The matter is worth examination, because it is not immediately clear exactly what either kind of idealism involves; by seeing how they relate to one another one can come to understand each of them better. In particular one can find in Kant's approach certain outstanding strengths, and also a fatal weakness. For Kant does have a point to make against Berkeley. But it is a point he cannot press home without destroying his own system entirely.

On the whole, I shall argue, Kant understood Berkeley's theory correctly, and did not misrepresent it (as has been suggested[3]) in order

[1] The discussion there has been in recent years starts from C. M. Turbayne, 'Kant's Refutation of Dogmatic Idealism', *Philosophical Quarterly* 1955 (reprinted as 'Kant's Relation to Berkeley' in L. W. Beck, ed., *Kant Studies Today*, La Salle, Open Court, 1969). Turbayne considers Kant to have been arguing in bad faith against Berkeley, since his own position is so similar. The articles I have found most useful are H. E. Allison, 'Kant's Critique of Berkeley', *Journal of the History of Philosophy* 1973; G. J. Matthey, 'Kant's Conception of Berkeley's Idealism', *Kant-Studien* 1983; and G. D. Justin, 'Re-relating Kant and Berkeley', *Kant-Studien* 1977. My debt to these, and particularly to the last, will be clear from what follows I am also indebted to Lesley Brown, Hugh Rice, John Kenyon, and the editors of this volume for valuable comments in discussion.
[2] References to the *Critique of Pure Reason* are given in the text in the customary fashion, 'A' referring to the first edition and 'B' to the second.
[3] Notably by C. M. Turbayne, op. cit. note 1 above.

to exaggerate its differences from his own. But we must notice at the outset that his first attempt to distinguish the two views does entirely mislocate the issue. This comes towards the end of the third note to section 13 of the *Prolegomena*, where he says that Berkeley's 'mystical and visionary' idealism is an idealism concerning the existence of things, whereas his own transcendental idealism is not. By 'things' here he means things in themselves, for he goes on to say that on his own view space, time, and appearances (*Erscheinungen*) in general are not 'things', but only 'the sensible representations of things'. So (Kant is claiming) Berkeley denies the existence of things in themselves, while he himself affirms it; and therein lies the difference.

This cannot be right (as has often been observed). If Berkeley had claimed there was nothing in the world but ideas Kant might reasonably have described him as denying things in themselves, but he is very far from claiming that: he is confident of the reality of a multitude of finite active spirits, and also of God, who causes our perceptions. Where he differs from Kant is not in denying a reality independent of and prior to the phenomenal world that we construct, but in asserting that we can know what that reality is like. Kant thinks it unknowable, because beyond the limits of possible experience. Berkeley, on the other hand, thinks that it consists of spirits, and that these spirits can be known by us: not, certainly, by way of ideas (for there can be no idea of an active thing), but by way of the notions we have of them. In *De Motu* and *Siris*, where his views on notions are most fully worked out, it appears that our knowledge of spirits and particularly of God is a kind of intuitive apprehension that cannot properly be called empirical.

But although here Kant mislocates the contrast between himself and Berkeley, he does better when he returns to the subject in the Appendix to the *Prolegomena*, which he wrote in reply to Garve's review of the *Critique*. What he says there is more complex. It is that Berkeley 'regarded space as a mere empirical representation', whereas both space and time are actually a priori forms of intuition; and that in consequence of this 'experience with Berkeley can have no criteria of truth', while on Kant's own view space and time 'prescribe their law a priori to all possible experience', which makes it possible to distinguish, within experience, truth from illusion.[4] There are thus

---

[4] *Prolegomena*, in the edition of *Kant's gesammelte Schriften* by the Preussische Akademie der Wissenschaften (Berlin, 1902– ; henceforth abbreviated 'Ak'.), iv. 374 f.; in the translation by P. G. Lucas (Manchester University Press, 1953). pp. 145 f.

two points here, one about the empirical character of space and the other about the criteria of truth, and the second is supposed to follow from the first.

Space for Berkeley is certainly an 'empirical representation', in the sense that we learn about space as we learn about colours, by observing features of our ideas and their relations. (The same applies to time, though since he does not mention time in the works Kant is likely to have read Kant was not aware of this.[5]) For Kant it is in this fashion that we learn how particular things and events are spatially and temporally related, but space and time themselves are imposed by the mind upon its experiences and not learnt about empirically. The contrast sounds clear enough. But it is not quite so clear what it comes to. Berkeley would no doubt agree with Kant that our ideas of spatial relationships depend in part on the nature of our own minds, as indeed he would hold also in the case of our ideas of colour. These ideas of ours may be caused in us by God, but they cannot altogether resemble their archetypes in the divine intellect, since in God 'there is no sense nor sensory'.[6] There must therefore be something in them which is due to our natures and the character of our senses. Berkeley does not speak of this something as a priori, or describe space as an a priori form of intuition, but could he not have done so if he had sought to express himself in Kantian terminology?

The answer is that he could not properly have done so, because Kant does not really regard the fact that space is in some sense contributed to experience by our minds as sufficient to make it a priori—although he does not always make this clear. The difference between Kant and Berkeley at this point is not so much over what the mind can be said to contribute, as over what the consequences are of its being thus involved in determining the character of experience. Kant's contention is that *because* space (and time) are contributed by us, 'space (and likewise time . . .) with all its determinations can be known by us a priori'.[7] It is this alleged consequence that is quite foreign to Berkeley, whatever he may think about the mind's own nature helping to determine what its sensory experience is like. This gives us a second significant difference between Kant and Berkeley.

[5] He says that 'Berkeley paid no attention to time' (ibid). He is likely to have read the *Dialogues, De Motu,* and *Siris;* cf. the articles by Turbayne, Allison, and Matthey referred to in note I above.

[6] *Siris,* 289; cf. *Dialogues,* 241.

[7] *Prolegomena,* loc. cit. note 4 above.

Kant thinks that synthetic a priori knowledge about space (and time) is possible, and Berkeley does not.

Kant goes on to say that it is because Berkeley does not that he is unable to distinguish empirical reality from illusion. The accusation that Berkeley is unable to distinguish reality from illusion has been made often enough, and Berkeley himself attempts a reply to it. Kant considers this reply to be ineffective, and for a fundamental reason: his failure to admit the Kantian synthetic a priori. 'For us space and time (in conjunction with the pure concepts of the understanding) prescribe their law a priori to all possible experience, and this yields at the same time the sure criterion for distinguishing truth in it from illusion.'[8]

What Berkeley does is to draw the distinction in two different, but complementary, ways. One appeals to an empirically discernible difference between veridical and non-veridical ideas. Veridical ideas are 'vivid and clear', and 'have not a like dependence on our will' with non-veridical ones.[9] Moreover (and perhaps more importantly) they are 'connected, and of a piece with the preceding and subsequent transactions of our lives'; when one mistakes an illusion for reality, one's mistake lies in inferring from the present perception that a certain pattern of others may be expected in future, or would be experienced under other conditions.[10] Veridical ideas, in other words, are ideas that belong to collections of an appropriately coherent sort, and such collections are what we commonly call objects. 'A *cherry*, I say, is nothing but a congeries of sensible impressions, or ideas perceived by various senses: which ideas are united into one thing (or have one name given them) by the mind; because they are observed to attend each other.'[11]

The other way of drawing the distinction draws it non-empirically, by reference to God. God is aware of all that there is, and he is the cause of our perceptions; veridical ideas are those that God produces in us to correspond to the appropriate archetypes in the divine intellect. 'The ideas imprinted on the senses by the Author of Nature are called *real things*.'[12] For Berkeley these two ways of seeing the matter go together naturally, since the 'steadiness, order, and

---

[8] Ibid.
[9] *Dialogues*, 235; cf. *Principles*, 29 ff.
[10] *Dialogues*, 235 and 238.
[11] *Dialogues*, 249.
[12] *Principles*, 33.

coherence' of our veridical ideas reflects and testifies to 'the wisdom and benevolence of its Author'.[13]

Kant has objections to both ways of drawing the distinction. His objection to the second we have already met: it takes us beyond the limits of possible experience, and therefore beyond the limits of possible knowledge. Neither God, nor the archetypes in the divine intellect, can be discovered by empirical means; in his later works Berkeley claims we can know them by some sort of intellectual apprehension,[14] but this is not a legitimate kind of knowing for Kant. In his preliminary notes for the *Prolegomena* he explicitly objects to Berkeley on this ground: 'Berkeley found nothing permanent, nor could he find anything that the understanding grasped in accordance with a priori principles; therefore he had to look for another [kind of] intuition, namely the mystical intuition of the divine ideas.'[15]

His objection to Berkeley's first way of distinguishing between veridical and non-veridical ideas is quite general, and does not depend on the particular suggestions that Berkeley makes, for it is an objection against any way of founding the distinction on straightforwardly empirical considerations—i.e. without the assistance of synthetic a priori principles. 'As truth rests on universal and necessary laws as its criteria, experience with Berkeley can have no criteria of truth because nothing was laid (by him) a priori at the ground of appearances in it, from which it then followed that it is nothing but illusion.'[16] But why does Kant think that something must be 'laid a priori at the ground of appearances' in order for the distinction to be possible?

Berkeley actually cites two different sorts of empirical test for determining whether ideas are veridical. On the one hand there is the comparison in terms of the internal qualities of the ideas themselves: how vivid they are, or how clear. On the other hand there is a more complex kind of comparison, that depends upon some form of inference (commonly inductive) that takes us beyond the internal qualities of the ideas presently before us. If someone is to make a judgement 'concerning the ideas that, from what he perceives at present, he imagines would be perceived in other circumstances',[17] he is making such an inference. So is he if he claims that certain of his

[13] *Principles*, 30.
[14] Particularly in *Siris*, 264, 294–5, 337, etc.; but also in *De Motu*, e.g. 71–2.
[15] Ak. xxiii. 58.
[16] *Prolegomena*, Ak. iv. 375, Lucas p. 146.
[17] *Dialogues*, 238.

present ideas belong to a pattern which has 'a steadiness, order, and coherence', and that they 'are not excited at random, as those which are the effects of human wills often are, but in a regular train or series'.[18] Kant's objection to Berkeley is that it is only those criteria which depend upon inference that are worth taking seriously, and that the principles of inference on which they rest must necessarily be synthetic and a priori—and hence not properly available to an empiricist like Berkeley. Or at least this is the first instalment of his objection.

He is right to claim that it is only the criteria which depend upon inference that are worth taking seriously. Vividness, clarity, and the like may serve us (in the right conditions) as evidence that our perceptions are veridical, but it cannot be in qualities such as these that their veridicality *consists*. More generally, no plausible analysis of the concept of objective reality could lead to the conclusion that this reality *consisted* in nothing more than some inspectable feature of particular perceptions, taken in isolation from their relationship to other perceptions at other times or circumstances. For whatever else the concept of objective reality involves, it must at least require that the existence of what is objectively real should not wholly depend on my present perception.

Is Kant then right to say that the inference beyond one's immediately present ideas must rely upon synthetic a priori principles? This again seems to be correct, though no doubt its correctness was less evident before Hume. If the inference is to be justifiable, it must be justifiable by reference to principles of inference, the validity of which cannot be simply given in present experience; and if they are to be more than just logical principles they must be (by definition) synthetic. No principle could ever be justified solely by appeal to the content of one's present experience, for a principle is in its nature general and one's present experience is ineluctably particular. Nor could the content of one's present experience, together with purely logical principles, warrant any conclusions about experiences at other times, or by other persons, or indeed any inferences beyond itself. It is true, of course, that an experience can be correctly described in such terms as 'the most memorable experience I had the day before I saw the great fire', and that from my having this experience, so described, it follows by logic alone that I saw the fire on the following day; but that is because this description does not give

---

[18] *Principles*, 30.

the content of the experience. Ascriptions of content are always intentional. It may no doubt be part of the content of an experience that the subject believes himself justified in inferring that he will see a fire tomorrow, or that God exists, and feels much confidence about these things; but such beliefs and such feelings are intentional states, and nothing about tomorrow's experiences or about God's existence is entailed by the subject's being in these states now. This, indeed, is why one's present experience is ineluctably particular. Even if the experience involves the belief that one intuits the truth of some universal proposition, the experience itself is a particular event, and its occurrence constitutes no justification for the universal proposition (save with the aid of some extra principle to the effect that such intuitions are warranted).

Thus if Berkeley is to give an account of reality which requires that certain inferences from one's present ideas to other (actual or possible) ideas be justifiable, these inferences must rest on principles which are non-logical and non-empirical; in Kantian terms, synthetic and a priori. He could avoid relying on such principles only by making a very radical move. This would be to claim that although our distinction between veridical and non-veridical ideas depends upon inferences these inferences are not justifiable: nothing more can be said about them than that we make them. All idea of justification would be abandoned, at least in this context, and we should be left— as Hume suggests and Quine at times proposes—with only the descriptive task of saying how human minds react and what inferences they tend to draw under what conditions.[19] One could observe that under such-and-such circumstances people do infer that their perceptions have the coherence, or connectedness, or whatever, that is considered appropriate for objectivity, and that under such-and-such others they do not; one would no longer seek to claim that they were ever justified in this, or even in the most elementary of inductive inferences.

If Berkeley had taken this line, as of course he never did, there can be no doubt that Kant would have regarded him as playing into his hands. He accused Berkeley of failing to provide criteria of truth: on the present suggestion there are no criteria of truth to provide. No criteria, that is, in the sense of means whereby we may justifiably determine how things are in the objective world. The present

---

[19] Quine, 'Epistemology Naturalized', in his *Ontological Relativity and Other Essays* (Columbia University Press, New York and London, 1969).

suggestion does not deny that there is an objective world, and that the things we say about it may be true, but it does deny that there is any way to justify our claims about it. In Kantian terms, this is to deny the possibility of knowledge about it, since for Kant one cannot be said to know in matters where justification is lacking. The objective world becomes as unknowable as the Kantian world of things in themselves, concerning which Kant himself thinks that people have certain natural beliefs, but which he thinks remains unknowable none the less, because there is no way in which these beliefs could be justified. Indeed, it can be equated with that world; which is tantamount to saying that empirical knowledge as Kant understands it, the empirical knowledge of an objective world, is on this view impossible.

To say this is not to reject the suggestion of Hume and Quine; it is only to say why Kant rejected it. It cannot be dismissed out of hand, and it properly requires an extended discussion. Such a discussion, however, would divert us from our present purpose, and would be more appropriate in an examination of Kant's relationship with Hume than in a comparison of his position with Berkeley's. It may be observed in any case that it is a counsel of despair. We normally seek to justify our inferences and the knowledge claims that depend upon them, and to distinguish those that can be justified from others that are foolish, irrational, the products of confusion or unthinking prejudice. If the suggested approach is correct this distinction is ill-founded, and the views we call rational are only those that accord with the habits of thought of a certain section of the population. This is a conclusion to which one might eventually be driven, but not one to be embraced while there is still a hope of making headway with epistemology as it has traditionally been conceived.

Berkeley, at any rate, has no wish to embrace it, and is therefore bound to rely upon principles of inference that Kant would call synthetic and a priori. He prefers, certainly, to make as modest a use of such principles as he can. The criterion he offers in terms of coherence or connectedness seems designed to make use of little more than induction: the expectation that a certain pattern of ideas will be continued, or 'would be perceived in other circumstances'[20] or by other spirits, being an inductive one. But the principle of induction is still a principle of inference, and one that (notoriously) lacks empirical justification; it therefore lacks any justification that is available to Berkeley, and hence (Kant concludes) Berkeley can be

[20] *Dialogues*, 238.

not unreasonably described as committed to the view that the objects of experience are 'nothing but illusion'.

There is some temptation to feel that this criticism is unfair, because empiricists should at least be allowed induction. Empiricists commonly do rely on inductive inference, and this creates the impression that they have a right to. Kant's point—or the first part of it—is that all such principles require defence, since their validity is not given to us in experience itself; this is one of the major messages of the *Critique*. He himself can provide such a defence, though it is one which places the principle of induction alongside a number of other synthetic a priori principles which are equally important and equally justifiable. And the second part of his point is that some of these other principles, left aside by Berkeley (as by other like-minded empiricists), are just as important as induction in distinguishing reality from illusion.

According to Kant synthetic a priori principles may be justified, despite their non-empirical character, if they can be justified 'transcendentally'. They can be justified transcendentally if it can be shown that they are required for the possibility of experience itself, or at any rate of experience of such a kind as ours is.[21] But it is important to notice that Kant recognizes two different ways in which a principle may be required for experience to be possible, and that he therefore admits two different kinds of transcendental justification, or (as he calls it) transcendental deduction.

In the first place, it may be a condition of the possibility of experience that the principle in question should actually be *true* (of the world as we know it, the world of appearances). The principles that have this status are those Kant calls the principles of pure understanding, like 'Every event has a cause', together with such subordinate truths as can be derived from them. It is on these that Kant concentrates in the first half of the *Critique*. Such principles are said to be constitutive of experience, because it is them that the mind uses in constructing the phenomenal world: they are guaranteed to be true of the phenomenal world just because that world has been constructed in that way.[22]

[21] A 92 ff./B 124 ff.; A 154 ff./B 193 ff.; and see further my *Kant* (Routledge and Kegan Paul, London, 1978), ch. 2.

[22] 'Phenomenal world' and 'world of appearances' I take to be equivalent; 'phenomenal' is not, of course, meant to suggest that any kind of phenomenalistic analysis is appropriate. Similarly I take 'noumenon' to be synonymous with 'thing in itself'.

The principle of induction is not amongst them. Unlike the principles of pure understanding, the principle of induction (in any plausible version) gives us no *assurance* that experience, or the world experienced, will take such-and-such a form. The principle of induction does not (in any plausible version) deny it is possible that the course of nature will change quite arbitrarily tomorrow; it says only that this is an *unreasonable* thing to expect. Roughly, it says something like this: 'Given a long run of A's that have been B's, and given that we have no other relevant information as to whether the next A will be a B or not, it is reasonable to expect that it will be.' A priori principles of this kind Kant calls regulative, rather than constitutive. We do not ensure their truth by reading them into the world of appearances, but we must nevertheless rely on them in the attempt to understand the world about us, for they provide us with a way of unifying things comprehensibly, and without that we should get nowhere. Kant argues that there is no alternative to seeking such comprehensible unity if we are to attain an understanding of things, and maintains also that the nature of reason—a faculty essential for any experience—leaves us no alternative to the search for as complete an understanding as possible. In this way he claims to provide a transcendental justification for the regulative principles as well; or in his own terminology, a transcendental deduction of the ideas of pure reason (A 669 ff./B 697 ff.).

Berkeley differs from Kant not only in having no way of justifying the synthetic a priori principles on which he needs to rely, but also in making no use of constitutive principles; only of regulative ones, and indeed rather few of those. Besides induction he makes use of a principle licensing inference to the simplest explanation, but that is also regulative, since it says that such inference is reasonable but not that it necessarily yields the truth. Because of this his attempted account of reality is a great deal simpler than Kant's, and a great deal too simple in Kant's opinion to be at all satisfactory. Just as Hume's empiricist account of causality was bound to fail because the concept of causality is a constitutive a priori concept, so on Kant's view Berkeley's account of empirical reality is bound to fail as well because it leaves out the constitutive a priori elements that are essential to the distinction between that reality and mere illusion.

Berkeley frequently says that an object *is* an idea. His position can be better expressed by saying that what we normally call an object is a collection of ideas, a collection which will typically include ideas in various finite minds and ideas in the mind of God.[23] (At one stage in his career he certainly thought it should include potential and non-actual ideas as well: whether this reflects his mature position is a matter for dispute.[24]) Membership in such a collection is determined by the criteria which distinguish veridical from illusory ideas: an idea of mine belongs to such a collection just in case it has the appropriate kind of coherence or connectedness with other ideas, and is produced in me by God to correspond to an archetype in the divine intellect. The coherence or connectedness in question can obtain without my being aware of it, but I can find out about it by relying on induction.

Kant's account is so totally different that it is very strange he has sometimes been said to be a phenomenalist along very much the lines just sketched—or at any rate to favour a phenomenalist account of the world of appearances. One way to show that this ascription is ill-founded is to go over the text, looking on the one hand at those passages which most seem to support a phenomenalistic view, and on the other at those which seem to offer an alternative. As this has been done elsewhere by various people, including myself,[25] I shall only observe here that those passages in which he speaks of objects as 'representations' or as 'totalities of representations' establish very little because the words are so vague, 'representation' (*Vorstellung*) in particular having all the unclarities and ambiguities of Locke's 'idea'. Moreover the references to the transcendental object in the first-edition Deduction suggest (if not perhaps in the perfect context) a much more sophisticated alternative view, whereby the non-empirical notion of an object serves as a kind of focus for uniting together the perceptions that Berkeley just concatenates.

Whether or not what is said in these passages reflects the detail of Kant's final view of the matter it does bring out the crucial element of difference. Details of text apart, Kant's whole theory of space, time, the categories, and their role in the construction of experience precludes him from giving a phenomenalistic account of objects in the way Berkeley or J. S. Mill did. In supplying the categories, as schematized in space and time, the mind supplies to its experience certain a priori concepts, like the concept of cause, in such a way as to

[23] He sometimes expresses it in this way himself. e.g. in the passage about the cherry quoted above from the *Dialogues*, 249.

[24] On this see G. Pitcher, *Berkeley* (Routledge and Kegan Paul, London, 1977), ch. 10.

[25] Cf. G. Bird, *Kant's Theory of Knowledge* (Routledge and Kegan Paul, London, 1962), ch. 1; and my *Kant*, ch. 8.

make true corresponding principles of an equally a priori character about the way in which those concepts are instantiated—principles like 'Every event has a cause'. These principles are constitutive of experience: we are assured (by transcendental arguments) not just that they are sensible to adopt in practice but that they are actually true of the world of appearances, true because our minds so construct that world that these principles are built into it and constitute its structure. The a priori concepts must include the concept of an object: necessarily so, because objects, no less than causes, are among the structural features of the phenomenal world. The corresponding principle is the principle 'That there exist objects in space outside me' (cf. B 275); and although the narrowness of Kant's architectonic prevents him from listing it in its proper place alongside the other principles of pure understanding, there is no room to doubt that it is as much a constitutive synthetic a priori principle as they are. The concept of an object does not appear on Kant's list of categories, but the concept of substance does, and a substance is a sort of super-object: ordinary objects exist independently of people's perceptions, but because substances are permanent they exist independently of all alterations there may be. The concept of an object is presumably to be derived from that of substance, in Kant's view. Such derived a priori concepts he calls predicables.[26]

Thus according to Kant the synthesis involved in putting together various of my perceptions as perceptions of a single object involves an a priori concept, the concept of an object. It is not simply a matter of collecting perceptions together into a set, as it was for Berkeley. Just as the concept of a cause is not to be analysed (or analysed away) along Humean lines, so the concept of an object is not simply the concept of a collection of perceptions; there would be nothing a priori about that over and above the (logical) notion of a set. Like Berkeley, Kant requires induction in order to decide in the *particular* case which perceptions go with which and what object, if any, they represent; presumably nearly everyone will agree with Berkeley that we *discover* which of our perceptions represent objective reality by seeing which of them will satisfy the appropriate inductive tests. (If, for instance, my present perception of a cup is veridical, induction leads me to expect like perceptions in other observers, at other angles, and at other times; the failure of these expectations is a reason for thinking there is no cup there.) Where Kant and Berkeley differ is over what

---

[26] A 81 f./B 107 f. On this see further my *Kant*, pp. 107-8.

the concept of an object involves. For Kant it is an a priori concept, instances of which are to be recognized empirically in the fashion just described, just as the concept of cause is an a priori concept the instances of which are to be recognized through constant conjunction. For Berkeley it is the concept of a collection of ideas, and there is nothing specifically a priori about it: Berkeley no more allows an a priori concept of an object than Hume allows an a priori concept of a cause.

There is an important sense in which Kant's world of physical objects is a construction and Berkeley's not. Berkeley's objects are nothing over and above ideas;[27] by introducing talk of objects we introduce a new and compendious way of talking about ideas, and that is all. For Kant objects are something additional, entities of a different kind from perceptions or collections of perceptions, whether the perceptions be actual or possible, human or of some other variety. And that additional something is genuinely there in the world of appearances, there because it has been put there by our minds in constructing that world. *How* our minds achieve such a feat is no doubt a problematic matter, and Kant's position is not without its difficulties here, but he clearly thinks they do achieve it.

And the distinction goes deeper. Berkeley's ideas are simply given: it is a fact that we have the ideas we do, though no doubt it is a fact which is partly determined by the nature of human sensibility. Kant on the other hand regards even the most elementary sense-data as constructions that our minds effect in accordance with space, time, and the categories.[28] Since the constructing is not undertaken voluntarily the question arose earlier—in connection with space—whether this amounts to more than a picturesque way of putting the Berkeleian point that the character of our ideas is in part a function of our human sensibility, but the answer was that it does, because it renders possible a priori knowledge about the world through our knowledge of what features our minds must contribute. Our minds so determine the material given in intuition as to make certain a priori concepts to apply, and certain a priori truths to hold, in the world as we experience it: in other words they create a coherent picture of the way the world is, a picture which we can treat (except for metaphysical purposes) not as a mere picture but as *constituting* the

[27] Realism about sets would be deeply foreign to him, of course.
[28] Otherwise there would be no place for a synthesis of apprehension. A 98 ff.; B 129 ff.; B 160 f.

objective reality we are concerned with every day. We can treat it in this way because the transcendental arguments which establish what our minds must contribute assure us that we must all construct similar pictures of the world, and must continue to do so as long as we have experience.

Kant's criticism of Berkeley in the Appendix to the *Prolegomena* was that he could not distinguish reality from illusion because he did not see that space (and time) were a priori respresentations and thus laid 'nothing . . . a priori at the ground of appearances'. It is slightly misleading of Kant to single out space and time in this way, for it is the categories quite as much as the forms of intuition which in his own system provide the necessary grounding, and yield the criterion of reality. He does so because he regards the a priori status of space and time as being particularly fundamental: it is *because* space and time are a priori that the categories can be applied a priori to intuition, and that experience can be constructed in accordance with the principles of pure understanding. 'For thus I can understand how I can judge a priori and with apodeictic certainty about objects of the senses.'[29]

In fact he has another reason as well for emphasizing that their difference over the status of space is central to the disagreement between Berkeley and himself. This is brought out in what he says about Berkeley at the start of the Refutation of Idealism, in the second edition of the *Critique*. His remarks here are very brief and have sometimes been found puzzling, but they fit in neatly with what has been said above. Berkeley is called a dogmatic idealist, who 'maintains that space, with all the things of which it is the inseparable condition, is something which is in itself (*an sich selbst*) impossible', and who 'therefore regards the things in space as merely imaginary entities' (B 274). Kant goes on to assert that 'Dogmatic idealism is unavoidable, if space be interpreted as a property that must belong to things in themselves. For in that case space, and everything to which it serves as condition, is a non-entity. The ground on which this idealism rests has already been undermined by us in the Transcendental Aesthetic' (ibid.). It needs, he clearly thinks, no further refutation, and the rest of what he says is devoted to the quite different 'problematic idealism' which holds the existence of objects in space to be doubtful but not impossible (and which he ascribes to Descartes).

The passage indicates, not that Kant was ignorant of Berkeley's views, but that he knew them well. Berkeley leaves us in no doubt that

[29] Ak. xxiii. 58.

he takes corporeal things to be essentially extended in space, and frequently uses this in arguing for his own position. On the view which he opposes, corporeal substance is independent of anyone's perceptions, and therefore space must be independent likewise. But that is contradictory, according to Berkeley, for extendedness and spatiality are features of our ideas, and cannot therefore belong to this alleged corporeal substance; so that space, with 'everything to which it serves as condition', must be ideal. So far Kant just reflects what Berkeley says himself. What is not obvious, if one reads only the passage in the *Critique*, is why Kant should think that by making them *ideal* Berkeley makes them *non-entities*. After all, he considers them ideal himself, and quite shares Berkeley's view that space is impossible *an sich selbst*, i.e. as something wholly independent of our cognitive faculties. But the *Prolegomena* has shown us what his reasons are: Berkeley lacks the criterion of truth, of reality within the world of appearances, which Kant is able to provide. It is unfortunate, but not uncharacteristic, that he should omit to explain this here. Perhaps, as G. J. Matthey has recently suggested, he sees no particular need to spell the matter out because Berkeley himself downgrades the reality of bodies in a work Kant may have known better than most philosophers do nowadays, namely *Siris*.[30]

Despite the emphasis on space, though, the basis of Kant's objection to Berkeley is (as we might have expected) an objection to his empiricism. Berkeley has his non-empirical moods, it is true—especially in *Siris*; in these moods he casts discretion aside and talks of an intuitive apprehension of God and of the ideas in the divine intellect. This 'mystical intuition' Kant dismisses as a gratuitous claim to insight into that unknowable realm which lies beyond the limits of possible experience. But the empiricist line of thought, very much the dominant one in Berkeley's earlier writings, is incapable of sustaining any distinction between illusion and objective reality. For if objective reality is to be discoverable, principles of inference are required in order to identify it, and these principles must be a priori;

---

[30] *Siris*, 266; Matthey, 'Kant's Conception of Berkeley's Idealism'. It is surprising that some have thought Kant did not read *Siris*; his summary of Berkeleian idealism in the *Prolegomena*—'All knowledge through the senses and through experience is nothing but illusion, and only in the ideas of pure understanding and reason is truth' (Ak. iv. 374, Lucas p. 145)—fits badly with the *Principles* and *Dialogues*, but is remarkably close to *Siris* 264. Matthey also points out that in Eschenbach's 1756 translation of the *Dialogues* into German, Berkeley is rendered as denying the reality of bodies.

even if reality were to be reductively handled along phenomenalist lines, induction at least would be required to find out about it, and the principle of induction cannot be empirical. If on the other hand objective reality is *not* discoverable, it must be consigned once more to the realm of the noumenal, leaving *us* with nothing better than illusion and with no criteria of truth.

As we have seen, the principle of induction is in Kant's terminology a regulative a priori principle. He differs from Berkeley not only in insisting on its a priori status but in admitting constitutive a priori principles as well, and a priori concepts whose application in experience is assured by the fact that experience is so constructed as to guarantee it. The concept of an object, and the principle that corresponds to it, are constitutive in this way, and the concept of an object is therefore not to be analysed in any phenomenalistic fashion. Since it is the constructive aspect of Kant's transcendental idealism that many people seem to find distasteful it is natural to ask how Kant would have replied to a Berkeley who so far modified his empiricism as to accept the regulative a priori, while rejecting the constitutive.

The answer is that he would have replied in two ways. First there is the objection that such a theory is too weak to accommodate our concepts of cause, object, and the like. The principle of induction in its regulative form may tell us what it is reasonable to expect, but it does not give us the concept of causation. In the same way, the concept of an object is not to be equated with that of a set of actual and possible perceptions; and against the phenomenalist who claims that it is, Kant can employ all the standard arguments against phenomenalism. In particular he can observe that the phenomenalist's proposed analysis cannot be carried through, because the conditionals required in specifying the relevant non-actual perceptions would be bound to make use in their antecedents of the concept of an object, the very concept which is supposed to be under analysis. For the possible perceptions that are relevant are not those that just anyone might have, however insane or deluded; they are the perceptions that would be experienced in the appropriate circumstances by someone who *perceived what was there*, and was not suffering from any kind of hallucination.[31] Objections of this kind to

---

[31] To be effective this would require more elaboration, of course. Cf. R. M. Chisholm, *Perceiving* (Cornell University Press, Ithaca, 1957). Appendix, and my *Kant*, pp. 107 f.

phenomenalism do not tell against Kant's own position, because for him the concept of an object is a priori and unanalysable.

The second reply, which goes deeper, is that one is not entitled to modify one's empiricism little by little, and choose what kinds of a priori principle to accept and what kinds to reject. One is not entitled to help oneself to the a priori at all without some defence, for otherwise there would be no answering those who adopted the strangest metaphysical positions, and no resolving the antinomies to which their differences lead. Since the defence cannot be empirical, Kant considers it can only be transcendental; the alternative Cartesian strategy of accepting as true whatever one very clearly and distinctly perceives being untenable, first because people take themselves clearly and distinctly to perceive different and conflicting things, and secondly because there can be no reason (short of divine benevolence) why a great confidence in some matter—even a great confidence shared by all the species—should ensure that matter's truth, when it lies beyond anyone's experience.[32] The principle of induction, therefore, must be justified transcendentally. We saw that he thinks it can be justified in that way; along with such other regulative principles as reason requires in its search for unity and completeness in the understanding of the world around us. But he also thinks (and devotes much of the central part of the *Critique* to arguing) that a like transcendental justification can be given for constitutive a priori principles, and for the application of the categories (and therefore the predicables) to the world of appearances. Thus his objection to the modified Berkeleian position, which admits the regulative a priori but not the constitutive, is that by admitting even the regulative it must concede the legitimacy of transcendental arguments, while arguments of just the same kind compel the acceptance of the constitutive too. It has moved away from the purest empiricism by accepting a priori principles that can be transcendentally justified, but fails to recognize that constitutive as well as regulative principles can be justified in that way.

Of course, this reply of Kant's will be effective only if the transcendental arguments that he claims to work actually do. Whether they do or not, or whether others can be found which will achieve the same objectives, is a large question and well beyond the scope of the present paper; but it has often been felt that most of the

[32] Cf. Kant's letter to Herz of 21 February 1772 (Ak. x. 123 ff.), or B 166 ff.

arguments Kant gives are less than adequate.[33] There is a possible answer to Kant here, then, for someone seeking to defend the modified Berkeleian position. It is conceivable that a defence may be available for the regulative a priori, but none for the constitutive. Conceivable; but (it must be admitted) very far from obvious.

But there is also another line of attack, which the Berkeleian can mount against Kant even if all Kant's transcendental arguments work. It turns on the fact that the principle of induction is not the only regulative a priori principle which Kant thinks he can justify, or on which Berkeley tacitly relies. The transcendental deduction of the ideas of pure reason gives us a general warrant for adopting such principles as enable us to see the world as a systematically unified totality, not by giving us any assurance that it really is such a totality, but by making clear that they provide the only way to satisfy a demand inevitably set before us by the nature of reason. Among these principles clearly belongs the one which licenses inference from given facts to the best explanation of those facts. It is a principle that Berkeley makes use of, as also—in a way that is rather crucial to his system—does Kant himself.

It is crucial to Kant's system because upon it rests his belief in things in themselves. Without it he can establish claims only about the world of appearances, and the standard neo-Kantian criticism, that he has no right to assert the existence of the noumenal world, becomes unavoidable. It is true that his account of how the mind acts in its construction of the phenomenal world gives him an alternative argument (of the transcendental kind) to the real existence of the 'I' that thinks, not as part of the phenomenal world but as the subject of it—a point sufficiently illustrated by the untenability of Fichte's early doctrine that the knowing self posits itself as well as the world that it knows; but Kant is firm in his insistence that there must also be things in themselves lying behind the objects of knowledge, as 'the ground of the sensible world and therefore also of its laws', since 'otherwise we should be landed in the absurd conclusion that there can be appearance without anything that appears' (B xxvi).[34] This as we saw was the basis of his first objection to Berkeley in the *Prolegomena*, where he accuses him of denying things in themselves and claims never to have doubted them. But his only reason for asserting their

---

[33] A considerable range of objections have been made against them. I have put some of them forward, and considered others, in my book *Kant*.

[34] See my *Kant*, pp. 131 ff.

existence is that otherwise there could be no source for the given, outside my own mind; no explanation for the shared *content* of experience between different percipients (for though his transcendental arguments may show that their minds must *structure* experience similarly, through the same forms of intuition and the same category-governed synthesis, they do nothing to ensure a similarity of empirical content). This is his only reason—but by his own standards it is a quite good enough reason, in view of the transcendental deduction of the ideas. It is as good a reason as we ever have for any explanation of a phenomenon, for although the Second Analogy guarantees that every event has a cause Kant is very clear that it does not determine a priori what causes what; this is to be found by examining the content of experience and employing regulative principles.[35]

Berkeley also makes great use of inference to the best explanation, for he depends on it to establish the existence of God. We find that many of our ideas of sense are not under our own control; 'there is therefore some other spirit that causes them, since it is repugnant that they should subsist by themselves'; the order, beauty, and harmony that they exhibit shows that this spirit must be God.[36] Berkeley is *not* inferring to the best explanation when he says that if they are caused they must be caused by some spirit, for he thinks he has arguments which show any other alternative to be impossible. But he is making use of such a principle when he infers from the orderliness that the spirit must be God, and also when he initially rejects as 'repugnant' the suggestion that the ideas should simply exist without a cause. In fact this argument of Berkeley's is very close to Kant's argument for things in themselves. To explain the regularities and similarities we find among perceptions both of them postulate a cause which cannot be more directly known; Kant insists that no more can be said of it than that it produces these effects, Berkeley argues that it is a unique, eternal, and omnipresent spirit, namely God.

[35] Kant often connects adopting a regulative principle with proceeding *as if* something were the case; it is therefore important to notice that regulative principles do enable us to make specific claims quite categorically (e.g. the claim that *this* causes *that*). These claims are not proved conclusively, but it is reasonable to believe them true; and this is not just a matter of treating them as if they were true. Kant's point is only that to regard e.g. the inductive principle as valid is tantamount to looking on the world *as if* it were created by a God who operates systematically (A 672 ff./B 700 ff.). We do not actually have to believe in such a God, though the natural dialectic of human reason pushes us in that direction.

[36] *Principles*, 146.

Kant's objection to this further move of Berkeley's was that it goes beyond the limits of possible experience. But this is a bad objection; bad in its own right, and bad from the point of view of Kant's system. To take it seriously would be to reject his ground for believing in things in themselves, for things in themselves lie equally beyond the limits of possible experience. And his ground is a perfectly good ground, for the rationality of that belief is assured by an a priori regulative principle which we rely on all the time, and which he regards as justifiable in the same transcendental fashion as the other synthetic a priori principles on which we depend. If he had objected only that Berkeley has no right to think God must be the cause of our perceptions, because the evidence leaves other explanations equally possible, that would have been another matter and an eminently discussable issue. But he is wrong to suppose that the regulative principle which makes reasonable a belief in things in themselves cannot also justify conclusions about what things in themselves are like. One cannot rule out in advance the idea that the best explanation will assign to them one character rather than another (a point which in a way he tacitly accepts when rejecting the thought that the only thing in itself is my knowing mind).

The trouble, of course, is that Kant never appreciated that his own methods do make it possible for knowledge to outrun the limits of possible experience; and not just in one way but in two. There is no reason in principle why transcendental arguments should not reach conclusions about what the world must be like in itself, as well as conclusions about what we must build into the world of appearances. It may be possible, in other words, to find arguments to the effect that the noumenally real world must be thus and so if experience is to be possible at all.[37] (Indeed Kant himself uses such arguments, without being explicit about it, when he infers that there must be an 'I' that thinks and that it must be active in synthesis.) And there is also no reason in principle why regulative principles, themselves justifiable transcendentally, should not entitle us to put forward claims about the noumenally real world by inference from what we can observe: claims we cannot be wholly sure of, any more than we can be wholly sure of a scientific explanation or of any conclusion which rests upon ordinary induction, but claims which can be perfectly reasonable and proper none the less. A sound transcendental idealism should make

---

[37] See my *Kant*, pp. 11, 131 ff.—developing a point of Stroud's in his paper 'Transcendental Arguments', *Journal of Philosophy* lxv (1968) pp. 252 f.

no such allegations as Kant is prone to, about the impossibility of justifying assertions about things in themselves. To take the alternative line and confine even regulative principles to a use wholly within the world of appearances would be a move for which Kant has no shadow of a justification to offer; and by depriving him of his own ground for believing in things in themselves it would render him liable to the accusation he once made against Berkeley, of holding a 'visionary idealism' which denies the ultimate reality of things and thus leaves us with 'the absurd conclusion that there can be appearance without anything that appears'.

TITLES IN THIS SERIES

James F. Ferrier, "Berkeley and Idealism," London: *Blackwood's Magazine* (June 1842).

John Stuart Mill, "Bailey on Berkeley's Theory of Vision," London: *Westminster Review*, 38 (1842).

Samuel Bailey, *A Letter to a Philosopher in Reply to Some Recent Attempts to Vindicate Berkeley's Theory of Vision, and in Further Elucidation of its Unsoundness*, London: James Ridgway, Piccadilly, 1843.

James F. Ferrier, "Mr. Bailey's Reply to an Article in Blackwood's Magazine," Edinburgh and London: *Blackwood's Magazine* (June 1843).

John Stuart Mill, "Rejoinder to Mr. Bailey's Reply," London: *Westminster Review*, 39 (1843).

8. George Berkeley, *Philosophical Commentaries, Transcribed from the Manuscript and Edited, with an Introduction and Index by George H. Thomas: Explanatory Notes by A. A. Luce*, printed by Mount Union College, 1976.

9. A. C. Crombie, *George Berkeley's Bicentenary, The British Journal for the Philosophy of Science*, 4 (May 1953). Edinburgh and London: Thomas Nelson and Sons Ltd.

10. Alexander Campbell Fraser, *Life and Letters of George Berkeley, Formerly Bishop of Cloyne, and an Account of His Philosophy. With Many Writings of Bishop Berkeley Hitherto Unpublished*, Oxford, At the Clarendon Press, 1871.

11. G. Dawes Hicks, *Berkeley*, New York: Russell & Russell, 1932.

12. G. A. Johnston, *The Development of Berkeley's Philosophy*, London: Macmillan and Co., 1923.

13. A. A. Luce, *Berkeley and Malebranche: A Study in the Origins of Berkeley's Thought*, Oxford, At the Clarendon Press, 1934.

14. C. B. Martin and D. M. Armstrong, eds., *Berkeley: A Collection of Critical Essays. The Articles from "Locke and Berkeley: A Collection of Critical Essays"*, Garden City, New York: Anchor Books, Doubleday & Company, Inc., 1968

15. I. C. Tipton, *Berkeley: The Philosophy of Immaterialism*, London: Methuen & Co. Ltd., 1974.